User's Guide to Cryptography and Standards

For quite a long time, computer security was a rather narrow field of study that was populated mainly by theoretical computer scientists, electrical engineers, and applied mathematicians. With the proliferation of open systems in general, and of the Internet and the World Wide Web (WWW) in particular, this situation has changed fundamentally. Today, computer and network practitioners are equally interested in computer security, since they require technologies and solutions that can be used to secure applications related to electronic commerce. Against this background, the field of computer security has become very broad and includes many topics of interest. The aim of this series is to publish state-of-the-art, high standard technical books on topics related to computer security. Further information about the series can be found on the WWW at the following URL:

http://www.esecurity.ch/serieseditor.html

Also, if you'd like to contribute to the series by writing a book about a topic related to computer security, feel free to contact either the Commissioning Editor or the Series Editor at Artech House.

For a listing of recent titles in the *Artech House Computer Security Series,* turn to the back of this book.

User's Guide to Cryptography and Standards

Alexander W. Dent
Chris J. Mitchell

Artech House
Boston ● London
www.artechhouse.com

Library of Congress Cataloging-in-Publication Data
Dent, Alexander W.
 User's guide to cryptography and standards/Alexander W. Dent, Chris J. Mitchell.
  p. cm — (Artech House computer security series)
 ISBN 1-58053-530-5 (alk. paper)
  1. Computer security. 2. Cryptography—Standards. 3. Computers—Access
control—Standards. I. Mitchell, Chris J. II. Title. III. Series

 QA76.9.A25D465 2004
 005.8–dc22

2004057411

British Library Cataloguing in Publication Data
Dent, Alexander W.
 User's guide to cryptography and standards—
 (Artech House computer security series)
 1. Data encryption (Computer science)
 I. Title II. Mitchell, Chris
 005.8'2

 ISBN 1-58053-530-5

Cover design by Yekaterina Ratner

© 2005 ARTECH HOUSE, INC.
685 Canton Street
Norwood, MA 02062

International Standard Book Number: 1-58053-530-5

10 9 8 7 6 5 4 3 2 1

Contents

Acknowledgments .... *xv*

1 Introduction 1

1.1 Scope and purpose   1

1.2 Structure of the book   3

1.3 Terminology   4

1.4 Modular arithmetic   5

1.5 Notes   7

References   7

2 Standards and the Standardization Process 9

2.1 Why bother with standards?   9

2.2 International standardization organizations   10

    2.2.1 International Organization for Standardization (ISO)   10

    2.2.2 International Electrotechnical Commission (IEC)   12

    2.2.3 International Telecommunication Union (ITU)   12

2.3 National standardization organizations   12

    2.3.1 American National Standards Institute (ANSI)   13

    2.3.2 British Standards Institute (BSI)   13

    2.3.3 National Institute of Standards and Technology (NIST)   13

2.4 Industrial standardization organizations   13

    2.4.1 Third Generation Partnership Project (3GPP)   14

    2.4.2 European Telecommunications Standard Institute (ETSI)   14

    2.4.3 Institute of Electrical and Electronics Engineers (IEEE) 14

    2.4.4 Internet Engineering Task Force (IETF)   14

    2.4.5 Standards for Efficient Cryptography Group (SECG)   15

    2.4.6 Public-Key Cryptography Standards (PKCSs)   15

2.5 Cryptographic evaluation bodies   16

2.6 Notes   17

References   17

3 **Security Mechanisms and Security Services** **19**

   3.1   Introduction   19
   3.2   Security standards   20
   3.3   A model for security   21
         3.3.1   Security policies   21

   3.4   Security services   22
         3.4.1   Authentication   23
         3.4.2   Access control   23
         3.4.3   Data confidentiality   24
         3.4.4   Data integrity   24
         3.4.5   Non-repudiation   25
         3.4.6   Other services   25
         3.4.7   Summary   25

   3.5   Security mechanisms   26
         3.5.1   Specific security mechanisms   26
         3.5.2   Pervasive security mechanisms   29
         3.5.3   Selection of security mechanisms   30

   3.6   Relating services to mechanisms   31

   3.7   Service and protocol layers   31
         3.7.1   The OSI model   31
         3.7.2   Layers versus security services   32
         3.7.3   The Internet model   33

   3.8   Security management   34
         3.8.1   System security management   35
         3.8.2   Security service management   35
         3.8.3   Security mechanism management   35
         3.8.4   Security of OSI management   36
         3.8.5   Assurance   36

   3.9   Security frameworks   36
         3.9.1   Frameworks overview   37
         3.9.2   Authentication framework   37
         3.9.3   Access control framework   37
         3.9.4   Non-repudiation framework   37
         3.9.5   Confidentiality framework   38
         3.9.6   Integrity framework   38
         3.9.7   Audit and alarms framework   38

   3.10 Notes   38
         References   40

4 **Encryption** **45**

4.1	Definitions and basic properties	46
	4.1.1 Symmetric ciphers	46
	4.1.2 Asymmetric ciphers	46
	4.1.3 Attacks against encryption schemes	47
4.2	Block ciphers	48
	4.2.1 The National Bureau of Standards and DES	49
	4.2.2 The ISO Register of Cryptographic Algorithms	51
	4.2.3 NIST and AES	52
	4.2.4 3GPP and KASUMI	52
	4.2.5 ISO/IEC 18033	53
4.3	Stream ciphers	53
4.4	Asymmetric ciphers	56
	4.4.1 The Rivest-Shamir-Adleman (RSA) scheme	57
	4.4.2 Industry Standards for Asymmetric Encryption	59
	4.4.3 IEEE 1363	60
	4.4.4 ISO/IEC 18033	61
4.5	Notes	63
	References	67

5 **Modes of Operation for Block Ciphers** **71**

5.1	Definitions and basic properties	71
5.2	Standards for modes of operation	72
5.3	Padding methods	72
5.4	ECB mode	73
5.5	Cipher block chaining (CBC) mode	74
5.6	CTR mode	77
5.7	OFB mode	79
5.8	CFB mode	81
5.9	Choosing a mode of operation	84
5.10	Other modes	86
	5.10.1 Triple-DES modes	86
	5.10.2 Authenticated encryption modes	87
5.11	Notes	87
	References	89

6 **Cryptographic Hash Functions** **93**

6.1	Definitions and basic properties	93
	6.1.1 The security of a hash function	93
	6.1.2 Iterative hash functions	95

6.2   Standards for hash functions   97
6.3   Hash functions based on block ciphers   98
    6.3.1   Padding methods   98
    6.3.2   Block cipher hash function 1   99
    6.3.3   Block cipher hash function 2   101
6.4   Dedicated hash functions   103
6.5   Hash functions based on modular arithmetic   105
6.6   Choosing a hash function   105
6.7   Notes   106
    References   109

7 Message Authentication Codes (MACs) 113

7.1   Definitions and basic properties   113
7.2   Standards for MACs   115
7.3   CBC-MACs   116
    7.3.1   SMAC—the simplest form of CBC-MAC   116
    7.3.2   Padding methods   117
    7.3.3   Output transformations   119
    7.3.4   Other CBC-MAC schemes   121
    7.3.5   MAC algorithm 4 from ISO/IEC 9797-1   123
    7.3.6   MAC algorithms 5 and 6 from ISO/IEC 9797-1 124
    7.3.7   XCBC, TMAC, and OMAC   124
    7.3.8   Choosing a CBC-MAC function   125
7.4   MACs based on hash functions   126
    7.4.1   The MDx-MAC functions   127
    7.4.2   HMAC   127
    7.4.3   MDx-MAC variant for short messages   128
    7.4.4   Choosing a hash-based MAC function   128
7.5   Other MAC functions   128
7.6   Notes   129
    References   131

8 Digital Signatures 135

8.1   Definitions and basic properties   135
    8.1.1   Deterministic and probabilistic signature schemes 138
    8.1.2   Reversible and nonreversible signature schemes   139
    8.1.3   Identity-based and certificate-based signature
        schemes   140
8.2   Standards for digital signatures   141
8.3   The Digital Signature Algorithm (DSA)   142

8.4   RSA-based signature schemes   144

8.5   Digital signatures and the law   147

    8.5.1   *U.S. legislation*   147

    8.5.2   *Certification authorities*   149

    8.5.3   *EU legislation*   149

8.6   Choosing a digital signature scheme   150

8.7   Notes   151

    References   156

9   **Non-Repudiation Mechanisms** **159**

9.1   Introduction   159

9.2   Standards for non-repudiation   160

9.3   Non-repudiation model and services   160

    9.3.1   *A model for non-repudiation*   161

    9.3.2   *Types of evidence*   162

    9.3.3   *Non-repudiation services*   162

    9.3.4   *Non-repudiation tokens*   163

9.4   Non-repudiation using symmetric cryptography   164

    9.4.1   *Non-repudiation of origin using MACs*   164

    9.4.2   *Non-repudiation of delivery using MACs*   166

    9.4.3   *Other mechanisms*   168

9.5   Non-repudiation using asymmetric cryptography   168

    9.5.1   *Non-repudiation of origin using signatures*   168

    9.5.2   *Non-repudiation of delivery using signatures*   169

    9.5.3   *Other mechanisms*   170

9.6   Time-stamping and non-repudiation   170

9.7   Notes   170

    References   171

10   **Authentication Protocols** **173**

10.1   Introduction   174

10.2   Standards for entity authentication protocols   175

10.3   Cryptographic mechanisms   176

    10.3.1   *Using symmetric encryption*   176

    10.3.2   *Using MACs*   177

    10.3.3   *Using digital signatures*   178

    10.3.4   *Zero-knowledge protocols*   178

    10.3.5   *Using asymmetric encryption*   178

    10.3.6   *Using other asymmetric cryptographic techniques*   179

10.4	Timeliness checking mechanisms	179
	10.4.1 Time-stamps	179
	10.4.2 Nonces	180
10.5	Authentication using symmetric cryptography	181
	10.5.1 Unilateral authentication protocols	181
	10.5.2 Mutual authentication protocols	185
	10.5.3 Third party–aided mechanisms	189
10.6	Authentication using asymmetric cryptography	194
	10.6.1 Unilateral authentication mechanisms	195
	10.6.2 Mutual authentication mechanisms	197
10.7	Manual authentication protocols	200
	10.7.1 Manual authentication using a short check-value	202
	10.7.2 Manual authentication using a full-length MAC function	203
10.8	Choosing an authentication protocol	205
10.9	Notes	207
	References	210

11   Key Management Frameworks 215

11.1	Standards for key management	215
11.2	Definitions and basic properties	216
	11.2.1 Threats and protection	216
	11.2.2 Basic definitions	217
	11.2.3 Key separation	218
	11.2.4 Key hierarchies	218
	11.2.5 Registration authorities	219
11.3	The general framework	219
	11.3.1 Key generation	221
	11.3.2 Key activation	223
	11.3.3 Key deactivation	223
	11.3.4 Key reactivation	224
	11.3.5 Key destruction	224
11.4	The ANSI X9.24 framework	225
	11.4.1 General requirements	225
	11.4.2 Key generation	227
	11.4.3 Key distribution	227
	11.4.4 Key utilization	227
	11.4.5 Key replacement	228
	11.4.6 Key destruction and archival	228
11.5	Notes	228
	References	229

12 **Key Establishment Mechanisms** **231**

12.1	Definitions and basic properties	231
	12.1.1 *Key establishment mechanisms and authentication protocols*	233
	12.1.2 *Properties of key establishment mechanisms*	234
12.2	Standards for key establishment	235
	12.2.1 *Standards using symmetric techniques*	235
	12.2.2 *Standards using asymmetric techniques*	236
12.3	Physical mechanisms	237
	12.3.1 *Dual control*	238
12.4	Mechanisms using symmetric cryptography	238
	12.4.1 *Direct communication*	239
	12.4.2 *Key distribution centers*	241
	12.4.3 *Key translation centers (KTCs)*	244
	12.4.4 *Key establishment between different security domains*	246
12.5	Mechanisms using asymmetric cryptography	246
	12.5.1 *The Diffie-Hellman function*	248
	12.5.2 *Key agreement mechanisms*	249
	12.5.3 *Key transport mechanisms*	253
12.6	Key establishment based on weak secrets	254
12.7	Key establishment for mobile networks	255
12.8	Choosing a key establishment scheme	258
12.9	Notes	259
	References	263

13 **Public Key Infrastructures** **267**

13.1	What is a PKI?	267
13.2	PKI standards	269
13.3	Certificate formats	271
	13.3.1 *X.509 public key certificates*	271
	13.3.2 *X.509 attribute certificates*	276
	13.3.3 *X.509 certificate profiles*	276
	13.3.4 *Other certificate formats*	278
13.4	Certificate management	278
	13.4.1 *The certificate management protocol (CMP)*	279
	13.4.2 *Certificate request messages*	281
	13.4.3 *Mechanisms for proof of possession*	282
	13.4.4 *Other certificate management standards*	282
13.5	Certificate storage and retrieval	283
	13.5.1 *X.500 directories*	283
	13.5.2 *Using LDAP version 2*	283

	13.5.3	*Using FTP and HTTP*	284
	13.5.4	*Delegating certification path discovery*	284
13.6	Certificate status discovery	284
	13.6.1	*Certificate revocation lists (CRLs)*	285
	13.6.2	*The on-line certificate status protocol (OCSP)*	285
	13.6.3	*Using proxies for status management*	285
13.7	Certificate policies and certification practice statements	286
13.8	Notes	287
	References	289

14   Trusted Third Parties **295**

14.1	Definitions and basic properties	295
14.2	Standards for managing TTPs	297
14.3	TTP requirements	297
	14.3.1	*Policy and practice statements*	297
	14.3.2	*TTP management*	298
	14.3.3	*Legal considerations*	299
14.4	TTP architectures	299
	14.4.1	*Two-party TTP architectures*	300
	14.4.2	*Interworking TTPs*	302
14.5	Time-stamping authorities	302
	14.5.1	*Time-stamping tokens*	303
	14.5.2	*Linked tokens*	304
14.6	Digital archiving authorities	305
14.7	Notes	305
	References	307

15   Cryptographic APIs **309**

15.1	Introduction	309
15.2	Standards for crypto APIs	311
15.3	GSS-API	312
	15.3.1	*Properties of the API*	313
	15.3.2	*Language bindings*	314
	15.3.3	*Authentication protocols*	314
15.4	PKCS #11	315
	15.4.1	*Data storage*	315
	15.4.2	*Access control*	316
	15.4.3	*Sessions and concurrency*	316
15.5	Security issues	316
15.6	Notes	318
	References	319

16   **Other Standards** **323**

16.1   Random bit generation   323

  16.1.1   Nondeterministic RBGs   324

  16.1.2   Deterministic RBGs   326

  16.1.3   Generating random numbers   327

16.2   Prime number generation   328

16.3   Authenticated encryption   329

  16.3.1   CTR and CBC-MAC (CCM) mode   330

  16.3.2   CTR and OMAC (EAX) mode   333

16.4   Security modules   336

  16.4.1   Security modules in the financial sector   336

  16.4.2   Security modules in the wider world   338

16.5   Standards for the use of biometric techniques   339

  16.5.1   General requirements of a biometric   340

  16.5.2   Common biometrics   341

  16.5.3   The general biometric architecture   343

  16.5.4   Supporting functions   344

  16.5.5   Biometric standards   344

16.6   Information security management   345

16.7   Notes   347

  References   350

17   **Standards: The Future** **355**

Appendix A: Table of Standards **359**

A.1   3GPP standards   359

A.2   ANSI standards   360

A.3   BSI standards   360

A.4   ETSI standards   361

A.5   IEEE standards   361

A.6   IETF requests for comments (RFCs)   361

A.7   ISO standards   363

A.8   ITU-T Recommendations   366

A.9   NIST FIPS   367

A.10   RSA PKCS   368

A.11   SECG standards   368

About the Authors **369**

Index **371**

Acknowledgments

This book has grown out of the course "Standards and Evaluation Criteria," given as part of the Royal Holloway masters degree in information security ever since its inception in 1992. This course was originally jointly taught by Dieter Gollmann and Chris Mitchell; for a while was given by Chris Mitchell alone; and most recently has been looked after by Alex Dent. While the coverage of this book is not the same as the scope of the course, there is a considerable overlap, and we would like to acknowledge the invaluable comments, advice and corrections given by many generations of students and fellow lecturers, including, of course, Dieter, as well the several visiting lecturers who have helped out over the years.

We are also very grateful for the many friends who have helped us enormously by reading and commenting on drafts of this book. Above all else, we would like to thank Bart Preneel, who somehow found time to read the whole book and provide us with many invaluable corrections and additions. We must also thank Niklas Borselius, Colin Boyd, Robert Carolina, Liqun Chen, Jason Crampton, Christine Dale, Simon Hurley, Kostas Markantonakis, Keith Mayes, Paulo Pagliusi, Tony Palmer, Geraint Price and Scarlet Schwiderski-Grosche for their input, as well as the many others who we have forgotten to mention. Of course, we remain responsible for the errors that remain in the book, but there would certainly be many more without the generous help we have received.

Another, often overlooked, group of people whose help we must acknowledge are the many anonymous experts who put in the long hours necessary to write and provide input to standards. Without them we would not have the material on which to base this book, and the users of standards would not have the guidance that they need.

Last, but by no means least, we would like to thank our families and friends for all the support and encouragement they have given us, without which this book would never have got off the ground.

Contents

1.1 Scope and purpose

1.2 Structure of the book

1.3 Terminology

1.4 Modular arithmetic

1.5 Notes

Introduction

This book is about standards, cryptography, and standards for cryptography. It has been written in the hope that it will serve a number of purposes, including the following.

- Perhaps most importantly, to provide a general introduction to standardized cryptography for the user of this technology (i.e., a designer or developer who wishes to build cryptographic methods into a system);

- To provide a guide to cryptography, based around the main standards, for students and others wishing to understand what services cryptography can provide.

It does not, however, try to describe how cryptography is used in specific application areas, nor does it cover standards for the use of cryptography in particular application domains. These issues are sufficiently large to require a book or books to themselves.

1.1 Scope and purpose

This book derives to a large extent from our joint experience in teaching a course on security standards as part of the Royal Holloway M.Sc. in information security. Over the 12 years during which the course has been run, the collection of cryptographic standards has grown hugely, and we have, within this text, attempted to provide a historical perspective for the development of cryptographic standards.

We have attempted to make this book accessible to the general reader, although it is not really designed for the reader completely unfamiliar with cryptography and its possible applications. We have certainly minimized the mathematical content of the material, and later in this introduction we provide a basic introduction to the mathematical concepts that we could not escape. However the reader is encouraged to get started on the book and only refer to the mathematical introduction if concepts arise with which they are not familiar.

Over the last 30 years, cryptography has grown from being a specialist technology used almost exclusively by governments and the military, to a technology underpinning the security of the electronic world. Cryptographic techniques, such as digital signature and data encryption algorithms, are used seamlessly without our knowledge in systems such as PC Web browsers, mobile telephones, and smart card–based credit cards.

Cryptography itself has grown into an important branch of applied mathematics and theoretical computer science. Indeed, in terms of volumes of published material, cryptography and its applications far outweigh parallel literature on coding and information theory. This is despite the fact that information theory has been an area of public research since the late 1940s, around 25 years longer than cryptography.

As mentioned at the beginning of this chapter, this book is about both cryptography and standards for cryptography. Over the last few years standards have been issued for most of the commonly used types of cryptographic schemes, and for the majority of the common uses of cryptography. This has enabled us to write a book that provides both an introduction to all types of cryptographic scheme and a guide to standardized techniques. One purpose of the book is to provide enough information to enable the standardized schemes to be used; in particular we have attempted to provide fairly exhaustive information on what standards there are, and what they contain. However, if conformance with a standard is being claimed, the reader is advised to refer to standards for fine details of the algorithms.

The book is not intended to provide a thorough grounding in the *theory* of cryptography, although pointers are provided to where more information may be found. Similarly, details of *cryptanalysis* of algorithms, although a vitally important subject, are not given in this volume. The main purpose, as stated above, is to enable users to choose algorithms for practical use, with confidence that the algorithms have been sufficiently well scrutinized by the academic community for them to be agreed standards. Of course, standardization does not in itself guarantee that any algorithm will not be the subject of an attack in the future, but in general standardized techniques represent the state of the art in cryptography. There are exceptions nevertheless, where a cryptographic technique is adopted that has not been scrutinized by the wider community—such exceptions tend to be in application-specific standards, and such standards are not covered here. As with all users of cryptography, users of standardized techniques are recommended to keep abreast of new developments in the field.

The reader should also be aware that certain standardized techniques are known to be weak unless used with care and are retained for legacy reasons alone. That is, there may be a large deployed base of systems using the suspect technique, and, while the technique should not be deployed in new systems, it remains secure if used in the appropriate way. In such a case, guidance is given in this book to avoid such techniques (and such guidance is also typically present in the standard itself). Of course, if a technique is always weak, no matter how carefully used, then it will normally be removed from the relevant standards.

Moreover, this book does not provide full implementation details for cryptographic techniques. For this the reader should either refer to the relevant standard, or to some of the other sources either cited in the notes at the end of the relevant chapter or mentioned on the book Web page (see below). This book is not intended to replace the standards to which it refers, and a system designer or developer wishing to claim conformance to a standard should always consult the text of the standard itself.

Each of the main chapters of this book is equipped with a reference *notes* section. In these notes pointers to the wider literature and further background reading are provided.

Finally, note that, as mentioned earlier, there is a Web page for the book: http://www.isg.rhul.ac.uk/ugcs/. We plan to maintain an up-to-date list of corrections to this book on this page, as well as additional material and pointers to other sources of information. We hope that this will be of use to all users of the book. If you find any errors in the book that have not been listed on the Web page, we would be very grateful if you could let us know by sending an e-mail to c.mitchell@rhul.ac.uk—we do not offer any financial incentives, but we will be happy to acknowledge on the Web page the first finder of every mistake.

1.2 Structure of the book

Following this introductory chapter are a total of 16 chapters covering different aspects of cryptography and its standardization. We now briefly review the contents of these chapters.

Chapters 2 and 3 are introductory in nature. Chapter 2 contains a review of the main relevant standardization bodies and provides a brief introduction to the main standardization processes. This is followed by Chapter 3, in which a set of terminology for the use of cryptography is defined. While most of the chapters in the book can be read in any order, we would recommend all readers to first work through these two chapters, since they provide the context and terminology for the whole of the remainder.

Chapters 4 through 8 are concerned with specific types of cryptographic algorithms and the relevant standards. Chapters 4 and 5 are concerned with encryption algorithms and their use for providing data confidentiality. Chapters 6 through 8 are concerned with cryptographic hash functions, message authentication codes, and digital signatures, respectively. These mechanisms can be used to protect the integrity and guarantee the origin of data.

Chapters 9 and 10 are a little different from the previous chapters. These two chapters respectively describe non-repudiation and authentication protocols. These involve the relevant parties exchanging a sequence of messages constructed using cryptographic algorithms, such as encryption algorithms and digital signatures. Successful completion of the protocol will provide the required security assurances to the protocol participants.

All cryptographic methods rely on the use and management of keys. Thus the topic of *key management* is absolutely fundamental to the use of cryptography. We devote Chapters 11 through 13 to this complex and sometimes difficult topic. Chapter 11 describes a standardized framework for key management. Protocols for establishing shared secret keys are the main focus of Chapter 12. The topic of public key infrastructures is the focus of Chapter 13.

Two further chapters cover issues relating to the use of cryptography: Chapter 14 considers standards governing the use of trusted third parties to support the use and management of cryptographic techniques. The standardization of cryptographic application program interfaces is then considered in Chapter 15.

Finally, Chapters 16 and 17 conclude the main part of the book. Chapter 16 summarizes a variety of other standards with relevance to cryptography. The future of cryptographic standardization is considered in Chapter 17. Appendix A provides numerical lists of all the standards discussed in this book, with references to the chapters in which they are discussed.

1.3 Terminology

In writing this book we have tried to use a consistent set of terminology. This has meant that we have had in some cases to change the terminology used in the standards themselves, although we have also tried to stay as close as possible to the original notation. We use the following notation throughout this book. In general, notations are also defined where they are used—this list is provided as a convenient point of reference.

- $X||Y$ denotes the block of bits obtained by concatenating the blocks X and Y.

- $X \oplus Y$ denotes the bit-wise exclusive-or of blocks of bits X and Y (of the same length).

- $X|_i$ represents the leftmost i bits of the block of bits X.

- $X|^i$ represents the rightmost i bits of the block of bits X.

- Cert_A denotes the public key certificate of entity A.

- d denotes a decryption algorithm. More specifically, d_K represents the particular symmetric decryption function corresponding to the secret key K, and $d_K(Y)$ denotes the symmetrically decrypted version of ciphertext Y using the key K.

- e denotes an encryption algorithm. More specifically, e_K represents the particular symmetric encryption function corresponding to the secret key K, and $e_K(X)$ denotes the symmetrically encrypted version of data X using the key K.

- $\mathcal{E}$ denotes an asymmetric encryption algorithm. More specifically, $\mathcal{E}(X, P_A)$ denotes the result of asymmetrically encrypting data block X using the public key P_A. For convenience, and for consistency with the notation used in published standards, we use $e_A(X)$ as a synonym for $\mathcal{E}(X, P_A)$, where the public key of entity A is assumed to be defined by the context.

▸ i_A denotes an identifier (e.g., a name) for entity A.

▸ K is used to denote a secret key for a symmetric cryptographic algorithm.

▸ K_{AB} denotes a secret key shared by entities A and B.

▸ $\mathrm{MAC}_K(X)$ denotes a MAC computed on data string X using the secret key K.

▸ n represents the block length of a block cipher (i.e., the number of bits in a ciphertext or plaintext block).

▸ P_A denotes the public key belonging to entity A.

▸ $\mathcal{S}$ denotes the signing function for a digital signature algorithm. Specifically $\mathcal{S}(m, s_A)$ denotes a digital signature computed on message m using the private signing key s_A. For convenience, and for consistency with the notation used in published standards, we use $\mathcal{S}_A(m)$ as a synonym for $\mathcal{S}(m, s_A)$, where the public key of entity A is assumed to be defined by the context.

▸ s_A denotes the private key belonging to entity A.

▸ $\mathcal{V}$ denotes the verification function for a digital signature algorithm.

▸ 1^i denotes a block of i bits all set to 1.

▸ The inclusion of fields within square brackets indicates that they are optional.

1.4   Modular arithmetic

We conclude this introductory chapter by introducing some elementary mathematics necessary for an understanding of the chapters dealing with asymmetric cryptography, particularly Chapters 4 and 8. Specifically we introduce the notion of *modular arithmetic* and discuss its implementation.

Modular arithmetic is a special type of arithmetic that can be performed using whole numbers (integers). To perform modular arithmetic it is first necessary to choose the *modulus*, which must be an integer greater than 1. We typically write n for the modulus. For any two integers a and b we then define

$$a \equiv b \quad (\mathrm{mod}\ n) \tag{1.1}$$

if and only if a and b leave the same remainder when they are divided by n.

For example, if $n = 2$, then we have $3 \equiv 5 \pmod{2}$ and $5 \equiv 9 \pmod{2}$, since 3, 5, and 9 all leave the remainder 1 when divided by 2. However, $3 \not\equiv 4 \pmod{2}$ and $7 \not\equiv 0 \pmod{2}$, since 4 and 0 leave remainder 0 when divided by 2, whereas 3 and 7 leave remainder 1. We can equivalently define $a \equiv b$ (mod n) if and only if n divides into $a - b$. That is, $8 \equiv 2$ (mod 3) since 3 divides into (is a factor of) $8 - 2 = 6$.

The symbol $\equiv$ defined in this way is what is known as an *equivalence relation*. When reading a formula such as $3 \equiv 18$ (mod 5), one should read it as "three is congruent to 18 modulo 5."

There is a second version of the "mod" notation, where "mod" acts as a binary operation. We write $a \bmod n$ for the smallest nonnegative integer b that satisfies $b \equiv a$ (mod n). Hence, 13 mod 4 = 1 and 12 mod 3 = 0.

Modular arithmetic is often used in the construction of asymmetric (public-key) schemes, including asymmetric encryption schemes (see Chapter 4) and digital signature schemes (see Chapter 8). In these cases it is very important to know which modular arithmetic operations can be computed efficiently, and which operations cannot be efficiently computed if suitably large numbers are involved. Of course, the term "efficiently" is subjective: The amount of computational effort required to do a certain computation may mean that this operation is efficient in one environment but inefficient in another, more limited, environment such as on a smart card. Furthermore, there is a whole mathematical theory that discusses the (theoretical) efficiency of algorithms. None of this theory, however, will be relevant to this book, and, for our purposes, it will be enough to note that there are some operations that are "easy" to compute, and others that are "hard" provided suitably large numbers are involved.

In general, simple modular arithmetic operations such as addition, subtraction, multiplication, and exponentiation are efficiently computable. Indeed, to compute

$$a \bmod n + b \bmod n \qquad (1.2)$$

it is only necessary to compute

$$(a + b) \bmod n \qquad (1.3)$$

and subtraction, multiplication, and exponentiation are defined in the same way. It is harder to define division using modular arithmetic. What does it mean to divide 5 by 2 modulo 7? Instead, we sidestep the issue by defining inversion. The inverse of a number x modulo n, written $x^{-1} \bmod n$, is the number such that $x \cdot x^{-1} \equiv 1$ (mod n). A number need not always have an inverse, but, when it does, that inverse is unique modulo n. In fact, a number x has an inverse modulo n if and only if there are no numbers bigger than one that divide into both x and n. If an inverse exists then it can be computed efficiently.

A lot of the cryptographic properties of modular arithmetic are based on the properties of prime numbers. A number is prime if it is bigger than one, and the only numbers that divide into it are one and the number itself. Methods for generating prime numbers suitable for use in cryptography are discussed in Chapter 16.

Not all operations that we can easily compute on "normal" numbers (i.e., ..., −1, 0, 1, 2, ...) can be efficiently computed using modular arithmetic. For example, it appears to be difficult to take logarithms modulo a large prime. In other words, if we know values g, y, and p such that p is a large prime and $g^x \equiv y \pmod{p}$, then, except for certain special cases, it is still difficult to compute x. This is known as the "discrete logarithm" (or "discrete log") problem.

It also appears to be difficult to compute the roots of a number in a modular arithmetic setting when the prime factorization of the modulus is unknown. This means that even if we know values e, y, and n such that $x^e \equiv y \pmod{n}$ then it is still difficult to compute x unless we know all of the prime numbers that divide into n. If we know all of the prime numbers that divide into n then computing x becomes easy.

1.5 Notes

Section 1.1

There are many useful books on cryptography—we mention just three. Murphy and Piper's book [1] provides a very simple introduction to cryptography. Schneier's book [2] is a very readable account of modern cryptography. In the notes in subsequent chapters we refer to books containing more detail on the topics covered in the particular chapter. Of particular importance in this respect is the *Handbook of Applied Cryptography* [3], which provides a detailed and meticulously researched account of cryptographic topics.

It is interesting to note that both modern cryptography and information theory owe a huge debt to the pioneering work of Shannon, who published enormously influential papers on both topics in the postwar years [4, 5].

Section 1.4

There are many books providing simple explanations of modular arithmetic and related concepts. Indeed, almost any book on modern cryptography will provide an explanation. Chapter 2 of [3] provides an extremely useful introduction to not only modular arithmetic but also many other mathematical concepts necessary to understand modern cryptography.

References

[1] Piper, F., and S. Murphy, *Cryptography: A Very Short Introduction*, Oxford, England: Oxford University Press, 2002.

[2] Schneier, B., *Applied Cryptography*, 2nd ed., New York: John Wiley and Sons, 1996.

[3] Menezes, A. J., P. C. van Oorschot, and S. A. Vanstone, *Handbook of Applied Cryptography*, Boca Raton, FL: CRC Press, 1997.

[4] Shannon, C. E., "A Mathematical Theory of Communication," *Bell System Technical Journal*, Vol. 27, 1948, pp. 379–423, 623–656.

[5] Shannon, C. E., "Communication Theory of Secrecy Systems," *Bell System Technical Journal*, Vol. 28, 1949, pp. 656–715.

Contents

2.1 Why bother with standards?

2.2 International standardization organizations

2.3 National standardization organizations

2.4 Industrial standardization organizations

2.5 Cryptographic evaluation bodies

2.6 Notes

Standards and the Standardization Process

This chapter is not concerned with cryptography directly but with the different organizations that produce cryptographic standards. A standard is a document that contains a series of rules or guidelines for a common task. In cryptography, standards provide common references for algorithms and protocols, advice on designing secure computer systems, and guidelines for managing cryptographic services and information.

There are a large variety of standards-making bodies, originally established for quite different reasons. For example, the International Telecommunication Union (ITU) (see Section 2.2.3) was set up to enable interworking between countries, essentially to enable international postal and telecommunications services to operate. The International Organization for Standardization (ISO) appears to have been originally set up to standardize the design of physical products (e.g., screw threads), to enable manufacturers to achieve greater levels of compatibility, and hence reduce costs and increase volumes. Other bodies appear to have originated to reflect the needs of particular industries or individual governments. Despite different origins, several standardization bodies have now produced standards governing the operation and use of cryptography, reflecting the broad importance of this technology.

2.1 Why bother with standards?

On its Web site the British Standards Institute (BSI) lists eight reasons why the use of standards might aid a business:

- Customer satisfaction;
- Cost and time effectiveness;
- Legal compliance;
- Better management;
- Integrity;

- Trust;

- Ability to prove a better brand;

- Ease of export and credibility as an international player.

Almost all of these advantages can, in some way, be gained by a business that chooses to use cryptographic standards. The most obvious advantages gained by the use of cryptographic standards are trust and cost- and time-effectiveness. A business that makes use of standardized cryptography—cryptographic schemes that have been scrutinized by a large number of experts—can trust that the schemes they are using are secure and need not spend time and money developing their own techniques.

From a cryptographic point of view, there are two main reasons why the use of products based on cryptographic standards is a good idea. The first is security—a business can trust that a product based on a cryptographic standard is secure, since the techniques it uses have been studied by a large number of experts. The second is interoperability. Interoperability occurs when two products made by different companies or designed to operate on different platforms can interact with each other. Cryptographic standards enable this to happen by precisely defining the format that data must take as it passes between different types of applications, and by precisely defining how each algorithm and protocol must run so that every product featuring that protocol will work in exactly the same way.

There are disadvantages to using standardized cryptographic techniques too. Due to their widespread use, they make attractive targets for both legitimate researchers and malicious attackers, and if a standardized scheme is broken then a company that advertises its compliance to a standard may find itself under attack very quickly. However, on balance, these disadvantages are comparatively minor compared to the advantages of using standardized schemes.

2.2 International standardization organizations

Most of the relevant cryptographic standardization bodies we shall discuss are international bodies (i.e., their standards are endorsed by many different countries, and the standards are produced based on inputs from an international panel of experts). We shall discuss each of the major bodies in turn.

2.2.1 International Organization for Standardization (ISO)

Many of the standards we will examine have been developed by ISO, whose name is derived from the Greek word "isos" meaning "equal"; it develops standards in a large number of completely separate fields. The standardization work undertaken by ISO is actually completed by a number of different technical committees (TCs), each concerned with a broad subject area. The technical committees further distribute the work to a series of subcommittees (SCs), which, in turn, distribute the work to various working groups (WGs).

Work on cryptographic standards within ISO is primarily conducted by two technical committees: TC68 and JTC1. The ISO/IEC Joint Technical

Committee (JTC1) is a collaboration between ISO and the IEC. The remit of this committee is huge, covering the whole of information technology! While most of the work that is being done by this committee is not security-related, there are several very important subcommittees that work with cryptography or security-related issues. These are JTC1/SC17, which works on security cards and personal identification; JTC1/SC27, whose remit is IT security techniques; and JTC1/SC37, which works on biometric techniques.

TC68 deals with the financial services industry and includes several subcommittees whose remits include the use of cryptography to secure financial data. Primarily, these subcommittees interpret the generic cryptography standards produced by ISO/IEC JTC1 and apply them to the financial sector. This interpretation often involves the selection of a single cryptographic scheme from the number that have been standardized by ISO/IEC JTC1 and making sure that all of the relevant information for that scheme, including such details as how to deal with starting variables and which hash function or block cipher algorithms are to be used with the scheme, are specified. However, TC68 also produces new cryptographic standards, particularly in areas for which there are no corresponding JTC1 standards.

ISO standards are numbered and are referred to by their standard number. For example, ISO 8730 is the ISO standard that details the requirements that a message authentication code must satisfy if it is to be used in the financial sector. Standards that have been split into multiple parts are referred to by their standard number and part number. For example, ISO 8731-1 is the first part of ISO 8731 and contains the specifications of a particular message authentication code algorithm. Standards that are published jointly by ISO and the IEC through the joint technical committee are referred to as ISO/IEC standards.

ISO also publishes technical reports. These are not standards, just guidelines for a particular task, and can be distinguished from ISO standards as they contain the letters "TR." For example, ISO/IEC TR 14516 is the technical report giving guidelines on the use of trusted third parties.

Most standardization bodies produce standards in roughly the same way, so we will only describe the process used by the ISO/IEC JTC1 technical committee. A standard begins life as a new work item (NWI) proposed by an ISO member body [such as the American National Standards Institute (ANSI) or British Standards Institute (BSI)—see Section 2.3]. If the new work item is accepted then an editor is appointed to produce a series of working drafts (WDs). Each working draft is circulated to the member bodies for comment, but member bodies are not yet required to vote on whether they think the draft would be acceptable as an international standard. Draft (unpublished) ISO/IEC standards in the WD stage are distinguished from published standards by the inclusion of the letters "WD." For example, ISO/IEC WD 19790 is the draft ISO/IEC standard on the security requirements for cryptographic modules.

Once the editor has produced a stable WD, which, although not complete, is accepted by the majority of the the ISO member bodies, the editor then produces a committee draft (CD). Draft ISO/IEC standards in the CD stage are distinguished from published standards by the inclusion of the letters "CD." For example, ISO/IEC CD 18031 is draft ISO/IEC standard on random bit generation. At this stage, ISO member bodies can still propose technical and editorial changes, and propose schemes to be included in the standard, although, unlike WDs, member bodies vote on the standard after each committee draft is produced. After the member bodies agree on the technical content of the standard, the editor produces a final committee draft (FCD) after which, if the FCD is approved by the member bodies, the technical content of the standard cannot be changed.

Last, the editor produces one or more distribution (DIS) drafts, concluding with a final distribution (FDIS) draft. Only editorial changes can be made to the standard at this stage, and each member body votes on whether the current draft is suitable for publication. The standard is only published if the majority of the member bodies approve of the FDIS draft.

For more information about ISO, and to purchase ISO standards, visit the ISO Web site: http://www.iso.ch/. ISO standards can also be purchased from ISO national member bodies, such as ANSI in the United States and BSI in the United Kingdom (see Section 2.3).

2.2.2   International Electrotechnical Commission (IEC)

The IEC produces standards for all electrical and electronic technologies. Its main standardization effort in cryptography and security-related issues is achieved through the joint technical committee it has formed with ISO, JTC1. For more information on JTC1, see Section 2.2.1. More information about the IEC and IEC standards is available from the IEC Web site: http://www.iec.ch/.

2.2.3   International Telecommunication Union (ITU)

The International Telecommunication Union (ITU) is a United Nations–sponsored organization that seeks to coordinate government and corporate efforts in producing global telecommunications networks and services. It is split into three main branches: the ITU-R, which deals with radio communication; the ITU-D, which deals with telecommunications development; and the ITU-T, which deals with telecommunications standards.

Our main focus will be the ITU-T standards and, specifically, the ITU-T X series of standards, which are concerned with data networks. These standards tend to be more focused on network design than on cryptography, but do cover such important topics as public-key infrastructures and the use of cryptographic services in networks. ITU-T standards are known as "recommendations."

More information about the ITU can be found on its Web site: http://www.itu.int/. More information on ITU-T standards can be found on a separate Web site: http://www.itu.int/ITU-T/.

2.3   National standardization organizations

Many countries have their own national standardization bodies. These bodies may produce standards of their own, and may also be part of, and contribute to, the work of international standardization bodies. National standardization bodies that contribute to the ISO standardization body are known as ISO member bodies.

2.3.1 American National Standards Institute (ANSI)

ANSI is the body that coordinates and administers voluntary standardization efforts in the United States. It is also the U.S. member body in ISO. More information about ANSI can be found on its Web site: http://www.ansi.org/.

ANSI is also responsible for developing standards of its own. It does this by accrediting other bodies with the task of studying and creating standards on ANSI's behalf. Within the area of cryptography, the ANSI X9 organization is probably the most prolific of the ANSI-accredited standardization bodies. X9 is responsible for developing, publishing, and promoting standards for the financial services sector and works closely with the International Organization for Standardization's TC68 committee. More information about the X9 organization can be found at the Web site: http://www.x9.org/. ANSI X9 standards are available from the Web site: http://webstore. ansi.org/.

2.3.2 British Standards Institute (BSI)

The BSI is the body that, among other things, manages the British standardization efforts. It is the U.K. member body in ISO. It also produces a series of standards of its own, although it does not have a history of developing technical cryptographic standards. BSI has nevertheless produced several influential standards on management techniques, including the two-part BS 7799 standard on information security management (see Chapter 16). Information about the BSI can be found on its Web site: http://www. bsi-global.com/. BSI standards can also be purchased from the site.

2.3.3 National Institute of Standards and Technology (NIST)

The National Institute of Standards and Technology (NIST) is another U.S. standards body. NIST is the federal standardization agency within the U.S. Commerce Department's technology administration. NIST has developed a variety of security standards, most notably the Advanced Encryption Standard (AES). NIST's output takes the form of federal information processing standards (FIPS). More information about NIST is available at its Web site: http://www.nist.gov/.

NIST FIPS can be freely downloaded from the NIST Computer Security Resource Center (CSRC) homepage at the following Web site: http://csrc. nist.gov/.

2.4 Industrial standardization organizations

It is not only governments and government-led organizations that produce cryptographic standards; occasionally the business community steps in to provide standards. The reasons for this can vary widely. It could be because the business community is best placed to develop these standards on its own, as often happens with sector-specific standardization efforts such as the 3GPP mobile telecommunication network standards or the IETF Internet standards, or it could be that the government is unable to provide or promote standards for political reasons.

We discuss some of the more important industrial standardization efforts that have developed cryptographic standards, including standards produced by a collection of businesses and those produced by single companies.

2.4.1 Third Generation Partnership Project (3GPP)

The 3GPP is a comparatively new standardization organization—it was only established in 1998—that brings together companies and other standardization bodies to work on the development of the third generation of mobile phone networks. Since security and privacy are major features of third generation networks, 3GPP has standardized both network security features and cryptographic schemes. The 3GPP standards are freely available from the 3GPP Web site: http://www.3gpp.org/.

2.4.2 European Telecommunications Standard Institute (ETSI)

ETSI, an independent collection of businesses with a mutual interest in developing standards for telecommunications, is one of the organizational partners that coordinate the 3GPP project. In many ways, it is the European equivalent of ITU-T (see Section 2.2.3). For more information about ETSI and to (freely) download ETSI standards, visit its Web site: http://www.etsi.org/.

2.4.3 Institute of Electrical and Electronics Engineers (IEEE)

The IEEE is an association of engineers that seeks to promote and share information in technical electrical and electronic engineering. Besides producing standards, it also hosts conferences and publishes books and journals. Membership is open to all professional electrical and electronic engineers. More information on IEEE standards can be found on the IEEE Web site: http://standards.ieee.org/. IEEE standards are also available for purchase through this Web site.

The IEEE forms groups of interested parties to coordinate its standardization activities. From a cryptographic point of view, there are two major standardization groups of interest. The first is the 1363 group, which produce standards related to asymmetric cryptography. Information about the 1363 group can be found at the Web site: http://grouper.ieee.org/groups/1363/.

The second is the 802 group, which produces standards relating to wireless local area networks (wireless LANs), and particularly the group that produces the 802.11 series of standards. Information about the 802.11 group can be found at the Web site: http://grouper.ieee.org/groups/802/11/.

2.4.4 Internet Engineering Task Force (IETF)

The Internet is the result of a long-term collaboration between governments, academia, and businesses seeking to create a truly worldwide communications network. For the Internet to function correctly it *must* be based upon standardized communication protocols and the IETF is the body that produces these standards. Its sister organization, the Internet Research Task Force (IRTF), is charged with studying long-term research problems in the Internet.

Internet standards are not the only publications that the IETF produces, it also produces an informal series of documents known as requests for comments (RFCs). For a scheme to become an Internet standard, it is first proposed as an RFC on the standardization track. RFCs in development can be temporarily made available as Internet drafts. All Internet standards begin life as RFCs on the standardization track, but there are also other classes of RFCs, most notably experimental and informational RFCs. IETF RFCs cover all of the topics of interest to an implementer working with the Internet, which would explain why there are so many of them (over 3,700 at the time of writing)!

Many of these describe security algorithms, protocols, or recommendations. IETF RFCs are freely available from many places on the Internet, including the IETF homepage: http://www.ietf.org/.

2.4.5   Standards for Efficient Cryptography Group (SECG)

During the early 1990s, a new style of public-key cryptography was being developed based on complex mathematical structures known as elliptic curves. The details of elliptic curve cryptography, as the subject became known, are far beyond the scope of this book; however, as we shall see, many traditional public-key cryptosystems have counterparts that work using elliptic curves.

A conglomeration of businesses, led by Certicom, were the first to try and make use of these new cryptographic techniques in business. In order to facilitate interoperability and to discuss the practical issues arising from elliptic curve cryptography, these businesses formed the SECG and, in 2000, published two standards: SEC 1, which standardized the use of elliptic curves in cryptography, and SEC 2, which recommended parameters for use with elliptic curve cryptography.

Since the publication of these standards in 2000, the group does not seem to have produced any new material and, as more well-established standardization bodies have started to publish standards on elliptic curve cryptography, it seems unlikely that SECG will continue its standardization efforts. More information about the SECG, and the two standards that it has produced, is available on the following Web site: http://www.secg.org/.

2.4.6   Public-Key Cryptography Standards (PKCSs)

It is not only collections of businesses that have produced industrial standards; sometimes standards have been produced by individual companies. In many cases, this proved to be an astute business move. A company that produces a standardized version of a protocol or algorithm that it has developed gains valuable advertising, promotes interoperability between their products and the products of other companies, and prevents the negative publicity that could be caused by a competitor poorly implementing a version of its scheme.

One of the few individual companies to have produced a wide-ranging series of standards on its own is RSA Laboratories. These PKCS started as simple standards on the use of the RSA encryption and signature schemes (see Chapters 4 and 8), but grew into a well respected series of standards that cover all areas of asymmetric cryptography. These standards can be freely downloaded from the Web site: http://www.rsasecurity.com/rsalabs/pkcs/index.html.

2.5 Cryptographic evaluation bodies

The large number of standardization bodies interested in cryptography is both a blessing and a curse. It certainly means that cryptographic algorithms and protocols are studied by a very large number of experts before becoming generally recognized as secure and useful schemes. However, this means that it can sometimes be difficult for good new schemes to gain acceptance in the general community.

After all, one of the key objectives of cryptographic standards is to promote interoperability between applications. However, the abundance of different cryptographic standards means that a scheme has to be included in several different standards for it to gain industry-wide acceptance, and each of these standards must contain *exactly* the same scheme—any variation between schemes in standards, no matter how small, may well mean that systems using the two standards are incompatible.

One solution to this problem is for several standardization bodies to take the advice of an independent evaluation body or project as to the best way of implementing a scheme. Such evaluation bodies are not common but can provide impartial advice as to the suitability of a scheme for standardization without being subject to the political problems that are associated with some standardization bodies.

The European Union has sponsored two evaluation projects: the RACE Integrity Primitives Evaluation (RIPE) project and the New European Schemes for Signatures, Integrity, and Encryption (NESSIE) project. The RIPE project only considered hash functions, MACs, and digital signature schemes (see Chapters 6 through 8, respectively). It was completed in 1992 and had some influence on subsequent standards activities, most notably the adoption of the RIPEMD hash functions into various standards. The NESSIE project was more wide-ranging, and considered encryption schemes, hash functions, MACs, and digital signature schemes (see Chapters 4 and 6 through 8, respectively) and was completed in 2003. More information about the NESSIE project, along with the results of the project, can be found on its Web site: http://www. cryptonessie.org/.

The Japanese government also sponsors an ongoing evaluation body known as CRYPTREC. This body has officially been set up to evaluate cryptographic primitives for use in an electronic government infrastructure; however, the CRYPTREC project has become established as a good source for impartial assessments of cryptographic primitives, and its recommendations are being considered by several standardization bodies. More information about the CRYPTREC project can be found on its Web site: http://www.ipa.go.jp/security/enc/CRYPTREC/index-e.html.

2.6   **Notes**

There are thousands of standards on a huge range of different topics (as a quick look on the ISO Web site will confirm) and all of them are designed to specify a common method of doing a routine task. The eight reasons for standardization given by the BSI and discussed in Section 2.1 are taken from the BSI Web site. A history of ISO standardization body is available on their Web site: http://www.iso.ch/iso/en/ aboutiso/introduction/fifty/fifty. html.

Several standards are mentioned during the discussion of standardization bodies: these will be discussed in detail later in the book. SEC 1 [1] and SEC 2 [2] will be discussed in Chapter 4; ISO 8370 [3] and ISO 8371 [4, 5] will be discussed in Chapter 7; ISO/IEC TR 14516 [6] will be discussed in Chapter 14; ISO/IEC WD 19790 [7], ISO/IEC CD 18031 [8], and BS 7799 [9, 10] will be discussed in Chapter 16.

The sister organization to the IETF, the Internet Research Task Force (IRTF), is also involved with cryptography. The IRTF conducts its research by creating small research groups to work on topics related to the Internet, and one such research group, the Crypto Forum Research Group (CFRG), is focused on cryptography. More information about the IRTF can be found at: http://www.irtf.org/, while information about the CFRG can be found on their homepage: http://www.irtf.org/cfrg/.

For more information about the IETF and its standardization efforts, the reader is referred to two of the IETF's own standards: RFC 1118 [11] and RFC 2026 [12]. For more general information on the standardization, Chapter 15 of [13] and the appendices of [14] both contain introductions to the subject.

References

[1]   Standards for Efficient Cryptography Group, *SEC 1: Elliptic Curve Cryptography*, September 2000.

[2]   Standards for Efficient Cryptography Group, *SEC 2: Recommended Elliptic Curve Domain Parameters*, September 2000.

[3]   International Organization for Standardization, *ISO 8730: 1986, Banking—Requirements for Message Authentication (Wholesale)*, 2nd ed., 1990.

[4]   International Organization for Standardization, *ISO 8731–1: 1987, Banking—Approved Algorithm for Message Authentication—Part 1: DEA*, 1987.

[5]   International Organization for Standardization, *ISO 8731–2: 1992, Banking—Approved Algorithm for Message Authentication—Part 2: Message Authenticator Algorithm*, 2nd ed., 1992.

[6]   International Organization for Standardization, *ISO/IEC TR 14516, Information Technology—Security Techniques—Guidelines for the Use and Management of Trusted Third Party Services*, 2002.

[7]   International Organization for Standardization, *ISO/IEC WD 19790, Information Technology—Security Techniques—Security Requirements for Cryptographic Modules*, 2004.

[8]   International Organization for Standardization, *ISO/IEC CD 18031, Information Technology—Security Techniques—Random Bit Generation*, 2004.

[9]   British Standards Institute (BSI), *BS 7799-1, Information Technology: Code of Practice for Information Security Management*, 2000.

[10] British Standards Institute (BSI), *BS 7799-2, Information Security Management: Specification with Guidance For Use*, 2002.

[11] Krol, E., *RFC 1118, The Hitchhiker's Guide to the Internet*, Internet Engineering Task Force, September 1989.

[12] Bradner, S., *RFC 2026, The Internet Standards Process—Revision 3*, Internet Engineering Task Force, October 1996.

[13] Menezes, A. J., P. C. van Oorschot, and S. A. Vanstone, *Handbook of Applied Cryptography*, Boca Raton, FL: CRC Press, 1997.

[14] Ford, W., *Computer Communications Security: Principles, Standard Protocols, and Techniques*, Upper Saddle River, NJ: Prentice Hall, 1994.

Contents

3.1 Introduction

3.2 Security standards

3.3 A model for security

3.4 Security services

3.5 Security mechanisms

3.6 Relating services to mechanisms

3.7 Service and protocols layers

3.8 Security management

3.9 Security frameworks

3.10 Notes

Security Mechanisms and Security Services

The main purpose of this chapter is to establish a framework within which we can discuss both the nature of cryptographic mechanisms and what they can be used for. It is important to make this distinction between *security mechanisms* (i.e., the means of achieving security goals) and *security services* (i.e., the security goals themselves).

The chapter is mainly based around a single standard, namely the OSI security architecture. This standard led the way in defining terms for security services and mechanisms, and the terms established in this standard have become very widely used.

3.1 Introduction

As stated earlier, this chapter is based around a single international standard, namely ISO 7498-2, the OSI security architecture. This, as its name implies, is a security-specific addition to the OSI network architecture, standardized in ISO/IEC 7498-1. A brief introduction to this network architecture, known as the *OSI model*, is provided in Section 3.7.

Although the OSI model, and network architectures generally, are outside the scope of this book, ISO 7498-2 defines many security-related terms and ideas that are of importance to a variety of application areas, including many not covered by the OSI model. Of particular importance is the terminology it introduces for the description of security services and mechanisms. This terminology is used throughout this book.

Following an introduction to relevant standards in Section 3.2, the security model implicit to ISO 7498-2 is explored in Section 3.3. This is followed in Sections 3.4 and 3.5 by detailed definitions of security services and mechanisms, as given in ISO 7498-2. Sections 3.6 and 3.7, respectively, consider which mechanisms can be used to provide which services, and which services it is appropriate to provide at the various layers of the OSI network architecture. A classification of security management issues is given in Section 3.8. Finally, security framework standards are briefly reviewed in Section 3.9.

3.2   Security standards

ISO 7498-2 (developed by JTC1 SC21) was intended to serve as a security-specific addition to ISO/IEC 7498-1, the OSI reference model. There are two other parts to this standard, namely ISO/IEC 7498-3, dealing with naming and addressing, and ISO/IEC 7498-4, covering management issues. A version of ISO 7498-2 has also been adopted as ITU recommendation X.800.

Following on from the pioneering work in ISO 7498-2, ISO/IEC JTC1/ SC21 set out to develop a seven-part "security frameworks" standard, ISO/ IEC 10181. This standard seeks to give general guidance on how particular security services, as defined in ISO 7498-2, may be provided. The titles of the seven parts are listed as follows:

- ISO/IEC 10181-1 (1996): Overview;

- ISO/IEC 10181-2 (1996): Authentication framework;

- ISO/IEC 10181-3 (1996): Access control framework;

- ISO/IEC 10181-4 (1997): Non-repudiation framework;

- ISO/IEC 10181-5 (1996): Confidentiality framework;

- ISO/IEC 10181-6 (1996): Integrity framework;

- ISO/IEC 10181-7 (1996): Security audit and alarms framework.

Seven identical ITU-T recommendations were published at around the same time, namely X.810-X.816.

Two further ISO/IEC documents dealing with security architectural issues are ISO/IEC 10745 and ISO/IEC TR 13594, the upper and lower layer security models, respectively. These two ISO documents have also been published as ITU-T Recommendations X.803 and X.802 respectively. ISO/IEC 10745 provides architectural guidance on the provision of security in the three uppermost layers of the OSI model (the application, presentation, and session layers), and ISO/IEC TR 13594 does the same for the other four layers (i.e., the transport, network, data link, and physical layer). See Section 3.7 for more details on the OSI model.

ITU-T Recommendation X.805 (which does not have a corresponding ISO/IEC standard) provides a general security architecture for systems providing end-to-end communications.

ISO/IEC 15816, also published as ITU-T Recommendation X.841, defines the format of data structures used for the purposes of access control. In particular it defines the format of a generic security label. This is not a topic addressed in detail in this book, although such data structures are fundamental to the access control mechanisms briefly discussed in Section 3.5.

Finally, note that ISO/IEC TR 15947 is a technical report on intrusion detection and provides an agreed framework for intrusion detection systems. (This is mentioned here because of its relevance to the "event detection" pervasive security mechanisms discussed in Section 3.5, although this is not a topic addressed in detail in this book.)

3.3 A model for security

The underlying model, implicit to the discussion in ISO 7498-2, is that there is a generic *security life cycle*, containing the following steps:

▸ Definition of a security policy, containing a potentially rather abstract series of security requirements for the system;

▸ A security requirements analysis, including a risk analysis, possibly using a tool such as CCTA risk analysis and management method (CRAMM), and an analysis of governmental, legal, and regulatory requirements;

▸ Definition of the security services necessary to meet the identified security requirements;

▸ System design and implementation, including selection of security mechanisms to provide the chosen security services;

▸ Continuing security management.

In the context of this model, a *security threat* is something that poses a danger to the security of a system. A *security service* is selected to meet an identified threat, and a *security mechanism* is the means by which a service is provided.

This distinction between a security service (i.e., a service that enhances system security in some way and is typically designed to address one of more threats) and a security mechanism (i.e., the means by which a service is provided) is of fundamental importance. Hence *data confidentiality* is a security service, whereas *encryption* is a security mechanism that can be used to provide the confidentiality service. In fact, encryption can be used to provide other services, and data confidentiality can also be provided by means other than encryption (e.g., by the physical protection of the means used to store the data).

3.3.1 Security policies

When designing a secure system, the scope of the system and the set of rules governing the security behavior of the system are of fundamental importance; these are the *security domain* and the *security policy*, respectively. A security policy is defined in ISO 7498-2 as "the set of criteria for the provision of security services." A security domain can be regarded as the scope of a single security policy. Importantly, security domains, and thus the scopes of security policies, can be nested or overlapping.

ISO 7498-2 gives the following statement as an example of a possible generic security policy statement regarding *authorization*.

Information may not be given to, accessed by, or permitted to be inferred by, nor may any resource be used by, those not appropriately authorized.

An initial generic policy of this type can then be refined, in conjunction with the results of a requirements analysis, into a detailed set of rules governing the operation and management of the system. Note that the above generic policy only deals with preventing unauthorized access (i.e., it does not make any statement about guaranteeing access to legitimate users). Thus it does not deal with *availability*, including denial of service threats.

In fact the issue of availability is not really covered by any of the standards discussed in this book. This is arguably a weakness in the coverage of the existing standards; however, one practical reason for this is that guaranteeing availability in the presence of network-based denial of service attacks is a very difficult problem to which no completely satisfactory solutions exist.

ISO 7498-2 distinguishes between two types of security policy: *identity-based* and *rule-based*, depending on how authorization is granted. Identity-based policies authorize system access on the basis of the identity of the client and the identity of the resource that the client wishes to use. Rule-based policies rely on global rules imposed on all users, with access decisions typically made using a comparison of the sensitivity of the resources with the user attributes (e.g., the "clearance" of the user).

3.4   Security services

ISO 7498-2 defines five main categories of security service:

- *Authentication*, which can be subdivided into *entity authentication*, the corroboration that the entity at the other end of a communications link is the one claimed, and *data origin authentication*, the corroboration that the source of data received is as claimed;

- *Access control* (i.e., the prevention of unauthorized use of a resource).

- *Data confidentiality* (i.e., the prevention of the disclosure of data to unauthorized entities);

- *Data integrity* (i.e., the prevention of unauthorized alteration or destruction of data by an unauthorized entity);

- *Non-repudiation* (i.e., the prevention of denial by an entity that it has taken a particular action, such as sending or receiving a message).

These services are next examined in a little more detail. However, it is first necessary to introduce a little terminology fundamental to an understanding of the ISO 7498-2 view of security. In the context of communications between two entities (e.g., two PCs) communications may be either *connection-oriented* or *connectionless*.

Connection-oriented communications describes the situation where, prior to sending any data, a communications link is established between the two parties—a simple example of a connection is a telephone call, where one party first establishes a call before the conversation starts. All data sent between the two parties is sent as part of this connection and will be protected by any security measures applied to the connection (e.g., by encryption if this is set up when the connection is established).

Connectionless communications, on the other hand, describes a situation where data sent between entities is divided into *data units* which are transmitted as self-contained entities, each with its own addressing information—analogous to the postal system, where each letter has its own address. Security services are then applied to individual data units.

Communications protocols may provide either a connection-oriented or a connectionless service. For example, some underlying communications technologies are inherently connectionless (e.g., LANs), whereas others are inherently connection-oriented (e.g., X.25 packed-switched networks (PSNs)). At higher layers in the protocol hierarchy (discussed in Section 3.7), the Internet protocol (IP) operates in a connectionless fashion, whereas the transmission control protocol (TCP) is connection-oriented.

3.4.1 Authentication

Entity authentication (or "peer entity authentication" as it is referred to in ISO 7498-2) provides corroboration to one entity that another entity is as claimed. This service may be used at the establishment of (or during) a communications connection to confirm the identities of one or more of the connected entities. This service provides confidence, at the time of use only, that an entity is not attempting to impersonate another entity or that the current communications session is an unauthorized replay of a previous connection.

Data origin authentication provides corroboration to an entity that the source of received data is as claimed. However, it does not, in itself, provide protection against duplication or modification of data. These latter properties are issues addressed by a data integrity service. Of course, in practice, data integrity and data origin authentication are usually provided using the same mechanism.

3.4.2 Access control

The access control service provides protection against the unauthorized use of resources. This protection may be applied to a variety of types of access and resources, such as the following:

- The use of a communications resource for the transmission of data;
- The reading, writing, or deletion of an information resource;
- The use of a processing resource to execute programs.

3.4.3 Data confidentiality

ISO 7498-2 defines four types of data confidentiality service; all these services provide for the protection of data against unauthorized disclosure. The four types are listed as follows:

> • *Connection confidentiality,* which provides for the confidentiality of all user data transferred using a connection;

> • *Connectionless confidentiality,* which provides for the confidentiality of all user data transferred in a single connectionless data unit (i.e., a data packet);

> • *Selective field confidentiality,* which provides for the confidentiality of selected fields within user data transferred in either a connection or a single connectionless data unit;

> • *Traffic flow confidentiality,* which provides for the confidentiality of information that might be derived from observation of traffic flows (e.g., the time at which data is sent, the volumes of data sent to or received by particular recipients, or the length of individual messages).

3.4.4 Data integrity

ISO 7498-2 defines five types of data integrity service; all these services counter active threats to the validity of transferred data. The five types are described as follows.

> • *Connection integrity with recovery:* This service provides integrity protection for all the user data transferred using a connection and detects any modification, insertion, deletion, or replay of data within an entire data unit sequence. The term *with recovery* means that if some form of modification is detected, then the service attempts to recover the correct data, typically by requesting that the data be resent.

> • *Connection integrity without recovery:* As previously but with no recovery attempted if an integrity failure is detected.

> • *Selective field connection integrity:* This service provides integrity protection for selected fields within the user data or within a data unit transferred over a connection.

> • *Connectionless integrity:* This service provides integrity assurance to the recipient of a data unit. More specifically, it enables the recipient of a connectionless data unit to determine whether that data unit has been modified. Additionally, a limited form of replay detection may be provided.

> • *Selective field connectionless integrity:* This service provides integrity protection for selective fields within a single connectionless data unit.

3.4.5 Non-repudiation

ISO 7498-2 defines two types of non-repudiation service.

▸ *Non-repudiation with proof of origin:* The recipient of data is provided with evidence of the origin of data. This will protect against any subsequent attempt by the sender to falsely deny sending the data. This service is usually abbreviated to *non-repudiation of origin*.

▸ *Non-repudiation with proof of delivery:* The sender of data is provided with evidence of delivery of data. This will protect against any subsequent attempt by the recipient to falsely deny receiving the data. This service is usually abbreviated to *non-repudiation of delivery*.

In both cases the evidence provided by the service must be of value in helping to resolve disputes using a trusted third party acting as an arbiter (e.g., a judge in a court of law). This means that, in the case of non-repudiation of origin, it must not be possible for evidence to be fabricated by the recipient, since otherwise the evidence will be of no value in dispute resolution. Similarly the evidence generated by a non-repudiation of delivery service must not be readily fabricated by the data sender or any party other than the recipient.

3.4.6 Other services

The list of five services provided in ISO 7498-2 is not complete; this is hardly surprising since it was compiled in the 1980s, and security technology and understanding has made considerable progress since then. However, it nevertheless covers the vast majority of *security* requirements arising in current systems. For completeness we mention two areas in which its coverage could be enhanced.

First, it does not address *privacy* requirements, including anonymity and related concepts such as pseudonymity and unlinkability of transactions. Of course, these are arguably not strictly security concerns, although it would almost certainly make sense to include such services within the scope of ISO 7498-2 if it were being written today. In connection with this, the architecture does not discuss what have become known as *privacy-enhancing technologies*, including methods for preserving anonymity, using pseudonyms, and protecting against linking of actions.

Second, it does not address *availability* services, including services and techniques designed to offer protection against *denial of service* attacks. In recent years there has been considerable effort devoted to devising authentication and key establishment protocols that offer a degree of such protection.

3.4.7 Summary

The five classes of security services are summarized in Table 3.1.

Table 3.1   The Five Classes of Security Service

Service	Types	Notes
Authentication	Entity authentication	Connection-oriented service; enables two entities to verify each other's identities
	Data origin authentication	Connectionless service; enables the origin of a data unit to be verified
Access control		Protects against unauthorized resource use
Data confidentiality	Connection confidentiality	Connection-oriented service; protects secrecy of all data transferred during connection
	Connectionless confidentiality	Connectionless service; protects secrecy of single data unit
	Selective field confidentiality	Protects selected parts of transferred data
	Traffic flow confidentiality	Conceals information about volume and destination of traffic
Data integrity	Connection integrity with recovery	Connection-oriented service; detects modifications to entire sequence of data units (and provides recovery)
	Connection integrity without recovery	Connection-oriented service; as above but no recovery
	Selective field connection integrity	Connection-oriented service; detects modifications to selected parts of sequence of data units
	Connectionless integrity	Connectionless service; protects integrity of single data unit
	Selective field connectionless integrity	Connectionless service; detects modifications to selected parts of a single data unit
Non-repudiation	Non-repudiation with proof of origin	Protects recipient against denial by sender
	Non-repudiation with proof of delivery	Protects sender against denial of receipt

3.5   Security mechanisms

Security mechanisms exist to provide and support security services. ISO 7498-2 divides mechanisms into two types:

▸ *Specific security mechanisms* (i.e., those specific to providing certain security services);

▸ *Pervasive security mechanisms* (i.e., those not specific to the provision of individual security services).

ISO 7498-2 then defines and describes eight types of specific security mechanisms and five types of pervasive security mechanisms. Most of the remainder of this book is concerned with examples of specific security mechanisms.

3.5.1   Specific security mechanisms

The eight types of specific security mechanisms are encipherment mechanisms (see Chapters 4 through 6); digital signature mechanisms (see Chapter 8); access control mechanisms; data integrity mechanisms, which include MACs (see Chapter 7); authentication exchange mechanisms (see

Chapter 10); traffic padding mechanisms; routing control mechanisms; and notarization mechanisms (see Chapters 9 and 14).

We now consider each of these eight classes in a little more detail. This provides the basis for the detailed consideration of standards for various types of security mechanisms in later chapters.

3.5.1.1 Encipherment mechanisms (information hiding transforms)

It is important to note that, here at least, *encipherment mechanism* means something subtly different from *encryption mechanism*. The class of encipherment mechanisms is defined to include all *information hiding transforms*. Encipherment mechanisms are subdivided into reversible and nonreversible transforms.

Reversible transforms are those for which an inverse transformation (a *decipherment transform*) exists. That is, such mechanisms essentially equate to encryption mechanisms, where we expect to be able to decrypt encrypted data. Encryption mechanisms can help provide confidentiality of either data or traffic flow information. They also provide the basis for some authentication and key management techniques (discussed in Chapters 10 and 12).

Nonreversible transforms are those for which it is impossible to recover the original data from the transformed data. One very important class of such transforms are the *cryptographic hash functions*, discussed in Chapter 6. Such functions are an essential part of the computation of almost all practical digital signature schemes (see Chapter 8).

It is important to note that the above definition of encipherment conflicts with common usage, where encipherment is used as a synonym for encryption. The broader, and potentially rather confusing, use of the term encipherment follows ISO 7498-2, and is restricted to this chapter.

3.5.1.2 Digital signatures

A digital signature mechanism consists of two operational procedures: a signing procedure and a verifying procedure, together with a procedure for generating pairs of keys. Such mechanisms can be used to provide non-repudiation, origin authentication, and integrity services, as well as serve as an integral part of some mechanisms to provide entity authentication. Signature mechanisms can be divided into two types, described as follows.

▸ Digital signatures "with message recovery," or *reversible signature schemes*, in which all or part of the message can be recovered from the signature;

▸ Digital signatures "with appendix," or *nonreversible signatures*, where none of the message can be recovered from the signature, and the entire message must be sent or stored with the signature.

3.5.1.3 Access control techniques

Access control mechanisms can be thought of as a means for using information associated with a client entity and a server entity to decide whether access to the server's resource should be granted to the client. Examples of types of access control mechanisms include: access control lists, capabilities, and security labels. A general framework for access control mechanisms can be found in ISO/IEC 10181-3 (the access control framework). Note that access control mechanisms are not discussed in detail in this book, as they are not cryptographic in nature.

3.5.1.4   Data integrity mechanisms

Two types of data integrity mechanisms exist: those concerned with the integrity of a single data unit and those concerned with protecting the integrity of an entire sequence of data units. The first type of mechanism (e.g., a MAC) can be used to help provide both data origin authentication and data integrity for a single data unit (as well as serve as an integral part of some authentication exchange and key management mechanisms).

Mechanisms of the second type, which must be used in conjunction with mechanisms of the first type, can be used to provide full connection-oriented integrity services. These mechanisms include sequence numbers and time stamps. These mechanisms are necessary since use of a MAC alone will not enable a recipient of a sequence of data units to detect replays of single data units, and, more generally, the manipulation of a sequence of data units (including replay, selective deletion, and reordering).

3.5.1.5   Authentication protocols

Authentication exchange mechanisms, otherwise known as authentication protocols, can be used to provide entity authentication (as well as serve as the basis of some key management mechanisms).

3.5.1.6   Traffic padding

The term traffic padding describes the addition of "bogus" data to conceal the volumes of real data traffic. It can be used to help provide traffic flow confidentiality. This mechanism can only be effective if the added padding is enciphered (or otherwise provided with confidentiality). As is the case for access control mechanisms, traffic padding techniques are not discussed further in this book, as they are not cryptographic in nature.

3.5.1.7   Routing control

Routing control mechanisms can be used to prevent sensitive data being sent via insecure communications paths. For example, depending on the data's sensitivity, routes can be chosen to use only secure network components (subnetworks, relays, or links). Data carrying certain security labels may be forbidden to enter certain network components. Again since they are not cryptographic in nature, routing control mechanisms are not discussed in detail in this book.

3.5.1.8 Notarization

The integrity, origin, and destination of transferred data can be guaranteed by the use of a notarization mechanism. A third-party notary, which must be trusted by the communicating entities, will provide the guarantee, typically by applying a cryptographic transformation to the transferred data.

3.5.1.9 Summary of specific mechanisms

The eight types of specific security mechanisms are summarized in Table 3.2.

3.5.2 Pervasive security mechanisms

The five types of pervasive security mechanism listed in ISO 7498-2 are trusted functionality, security labels, event detection, security audit trails, and security recovery. We next briefly define these mechanisms. While these mechanisms are fundamental to the provision of secure systems, they are not cryptographic in nature and thus are not considered in detail in this book.

3.5.2.1 Trusted functionality

Trusted functionality is used in conjunction with other security mechanisms. Any functionality providing or accessing security mechanisms should be trustworthy. Trusted functionality may involve some combination of software and hardware.

Table 3.2 The Eight Types of Specific Security Mechanisms

Mechanism	Types	Notes
Enciherment mechanisms	Reversible (i.e., encryption mechanisms)	See Chapters 4 and 5
	Nonreversible (i.e., hash functions)	See Chapter 6
Digital signatures	Reversible signatures	See Chapter 8
	Nonreversible signatures	See Chapter 8
Access control techniques		Discussed in ISO/IEC 10181-3 (the access control framework)
Data integrity mechanisms	Mechanisms protecting the integrity of a single data unit (e.g., MACs and signatures)	See Chapters 7 and 8
	Mechanisms protecting the integrity of a sequence of data units	Sequence numbers, timestamps, end-of-sequence flags
Authentication protocols		See Chapter 10
Traffic padding		Discussed in ISO/IEC 10181-5 (the confidentiality framework)
Routing control		Discussed in ISO/IEC 10181-5 (the confidentiality framework)
Notarisation		An example of a trusted third party mechanism; see Chapters 9 and 14

3.5.2.2 Security labels

Any resource (stored data, processing power, or communications bandwidth) may have a security label associated with it to indicate its "security sensitivity." Transferred data may need to have its associated security label transferred with it in a secure fashion (typically by binding the label to the data using a cryptographic function). The format of such labels is standardized in ISO/IEC 15816 and ITU-T X.841.

3.5.2.3 Event detection

Security-relevant event detection includes detecting attempted security violations (and whether they succeeded) as well as legitimate security-related activity. Detection may cause local and remote event reporting, event logging, and recovery actions. While not discussed here, ISO/IEC TR 15947 provides a framework for intrusion detection techniques, a special class of event detection mechanisms.

3.5.2.4 Security audit trails

A security audit trail consists of a log of past security-related events. Audit trails permit the detection and investigation of security breaches.

3.5.2.5 Security recovery

This covers mechanisms put in place to handle requests from management functions (and event-handling mechanisms) to recover from security failures. This may, for example, involve the immediate abort of operations (disconnection), the temporary invalidation of an entity, or the addition of an entity to a blacklist.

3.5.3 Selection of security mechanisms

At various places in this book references are made to computational infeasibility in the context of the "strength" of a security mechanism. This follows many standards for cryptographic mechanisms, which make similar references to computational infeasibility. That is, typically, it should be computationally infeasible for an opponent to successfully attack a scheme.

This notion of infeasibility is somewhat vague, and to some extent this is deliberate. What is feasible in some environments (e.g., when the potential attackers have significant computing resources) may be infeasible in others (e.g., where the scheme is only used for a very limited period for messages with relatively small value). Hence the notion of feasibility must be assessed in the context of the environment in which the system is used. This means that algorithms that are perfectly adequate in some situations will be inadequate in others.

This raises an important question: Why would anyone ever use a weaker mechanism, although it may be adequate for their application, when a stronger one is available? In fact the answer to this question is not simple, and the selection of a cryptographic mechanism is often based on a host of factors, not all of them technical. Perhaps most significant in this respect is compatibility with legacy applications and large installed bases of existing hardware which already use an algorithm. Other issues that may influence the choice of algorithm include complexity of computation and intellectual property issues.

3.6   Relating services to mechanisms

ISO 7498-2 gives an indication of which mechanisms are appropriate to the provision of which services in the form of a table—see Table 3.3. ISO 7498-2 makes it clear that this table is illustrative and not definitive.

There are some surprising omissions from Table 3.3. They include the possible use of data integrity mechanisms to help provide entity authentication and data origin authentication services and the possible use of encryption to help provide non-repudiation services (as part of a notarization mechanism).

3.7   Service and protocol layers

ISO 7498-2 lays down which security services may be provided in what parts of the OSI model. Before presenting details of this mapping we first briefly introduce the seven-layer open systems interconnection (OSI) model. We also present the parallel Internet layered model.

It is important to note that, in practice, the Internet model has "won" and is almost universally used to the exclusion of the OSI model. However, the OSI model still provides a useful reference for layered network architectures; it is also particularly important here since there is no Internet security architecture analogous to ISO 7498-2. Of course, if such an architecture existed (and was at least as complete as ISO 7498-2), then it would probably make more sense to use it as the basis of this chapter.

3.7.1   The OSI model

The aim of the OSI model is to provide a standardized means of communication between diverse computer systems. As a basis for the development of OSI standards, ISO has developed a *reference model*, defined in ISO/IEC 7498-1,

Table 3.3   Relating Services to Mechanisms

Service	Relevant Mechanisms
Entity authentication	Encipherment, digital signature, authentication protocol
Data origin authentication	Encipherment, digital signature
Access control	Access control mechanism
Connection confidentiality	Encipherment, routing control
Connectionless confidentiality	Encipherment, routing control
Selective field confidentiality	Encipherment
Traffic flow confidentiality	Encipherment, traffic padding, routing control
Connection integrity with recovery	Encipherment, data integrity
Connection integrity without recovery	Encipherment, data integrity
Selective field connection integrity	Encipherment, data integrity
Connectionless integrity	Encipherment, digital signature, data integrity
Selective field connectionless integrity	Encipherment, digital signature, data integrity
Non-repudiation of origin	Digital signature, data integrity, notarization
Non-repudiation of delivery	Digital signature, data integrity, notarization

to partition the problem into discrete layers, and to provide a conceptual framework for understanding the complex problems involved.

The reference model has seven layers; from the "bottom up" they are as follows: (1) *physical layer,* (2) *link layer,* (3) *network layer,* (4) *transport layer,* (5) *session layer,* (6) *presentation layer,* and (7) *application layer.* The reference model specifies the functionality of each layer and the interfaces between adjacent layers. It also defines methods for achieving layer-specific functionality between cooperating computer systems.

The lowest three layers (physical, data link, and network) are concerned with the provision of data transmission. The physical layer models the interface of a computer system to the physical medium. It includes such aspects as physical connectors and voltage levels. The data link layer provides a framework for the data transmitted by the physical layer, and the detection and correction of errors may be performed by this layer. The network layer is particularly concerned with routing and relaying. The services offered by the network layer to the transport layer conceal from it the numbers and types of subnetworks that may be involved in the communication.

The transport layer operates end-to-end between computer systems and one of its concerns is the issue of quality of service (QoS). The transport layer is responsible for providing the session layer with a reliable data transmission service.

The session layer assumes reliable data transmission services between computer systems (i.e., end-to-end communications). It occupies the area between the application-oriented upper layers and the "real-time" data communication environment. It provides services for the management and control of data flow between two computer systems. The function of the presentation layer is to provide a common representation of information while in transit between computer systems.

The application layer provides the communication-based service to end users. The other six layers of the model only exist to support and make possible the activities that take place at the application layer.

3.7.2 Layers versus security services

The ISO 7498-2 layer/service specifications are summarized in Table 3.4, which indicates which security services may be placed in which layers of the OSI model.

Essentially, the following are true:

▸ Layers 1 and 2 are restricted to providing certain types of confidentiality services.

▸ Layers 3 and 4 can provide authentication, access control, confidentiality, and integrity services.

▸ No security services can be provided in layer 5 or layer 6, although layer 6 may contain facilities to support the provision of services at layer 7.

▸ All security services may be provided at layer 7.

Table 3.4 OSI Layers Versus Security Services (7498-2 Version)

Service	Layer						
	1	2	3	4	5	6	7
Entity authentication	–	–	Y	Y	–	–	Y
Data origin authentication	–	–	Y	Y	–	–	Y
Access control	–	–	Y	Y	–	–	Y
Connection confidentiality	Y	Y	Y	Y	–	–	Y
Connectionless confidentiality	–	Y	Y	Y	–	–	Y
Selective field confidentiality	–	–	–	–	–	–	Y
Traffic flow confidentiality	Y	–	Y	–	–	–	Y
Connection integrity with recovery	–	–	–	Y	–	–	Y
Connection integrity without recovery	–	–	Y	Y	–	–	Y
Selective field connection integrity	–	–	–	–	–	–	Y
Connectionless integrity	–	–	Y	Y	–	–	Y
Selective field connectionless integrity	–	–	–	–	–	–	Y
Non-repudiation of origin	–	–	–	–	–	–	Y
Non-repudiation of delivery	–	–	–	–	–	–	Y

There are good reasons for varying the position of security functionality within the OSI layer hierarchy depending on the type of network in use. For the maximum degree of traffic flow confidentiality, data encryption needs to be placed at the lowest possible layer (to hide the protocol addresses). Low-level placement also offers common security support for all the different applications running across the network. However, if end-to-end security is required, then the security services must be placed in layer 3 or above. Moreover, if application-specific security services are required, then the security must be placed in layer 7.

It is interesting to note that, although X.800 is supposedly technically aligned with ISO 7498-2, the table corresponding to Table 3.4 in X.800 is slightly different. Specifically, X.800 permits the first three of the four confidentiality services to be provided in the presentation layer. Why this difference exists is not clear. Further differences arise in X.800 amendment 1, in which, in the context of LANs, a number of additional security services are permitted to be provided at layer 2, including authentication, access control, and integrity services. This reflects the fact that, in some environments, applications may be built directly on LAN protocols.

Finally, it is important to observe that there are significant interactions between the layers at which services are provided and the operation of network security devices such as *firewalls*. A firewall will typically operate at one layer in the network protocol hierarchy and will examine data being handled by the relevant protocol. If, for example, data is encrypted at a higher layer in the protocol hierarchy, then such data will be unavailable to the firewall, which must either block all such data or permit it to pass through unchecked. The choice of location of security mechanisms must therefore take into account the location and functioning of such security devices.

3.7.3 The Internet model

The seven-layer OSI model has significant differences to the four-layer Internet model, which is the basis of the vast majority of modern data communications. The four layers of the Internet model are essentially as follows.

> *Application layer:* This corresponds to the three upper layers of the OSI model (i.e., the session, presentation, and application layers). Example application layer protocols include file transfer protocol (FTP), hypertext transfer protocol (HTTP), and simple mail transfer protocol (SMTP).

> *Transport layer:* This corresponds to the OSI transport layer. The two most commonly used transport protocols are the connection-oriented transmission control protocol (TCP) and the connectionless user datagram protocol (UDP).

> *Internet protocol:* This layer covers a subset of the functionality in the OSI network layer; the primary example protocol for this layer is the connectionless Internet protocol (IP).

> *Interface layer:* This covers the functionality in the lowest two layers of the OSI protocol hierarchy.

Mapping these layers to the security services (Table 3.4) means that all security services can be provided at the application layer, most services (excluding non-repudiation and selective field services) can be provided in the middle two layers, and the bottom layer is restricted to confidentiality services (except in the case of LANs). Of course, protocols making up the Internet are not bound by the OSI security architecture, but the derived mappings of services to layers would appear to make sense in most circumstances.

3.8 Security management

ISO 7498-2 defines security management as the control and distribution of information for use in "providing security services and mechanisms (e.g., distributing access rights information), reporting on security services, and mechanisms, and reporting security-related events."

ISO 7498-2 also introduces the concept of a security management information base (SMIB), which is part of the management information base (MIB). The MIB, discussed in detail in ISO/IEC 7498-4, is a term used to describe the collection of information needed to manage all the devices in a network. Typically there will not be a single physical MIB; instead the MIB will exist as a set of information repositories distributed across the devices within a network.

The SMIB is simply the part of the MIB that manages security functionality, and will again typically exist in a distributed form. A network SMIB may include tables of data, including cryptographic keys and other parameters, files, and data or rules embedded within software or hardware.

ISO 7498-2 divides security management functions into four categories, namely the following.

> System security management;

> Security service management;

> ▸ Security mechanism management;

> ▸ Security of OSI management.

The scope of each of these categories is now briefly reviewed.

3.8.1 System security management

This function is concerned with the management of security aspects of the entire OSI system and typically includes the following.

> ▸ Security policy management;

> ▸ Interaction with other OSI management functions (e.g., accounting and fault management);

> ▸ Event-handling management;

> ▸ Security audit management;

> ▸ Security recovery management;

> ▸ Access control policy management.

Of particular importance here is the security audit, which is defined in ISO 7498-2 as follows.

> An independent review and examination of security records and activities in order to test for adequacy of system controls, to ensure compliance with established policy and operational procedures, and to recommend any necessary changes in control, policy and procedures.

This process normally uses one or more security audit trails. Security audit management includes the selection of events to be logged, the enabling/disabling of audit trail logging of certain events, and the preparation of audit reports.

3.8.2 Security service management

This refers to the management of particular security services (e.g., confidentiality and authentication) and typically includes the selection of the security mechanisms to be used to provide a requested service and the negotiation of available security mechanisms.

3.8.3 Security mechanism management

This is concerned with the management of individual security mechanisms and typically includes key management as well as management functions for the individual security mechanisms in use. Key management is fundamental to any cryptography-based security services, and includes the following.

> Determination of when key updates are required;

> Generation of keys as required;

> Secure distribution of keys.

Key management is the focus of Chapters 11 and 12.

3.8.4 Security of OSI management

This is the security of the management functions themselves and the security of communicated management information. For example this will include provisions for the protection of the MIB and for security of communications between parts of a distributed MIB.

3.8.5 Assurance

For completeness we mention a topic of fundamental importance that has been omitted from ISO 7498-2, except for the brief discussion of trusted functionality (one of the five pervasive security mechanisms). When designing a secure system, there are two fundamental considerations: system functionality and system assurance (i.e., the level of assurance that the functionality is implemented and operates as specified).

Examples of security systems failing to deliver claimed functionality are well-known; for example, access control schemes in operating systems often fail to prevent unauthorized access to resources. To assess the correctness of implementation of functionality, and so give users some measure of assurance in the functioning of a product, various bodies have devised criteria for evaluating products. Examples include the U.S. Department of Defense (DoD) Orange Book, and other more recent security evaluation criteria, such as the ISO/IEC common criteria.

3.9 Security frameworks

We conclude this chapter by considering the ISO/IEC multipart security frameworks standard, ISO/IEC 10181. Work commenced within ISO/IEC JTC1/SC21 on ISO/IEC 10181 in 1988, as soon as work finished on the OSI security architecture, ISO 7498-2. The scope of ISO/IEC 10181 is wider than that of ISO 7498-2, in that it is designed to cover all open systems, and not just those conforming to the OSI model. Each part of ISO/IEC 10181 discusses in detail how one particular security service (e.g., authentication and confidentiality) should be provided and attempts to classify the main types of mechanisms relevant to the provision of the service. The fit to the actual security mechanisms in existence is not always perfect, as the frameworks were developed in parallel with many recent developments in cryptography.

Of the seven parts of ISO/IEC 10181, five correspond to the five security services identified in ISO 7498-2; of the other two parts, one (part 1) is a general introduction, and the other (part 7) covers an important topic not really addressed in ISO 7498-2, namely security audit and alarms.

The frameworks' main role is to provide an agreed set of concepts and terminology. The frameworks are not directed at implementers but primarily at the developers of other standards, as well as the developers of proprietary security systems.

One framework that "escaped" from ISO/IEC 10181 is the key management framework. This framework was developed by ISO/IEC JTC1/SC27 as part 1 of the key management standard (ISO/IEC 11770), and this standard is discussed in Chapter 11.

3.9.1 Frameworks overview

There are two main purposes of part 1 of ISO/IEC 10181 (the frameworks overview). It serves as a general introduction to the multipart standard, and it defines a number of general security concepts and information types, including the following.

> *Security policy*. A security policy is a high-level set of rules that govern the security-relevant activities of one or more sets of elements (where an element might, for example, be a network component or a computer). A security policy applies within a security domain and may also cover interactions between domains.

> *Security authority*. A security authority is responsible for the implementation of a security policy.

> *Security domain*. A security domain is a set of elements governed by a given security policy administered by a single security authority for some specific security-relevant activities.

3.9.2 Authentication framework

The authentication framework was the first part of ISO/IEC 10181 to be completed. It provides a set of terminology to describe principles and architectures governing the provision of authentication services. It also provides a high-level classification scheme for the various types of authentication exchange mechanisms.

3.9.3 Access control framework

The access control framework was completed shortly after the authentication framework. These two parts received the most effort during the first few years of the development of ISO/IEC 10181. The access control framework is one of the most useful of the framework standards, in that it provides a set of useful concepts for discussing the provision of access control, concepts that are not really covered by other ISO/IEC standardization activity.

3.9.4 Non-repudiation framework

This framework "expands upon the concepts of non-repudiation services described in ISO 7498-2 and describes how they may be applied." It defines the entities involved in generating and managing evidence, as required to support non-repudiation services. It also provides a model for dispute resolution. Mechanisms for non-repudiation are discussed in detail in Chapter 9.

3.9.5 Confidentiality framework

The confidentiality framework discusses at a high level a variety of different approaches to providing confidentiality services. Three main classes of mechanisms are identified:

▸ *Access protection*, covering physical media protection and routing control;

▸ *The use of encryption*, including data padding, introduction of dummy events, data unit header protection, and the use of time-varying fields;

▸ *Contextual location*, including steganography and spread spectrum techniques.

3.9.6 Integrity framework

The cryptographic techniques that can be used to provide data integrity services are discussed, including MACs, signatures, and the encryption of redundant data. Surprisingly, there is little or no discussion of the mechanisms that need to be used to provide integrity protection for an entire connection; the focus is almost exclusively on cryptographic mechanisms, which can typically only be used to protect individual data units. Moreover, the discussion of the use of encryption for data integrity protection is rather naive and does not fully highlight the dangers of such an approach.

3.9.7 Audit and alarms framework

The final part of the frameworks standard provides a general model for security audit and alarm. The roles of the participants in the model are described, as are the various phases involved in security audit and alarm services.

3.10 Notes

Section 3.1

The OSI model is specified in ISO/IEC 7498-1, the second edition of which was published in 1994 [1]. Ford's book [2] provides an excellent standards-based introduction to network security that is essentially complementary to the scope of this book. Section 1.2 of [3] and the foreword to [4] also provide brief introductions to security services and mechanisms.

Section 3.2

ISO 7498-2 [5] was published in 1989 as one part of the OSI "basic reference model," and a version of this document was also adopted as CCITT Recommendation X.800 in 1991 [6] (an amendment to this latter recommendation, addressing LAN security issues, was published in 1996 [7]).

The seven part ISO/IEC security frameworks standard, ISO/IEC 10181, was published in 1996–1997 [8–14]. The identical ITU-T recommendations, X.810–X816, were published a little earlier [15–21].

ISO/IEC TR 13594 [22], the lower layers security model (see also X.802 [23]), and the upper layers security model ISO/IEC 10745 [24] (see also X.803 [25]) are not discussed in detail here. However, Ford [2] provides a comprehensive description of lower and upper layer security.

The ITU-T security architecture for end-to-end systems (i.e., X.805) was published in 2003 [26]. ISO/IEC 15816, standardizing security labels, was published in 2001 [27], and the identical ITU-T recommendation, X.841, was published a few months earlier, [28].

Section 3.3

The CRAMM risk assessment methodology originated from a U.K. government initiative, but today is a commercial product. For more information about CRAMM, see http://www.cramm.com.

Section 3.4

The discussion of security services in this chapter is very much oriented towards communications security issues. This contrasts with the common division of security services into Confidentiality, Integrity, and Availability (CIA) in a computer security context. For more details of this approach see, for example, Chapter 1 of Gollmann [29] or Chapter 1 of Pfleeger [30].

The division of non-repudiation into two subservices contrasts with the approach in ISO/IEC 13888-1 (see Chapter 9), where a total of eight non-repudiation services are defined. A description of LAN protocols, X.25 PSNs, IP and TCP can be found in just about any book on computer networking; see, for example, Stallings [31].

Section 3.5

Defining encryption mechanisms to be a special case of encipherment mechanisms, and defining hash-functions as a separate class of encipherment mechanisms, departs somewhat from common use of these terms. Indeed, most cryptographers would equate encipherment and encryption and would regard hash-functions as being something else entirely. The reason we have departed from the commonly used terminology is that the usage here would appear to be the only way to apply the ISO 7498-2 classification of mechanisms without making major modifications to it.

Although access control mechanisms are not discussed in this book, they are extremely important and have been the focus of a huge amount of research effort. For further details of some of this work, see Bishop [32] or Ferraiolo, Kuhn, and Chandramouli [33].

ISO/IEC TR 15947 [34] provides a framework for intrusion detection systems; intrusion detection is also the focus of the IETF idwg working group (the Intrusion Detection Exchange Format working group).

Section 3.6

For further information about OSI, see, for example, Henshall and Shaw's book [35], and for a review in the context of security issues, see Ford [2].

Section 3.7

Firewalls are a very widely used type of network security device. Books on firewalls include those of Cheswick, Bellovin, and Rubin [36] and Zwicky, Chapman, and Cooper [37].

The description of the Internet protocol hierarchy is based on Ford [2]. In fact, this protocol hierarchy is described in just about any modern book on computer networking (see, for example, [31]).

Section 3.8

The OSI management framework, ISO/IEC 7498-4 [38], was published in 1989. The U.S. DoD "Orange Book" [39], published in 1985, was the first standard for security system evaluation. More recently, the internationally harmonized "Common Criteria," have been developed and standardized in ISO/IEC 15408, parts 1–3 [40–42]. There are many books describing the various evaluation criteria. Ford [2] provides an introduction, as does Gollmann [29].

Section 3.9

Chapter 6 of Ford's book [2] is relevant to the discussion of the access control framework. Many of the ideas in the access control framework come in fact from earlier prestandardization efforts by ECMA [43].

References

[1]   International Organization for Standardization, *ISO/IEC 7498–1: 1994, Information Technology—Open Systems Interconnection—Basic Reference Model—The Basic Model*, 2nd ed., 1994.

[2]   Ford, W., *Computer Communications Security: Principles, Standard Protocols, and Techniques*, Upper Saddle River, NJ: Prentice Hall, 1994.

[3]   Menezes, A. J., P. C. van Oorschot, and S. A. Vanstone, *Handbook of Applied Cryptography*, Boca Raton, FL: CRC Press, 1997.

[4]   Simmons, G. J., (ed.) *Contemporary Cryptology: The Science of Information Integrity*, New York: IEEE Press, 1992.

[5]   International Organization for Standardization, *ISO 7498–2: 1989, Information Processing Systems—Open Systems Interconnection—Basic Reference Model—Part 2: Security Architecture*, 1989.

[6]   International Telecommunication Union, *CCITT Recommendation X.800 (1991), Data Communication Networks: Open Systems Interconnection (OSI); Security, Structure and Applications—Security Architecture for Open Systems Interconnection for CCITT Applications*, 1991.

[7]   International Telecommunication Union, *ITU-T Recommendation X.800 Amendment 1 (10/96), Security Architecture for Open Systems Interconnection for CCITT Applications—Amendment 1: Layer Two Security Service and Mechanisms for LANs*, 1996.

[8] International Organization for Standardization, *ISO/IEC 10181–1: 1996, Information Technology—Open Systems Interconnection—Security Frameworks for Open Systems—Part 1: Overview*, 1996.

[9] International Organization for Standardization, *ISO/IEC 10181–2: 1996, Information Technology—Open Systems Interconnection—Security Frameworks for Open Systems—Part 2: Authentication Framework*, 1996.

[10] International Organization for Standardization, *ISO/IEC 10181–3: 1996, Information Technology—Open Systems Interconnection—Security Frameworks for Open Systems—Part 3: Access Control Framework*, 1996.

[11] International Organization for Standardization, *ISO/IEC 10181–5: 1996, Information Technology—Open Systems Interconnection—Security Frameworks for Open Systems—Part 5: Confidentiality Framework*, 1996.

[12] International Organization for Standardization, *ISO/IEC 10181–6: 1996, Information Technology—Open Systems Interconnection—Security Frameworks for Open Systems—Part 6: Integrity Framework*, 1996.

[13] International Organization for Standardization, *ISO/IEC 10181–7: 1996, Information Technology—Open Systems Interconnection—Security Frameworks for Open Systems—Part 7: Security Audit and Alarms Framework*, 1996.

[14] International Organization for Standardization, *ISO/IEC 10181–4: 1997, Information Technology—Open Systems Interconnection—Security Frameworks for Open Systems—Part 4: Non-Repudiation Framework*, 1997.

[15] International Telecommunication Union, *ITU-T Recommendation X.810 (11/95), Data Networks and Open System Communications—Security—Information Technology—Open Systems Interconnection—Security Frameworks for Open Systems: Overview*, 1995.

[16] International Telecommunication Union, *ITU-T Recommendation X.811 (04/95), Data Networks and Open System Communications—Security—Information Technology—Open Systems Interconnection—Security Frameworks for Open Systems: Authentication Framework*, 1995.

[17] International Telecommunication Union, *ITU-T Recommendation X.812 (11/95), Data Networks and Open System Communications—Security—Information Technology—Open Systems Interconnection—Security Frameworks for Open Systems: Access Control Framework*, 1995.

[18] International Telecommunication Union, *ITU-T Recommendation X.814 (11/95), Data Networks and Open System Communications—Security—Information Technology—Open Systems Interconnection—Security Frameworks for Open Systems: Confidentiality Framework*, 1995.

[19] International Telecommunication Union, *ITU-T Recommendation X.815 (11/95), Data Networks and Open System Communications—Security—Information Technology—Open Systems Interconnection—Security Frameworks for Open Systems: Integrity Framework*, 1995.

[20] International Telecommunication Union, *ITU-T Recommendation X.816 (11/95), Data Networks and Open System Communications—Security—Information Technology—Open Systems Interconnection—Security Frameworks for Open Systems: Security Audit and Alarms Framework*, 1995.

[21] International Telecommunication Union, *ITU-T Recommendation X.813 (10/96), Data Networks and Open System Communications—Security—Information*

Technology—Open Systems Interconnection—Security Frameworks for Open Systems: Non-Repudiation Framework, 1996.

[22]   International Organization for Standardization. *ISO/IEC TR 13594: 1995, Information Technology—Lower Layers Security*, 1995.

[23]   International Telecommunication Union, *ITU-T Recommendation X.802 (04/95), Data Networks and Open System Communications—Security—Information Technology—Lower Layers Security Model*, 1995.

[24]   International Organization for Standardization, *ISO/IEC 10745: 1995, Information Technology—Open Systems Interconnection—Upper Layers Security Model*, 1995.

[25]   International Telecommunication Union, *ITU-T Recommendation X.803 (07/94), Data Networks and Open System Communications—Security—Information Technology—Open Systems Interconnection—Upper Layers Security Model*, 1994.

[26]   International Telecommunication Union, *ITU-T Recommendation X.805 (10/2003), Security—Security Architecture for Systems Providing End-to-End Communications*, 2003.

[27]   International Organization for Standardization, *ISO/IEC 15816: 2001, Information Technology—Security Techniques—Security Information Objects for Access Control*, 2001.

[28]   International Telecommunication Union, *ITU-T Recommendation X.841 (10/2000), Security—Information Technology—Security Techniques—Security Information Objects for Access Control*, 2000.

[29]   Gollmann, D., *Computer Security*, New York: John Wiley and Sons, 1999.

[30]   Pfleeger, C. P., *Security in Computing*, 2nd ed., Upper Saddle River, NJ: Prentice Hall, 1997.

[31]   Stallings, W., *Data and Computer Communications*, 7th ed., Upper Saddle River, NJ: Prentice Hall, 2004.

[32]   Bishop, M., *Computer Security: Art and Science*, Reading, MA: Addison-Wesley, 2002.

[33]   Ferraiolo, D. F., D. R. Kuhn, and R. Chandramouli, *Role-Based Access Control*, Norwood, MA: Artech House, 2003.

[34]   International Organization for Standardization, *ISO/IEC TR 15947: 2002, Information Technology—Security Techniques—IT Intrusion Detection Framework*, 2002.

[35]   Henshall, J., and S. Shaw, *OSI Explained*, Chichester, England: Ellis Horwood, 1988.

[36]   Cheswick, W. R., S. M. Bellovin, and A. D. Rubin, *Firewalls and Internet Security: Repelling the Wily Hacker*, 2nd ed., Reading, MA: Addison-Wesley, 2003.

[37]   Zwicky, E. D., D. B. Chapman, and S. Cooper, *Building Internet Firewalls*, 2nd ed., Sebastapol, CA: O'Reilly, 2000.

[38]   International Organization for Standardization, *ISO/IEC 7498–4: 1989, Information Processing Systems—Open Systems Interconnection—Basic Reference Model—Part 4: Management Framework*, 1989.

[39]   U.S. Department of Defense, *DoD 5200.28-STD, Trusted Computer System Evaluation Criteria*, 1985.

[40]   International Organization for Standardization, *ISO/IEC 15408–1: 1999, Information Technology—Security Techniques—Evaluation Criteria for IT Security—Part 1: Introduction and General Model*, 1999.

[41]   International Organization for Standardization, *ISO/IEC 15408–2: 1999, Information Technology—Security Techniques—Evaluation Criteria for IT Security—Part 2: Security Functional Requirements*, 1999.

[42]   International Organization for Standardization, *ISO/IEC 15408–3: 1999, Information Technology—Security Techniques—Evaluation Criteria for IT Security—Part 3: Security Assurance Requirements*, 1999.

[43]   European Computer Manufacturers Association, *ECMA TR/46, Security in Open Systems: A Security Framework*, July 1988.

Encryption

Contents

4.1 Definitions and basic properties

4.2 Block ciphers

4.3 Stream ciphers

4.4 Asymmetric ciphers

4.5 Notes

The term "cryptography" is often mistakenly used as a synonym for "encryption" and vice versa. Cryptography is the study of algorithms that provide a security service, and includes, among others, the study of algorithms that protect the integrity of data, algorithms that guarantee the authenticity of the source of data, and algorithms that provide confidentiality for data (encryption algorithms).

Encryption schemes, on the other hand, are only concerned with the provision of confidentiality. In other words encryption algorithms transform data, sometimes called *messages* or *plaintext,* into *ciphertext,* which can be transmitted over a public network and from which no unauthorized entity can determine any information about the message (except, possibly, its length). When the ciphertext reaches its intended recipient, he or she can undo the encryption operation and recover the message from the ciphertext. It is easy to see that, in order to do this, the recipient must have some kind of extra, secret information that is not known to any unauthorized person. This is known as a *key.*

It is important to understand that, in general, an encryption scheme only provides confidentiality. It does not make any claim that the message that arrives will not have been altered in some way (integrity) or has come from the source that claims to have sent it (data origin authentication), only that the message that arrives has not been read by anybody else along the way. (Although some encryption algorithms do provide some measure of integrity protection, this is considered a bonus rather than an objective of the scheme.) Unauthorized entities that try to find out information about a message from its ciphertext are known as *attackers* or *eavesdroppers.*

It should be noted that encryption schemes are not the only method of providing confidentiality. For more information about which security mechanisms can be used to provide security services, see Chapter 3.

4.1 Definitions and basic properties

As we have already mentioned, for an encryption scheme to work, the intended recipients must know some secret key that will allow them to recover messages from ciphertexts. We can now split encryption schemes into two types. If the message sender knows this secret key then the scheme is said to be *symmetric*. If the message sender does not know the secret key then the scheme is said to be *asymmetric* or *public-key*. The relationships between the various types of ciphers are shown in Figure 4.1.

4.1.1 Symmetric ciphers

The two types of ciphers are very different. Symmetric ciphers are typically designed to minimize the computation required to encrypt or decrypt data and hence can be implemented in such a way as to operate at high speeds. Their main drawback comes from the fact that both the sender and receiver need to know the secret key. If one party (say, the sender) generates this key then he or she has the problem of getting it securely to the receiver without any attacker intercepting it—and they cannot use symmetric encryption to do this unless they already share a secret key! This problem of key distribution will be addressed in Chapters 11 and 12.

We can further categorize symmetric ciphers into two types: *block ciphers* and *stream ciphers*. Block ciphers operate on messages of a fixed length and produce a ciphertext of the same length. This fixed length is block cipher's *block length* and is typically 64 or 128 bits. Stream ciphers are symmetric ciphers that produce ciphertext from plaintext in a continuous manner and that do not have any restrictions on the size of the plaintext. Stream ciphers are often built using block ciphers.

4.1.2 Asymmetric ciphers

Keys for asymmetric ciphers consist of two values. The first is a public key that contains all the information required by a sender to encrypt a message

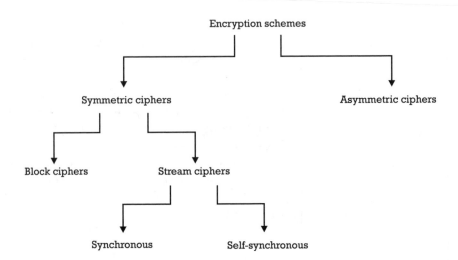

Figure 4.1 An encryption scheme family tree.

but no information that would allow anyone to recover the message from the ciphertext. This key can and should be distributed to everybody who wishes to be able to send confidential messages to the recipient. The second key is known as the private key and should only be known to the recipient. The private key contains all the information required to recover messages from ciphertexts.

Asymmetric ciphers are almost always based on complicated mathematical problems and are typically very slow when compared to symmetric ciphers. The main problem with asymmetric ciphers is not key distribution—if the recipients generate the public and private keys then they can keep the private key to themselves and make the public key available by way of the Internet, say—but a problem of authenticity. Anybody who wishes to send a message must first get hold of an authentic copy of the recipient's public key. This may not be as easy as it sounds! Again, this problem will be discussed more thoroughly when we talk about the management of asymmetric keys in Chapters 11 and 13.

Regardless of whether we are talking about symmetric or asymmetric schemes, an encryption scheme consists of three distinct algorithms:

▸ A key generation algorithm that describes how to generate the key (or keys) to be used with the scheme;

▸ An encryption algorithm that describes how to encrypt a message to give a ciphertext;

▸ A decryption algorithm that describes how to recover a message from a ciphertext.

The key generation algorithm is generally very simple for block ciphers, where the secret key is usually just a randomly chosen bit string of some fixed length (typically 64 or 128 bits). Stream ciphers also have keys that start off as a fixed length, randomly chosen bit string, but often these need to be changed (or "loaded") before they can be used by the stream cipher algorithms. Stream ciphers also typically need some kind of initializing value [known as an starting variable (SV)]. This is usually a fixed length, randomly chosen bit string too, but, unlike a stream cipher's key, an SV is not usually kept secret. Asymmetric encryption schemes have more complicated keys and need complex mathematical key generation algorithms.

All key generation algorithms require good random bit generators. Standardized random bit generation techniques will be discussed in Chapter 16.

4.1.3 Attacks against encryption schemes

There are two types of attack to which an encryption scheme can be subjected. The first is known as a *key recovery* attack. In a key recovery attack some unauthorized party attempts to determine the recipient's secret or private key. The cipher has to remain secure even if the unauthorized party can somehow get hold of encryptions and decryptions of certain messages of their choice (and the public key, if the encryption scheme is asymmetric).

The second type of attack is known as a *message recovery* attack. In a message recovery attack some unauthorized party intercepts the encryption of some unknown message and tries to find out some (any!) information about the message from the ciphertext. Again we assume that the unauthorized parties can somehow get hold of encryptions and decryptions of certain messages of their choice (and the public key, if the scheme is asymmetric).

Traditionally, a message recovery attack is only valid if it recovers the whole message from a ciphertext. Nowadays the attack is deemed to have succeeded if the attacker can determine any information about the message from the ciphertext. This is known as *semantic security,* and it can be shown that a cipher is semantically secure if attackers are unable to decide whether a given ciphertext is an encryption of one message or another, even when they can request the decryption of any other ciphertext.

4.2 Block ciphers

The block cipher is probably the simplest type of encryption algorithm to understand and one of the most widely used. Block ciphers are not only used to protect confidentiality but are often used as building blocks for creating other algorithms; in particular, block ciphers can be used to build hash functions (see Chapter 6) and MACs (see Chapter 7).

We will therefore take this opportunity to introduce some notations that will be used throughout this book. A block cipher takes as input messages that are precisely n-bits long and produce outputs of the same length. The secret key will be a bit-string K of some fixed length, called the key length. The encryption function (using the key K) will be denoted e_K; hence, if X is an n-bit block then $e_K(X)$ will be the encryption of X using the key K. Similarly the decryption function (using the key K) will be denoted d_K and the decryption of an n-bit block Y will be written as $d_K(Y)$. For the encryption scheme to be useful we demand that for any key K of the correct length and any n-bit block X we have

$$Y = e_K(X) \text{ if and only if } X = d_K(Y) \qquad (4.1)$$

This notation is summarized in Table 4.1.

The major problem with block ciphers is that the block length, n, is very small—typically only 64 or 128 bits. Therefore, on its own, one can only use a block cipher to encrypt very short messages.

Table 4.1 Notation for Block Ciphers

Variable	Definition
n	The block length
K	A symmetric key
e_K	The encryption function using the key K
$e_K(X)$	The encryption of the n-bit block X using the key K
d_K	The decryption function using the key K
$d_K(Y)$	The decryption of the n-bit block Y using the key K

The short block length can also lead to other problems. If a block cipher is ever used to encrypt the same message block twice under the same key then the same ciphertext block will result in both cases. Therefore, any attacker who sees two equal ciphertexts being passed between a sender and a receiver will know that the same message has been sent (although he or she may not know what that message is!). Since n is fairly small, if a lot of data is transmitted then it is fairly likely that such a repetition will occur and so the attacker gains some information about the structure of the messages being sent.

Both of these problems can be avoided by using a *mode of operation* for a block cipher. A mode of operation for a block cipher is a method of using a block cipher iteratively to encipher long messages while (generally) avoiding the problems associated with sending the same message twice. Modes of operations for a block cipher are discussed in detail in Chapter 5. In this way, block ciphers can be thought of as building blocks for larger confidentiality services.

Technically, a block cipher is trying to emulate a random permutation of the message space. A block cipher is indistinguishable from a random permutation if an attacker cannot distinguish between messages that have been encrypted using the block cipher (with some secret key) and an algorithm that assigns ciphertexts to messages randomly. None of the standardized block ciphers have been proved to be indistinguishable from a random permutation but most are thought to be so.

It can be shown that many of the modes of operation of a block cipher are secure, providing the block cipher that they use is indistinguishable from a random permutation.

4.2.1 The National Bureau of Standards and DES

The first real standardization effort for any type of cryptographic algorithm was launched in 1974 when the U.S. National Bureau of Standards (NBS) asked businesses and academics to submit proposals for a new standardized block ciper. This block cipher was to be recommended for use with any type of nonclassified data. In 1977 a variant of the Lucifer block cipher, submitted by IBM, was finally chosen for standardization. This encryption scheme became the data encryption standard and is almost uniformly known as DES[1] now.

The cipher became a FIPS standard (NBS FIPS Pub. 46) and later an ANSI standard (ANSI X3.92). It has been widely adopted, most notably in the banking industry where almost all the cryptography used is based in some way on DES.

DES is a 64-bit block cipher (i.e., it takes 64-bit blocks as inputs) and technically has a 64-bit key. However eight bits of the 64-bit key are not randomly generated but computed from the remaining 56 bits. These eight bits act as a check value, allowing users to check that the key that they have been given is indeed a valid DES key and has not, say, been corrupted

---

1. Technically the cipher should be called "the DES" but, as this sounds somewhat odd, most people prefer to call it just DES.

in transit. Unfortunately this means that any attacker who is trying to guess the key does not need to guess all 64 bits but only needs to guess 56 key bits, a feat that is 256 times easier than trying to guess a 64-bit key. Even at the time a 56-bit key was thought to be too small for long-term purposes. Nowadays, although trying all 2^{56} possible keys is still beyond the abilities of most casual attackers, it is certainly not beyond the means of most serious organizations.

The first practical demonstration that the key length of DES was too small to provide adequate security was demonstrated by Curtin and Dolske in 1997. In response to a challenge set by RSA Laboratories, and for a prize of $10,000, Curtin and Dolske coordinated a distributed brute force key recovery attack against DES—the attack combined the computing power of thousands of computers linked via the Internet, and each computer checked a number of DES keys to see if that key was the correct one.

After this, in 1998, the Electronic Frontier Foundation (EFF) demonstrated that for $250,000, it was possible to build a specialist machine that would complete an exhaustive search for a DES key in about a week. On average the machine would recover a DES key in about three days. In 1999 the EFF took this one step further and, by combining its "DES cracker" with thousands of other computers connected via the Internet, completed an exhaustive search for a DES key in under 24 hours.

Exhaustive key search is not the only possible attack on DES. DES has also been attacked using complicated cryptanalytic attacks called "differential cryptanalysis" and "linear cryptanalysis." While it is not the intention of this book to explain these attacks in detail, it should be noted that these attacks (and linear cryptanalysis in particular) severely weaken DES, and it is generally agreed that DES should not be used to provide confidentiality on its own.

These attacks were published in the 1980s and caused many problems. In the time between the NBS publishing the data encryption standard and the attacks against DES being published, many large companies had invested huge amounts of money on international computer systems whose security was based on DES. In order to avoid a similar amount of money having to be spent to update these networks, the NBS published a new FIPS standard (FIPS Pub. 46-3) which standardized a new way of using DES called Triple DES. Triple DES, as one might expect, involves encrypting an n-bit block of data three times using DES. Encryption of an n-bit block of data X is given by

$$Y := e_{K_3}(d_{K_2}(e_{K_1}(X))) \qquad\qquad (4.2)$$

Decryption is given by

$$X := d_{K_3}(e_{K_2}(e_{K_1}(Y))) \qquad\qquad (4.3)$$

The FIPS standard insisted that K_1 and K_2 be independent and randomly generated DES keys but allowed K_3 to either be an independent and randomly generated key or equal to K_1.

Triple DES has a larger key (since K_1 and K_2 must be randomly generated, any party attempting to guess the key must now guess 112 key bits rather than 56 key bits), which means that exhaustive key search is no longer possible, and its more complicated structure means that it is more resistant to differential and linear cryptanalysis. Unfortunately, because Triple DES was not designed from scratch, it is not very efficient and runs a lot more slowly than most modern block ciphers.

4.2.2 The ISO Register of Cryptographic Algorithms

ANSI is a member body of ISO, so it is not surprising that the ANSI-standardized DES algorithm was proposed for inclusion within an ISO standard in the mid-1980s. This nearly succeeded, but, in the end, the effort had to be abandoned for political reasons. At that time, many of the member countries had legislation that restricted the use of strong cryptography. For example, the use of all cryptography was banned in France, and even the United States controlled the export of strong cryptographic schemes.

So, instead of actually standardizing encryption schemes, ISO instead started a register of cryptographic algorithms (ISO/IEC 9979). This provided a common reference point for the identification of cryptographic schemes by a unique name but made no attempt to judge the quality of any scheme contained in the register. Submission of an entry to the register can be made by an ISO member body, an ISO technical committee, or a liaison organization and the entry must include the following:

- The algorithm's name(s);
- The intended range of applications;
- Interface parameters;
- Test values;
- Registration information (such as who requested the registration and when registration was requested);
- Patent information.

It should be noted that an entry need not actually specify how an algorithm works, only the input and output characteristics! Additionally, the register can store any other information that the registering entity wants, including the following:

- A description of the algorithm;
- Information on the modes of operation for the algorithm;
- References to associated algorithms.

Although the register is not restricted to block ciphers, or even encryption schemes, it is mainly used to store information about these ciphers, and most of the historically important block ciphers are included on the register. Examples include DES, MISTY1, and IDEA.

The ISO register is still running and is publicly available through the Internet. However, the increasingly liberal attitude of governments toward cryptography and more recent standardization efforts have meant that the register has been somewhat neglected of late. There are only 24 algorithms contained on the register, and no new algorithms have been added since 2001. The register does not even contain an entry for AES.

4.2.3 NIST and AES

In 1988 the U.S. National Bureau of Standards changed its name to the National Institute of Standards and Technology (NIST). In 1997 it launched the next major block cipher standardization effort and called for academics and businesses to submit proposals for a new Advanced Encryption Standard (AES) to replace the outdated DES. The new scheme had to work with on 128-bit data blocks and be able to support 128-bit, 192-bit, and 256-bit keys.

There were 22 submissions to the AES standardization process, but seven of these did not fulfill all of the entry requirements specified by NIST and were not considered. This left 15 algorithms. In 1999 this list was reduced to five finalists. These were MARS, RC6, Rijndael, Serpent, and Twofish. The eventual winner was Rijndael—a very efficient, flexible algorithm proposed by two Belgians: Joan Daemen and Vincent Rijmen. The new standard, NIST FIPS Pub. 197, was published in 2002.

Since then AES has received an enormous amount of attention, and, even now, cryptographers are beginning to notice certain mathematical anomalies in the way that the cipher works. It is unclear yet whether these anomalies will give rise to actual attacks against AES, and the security of AES remains a contentious issue within the cryptographic community. Despite the concerns of the academic community, the U.S. government has declared that AES is secure enough to be used to protect classified information up to secret and top secret levels.

4.2.4 3GPP and KASUMI

Whilst NIST was busy standardizing a 128-bit block cipher, another important standardization event was happening: The 3GPP partnership was choosing a 64-bit block cipher that would be used as a basis for confidentiality and integrity algorithms within the third generation of mobile phones.

Due to the limited computational power of mobile devices and the need for encryption of data that may be appearing in real time (e.g., voice data) the block cipher in question has to be fast, simple, and, obviously, secure. Beyond this the algorithm's designers had to be prepared to give up the ownership of the algorithm to the 3GPP consortium, which would then grant royalty-free licenses to the mobile phone companies.

The algorithm 3GPP finally agreed on was KASUMI. KASUMI is a variant of the MISTY1 block cipher that appears the ISO register of cryptographic algorithms and is likely to be contained in the ISO standard on encryption. It uses 64-bit plaintext blocks and encrypts them under a 128-bit key.

4.2.5   ISO/IEC 18033

In 2001 ISO decided that the political situation had changed sufficiently for it to begin work on a standard for encryption schemes. The standard, named ISO/IEC 18033, has four parts:

▸ Part 1: General;

▸ Part 2: Asymmetric ciphers;

▸ Part 3: Block ciphers;

▸ Part 4: Stream ciphers.

The first part, ISO/IEC 18033-1, only sets out some general ideas and terminology that are used by the other three parts. It details the criteria that ISO has used in selecting ciphers for inclusion in the standard. It states that each proposed cipher should be evaluated with respect to its security, speed, patent situation, maturity (i.e., its age), and its level of adoption by other standards bodies and by the cryptographic community in general. The number of schemes in each part is also to be kept as small as possible.

Obviously the smallest number of ciphers it is possible to have in each part of the standard is one. The idea is that each part will only contain more than one algorithm if each algorithm has an advantage over all the others in some way. It could be, for example, that a cipher is particularly suited for implementation on smart cards or that it is particularly strong but slightly slower than other algorithms. Two algorithms with similar characteristics can be included only if they are based on totally different principles, so that if one algorithm is broken then the other will still be secure.

It is unclear at the moment which algorithms will be included in the final version of 18033-3. Currently the standard splits the schemes between those that work on 64-bit blocks (like Triple DES) and those that work on 128-bit blocks (like AES). It seems likely that the standard will contain at least Triple DES and MISTY1 (as 64-bit block ciphers) and AES (as a 128-bit block ciphers).

4.3   Stream ciphers

There have not been many attempts to standardize stream ciphers. There are two major reasons for this. First, secure stream ciphers are notoriously difficult to design. Speed is a major factor in the design of stream ciphers, and designers often find it hard to produce ciphers that are both secure and fast. This sometimes means that the security of the cipher can suffer as designers build ciphers on untested principles. It should also be remembered that the term "speed" is relative: What may be impractical at one point in time, may be totally feasible 5 years later. Hence, older stream ciphers may now run incredibly quickly but also may find it harder to resist attacks launched by unauthorized parties with vastly improved computers.

The second reason is that many stream ciphers that are commonly used have not been released into the public domain. Many owners prefer to keep their algorithms secret to stop them from being broken. Any unauthorized party who then wishes to break the cipher first needs to figure out what the cipher is before he or she can even start to think about attacking it.

One good example of this is in the use of stream ciphers to encrypt GSM mobile telephone communications. For confidentiality GSM standardized the use of three stream ciphers (named A5/1, A5/2, and A5/3) for encryption. The descriptions of A5/1 and A5/2 were never released to the public, yet in both cases the algorithms were reverse-engineered from their implementations and the schemes subsequently broken. The specification for the last encryption algorithm, A5/3, has been made public and is based on a mode of operation of the KASUMI block cipher (see Section 4.2.4). Although the A5/3 stream cipher has not been broken, some problems with the way in which it is implemented (combined with the weaknesses of A5/1 and A5/2) mean that the confidentiality of data sent over a mobile telephone cannot be assured.

Currently, 3GPP recommends the use of a stream cipher based on the counter mode and output feedback mode (see Chapter 5) to provide confidentiality for mobile telephone communications. Furthermore, 3GPP recommends the use of the KASUMI block cipher with these modes. This algorithm is known as $f8$.

Despite the difficulties historically associated with standardizing stream ciphers, ISO has decided to attempt to produce a standard: ISO/IEC 18033-4. All stream ciphers conform to the same basic model. A stream cipher is composed of two basic parts: a *keystream generator* and a *mode of operation*. The keystream generator is set up using the secret key and a (possibly secret) starting variable (SV).

Whenever some party wishes to use the stream cipher the keystream generator outputs a block of keystream—a fixed size block of random looking bits that will be used to encrypt a block of plaintext. Usually the keystream block is the same size as the plaintext block. Theoretically the keystream generator could continue to produce keystream blocks forever but after a while the blocks must start to repeat, so it is important to update the secret key and the starting variable before this happens.

The purpose of a starting variable is to allow the keystream generator to be initialized and reinitialized easily. Since the initial setup of a keystream generator depends upon the starting variable, different starting variables cause the keystream generator to output different blocks of keystream; while using the same starting variable (and key) twice causes the keystream generator to output the same blocks of keystream. Hence using a different starting variable whenever the keystream generator is restarted makes sure that the same keystream is never used to encrypt two different messages.

Of course, one could also ensure that the keystream generator produced different keystream blocks by changing the key instead of the starting variable; while this is a solution to the problem, any operations that involve changing or updating a key need to be done with a very high level of security (see Chapter 11), and it is usually easier to change the starting variable than the key.

A mode of operation is a way of combining a block of keystream data and a block of plaintext to create a block of ciphertext. The mode of operation has to be reversible (i.e., if we use a block of keystream data to encrypt a block of plaintext then the resulting block of ciphertext must give the same block of plaintext when decrypted using the same block of keystream).

Thus, to encrypt a message m using a secret key K and a starting variable SV the following steps are performed:

1. *Splitting:* The message m is split into message blocks $m_0, m_1, \ldots, m_l$.

2. *Initialization:* The keystream generator is initialized using the secret key K and the starting variable SV. A counting variable i is set to 0.

3. *Keystream generation:* The keystream generator outputs a block of keystream Z_i.

4. *Encryption:* The mode of operation is used to encrypt the message block m_i with keystream block Z_i to get a ciphertext block C_i.

5. *Looping:* If $i < l$, then i is increased by one and steps 3–5 are repeated.

6. *Output:* The ciphertext $C = C_0 || C_1 || \ldots || C_l$ is output.

Decryption of a ciphertext C using a secret key K and a starting variable SV is very similar:

1. *Splitting:* The ciphertext C is split into ciphertext blocks $C_0, C_1, \ldots, C_l$.

2. *Initialization:* The keystream generator is initialised using the secret key K and the starting vairable SV. A counting variable i is set to 0.

3. *Keystream generation:* The keystream generator outputs a block of keystream Z_i.

4. *Decryption:* The mode of operation is used to decrypt the ciphertext block C_i with keystream block Z_i to get a message block m_i.

5. *Looping:* If $i < l$, then i is increased by one and steps 3–5 are repeated.

6. *Output:* The message $m = m_0 || m_1 || \ldots || m_l$ is output.

Stream ciphers can be divided into two types depending on the way that the keystream generator works. In a *synchronous* stream cipher the keystream generator produces keystream blocks that only depend upon the secret key K and the starting variable. In a *self-synchronous* stream cipher each keystream block produced depends not only on the secret key and the starting variable but also on the ciphertexts that have previously been produced by the algorithm (hence, in some way, on the previous message blocks).

Currently, there are three keystream generators based on block ciphers included in the draft of ISO 18033-4. These correspond to the ciphertext feedback (CFB), output feedback (OFB), and counter (CTR) modes of operation for a block cipher (see Chapter 5). OFB mode and CTR mode are synchronous stream ciphers, while CFB mode is a self-synchronous stream cipher. It is unclear at the moment whether any "dedicated" stream ciphers (stream ciphers that are not built using block ciphers or any other type of cryptographic function) will be included in the standard.

The standard also contains two modes of operation for a stream cipher. The first involves simply combining equal-sized plaintext and keystream blocks using the exclusive-OR (XOR) operation. (This is obviously reversible as the message block is the XOR of the ciphertext block and the appropriate keystream block.) The second mode of operation is called MULTI-S01. MULTI-S01 is a more complex mode of operation for a stream cipher, but it is designed to ensure the integrity of the data as well as the confidentiality (see Chapter 16).

The formal security definition of a stream cipher states that an attacker should not be able to distinguish the output of the keystream generator (for some random secret key) from a string of randomly generated bits. A keystream generator that satisfies this property is said to be indistinguishable from random, and it can be shown that the symmetric cipher composed of a keystream generator that is indistinguishable from random and the XOR mode of operation is semantically secure.

It has been proven that all of the standardized keystream generators based on block ciphers are indistinguishable from random provided that the underlying block cipher is indistinguishable from a random permutation (see Chapter 5 for more information on security proofs for the modes of operation of a block cipher). None of the "standard" dedicated keystream generators have been proven to be indistinguishable from random (although all of them are believed to be secure).

4.4 Asymmetric ciphers

Asymmetric ciphers are much more mathematically complex than symmetric ciphers. They are based on the difficulties involved in solving certain mathematical problems. They are also often probabilistic (i.e., may generate random numbers or bits as part of their algorithms) instead of deterministic (i.e., do not use any kind of random information).

In a deterministic encryption algorithm (such as a block cipher) there is only one possible ciphertext for each message, so whenever we encrypt a message we will always get the same ciphertext. In a probabilistic encryption scheme there are many different ciphertexts that can be the encryption of a message, and we would expect to get a different ciphertext every time we encrypt that message. Which ciphertext is given in any execution of the encryption algorithm depends on the random bits that the encryption algorithm uses. The generation of random bits and random numbers has to be done with care or an otherwise secure scheme may be weakened. The generation of random bits and numbers is dealt with in Chapter 16.

Formally, an asymmetric encryption scheme is only considered secure if it is semantically secure (i.e., if an attacker cannot decide if a given ciphertext is an encryption of one message or another). This is why modern asymmetric encryption schemes must be probabilistic: If a scheme was deterministic then an attacker could tell if a given ciphertext was an encryption of a message by encrypting that message using the public key and comparing the result to the ciphertext.

4.4.1 The Rivest-Shamir-Adleman (RSA) scheme

While the NBS were making the revolutionary move of standardizing DES, another revolution was happening in the world of cryptography: the development of asymmetric cryptography. Previous to the work of Whitfield Diffie and Martin Hellman, it was assumed that it was impossible for two people to communicate confidentially without sharing some secret key. The Diffie-Hellman key agreement protocol (see Chapter 12) changed this by showing that it was possible to have a scheme that used two keys: a public key that could be freely distributed and a private key that had to be kept secret. The security of these schemes depends upon it being difficult to solve complex, underlying mathematical problems.

The arrival of the Diffie-Hellman key agreement protocol was quickly followed by the first asymmetric encryption scheme: RSA. The history of RSA and standards is a bizarre one. As we have already mentioned, in the late 1970s and 1980s few countries were comfortable with standardizing encryption algorithms and so RSA was not officially standardized as a method of confidentiality for many years. However, RSA can also be used as a method of providing digital signatures (see Chapter 8), and it was not long until it was standardized as a digital signature algorithm. Since there are very few differences between the digital signature and encryption schemes, one could suggest that RSA snuck into international standards very quickly through the "back door" of digital signatures.

The RSA scheme was developed by three academics—Ron Rivest, Adi Shamir, and Len Adleman—at MIT in 1978. As it will be useful later on, we give a quick description of the RSA scheme. Remember that an encryption scheme is actually the combination of three algorithms: the key generation algorithm, the encryption algorithm, and the decryption algorithm.

Key generation   Key generation for any cipher is difficult. It forms an important part of a key's life cycle (see Chapter 11) and should always done with care and only by authorized parties (such as a systems administrator or the intended recipient of the private key). To generate an RSA key the authorized party must do the following things:

1. Generate two large prime numbers p and q of the same size. We insist that p and q are distinct (i.e., $p \neq q$). For more information about generating prime numbers, see Chapter 16.

2. Set $n = pq$. The value n is known as the *modulus*.

3. Choose, or generate randomly, an *encryption exponent e* that is co-prime to $p - 1$ and $q - 1$.

4. Find a value d between 1 and $n-1$ such that $ed \equiv 1 \bmod (p-1)$ $(q-1)$. d is known as the *decryption exponent*. There are fast mathematical algorithms that can do this if they are given p and q as well as n and e.

5. The public key consists of the modulus n and the encryption exponent e.

6. The private key is the decryption exponent d.

Note that the two primes p and q are no longer needed after they are used to compute the decryption exponent d. After this they need to be safely and securely destroyed.

Encryption   We consider how to encrypt a message m using a public key consisting of a modulus n and an encryption exponent e. The message m must be represented as an integer between 1 and $n-1$. The sender generates the ciphertext C (also a number between 1 and $n-1$) by computing

$$C = m^e \bmod n \tag{4.4}$$

The ciphertext C can now be sent to the intended recipient safe in the knowledge that nobody who accidently observes C in transit can recover m without knowing the private key.

Decryption   When a recipient receives a ciphertext C (a number between 1 and $n-1$), he or she can recover the message using the modulus n and the (secret) decryption exponent d. The recipient computes the message m' by computing

$$m' = C^d \bmod n \tag{4.5}$$

Provided that the key generation algorithm has worked properly, the decrypted message m' will be the same as the message m that was sent.

Although RSA is still considered to be secure in some sense, in the very basic form given above it is does not give the high levels of security that are required from modern encryption schemes. Since it is deterministic and not probabilistic, we can immediately see that it is not semantically secure, but it also suffers from many other problems. For example, the basic version of RSA cannot be used to encrypt small numbers as if $0 \leq m < \sqrt[e]{n}$ then

$$C = m^e \bmod n = m^e \tag{4.6}$$

and so it is very easy to recover $m = \sqrt[e]{C}$.

It is also very easy to establish relationships between different messages that have related ciphertexts when using RSA. For example, if C is the encryption of a message m and C' is the encryption of a message m' then

$$C' = 2^e C \bmod n \qquad \text{if and only if} \qquad m' = 2m \bmod n \tag{4.7}$$

These days RSA is most commonly used as a building block for more complicated encryption or digital signature schemes.

4.4.2 Industry Standards for Asymmetric Encryption

While RSA may have crept into international standards quietly via digital signatures, it still took a significant amount of knowledge to be able to recognize this and to be able to adapt the algorithms to provide confidentiality. During the 1980s this knowledge was not readily available within the software development community, which was trying to produce products with encryption capabilities. This led several industrial bodies (generally those that owned patents on various asymmetric encryption techniques) to produce their own standards. This was a shrewd move on the part of these companies: Not only did they raise the profile of their algorithms and earn royalties, they also reduced the possibility of losing their reputations as security experts because some third party had implemented the algorithms badly.

The first successful attempt to standardize asymmetric encryption algorithms was made in 1991 by RSA Labs., the company that owned the patent on the RSA encryption scheme. It produced a series of standards under the title Public-Key Cryptography Standards (PKCS). The first standard (PKCS #1) only dealt with the RSA scheme and its variants, but subsequent standards have had a broader scope, and PKCS now covers such areas as Diffie-Hellman key agreement and the syntax of various asymmetric data types. A more detailed description of the PKCS range is given in Table 4.2.

Just as with DES, the existence of a standardized version of RSA really gave the cryptographic community a target to attack and there have been several attacks directed specifically against the implementations of RSA given in PKCS #1. As we have already mentioned, the RSA scheme on its own is not good enough to provide confidentiality in the modern world—it needs to be combined with some other techniques. The attacks against PKCS #1 have all exploited weaknesses in these other techniques rather than breaking the RSA scheme in general.

Table 4.2 Selected PKCS Standards

Standard	Description	First Published	Last Revised
PKCS #1	Asymmetric schemes based on RSA (including both encryption and signature schemes)	1991	2002
PKCS #3	The Diffie-Hellman key agreement protocol and its variants (see Chapter 12)	1991	1993
PKCS #5	Asymmetric encryption schemes that can be derived from a weak secret (such as a password)	1991	1999
PKCS #7	Syntax for messages and other cryptographic data	1991	1997
PKCS #8	Syntax for private keys for asymmetric encryption schemes	1991	1993
PKCS #11	A standardized interface for accessing a systems cryptographic functions (see Chapter 15)	1995	2004
PKCS #13	Elliptic curve cryptography (including both encryption and signature schemes)	TBC	TBC

The RSA PKCS standards were not the only industrial encryption standards produced but they were one of the most successful. Another successful industry standard was published by the Standards in Efficient Cryptography Group (SECG)—a loose conglomeration of interested business including Certicom, VeriSign, and NIST. This group was primarily focused on standardizing the use of elliptic curves in asymmetric cryptography.

Elliptic curves are very complicated mathematical structures with some properties similar to modular arithmetic. These properties make them very attractive as a basis for certain types of asymmetric cryptography, but, because they are so complicated, without standardization it would be very difficult to guarantee their security or to have any kind of interoperability between different products. The work of the SECG has laid the foundations for several other elliptic curve standards including one by ISO. At the moment there does not seem to be any more work being done by the SECG, and, owing to the mathematical nature of elliptic curve cryptography, we will not be discussing elliptic curve standards any further in this book.

4.4.3   IEEE 1363

While the PKCS standards produced by RSA Labs. are hugely respected, they are still only produced by single company, and so only represent the views and interests of that company; they can also sometimes be a little slow to adopt newer techniques. In response to this, the IEEE formed a working group of individuals and businesses to standardize asymmetric cryptography techniques. This group (IEEE 1363) is not only concerned with asymmetric encryption but all of asymmetric cryptography including encryption schemes, digitial signatures (see Chapter 8), and key distribution (see Chapter 12).

IEEE 1363 has published two standards and is currently working on two more. The published standards are concerned with the traditional uses and techniques of asymmetric cryptography including the use of the Diffie-Hellman key agreement protocol and the RSA scheme. These standards are listed as follows:

- IEEE 1363: Standard Specifications for Public Key Cryptography;

- IEEE 1363a: Standard Specifications for Public Key Cryptography— Amendment 1: Additional Techniques.

The second standard (IEEE 1363a) contains several extra mechanisms that have commercial applications but were, at the time IEEE 1363 was published, considered too immature to be included in the standard. The two standards currently being developed by IEEE 1363 are concerned with newer technologies (the "P" is added to denote a draft or incomplete standard):

- IEEE P1363.1: Standard Specification for Public Key Cryptographic Techniques Based on Hard Problems over Lattices;

- IEEE P1363.2: Standard Specification for Password-Based Public Key Cryptographic Techniques.

Lattice-based cryptography is new style of cryptography based on mathematical structures called lattices. The main advantage of lattice-based cryptography is that it seems to resist attacks made by quantum computers. Quantum computers are theoretical systems that use the properties of atomic particles to solve problems. Currently no quantum computers exist[2], but there are estimates that suggest that one could be built in as little as 10–15 years[3]. If a quantum computer could be built then it has already been shown that it would be able to break all cryptosystems based on the Diffie-Hellman key agreement protocol and the RSA scheme. Obviously this would cause major problems! Lattice based cryptosystems are being developed as an alternative that could be used if quantum computers ever become a credible threat.

Password-based cryptosystems are concerned with the distribution of secret keys in the situation where the users only share a weak secret like a guessable password. We will briefly return to this issue in Chapter 12.

4.4.4 ISO/IEC 18033

As has already been mentioned, in 2001 ISO began work on standardizing all kinds of encryption schemes. The standard on asymmetric encryption, ISO/IEC 18033-2, has a couple of unusual features. In particular it embraces the use of a particular type of hybrid cipher called a KEM/DEM cipher.

A hybrid cipher is an asymmetric encryption scheme that uses both symmetric and asymmetric techniques. Typically this is done by generating a random symmetric key, encrypting the message using a symmetric encryption scheme and the newly generated symmetric key, and then encrypting the symmetric key using asymmetric techniques. The recipient can then recover the symmetric key using asymmetric techniques and then decrypt the message with the symmetric key. This gives the user the best of both worlds—the use of asymmetric cryptography means that we do not need to worry about the problem of distributing secret symmetric keys securely, while the use of symmetric encryption means that we can still encrypt/decrypt long messages quickly (traditionally a problem with asymmetric encryptions schemes).

A KEM/DEM hybrid scheme is even more specialized. It consists of two entirely separate and independent parts: an asymmetric *key encapsulation mechanism* or KEM, and a symmetric *data encapsulation mechanism* or DEM. The KEM has three parts:

> ▸ A key generation algorithm, which generates the asymmetric keys that the KEM will use. This works in exactly the same way as the

---

2. Technically, quantum computers have been built but only for very small numbers of quantum bits (qubits), and the techniques used to develop these machines do not seem to be easily adaptable to produce machines that have a larger number of qubits. Therefore when we say "no quantum computers exist" we actually mean "no quantum computers with a significant amount of computing power exist."

3. This is a "best case" scenario. There are also estimates that suggest that building a practical quantum computer would take a lot longer or that building quantum computers is impossible.

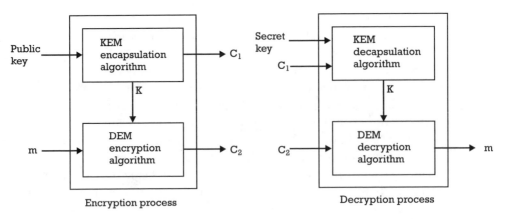

Figure 4.2   Encrypting and decrypting using a KEM/DEM cipher.

key generation algorithm of an asymmetric encryption scheme (see Section 4.1).

▶ An encapsulation algorithm, which (using the public key) generates a random symmetric key and an encryption or *encapsulation* of that key.

▶ A decapsulation algorithm, which (using the private key) recovers a symmetric key from an encapsulation.

The DEM has two parts:

▶ An encryption algorithm that takes as input a message and a symmetric key and outputs an encryption of that message under that key;

▶ A decryption algorithm that takes as input a ciphertext and a symmetric key and recovers the message from the ciphertext.

This allows us to build a hybrid cipher in the obvious way. Once the asymmetric keys are generated, anyone with the public key can encrypt a message m by using the KEM encapsulation algorithm to produce a symmetric key K and an encapsulation C_1 and then encrypting the message m with the DEM encryption algorithm and the key K to give a ciphertext C_2. The user then sends both C_1 and C_2 to the intended recipient.

Decryption of C_1 and C_2 is given by using the KEM decapsulation algorithm and the private key to recover the symmetric key K from C_1, then recovering the message m by decrypting C_2 under the DEM decryption algorithm and the key K. This process is shown graphically in Figure 4.2.

Just as for ISO/IEC 18033-3 (the block ciphers part of the ISO encryption standard), it is not yet clear which algorithms are going to be included in the standard. It seems likely however that at least one algorithm based on RSA (RSA-KEM) and one based on the Diffie-Hellman key agreement protocol (ECIES-KEM and/or PSEC-KEM) will be included. At the moment no asymmetric encryption schemes based on the use of lattices have been proposed for inclusion.

4.5 Notes

Section 4.1

This chapter is only meant to act as an introduction to the world of encryption, not as an exhaustive study of the subject. In terms of the study of standardization, very little is actually gained by describing the actual encryption schemes that we have discussed—their methodologies are not easily understood and they are remarkably unenlightening on their own.

Semantic security was formally introduced by Goldwasser and Micali [1] and studied further by Micali, Rackoff, and Sloan [2]. The more modern notions of security for symmetric and asymmetric ciphers and the relationships between these notions are discussed in two excellent papers: one for symmetric ciphers [3] and one for asymmetric ciphers [4].

The reader who is looking for a more comprehensive academic treatment of encryption schemes is referred to one of the many introductory books on the subject [5–10]. The reader who is looking for an algorithmic description of many cryptographic algorithms is referred to Menezes et al. [11].

Section 4.2.1

The latest version of the Data Encryption Standard is contained in NIST FIPS Pub. 46-3 [12] and the corresponding ANSI standard [13]. This version standardizes both the original version and the Triple-DES variant, although the original version is not actually recommended for use as a confidentiality algorithm. Triple-DES is also standardized in the draft ISO/IEC 18033-3 standard [14]. Details of the exhaustive key search performed by Curtin and Dolske can be found in [15].

The idea of building a dedicated machine for cracking DES by exhaustively searching all possible keys—a DES cracker—was first suggested by Wiener [16]. The Electronic Frontier Foundation, the organization that practically demonstrated the practical weakness of 56-bit DES keys so effectively by building the DES cracker, is contactable through its Web site http://www.eff.org/, and details about the DES cracker in particular can be found at http://www.eff.org/descracker. The existence of the DES cracker has put the final nail in the coffin of DES. It is interesting that it is the short key, an issue which was brought up during the standardization process itself, rather than any later cryptographic developments, which has caused the cipher to fall.

The two greatest developments in the cryptanalysis of block ciphers were the discoveries of differential and linear cryptanalyses. Differential cryptanalysis was introduced into the public domain by Biham and Shamir [17], although their work is similar to an unpublished attack against DES by Davies (later published by Davies and Murphy [18]). Biham and Shamir went on to use differential cryptanalysis to break DES [19], even though it seems as if one of the design conditions for the cipher was its resistance to exactly this kind of cryptanalysis. Linear cryptanalysis was introduced by Matsui [20] and has also been applied to DES.

Section 4.2.2

The ISO register of cryptographic algorithms can be found on the Internet at http://www.iso-register.com/. The register is currently maintained by Royal Holloway on behalf of the BSI and ISO. The procedures for registering a cryptographic algorithm are given in ISO/IEC 9979 [21].

The block cipher IDEA [11] was one of the original choices for use with the PGP e-mail encryption system and is the subject of a Swiss National Standard. The block cipher MISTY1 [22] is the primary recommendation of the NESSIE algorithm analysis project for a 64-bit block cipher and is contained in an IETF RFC [23]. Both algorithms have been proposed (along with Triple-DES) for inclusion in the ISO encryption standard [14].

For more information on the history and politics of cryptography, the reader is referred to Diffie and Landau [24] and Hoffman [25].

Section 4.2.3

The AES is available as NIST FIPS Pub. 197 [26]. It is the primary recommendation of the NESSIE algorithm analysis project for a 128-bit block cipher. It appears that the main reasons why Rijndael was selected as the AES are its flexibility and its efficiency on a wide variety of software and hardware platforms—it is especially well designed for use with smart cards, for example. A good overview of the AES standardization process is given in Burr [27] and Danielyan [28].

However, recently there have been some interesting papers that have shown up some unusual properties of Rijndael. The most of interesting of these are by Courtois and Pieprzyk [29] and by Murphy and Robshaw [30]. Both of these rely on the fact that the inner structure of the AES can be easily represented as a simple algebraic structure, thus giving rise to a description of the cipher as a series of simple, low-degree algebraic equations. Whether these properties will give rise to practical attacks against the AES is not yet known; however, this does not seem to be stopping the standardization or implementation of the cipher.

Despite these unusual properties, AES has been approved by the U.S. government to protect confidential information [31].

Section 4.2.4

The criteria for the cryptographic algorithms used in third generation mobile phones were first set down in June 1999 [32]. Since then it has been updated several times, the latest version having been released in July 2001.

The cryptographic algorithm requirements do not specifically mention the need for a block cipher but only specify the properties that the confidentiality and integrity functions $f8$ and $f9$ should have. It is the specification of $f8$ and $f9$ [33] that contains the first explicit references to the KASUMI block cipher [34].

Section 4.2.5

The general guidelines for the selection of encryption algorithms for standardization by ISO is given in ISO/IEC 18033-1 [35]. The part concerning block ciphers is ISO/IEC 18033-3 [14].

Section 4.3

The A5/1 and A5/2 stream ciphers were reverse engineered by Briceno, Goldberg, and Wagner [36] and have been attacked by numerous authors, the most recent and damning of which is by Barkan, Biham, and Keller [37]. This final attack is rather devastating, recovering the secret key by observing encrypted ciphertexts as they are transmitted and relatively quickly. The A5/3 stream cipher [38] has not yet been broken.

There are no known weaknesses in the third generation confidentiality algorithm, $f8$ [33]. The general model for a stream cipher is adapted from the draft ISO/IEC 18033-4 standard on stream ciphers [39]. More information on the history and properties of the CFB, OFB, and CTR modes of operation for a block cipher can be found in Chapter 5.

Section 4.4

While the first-ever asymmetric encryption scheme was the hugely successful RSA scheme, introduced in 1978 [40]. The first probabilistic encryption scheme was introduced by Goldwasser and Micali [1] in 1984. Today almost all proposed asymmetric encryption schemes are probabilistic because it has been found that deterministic schemes can not meet the high security criteria demanded of modern ciphers (i.e., deterministic schemes cannot be semantically secure). More information about the security requirements for modern asymmetric ciphers can be found in [4].

Section 4.4.1

The first asymmetric algorithm (and the introduction of the concept of asymmetric algorithms) was given in a paper by Diffie and Hellman [41]. This paper contained the Diffie-Hellman key agreement protocol but stopped short of giving an encryption scheme. The first asymmetric encryption scheme was given by Rivest, Shamir, and Addleman [40]. Since its inception, there have been numerous attacks made against the RSA cipher but none of them have proved enough to break the scheme completely. There are, however, too many to detail here. A good survey of the attacks against RSA can be found in [42].

Section 4.4.2

Both the RSA PKCS and the SECG standards are freely available on the Internet (see Chapter 2 for more information about obtaining standards). The most famous attack against RSA PKCS was by Bleichenbacher [43] and attacked not the RSA scheme itself but the padding system used to format messages before they were encrypted using RSA. After the initial efforts of the SECG, elliptic curve cryptography has been quickly accepted by the both cryptographers and implementors. It is now also standardized by the IEEE

1363 group [44, 45], ISO/IEC JTC1 [46], and is now even being included in the RSA PKCS. A good introduction to elliptic curve cryptography is given by Hankerson, Menezes, and Vanstone [47]. More technical issues associated with elliptic curves are discussed in Blake, Seroussi, and Smart [48, 49].

Section 4.4.3

There are two IEEE standards published [44, 45] and two more in development. Of the two standards in development, only the draft standard on lattice-based techniques proposes any kind of encryption scheme.

Lattice-based cryptography seems to have been developed in a rather bizarre fashion. Initially lattices were only used as a tool for attacking certain types of cryptosystem (particularly "knapsack" cryptosystems; see [10]). It wasn't until the NTRU public-key cryptosystem was proposed during the rump session of the Crypto '96 Conference that it was considered a viable basis for a cryptographic scheme. The NTRU encryption scheme was shown to be equivalent to a particular lattice problem [50] and it seems that, for suitably chosen parameters, this problem would be hard to solve, thus showing the security of the cryptosystem. Despite this "security proof," there have been many problems with NTRU and it has not yet been fully accepted by the cryptographic community. Other lattice schemes have since been proposed, for example, [51] proposed by IBM Research, but these have similarly failed to be universally accepted.

As we have stated, one of the main strengths of lattice-based cryptography is that it seems to be resistent to attacks made by quantum computers. Quantum computing is a vastly complex subject that takes in elements of mathematics, atomic physics, and cryptography, and is far beyond the scope of this book. It is known, however, that a quantum computer would be able to efficiently break both the RSA and the Diffie-Hellman schemes [52]. For more information, the reader is referred to [53].

Section 4.4.4

The ISO standard on asymmetric encryption [54] is the first to so fully embrace the use of hybrid ciphers. Of the seven algorithms proposed for inclusion, only two are not hybrid ciphers, and, of the five hybrid ciphers proposed, four are KEM/DEM constructions. The idea of a hybrid asymmetric encryption scheme has been cryptographic folklore for years and almost all practical uses of asymmetric encryption involve hybrid schemes (including the PGP encryption scheme, SSL/TLS encryption and IPsec). However, it has only recently been formalized.

While a KEM/DEM construction is far from being the only way in which one can construct a hybrid cipher, it does have certain attractive security features. The concept was introduced by Shoup [55] in 2000. It now appears likely that the ISO/IEC standard will contain at least one KEM based on RSA (RSA-KEM) and at least one KEM based on the Diffie-Hellman key agreement protocol (ECIES-KEM and/or PSEC-KEM). PSEC-KEM was the primary choice of the NESSIE evaluation project for an asymmetric encryption scheme.

References

[1]   Goldwasser, S., and S. Micali, "Probabilistic Encryption," *Journal of Computer and System Science*, Vol. 28, 1984, pp. 270–299.

[2]   Micali, S., C. Rackoff, and B. Sloan, "The Notion of Security for Probabilistic Cryptosystems," *SIAM Journal on Computing*, Vol. 17, 1988, pp. 412–426.

[3]   Bellare, M., et al., "A Concrete Security Treatment of Symmetric Encryption," *Proceedings of the 38th IEEE Symposium on Foundations of Computer Science*, 1997, pp. 394–403.

[4]   Bellare, M., et al., "Relations Among Notions of Security for Public-Key Encryption Schemes," in H. Krawczyk, (ed.), *Advances in Cryptology—Crypto '98*, Vol. 1462, *Lecture Notes in Computer Science*, Springer-Verlag, 1998, pp. 26–45.

[5]   Goldreich, O., *Foundations of Cryptography: Basic Tools*, Cambridge, England: Cambridge University Press, 2001.

[6]   Goldreich, O., *Foundations of Cryptography: Basic Applications*, Cambridge, England: Cambridge University Press, 2004.

[7]   Piper, F., and S. Murphy, *Cryptography: A Very Short Introduction*, Oxford, England: Oxford University Press, 2002.

[8]   Schneier, B., *Applied Cryptography*, 2nd ed., New York: John Wiley and Sons, 1996.

[9]   Stinson, D. R., *Cryptography: Theory and Practice*, Boca Raton, FL: CRC Press, 1995.

[10]   Welsh, D., *Codes and Cryptography*, Oxford, England: Oxford University Press, 1988.

[11]   Menezes, A. J., P. C. van Oorschot, and S. A. Vanstone, *Handbook of Applied Cryptography*, Boca Raton, FL: CRC Press, 1997.

[12]   National Institute of Standards and Technology, (NIST), *Federal Information Processing Standards Publication 46-3 (FIPS PUB 46-3): Data Encryption Standard*, October 1999.

[13]   American National Standards Institute, *ANSI INCITS 92–1981 (R1998), Data Encryption Algorithm (formerly ANSI X3.92–1981 (R1998))*, 1998.

[14]   International Organization for Standardization, *ISO/IEC CD 18033–3, Information Technology—Security Techniques—Encryption Algorithms—Part 3: Block Ciphers*, 2003.

[15]   Curtin, M., and J. Dolske, "A Brute Force Search of DES Keyspace," *; login:—The Magazine of the USENIX Association*, May 1998, http://www.interhack.net/pubs/des-key-crack/.

[16]   Wiener, M. J., *Efficient DES Key Search*, Technical Report TR–244, Carleton University, 1993, http://www.ja.net/CERT/Wiener/des_key_search.ps.

[17]   Biham, E., and A. Shamir, "Differential Cryptanalysis of DES-Like Cryptosystems," in A. J. Menezes and S. A. Vanstone, (ed.), *Advances in Cryptology—Crypto '90*, Vol. 537, *Lecture Notes in Computer Science*, 1990, pp. 2–21.

[18]   Davies, D. W., and S. Murphy, "Pairs and Triplets of DES S-Boxes," *Journal of Cryptology*, Vol. 8, 1995, pp. 1–25.

[19]   Biham, E., and A. Shamir, "Differential Cryptanalysis of the Full 16-Round DES," E. F. Brickell, (ed.), *Advances in Cryptology—Crypto '92*, Vol. 740, *Lecture Notes in Computer Science*, Springer-Verlag, 1992, pp. 487–496.

[20]   Matsui, M., "Linear Cryptanalysis Method for DES Cipher," in T. Helleseth, (ed.), *Advances in Cryptology—Eurocrypt '93*, Vol. 765, *Lecture Notes in Computer Science*, Springer-Verlag, 1993, pp. 386–397.

[21]   International Organization for Standardization, *ISO/IEC 9979, Information Technology—Security Techniques—Procedures for the Registration of Cryptographic Algorithms*, 2nd ed., April 1999.

[22]   Matsui, M., "New Block Encryption Algorithm MISTY," in E. Biham, (ed.), *Fast Software Encryption—4th International Workshop (FSE '97)*, Vol. 1267, *Lecture Notes in Computer Science*, Springer-Verlag, 1997, pp. 54–68.

[23]   Ohta, H., and M. Matsui, *RFC 2994, A Description of the MISTY1 Encryption Algorithm*, Internet Engineering Task Force, November 2000.

[24]   Diffie, W., and S. Landau, *Privacy on the Line*, Cambridge, MA: MIT Press, 1999.

[25]   Hoffman, L. J., (ed.), *Building in Big Brother*, New York: Springer-Verlag, 1995.

[26]   National Institute of Standards and Technology (NIST), *Federal Information Processing Standards Publication 197 (FIPS PUB 197): Specification for the Advanced Encryption Standard (AES)*, November 2001.

[27]   Burr, W. E., "Selecting the Advanced Encryption Standard," *IEEE Security and Privacy*, Vol. 1, No. 2, March/April 2003, pp. 43–52.

[28]   Danielyan, E., "Goodbye DES, Welcome AES," *The Internet Protocol Journal*, Vol. 4, No. 2, June 2001, pp. 15–21.

[29]   Courtois, N. T., and J. Pieprzyk, "Cryptanalysis of Block Ciphers with Overdefined Systems of Equations," in Y. Zheng, (ed.), *Advances in Cryptology—Asiacrypt 2002*, Vol. 2501, *Lecture Notes in Computer Science*, Springer-Verlag, 2002, pp. 267–287.

[30]   Murphy, S., and M. Robshaw, "Essential Algebraic Structure Within the AES," in M. Yung, (ed.), *Advances in Cryptology—Crypto 2002*, Vol. 2442, *Lecture Notes in Computer Science*, Springer-Verlag, 2002, pp. 1–16.

[31]   Committee on National Security Systems. *CNSS Policy No. 15, Fact Sheet No. 1: National Policy on the Use of the Advanced Encryption Standard (AES) to Protect National Security Systems and National Security Information*, June 2003. Available from http://www.nstissc.gov/Assets/pdf/fact sheet.pdf.

[32]   European Telecommunications Standards Institute (ETSI), *3GPP TS 33.105, Third Generation Partnership Project; Technical Specification Group Services and System Aspects; 3G Security; Cryptographic Algorithm Requirements*, June 2001.

[33]   European Telecommunications Standards Institute (ETSI), *3GPP TS 35.201, 3rd Generation Partnership Project; Technical Specification Group Services and System*

Aspects; 3G Security; Specification of the 3GPP Confidentiality and Integrity Algorithms; Document 1: f8 and f9 Specification, June 2002.

[34] European Telecommunications Standards Institute (ETSI), *3GPP TS 35.202, 3rd Generation Partnership Project; Technical Specification Group Services and System Aspects; 3G Security; Specification of the 3GPP Confidentiality and Integrity Algorithms; Document 2: KASUMI Specification,* June 2002.

[35] International Organization for Standardization, *ISO/IEC CD 18033–1, Information Technology—Security Techniques—Encryption Algorithms—Part 1: General,* 2003.

[36] Briceno, M., I. Goldberg, and D. Wagner, "A Pedagogical Implementation of the GSM A5/1 and A5/2 'Voice Privacy' Encryption Algorithms," http://cryptome.org/gsm-a512.htm, 1999.

[37] Barkan, E., E. Biham, and N. Keller, "Instant Ciphertext-Only Cryptanalysis of GSM Encrypted Communications," in D. Boneh, (ed.), *Advances in Cryptology—Crypto 2003,* Vol. 2729, *Lecture Notes in Computer Science,* Springer-Verlag, 2003, pp. 600–616.

[38] European Telecommunications Standards Institute (ETSI), *3GPP TS 55.216, 3rd Generation Partnership Project; Technical Specification Group Services and System Aspects; 3G Security; Specification of the A5/3 Encryption Algorithm for GSM and ECSD, and the GEA3 Encryption Algorithm for GPRS; Document 1: A5/3 and GEA3 Specifications,* September 2003.

[39] International Organization for Standardization, *ISO/IEC FCD 18033–4, Information Technology—Security Techniques—Encryption Algorithms—Part 4: Stream Ciphers,* 2003.

[40] Rivest, R. L., A. Shamir, and L. Adleman, "A Method for Obtaining Digital Signatures and Public-Key Cryptosystems," *Communications of the ACM,* Vol. 21, 1978, pp. 120–126.

[41] Diffie, W., and M. E. Hellman, "New Directions in Cryptography," *IEEE Transactions on Information Theory,* Vol. 22, 1976, pp. 644–654.

[42] Boneh, D., "Twenty Years of Attacks on the RSA Cryptosystem," *Notices of the American Mathematical Society (AMS),* Vol. 46, No. 2, 1999, pp. 203–213.

[43] Bleichenbacher, D., "Chosen Ciphertext Attacks Against Protocols Based on the RSA Encryption Standard PKCS# 1," H. Krawczyk, (ed.), *Advances in Cryptology—Crypto '98,* Vol. 1462, *Lecture Notes in Computer Science,* Springer-Verlag, 1998, pp. 1–12.

[44] Institute of Electrical and Electronics Engineers, Inc., *IEEE Standard Specifications for Public-Key Cryptography,* 2000.

[45] Institute of Electrical and Electronics Engineers, Inc., *IEEE Standard Specifications for Public-Key Cryptography—Amendment 1: Additional Techniques,* 2004.

[46] International Organization for Standardization, *ISO/IEC 15946, Information Technology—Security Techniques—Cryptographic Techniques Based on Elliptic Curves,* 2002.

[47] Hankerson, D., A. J. Menezes, and S. Vanstone, *Guide to Elliptic Curve Cryptography,* New York: Springer-Verlag, 2004.

[48] Blake, I., G. Seroussi, and N. Smart. *Elliptic Curves in Cryptography,* Cambridge, England: Cambridge Univeristy Press, 1999.

[49]   Blake, I., G. Seroussi, and N. Smart. *Elliptic Curves in Cryptography II: Further Topics*, Cambridge, England: Cambridge University Press, 2004.

[50]   Coppersmith, D., and A. Shamir, "Lattice Attacks on NTRU," W. Fumy, (ed.), *Advances in Cryptology—Eurocrypt '97*, Vol. 1233, *Lecture Notes in Computer Science*, Springer-Verlag, 1997, pp. 52–61.

[51]   Goldreich, O., S. Goldwasser, and S. Halevi, "Public-Key Cryptosystems from Lattice Reduction Problems," in B. Kaliski, (ed.), *Advances in Cryptology—Crypto '97*, Vol. 1294, *Lecture Notes in Computer Science*, Springer-Verlag, 1997, pp. 165–179.

[52]   Shor, P. W., "Algorithms for Quantum Computation: Discrete Logarithms and Factoring," *Proceedings of the IEEE 35th Annual Symposium on Foundations of Computer Science*, 1994, pp. 124–134.

[53]   Nielsen, M. A., and I. L. Chuang, *Quantum Computation and Quantum Information*, Cambridge, England: Cambridge University Press, 2000.

[54]   International Organization for Standardization, *ISO/IEC CD 18033–2, Information Technology—Security Techniques—Encryption Algorithms—Part 2: Asymmetric Ciphers*, 2003.

[55]   Shoup, V., "Using Hash Functions as a Hedge Against Chosen Ciphertext Attack," in B. Preneel, (ed.), *Advances in Cryptology—Eurocrypt 2000*, Vol. 1807, *Lecture Notes in Computer Science*, Springer-Verlag, 2000, pp. 275–288.

Contents

5.1 Definitions and basic properties

5.2 Standards for modes of operation

5.3 Padding methods

5.4 ECB mode

5.5 Cipher block chaining (CBC) mode

5.6 CTR mode

5.7 OFB mode

5.8 CFB mode

5.9 Choosing a mode of operation

5.10 Other modes

5.11 Notes

Modes of Operation for Block Ciphers

A mode of operation is a recommended way in which to use a block cipher to encrypt a string of data bits (*plaintext*), sometimes also referred to as a "message," to obtain *ciphertext*. Such a mode is necessary since, as discussed in Chapter 4, a block cipher just provides a method of encrypting a single string of n bits, not a message of arbitrary length. Moreover, even when it is only necessary to encrypt a string of n bits, a mode of operation should be employed to avoid information leakage arising from repeated n-bit plaintexts (see Section 5.4).

5.1 Definitions and basic properties

Following Chapter 4, we use the following notation for block cipher encryption and decryption. We write e for the encryption operation of an n-bit block cipher, where n is the number of bits in a plaintext or a ciphertext block, and d for the decryption operation of a block cipher.

We can thus write $C = e_K(P)$, where C is an n-bit ciphertext block, K is a secret key, and P is an n-bit plaintext block. Conversely we have $P = d_K(C)$, and hence $P = d_K(e_K(P))$ for any K and P.

We also use the following notation throughout this chapter:

- $X||Y$ denotes the block of bits obtained by concatenating the blocks X and Y.

- $X \oplus Y$ denotes the bit-wise exclusive-or of blocks of bits X and Y (of the same length).

- $X|_i$ represents the leftmost i bits of the block of bits X.

- $X|^i$ represents the rightmost i bits of the block of bits X.

- 1^i denotes a block of i bits all set to 1.

5.2 Standards for modes of operation

Four modes of operation, namely electronic codebook (ECB), cipher block chaining (CBC), OFB and CFB, were originally standardized in the United States in 1980. These modes were introduced specifically for use with the DES block cipher, although they have since been adopted for use with other block ciphers. The four modes were first specified in the U.S. federal modes of operation standard, NBS FIPS Pub. 81, which was followed by the U.S. national standard ANSI X3.106 in 1983. This latter standard is no longer available, having been superseded by the ISO standards.

These four modes are described in Sections 5.4, 5.5, 5.7 and 5.8, respectively. A fifth, more recently standardized, mode, known as CTR mode, is discussed in Section 5.6. Three other standardized modes, all designed specifically for use with triple-DES, are discussed briefly in Section 5.10.

Once these modes were established, they rapidly became de facto international standards, particularly in the financial industry. Thus, in the early and mid 1980s, work started within ISO to produce a corresponding international standard for modes of operation for DES; this was originally designed as a companion to the international DES standard that was being developed in parallel. When the ISO work on DES ceased, as described in Chapter 4, work on modes of operation continued, but now directed toward any block cipher algorithm.

This work resulted in two standards: ISO 8372, standardizing modes of operation for a 64-bit block cipher algorithm, and ISO/IEC 10116, specifying modes of operation for an n-bit block cipher algorithm (for any n). These standards contain the same four modes as originally standardized for DES. The first edition of ISO/IEC 10116 appeared in 1991; a revised version was published in 1997 containing a slightly enhanced version of CFB mode. A third edition, currently nearing completion, contains an additional mode of operation, namely the CTR mode (see Section 5.6), and makes some minor adjustments to two of the other four modes. This CTR mode has long been known as a "nonstandard" mode (it was originally proposed by Diffie and Hellman in 1979), and appears in the recent NIST recommendation for modes of operation, NIST SP800-38A. A modified version of OFB mode appears in the ETSI 3GPP specifications, where it is known as function $f8$.

Finally, note that there is also a U.S. national standard, ANSI X9.52, that standardizes seven different modes of operation specifically for use with triple-DES. Four of these seven modes are the same as the modes originally standardized for DES, namely ECB, CBC, OFB, and CFB. The other three modes, called TCBC-I, TCFB-P, and TOFB-I, are modes designed specifically for use with triple-DES.

5.3 Padding methods

All five of the ISO/IEC standardized modes of operation require the plaintext to be divided into a series of blocks of a certain length—j, for example. This is achieved by simply letting the first j bits of plaintext constitute the first block, the next j bits the second block, and so on. Clearly, this means that the final block might contain less than j bits. While this does not matter for three of the five modes of operation specified in ISO/IEC 10116, namely CTR, OFB, and CFB, this does cause a problem with the other two modes, ECB and CBC.

To resolve this problem, a padding method needs to be agreed by the sender and recipient. A padding method involves adding bits to the plaintext according to an agreed formula and in such a way that the padded data will contain a multiple of j bits. ISO/IEC 10116 does not specify how this should be achieved.

What is important to note is that the recipient of the ciphertext will, after decryption, recover the padded plaintext, and not the plaintext itself. This means that, whatever padding method is used, the recipient needs to have a way to unambiguously remove the padding bits. This can be achieved in two main ways.

Zero padding   Removing padding is elementary if the data is structured in such a way that the recipient can unambiguously determine the end of the data string. Most obviously this applies when the plaintext is always of a fixed length. Alternatively, a "special" string of bits could be used to indicate the end of the data, where this string is never used elsewhere in the message. In such a case any padding method can be used—the most simple being the addition of the minimum number of zeros to the end of the data to ensure that the length of the padded string is a multiple of j bits. (This is padding method 1 in ISO/IEC 9797-1.)

Although zero padding should not present major problems in the case where messages have fixed length, in general its use is to be discouraged. This is because general adoption of a method that is only appropriate for certain types of message carries significant risks, not least the accidental use of this technique in inappropriate circumstances.

Unambiguous padding   The padding method may be designed such that, regardless of the data string, the padding can be removed in an unambiguous way. One example of such a method, also defined as padding method 2 in ISO/IEC 9797-1, is to always add a single 1-bit to the end of the message, followed by the minimum number of zeros to ensure that the padded plaintext has a length that is a multiple of j. If the recipient knows that such a padding method has been used, removing the padding correctly is trivial.

The only disadvantage of the padding method described, and indeed of just about any "unambiguous" padding method, is that sometimes an extra block will be created by comparison with the zero padding method.

5.4 ECB mode

To use this mode the plaintext must be in the form of a sequence of n-bit blocks $P_1, P_2, \ldots, P_q$ (i.e., unless the data is guaranteed to always be of an appropriate length, a padding method is required). The ciphertext is then

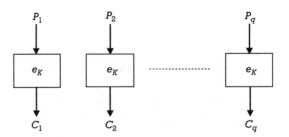

Figure 5.1 Electronic code book (ECB) mode encryption.

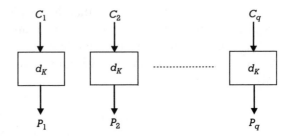

Figure 5.2 Electronic code book (ECB) mode decryption.

defined to be the sequence of blocks $C_1, C_2, \ldots, C_q$, where $C_i = e_K(P_i)$ for every i ($1 \le i \le q$). The encryption process is shown pictorially in Figure 5.1.

Decipherment works analogously [i.e., $P_i = d_K(C_i)$ for every i ($1 \le i \le q$)]. The decryption process is shown pictorially in Figure 5.2.

Properties   In ECB mode, if the same plaintext block is encrypted twice (using the same key) then the same ciphertext block results. This is a problem if highly redundant plaintext is being encrypted, since the probability of two identical plaintext blocks occurring may be high. For example, if the plaintext is a binary version of a document in English, then the probability that a message will contain two identical blocks will be very high unless the document is very short, since repeated words and phrases are very common. Thus, in general, ECB mode should only be used in very special circumstances (see also Section 5.9).

Use of this mode of operation also results in a phenomenon known as *error propagation*. That is, if a single bit error occurs when transmitting the ciphertext, then, when decrypted, an entire block of plaintext will be corrupted.

5.5   Cipher block chaining (CBC) mode

As with ECB mode, CBC mode encryption requires that the plaintext is first padded so that its length is a multiple of n bits, and then divided into a series of n-bit blocks: $P_1, P_2, \ldots, P_q$. An SV is also required. If the chosen SV is denoted by S, then encryption involves computing a sequence of ciphertext blocks $C_1, C_2, \ldots, C_q$, as follows:

$$C_1 = e_K(P_1 \oplus S), \quad C_i = e_K(P_i \oplus C_{i-1}), \quad (i > 1) \tag{5.1}$$

The CBC mode encryption process is shown in Figure 5.3.

Decipherment operates as follows:

$$P_1 = d_K(C_1) \oplus S, \quad P_i = d_K(C_i) \oplus C_{i-1}, \quad (i > 1) \tag{5.2}$$

The CBC mode decryption process is shown in Figure 5.4.

Properties   In CBC mode, if the same message is enciphered twice then the same ciphertext will result, unless the SV is changed. Moreover, if two messages agree for the first t blocks, for some t, then the first t blocks of ciphertext will be the same (unless a different SV is used). Hence the SV S should be different for every message. To maximize security S should also be secret.

Managing SVs is clearly a nontrivial issue for the user. One way of achieving the use of a different value of S for every encrypted message is simply

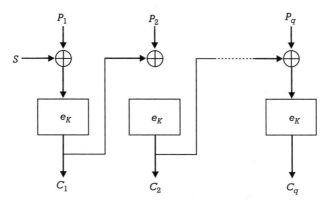

Figure 5.3   Cipher block chaining (CBC) mode encryption.

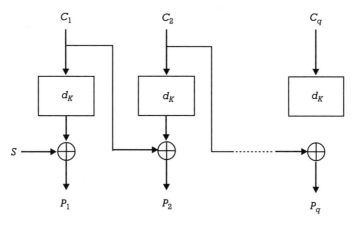

Figure 5.4   Cipher block chaining (CBC) mode decryption.

to generate a random value for S, and to send this with the encrypted message. However this does not meet the requirement that SVs should ideally be secret. Providing a different secret SV for every message can be achieved in a variety of ways (e.g., sending a counter with the message and using an encrypted version of this counter as the SV), or generating a random value for every message and encrypting it (e.g., using ECB mode) before sending it to the recipient with the encrypted message.

The major advantage of CBC mode over ECB mode is that if the same plaintext block is encrypted twice (using the same key), then different ciphertext blocks result.

As with ECB, use of this mode of operation results in error propagation. That is, a single bit error in the ciphertext will result in the loss of an entire block of plaintext. Moreover, the corresponding single bit in the next plaintext block will also be in error. To see why this holds, consider the decryption step used to yield P_i (for any i), namely:

$$P_i = d_K(C_i) \oplus C_{i-1} \tag{5.3}$$

First note that P_i is a function of just two ciphertext blocks: C_i and C_{i-1}. Also, if C_i contains one or more bit errors, then P_i will be completely garbled because of the randomizing effects of the block cipher. Finally, if C_{i-1} contains one bit error, then this will affect the recovered value of P_i in precisely the same bit position.

Padding issues   Just as with ECB mode, the CBC mode of operation requires the plaintext to be "padded" to the right length. This means that the ciphertext is often longer than the plaintext; indeed, depending on the chosen padding method, this may always be the case. In some applications (e.g., where encryption is applied to a data record and the encrypted data string is required to "fit" back into the space where the plaintext was stored), this is not acceptable. As a result, an annex to the second edition of ISO/IEC 10116 describes the following two methods for avoiding message extension when using CBC mode. To describe these methods, we first suppose that the "unpadded" plaintext results in a final block P_q of j bits (where $j < n$).

Method 1 modifies the encipherment of the last "short" block. The encipherment (and decipherment) methods for this block are as follows:

$$C_q = P_q \oplus (e_K(C_{q-1})|_j) \tag{5.4}$$

and

$$P_q = C_q \oplus (e_K(C_{q-1})|_j) \tag{5.5}$$

Method 1 essentially equates to the use of OFB mode for the final block. As such it is subject to the same weaknesses as this mode, and is hence subject to a possible "chosen plaintext" attack if the SV is not secret or has been used more than once with the same key.

Method 2 does not have this problem. This method (also known as *ciphertext stealing*) modifies the encipherment of the last block as follows:

$$C_q = e_K((C_{q-1}|^{n-j})||P_q) \tag{5.6}$$

and the last two ciphertext blocks are then $C_{q-1}|_j$ and C_q. It is necessary to decipher the final block C_q before C_{q-1}. Deciphering C_q enables the discovery of the rightmost $n - j$ bits of C_{q-1}, and then C_{q-1} can be deciphered.

Parallelized CBC mode   Finally, note that the latest (third) edition of ISO/IEC 10116, allows a generalized version of CBC mode. This involves selecting an additional parameter m, where $1 \le m \le 1,024$. The purpose of this generalization is to allow the mode to be implemented in a parallel (or "pipelined" fashion). In the mode as described above, the encryption of block P_i cannot take place until C_{i-1} has been computed, preventing any parallel computation. The generalized mode allows m parallel computations to take place.

The generalized mode requires a total of m SVs (each of n bits), denoted $S_1, S_2, \ldots, S_m$. Encryption then operates as follows:

$$C_i = e_K(S_i), \quad (1 \le i \le m) \tag{5.7}$$
$$C_i = e_K(P_i \oplus C_{i-m}) \quad (m < i \le q) \tag{5.8}$$

Note that when $m = 1$ the generalized mode corresponds to the mode as previously described.

5.6   **CTR mode**

CTR mode is one of two modes, the other being OFB mode, that enable a block cipher to be used as a component in a key stream generator for a synchronous stream cipher (see Chapter 4). To use this mode, it is first necessary to choose the parameter j $(1 \le j \le n)$ (i.e., the number of bits of plaintext encrypted per block cipher operation). Before encrypting the message it is necessary to split it into a series of blocks; if the message contains $(q - 1)j + t$ bits $(1 \le t \le j)$ then divide the plaintext into a series of q blocks: $P_1, P_2, \ldots, P_q$, where P_1 is the first j bits of the message, P_2 is the next j bits, and so on. The last block, P_q, is equal to the final $t \le j$ bits. Again, as with CBC mode, let S be an n-bit SV. The computations also use variables X_i $(1 \le i \le q)$, each of n bits.

Encryption operates as follows. First let $X_1 = S$. Then, for $i = 1, 2, \ldots, q - 1$, calculate:

$$C_i = P_i \oplus (e_K(X_i)|_j) \tag{5.9}$$
$$X_{i+1} = X_i + 1 \pmod{2^n} \tag{5.10}$$

where, in the second step, the block of bits X_i is treated as the binary representation of an integer between 0 and $2^n - 1$. Finally, let

$$C_q = P_q \oplus (e_K(X_q)|_t) \tag{5.11}$$

The CTR mode encryption process is shown in Figure 5.5.

Decryption operates almost identically to encryption. First let $X_1 = S$. Then, for $i = 1, 2, \ldots, q - 1$ calculate:

$$P_i = C_i \oplus (e_K(X_q)|_j) \tag{5.12}$$

$$X_{i+1} = X_i + 1 \pmod{2^n} \tag{5.13}$$

where, as for encryption, in the second step the block of bits X_i is treated as the binary representation of an integer between 0 and $2^n - 1$. Finally, let

$$P_q = C_q \oplus (e_K(X_i)|_t) \tag{5.14}$$

The CTR mode decryption process is shown in Figure 5.6.

Properties   If the same message is enciphered twice using CTR mode then the same ciphertext will result, unless the SV is changed. Note that if two messages agree for the first u bits, for some u, then the ciphertexts will also agree for the first u bits. Hence, just as for CBC mode, the SV should be different for every message.

This leads to a more significant point, namely that if the same counter-value is ever used twice, then the same pseudorandom bits will be ex-ored

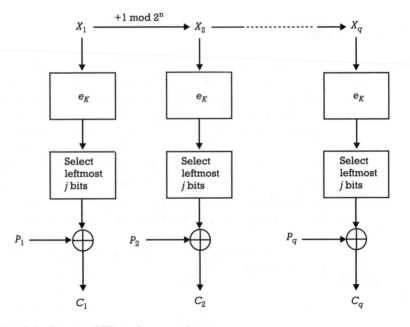

Figure 5.5   Counter (CTR) mode encryption.

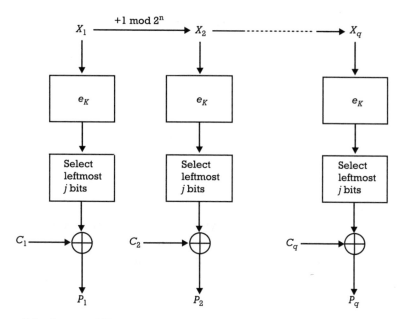

Figure 5.6 Counter (CTR) mode decryption.

with the plaintext to obtain the ciphertext. If this ever occurs and the attacker has information about either of the plaintexts, then this can potentially be used to derive information about the other plaintext. Hence it is extremely important that the SVs should be chosen so that the same value of X_i never recurs during the lifetime of a key.

There is no need for padding of messages. Thus the ciphertext will always be the same length as the plaintext. Moreover, as with all synchronous stream ciphers, there is no error propagation associated with use of this mode of operation. A single bit error in the ciphertext will result in a single bit error in the plaintext.

Observe that CTR mode is inherently parallelizable, since the encryption of one block does not depend in any way on the encryption of previous blocks. Finally, note that the ETSI 3GPP standard (TS 35.201) also uses a version of CTR mode. The 3GPP block cipher (known as KASUMI—see Chapter 4) is used with CTR mode to instantiate a function known as $f8$.

5.7 OFB mode

Like CTR mode, OFB mode allows a block cipher to be used as the basis of a keystream generator for a synchronous stream cipher (see Chapter 4). To use this mode it is first necessary to choose the parameter j $(1 \le j \le n)$ (i.e., the number of bits of plaintext encrypted per block cipher operation). Before encrypting the message it is necessary to split it into a series of blocks; if the message contains $(q-1)j+t$ bits $(1 \le t \le j)$ then divide the plaintext into a series of q blocks: $P_1, P_2, \ldots, P_q$, where P_1 is the first j bits of the message, P_2 is the next j bits, and so on. The last block, P_q, is equal to the final $t \le j$ bits.

Let S be an n-bit SV. The computations also use the variables X_i $(1 \leq i \leq q)$, each of n bits.

Encryption operates as follows. First, let $X_1 = S$. Then, for $i = 1, 2, \ldots,$ $q - 1$ calculate:

$$C_i = P_i \oplus (e_K(X_i)|_j) \tag{5.15}$$

$$X_{i+1} = e_K(X_i) \tag{5.16}$$

Finally, let

$$C_q = P_q \oplus (e_K(X_q)|_t) \tag{5.17}$$

The OFB mode encryption process is shown in Figure 5.7.

Decryption operates almost identically to encryption. First, let $X_1 = S$. Then, for $i = 1, 2, \ldots, q - 1$ calculate:

$$P_i = C_i \oplus (e_K(X_i)|_j) \tag{5.18}$$

$$X_{i+1} = e_K(X_i) \tag{5.19}$$

Finally, let

$$P_q = C_q \oplus (e_K(X_q)|_t) \tag{5.20}$$

The OFB mode decryption process is shown in Figure 5.8.

Properties The properties of OFB mode with respect to the use of the SV and error propagation are identical to those of CTR mode, since they are both examples of synchronous stream ciphers.

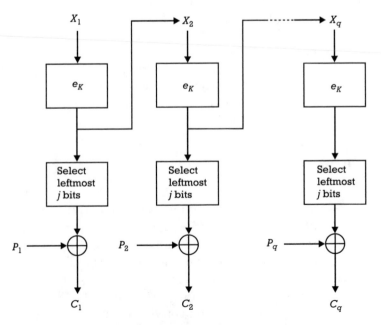

Figure 5.7 Output feedback (OFB) mode encryption.

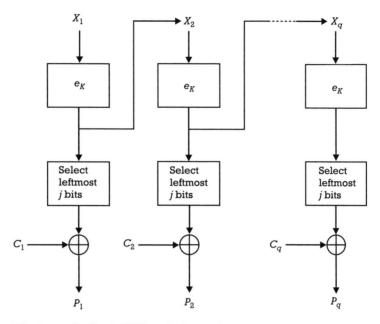

Figure 5.8 Output feedback (OFB) mode decryption.

Analogously to CTR mode, the SVs should be chosen so that the same value of X_i is never used twice within the lifetime of a key. However, this is very difficult to ensure, and it is normally managed in a probabilistic fashion. That is, if the number of blocks enciphered with a single key is significantly less than $\sqrt{2^n}$, then the probability of reusing a value of X_i is small—this, of course, limits the amount of data that should be encrypted with a single key.

5.8 CFB mode

This mode enables a block cipher to be used as the main element in a keystream generator for a self-synchronous stream cipher. To use this mode it is first necessary to choose two parameters: k ($1 \le k \le n$), the size of the *feedback variable*, and j ($1 \le j \le k$), the number of bits of plaintext encrypted for each block cipher operation.

In practice it would appear sensible to always choose $j = k$. In fact, this is recommended by the second edition of ISO/IEC 10116, and any other choice would appear to reduce the overall level of security of the scheme.

The original CFB mode   As specified in the original 1991 (first) edition of ISO/IEC 10116, CFB mode operates as follows: Divide the plaintext into a series of j-bit blocks: $P_1, P_2, \ldots, P_q$, where, as for OFB and CTR modes, P_q will contain $t \le j$ bits. Let S be an n-bit SV. The computations also use the variables X_i ($1 \le i \le q$), each of n bits.

Encryption operates as follows. First let $X_1 = S$. Then, for $i = 1, 2, \ldots, q$

calculate:

$$C_i = P_i \oplus (e_K(X_i)|_j) \tag{5.21}$$
$$X_{i+1} = (X_i || 1^{k-j} || C_i)|^n \tag{5.22}$$

When $i = q$, two points should be noted: First, P_q may contain $t < j$ bits, and in such a case in the first step P_q is ex-ored with $e_K(X_i)|_t$ to obtain a t-bit C_q; secondly, the second step is not performed. The CFB mode encryption process is shown in Figure 5.9.

Decryption operates as follows. First let $X_1 = S$. Then, for $i = 1, 2, \ldots, q$ calculate:

$$P_i = C_i \oplus (e_K(X_i)|_j) \tag{5.23}$$
$$X_{i+1} = (X_i || 1^{k-j} || C_i)|^n \tag{5.24}$$

As for encryption, the second step is not performed when $i = q$. The CFB mode decryption process is shown in Figure 5.10.

Pipelined CFB mode   In the second (1997) edition of ISO/IEC 10116, a generalized version of the CFB mode has been included; this version has been further generalized in the third edition. This method allows "pipelining" to take place. In the original version of CFB mode, each j-bit ciphertext block needs to be computed before the next plaintext block can be processed. This

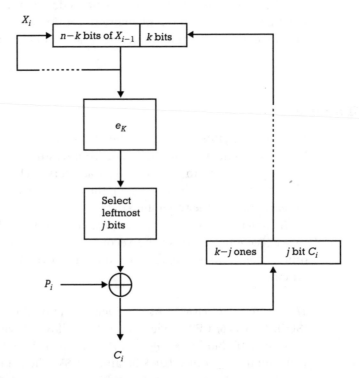

Figure 5.9 Cipher feedback (CFB) mode encryption.

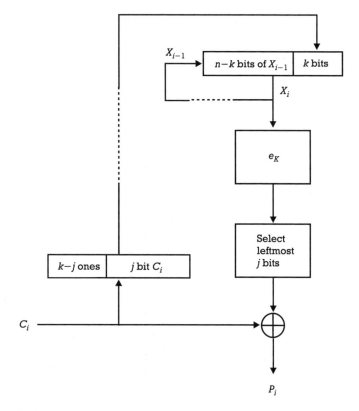

Figure 5.10 Cipher feedback (CFB) mode decryption.

means that it is impossible to pipeline calculations (i.e., start on the encryption of one block before the processing of the previous block is complete). To avoid this problem, in the new version of CFB mode an r-bit *feedback buffer* is introduced, where $n \leq r \leq 1024n$; the successive contents of this buffer are labelled $F_1, F_2, \ldots$. An r-bit SV is now also needed.

After setting $F_1 = S$, the encipherment process becomes:

$$X_i = F_i|_n \tag{5.25}$$

$$C_i = P_i \oplus (e_K(X_i)|_j) \tag{5.26}$$

$$F_{i+1} = (F_i||1^{k-j}||C_i)|^r \tag{5.27}$$

where the final step is not performed in the case $i = q$. The generalized CFB mode encryption process is shown in Figure 5.11.

Properties   If the same message is enciphered twice using CFB mode then the same ciphertext will result, unless the SV is changed. (Note that if two messages agree for the first s bits, for some s, then the ciphertexts will also agree for the first s bits. Hence, just as for CBC mode, the SV should be different for every message.

There is no need to pad a message, since we have shown how to handle

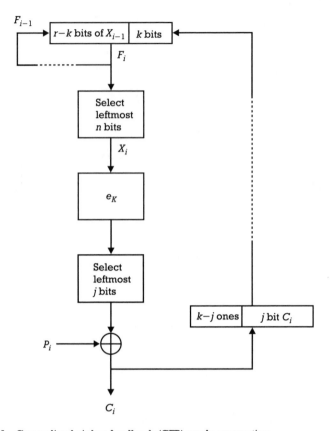

Figure 5.11 Generalized cipher feedback (CFB) mode encryption.

a final plaintext block of less than j bits. Thus the ciphertext will always be the same length as the plaintext.

Finally, as with all self-synchronous stream ciphers, this mode of operation *does* result in error propagation. A single bit error in the ciphertext will result in the loss of one or more entire j-bit blocks of plaintext. Decryption will remain corrupted until the erroneous ciphertext bit is shifted out of the feedback register.

5.9   Choosing a mode of operation

We now consider how a user of ISO/IEC 10116, or any of the other standards specifying modes of operation, should choose which mode of operation to use. Note here that we discuss CTR mode as if it is a standardized mode, as this will be the case once the third edition of ISO/IEC 10116 is published.

Choosing the block cipher   The first decision that needs to be made is almost certainly which block cipher to use. This issue is discussed in more detail in Chapter 4, and so we do not repeat the discussion here, except to say that longer block lengths (i.e., of 128 bits or more) have potentially significant advantages, especially if large quantities of data are to be encrypted.

Choosing the mode   Probably the next decision is whether or not error prop-agation is acceptable. In many cases error propagation is not a problem (it may even be desirable) since if there is a single error in the recovered data, then it will be necessary to retransmit the entire message.

However, in some cases (e.g., where the data represents digitized voice), a small number of errors in the recovered plaintext are acceptable. In such a case, error propagation is typically unacceptable, since a small number of errors in the ciphertext will typically result in a large number of errors in the decrypted plaintext.

If error propagation is unacceptable then one of the two (synchronous) stream cipher modes (i.e., CTR or OFB), should be used. If, on the other hand, error propagation is acceptable, or even desirable, then typically the choice is between CFB and CBC. The CFB mode has the advantage that, if it is used with $j = 1$, then it can recover from bits being lost or gained in transmission (i.e., after a short "burst of errors," decryption will continue successfully even if one or more bits are inserted into, or deleted from, the ciphertext). By comparison, if ciphertext bits are gained or lost when using OFB or CTR mode, then synchrony will never be recovered. On the other hand, CBC is maximally efficient in terms of minimizing the number of block cipher operation to be performed, since n bits are encrypted for every block cipher iteration.

Finally note that ECB mode is only acceptable for very short and highly random messages (e.g., keys), because of the danger of leaking information about the plaintext if the same plaintext block is ever encrypted twice using the same key. Even in the case of key encryption, where repetition of blocks is unlikely, it is typically necessary to also guarantee the integrity of the key, and hence an authenticated encryption mode (see Section 5.10.2) would be more appropriate.

Parameter choice   Having chosen the mode of operation, it is also neces-sary to choose the parameters. The ECB and CBC modes do not have any operational parameters. The OFB and CTR modes have a single parameter, namely the number of bits (j) from each encryption operation to be used to encrypt the data. In many cases it will be appropriate to choose the maximum possible value (i.e., $j = n$), since this will maximize throughput; however, such a choice will potentially provide the cryptanalyst with large numbers of known plaintext/ciphertext pairs for the block cipher. Nevertheless, if a suitably strong block cipher is used, then this should not be a problem. Of course, choosing j to be significantly less than n, say, $j = n/2$, does reduce this risk, and in some cases might be an appropriate additional precaution.

The situation is a little more complicated for CFB mode. Here there are three parameters (i.e., r, j, and k). First, as noted earlier, it is sound prac-tice to choose $j = k$. Second, unless it is necessary to parallelize opera-tion of CFB mode, there is no reason not to choose $r = n$. This leaves the choice of j. As previously, choosing $j = n$ will maximize throughput and will not cause any weaknesses as long as the block cipher is resistant to known and chosen plaintext attacks; however, in this case CFB offers no significant advantages over CBC mode. The main advantage of CFB mode arises from its self-synchronizing property. That is, after a delay dependent on r, a receiver can start to correctly decrypt an encrypted message even if the beginning of the message is lost, or if bits are lost (or added) during transmission. This property only holds if the receiver knows where the j-bit "boundaries" are in the ciphertext. Thus choosing $j = 1$ for this mode has a major advantage, as does $j = 7$ or $j = 8$ in the case where transmissions are in the form of 7 or 8 bit symbols.

SVs and key management   Finally note that all of the modes, except for ECB, require a SV to be established for each communications session. As discussed above, this SV should be different for every message; moreover, where possible, this variable should be secret. In particular, it is strongly recommended to use a secret SV with CBC mode (otherwise the proof of security does not hold).

Finally, regardless of the mode, it is strongly recommended never to use a single key to perform more than $\sqrt{2^n}$ encryption operations. The key management system should be designed to ensure that this rule is followed. Of course, if $n \geq 128$ then it is unlikely that special precautions will be required.

5.10   Other modes

We conclude the main part of this chapter by briefly mentioning certain other standardized modes of operation. These modes of operation fall into two main classes: modes designed specifically for use with triple DES and modes providing combined confidentiality and integrity.

5.10.1   Triple-DES modes

As mentioned in Section 5.2, ANSI X9.52 specifies three modes of operation, namely TCBC-I, TCFB-P, and TOFB-I, specifically designed for use with triple-DES.

TCBC-I (CBC interleaved mode) is actually nothing new. The effect of using this mode is precisely the same as using the parallelized CBC mode with $m = 3$. The objective is to allow TCBC-I mode computations to proceed as fast as single DES CBC mode, by using three parallel DES encryption modules. The detailed description in ANSI X9.52 shows how to use the three modules to achieve this effect.

TCFB-P (CFB pipelined mode) is again consistent with the pipelined CFB mode specified in Section 5.8. This mode is precisely equivalent to the mode in the third edition of ISO/IEC 10116 for the case where $r = 3n$ (in fact $r = 192$, since ANSI X9.52 is restricted to triple-DES where $n = 64$).

Finally, TOFB-I (interleaved OFB mode) is a parallelized version of OFB mode. This interleaved mode is *not* standardized in the third edition of ISO/IEC 10116. However, the same effect as TOFB-I can be achieved using the "normal OFB mode," as specified in Section 5.7, by dividing the message to be encrypted into three parallel streams, and then encrypting each stream using OFB mode (and hence three SVs are required).

5.10.2 Authenticated encryption modes

In recent years several "authenticated encryption modes" have been devised. These modes are designed to simultaneously encrypt a message (to provide confidentiality) and guarantee the origin and integrity of the message, by including cryptographically protected redundancy.

A first working draft for an ISO/IEC standard (ISO/IEC WD 19772) has recently been produced containing three such authenticated encryption modes, namely those known as OCB, CCM, and AES key wrap. The OCB mode is approximately twice as efficient as simply encrypting and computing a MAC on a message (it requires one pass through the data instead of two).

Apart from their inclusion in WD 19772, these three "modes" are also included in various other standards documents. The CCM mode is included in a NIST draft standard, NIST SP800-38C, and OCB and AES key wrap are included in Internet RFCs. Authenticated encryption modes are discussed in greater detail in Chapter 16.

5.11 Notes

Section 5.1

For a more detailed treatment of modes of operation for block ciphers, the reader is referred to Chapter 7 of [1].

Section 5.2

The original NBS FIPS on block cipher modes of operation [2] was published in 1980, and ANSI X3.106 [3] followed in 1983. The ISO 64-bit modes of operation standard ISO 8372 (now withdrawn), based very closely on ANSI X3.106, appeared in 1987 [4]. The n-bit version of this latter standard, namely, ISO/IEC 10116, has been through three revisions [5–7].

The most recent (third) edition of ISO/IEC 10116 [7], which was scheduled to be published in late 2004 or 2005, contains the CTR mode (first proposed by Diffie and Hellman in 1979 [8]), which is also contained in NIST Special Publication 800-38A [9]. An overview of the NIST standardization effort that led to NIST Special Publication 800-38A can be found in [10].

The 3GPP standard 3GPP TS 35.201 [11] contains a modified version of the OFB mode.

Section 5.3

Vaudenay [12] pointed out the possibility of attacks on messages encrypted using CBC mode in a special scenario where an attacker can modify messages and send them to the authorized decryptor, and then observe error messages indicating formatting failures in decrypted messages. In such a case, an attacker can, by repeating this process, learn information about the plaintext. This attack takes advantage of a particular choice for a padding method. Paterson and Yau [13] have extended this attack to other padding techniques. These attacks show that it is important for error messages to be handled with great care.

Section 5.4

The ECB mode should not be used even for short messages unless the data being encrypted is highly random or unless a single key is only used to encrypt a small number of blocks. To see why, suppose a 64-bit block cipher is used to encrypt single blocks, each made up of eight letters. There will thus be only $26^8 \simeq 2 \times 10^{11}$ possible different plaintext blocks, and hence, after only around $26^4 \simeq 500,000$ plaintext blocks have been encrypted, the same block is likely to occur twice.

Section 5.5

A "proof of security" for the CBC mode was published by Bellare et al. in 1997 [14]. This proof requires the starting variable to be a secret (known only to the legitimate sender and receiver).

The modification to CBC mode known as ciphertext stealing is attributed to Meyer and Matyas [15]. Mitchell and Varadharajan [16] pointed out the hazards of using OFB mode to encrypt the final block.

Section 5.6

A formal treatment of CTR mode has been presented by Bellare et al. in [14].

Section 5.7

The probability of the same sequence of bits being used to encrypt two different messages can be reduced by not "restarting" OFB every time a message is encrypted. That is, after encrypting a message, the encrypter stores the final value of X_i to be used as the starting variable for the next message. However, even with this approach, a single key should not be used to encrypt more than $\sqrt{2^n}$ blocks for the following reason. Knowledge that the keystream will, with high probability, not repeat leaks information about the plaintext (see Bellare et al. [14]).

A proof of security for the version of OFB contained in the 3GPP standard [11] was published by Kang et al. in 2001 [17]. However, this proof was shown to be incorrect by Iwata and Kurosawa in 2003 [18], although this does not mean that any significant weakness has been found in this function. Indeed, by making a slightly stronger assumption about the security of the block cipher, Iwata and Kohno [19] have recently provided a new proof of security for this modified OFB mode.

Section 5.8

The CFB mode is an example of what is known as a "self-sychronizing stream cipher"; such systems have a long history (see also Chapter 4). In fact, a version of CFB mode was first proposed by Diffie and Hellman in 1979 [8]. If used with $j = 1$, then this technique will, after a delay, recover from all types of errors, including insertion or deletion of bits (see Chapter 6 of [1]).

Section 5.9

Error propagation is probably only desirable if data integrity and data origin authentication services are to be based on a combination of encryption and the addition of redundancy. Unfortunately, none of the known constructions of this type (i.e., which simply involve adding redundancy to data prior to applying encryption using one of the standard modes) satisfy any of the reasonable security definitions (see, for example, [20, 21]). Reliably achieving confidentiality and integrity would appear to require a somewhat more sophisticated approach [e.g., as provided by the authenticated-encryption modes (briefly discussed in Section 5.10.2)].

Section 5.10

Prior to the publication of ANSI X9.52 in 1998 [22], various other modes of operation specifically designed for use with triple DES had been proposed, and some of them appeared in draft versions of this standard. One of them, known as CBCM, was shown to be weak by Biham and Knudsen [23, 24] and was removed from the published standard.

The first working draft of ISO/IEC 19772 appeared in early 2004 [25]. The OCB mode was originally proposed by Rogaway, Bellare, and Black [26]. The CCM mode is contained in RFC 3610 [27] and in NIST special publication 800-38C [28], a draft NIST recommendation for an authenticated encryption mode. AES key wrap is specified in Internet RFC 3394 [29].

References

[1]   Menezes, A. J., P. C. van Oorschot, and S. A. Vanstone, *Handbook of Applied Cryptography*, Boca Raton, FL: CRC Press, 1997.

[2]   National Institute of Standards and Technology (NIST), *Federal Information Processing Standards Publication 81 (FIPS PUB 81): DES Modes of Operation*, December 1980.

[3]   American National Standards Institute, *ANSI X3.106–1983, American National Standard for Information Systems—Data Encryption Algorithm—Modes of Operation*, 1983.

[4]   International Organization for Standardization, *ISO 8372: 1987, Information Processing—Modes of Operation for a 64-Bit Block Cipher Algorithm*, 1987.

[5]   International Organization for Standardization, *ISO/IEC 10116: 1991, Information Technology—Modes of Operation for an n-Bit Block Cipher Algorithm*, 1991.

[6]   International Organization for Standardization, *ISO/IEC 10116: 1997, Information Technology—Security Techniques—Modes of Operation for an n-Bit Block Cipher*, 2nd ed., 1997.

[7]   International Organization for Standardization, *ISO/IEC FCD 10116, Information Technology—Security Techniques—Modes of Operation for an n-Bit Block Cipher*, 3rd ed., 2004.

[8]   Diffie, W., and M. E. Hellman, "Privacy and Authentication: An Introduction to Cryptography," *Proceedings of the IEEE*, Vol. 67, 1979, pp. 397–427.

[9]   National Institute of Standards and Technology (NIST), *NIST Special Publication 800-38A, Recommendation for Block Cipher Modes of Operation: Methods and Techniques*, December 2001.

[10]   Burr, W. E., "Selecting the Advanced Encryption Standard," *IEEE Security and Privacy*, Vol. 1, No. 2, March/April 2003, pp. 43–52.

[11] European Telecommunications Standards Institute (ETSI), *3GPP TS 35.201, Third Generation Partnership Project; Technical Specification Group Services and System Aspects; 3G Security; Specification of the 3GPP Confidentiality and Integrity Algorithms; Document 1: f8 and f9 Specification*, June 2002.

[12] Vaudenay, S., "Security Flaws Induced by CBC Padding—Applications to SSL, IPSEC, WTLS ...," in L. R. Knudsen, (ed.), *Advances in Cryptology—Eurocrypt 2002*, Vol. 2332, *Lecture Notes in Computer Science*, Springer-Verlag, 2002, pp. 534–545.

[13] Paterson, K. G., and A. Yau, "Padding Oracle Attacks on the ISO CBC Mode Encryption Standard," in T. Okamoto, (ed.), *Topics in Cryptology—CT-RSA 2004*, Vol. 2964, *Lecture Notes in Computer Science*, Springer-Verlag, 2004, pp. 305–323.

[14] Bellare, M., et al., "A Concrete Security Treatment of Symmetric Encryption," *Proceedings of the 38th IEEE Symposium on Foundations of Computer Science*, 1997, pp. 394–403.

[15] Meyer, C. H., and S. M. Matyas, *Cryptography: A New Dimension in Computer Data Security*, New York: John Wiley and Sons, 1982.

[16] Mitchell, C. J., and V. Varadharajan, "Modified Forms of Cipher Block Chaining," *Computers and Security*, Vol. 10, 1991, pp. 37–40.

[17] Kang, J.-S., et al., "Provable Security of KASUMI and 3GPP Encryption Mode f8," in C. Boyd, (ed.), *Advances in Cryptology—Asiacrypt 2001*, Vol. 2248, *Lecture Notes in Computer Science*, Springer-Verlag, 2001, pp. 255–271.

[18] Iwata, T., and K. Kurosawa, "On the Correctness of Security Proofs for the 3GPP Confidentiality and Integrity Algorithms," in K. G. Paterson, (ed.), *Cryptography and Coding, 9th IMA International Conference*, Vol. 2898, *Lecture Notes in Computer Science*, Springer-Verlag, 2003, pp. 306–318.

[19] Iwata, T., and T. Kohno, "New Security Proofs for the 3GPP Confidentiality and Integrity Algorithms," in W. Meier and B. Roy, (eds.), *Proceedings of FSE 2004*, Vol. 3017, *Lecture Notes in Computer Science*, Springer-Verlag, 2004, pp. 427–444.

[20] An, J. H., and M. Bellare, "Constructing VIL-MACs from FIL-MACs: Message Authentication Under Weakened Assumptions," in M. J. Wiener, (ed.), *Advances in Cryptology—Crypto '99*, Vol. 1666, *Lecture Notes in Computer Science*, Springer-Verlag, 1999, pp. 252–269.

[21] Katz, J., and M. Yung, "Unforgeable Encruption and Chosen Ciphertext Secure Modes of Operation," in B. Schneier, (ed.), *Fast Software Encryption, 7th International Workshop, FSE 2000*, Vol. 1978, *Lecture Notes in Computer Science*, Springer-Verlag, 2001, pp. 284–299.

[22] American Bankers Association, *ANSI X9.52–1998, Triple Data Encryption Algorithm Modes of Operation*, 1998.

[23] Biham, E., and L. R. Knudsen, "Cryptanalysis of the ANSI X9.52 CBCM Mode," in K. Nyberg, (ed.), *Advances in Cryptology—Eurocrypt '98*, Vol. 1403, *Lecture Notes in Computer Science*, Springer-Verlag, 1998, pp. 100–111.

[24] Biham, E., and L. R. Knudsen, "Cryptanalysis of the ANSI X9.52 CBCM Mode," *Journal of Cryptology*, Vol. 15, 2002, pp. 47–59.

[25] International Organization for Standardization, *ISO/IEC WD 19772: 2004, Information Technology—Security Techniques—Authenticated Encryption Mechanisms*, 2004.

[26] Rogaway, P., M. Bellare, and J. Black, "OCB: A Block-Cipher Mode of Operation for Efficient Authenticated Encryption," *ACM Transactions on Information and System Security*, Vol. 6, 2003, pp. 365–403.

[27] Whiting, D., R. Housley, and N. Ferguson, *RFC 3610, Counter with CBC-MAC (CCM)*. Internet Engineering Task Force, September 2003.

[28] National Institute of Standards and Technology (NIST), *NIST Special Publication 800-38C, Draft Recommendation for Block Cipher Modes of Operation: The CCM Mode For Authentication and Confidentiality*, September 2003.

[29] Schaad, J., and R. Housley, *RFC 3394, Advanced Encryption Standard (AES) Key Wrap Algorithm*, Internet Engineering Task Force, September 2002.

CHAPTER

6

Contents

6.1 Definitions and basic properties

6.2 Standards for hash functions

6.3 Hash functions based on block ciphers

6.4 Dedicated hash functions

6.5 Hash functions based on modular arithmetic

6.6 Choosing a hash function

6.7 Notes

Cryptographic Hash Functions

Hash functions are a curious type of cryptographic algorithm. In its simplest form a hash function is an algorithm that takes an input of any size and outputs a fixed-length "hash code" that is, in some sense, difficult to predict in advance. The odd thing about the use of hash functions in cryptography is that they do not usually depend on any secret keys, and so they can only provide a limited set of security services on their own. In fact, they are usually only used as a building block for other mechanisms. However their role in cryptography as a building block is absolutely vital—a huge number of cryptographic schemes use a hash function at some point, and in most cases the use of a weak hash function destroys the security of the entire scheme.

In particular we use hash functions to help provide data integrity in MACs (see Chapter 7), to produce message digests for use with digital signature schemes (see Chapter 8) and to produce manipulation detection codes (MDCs) in entity authentication and key establishment schemes (see Chapters 10 and 12).

Hash functions were one of the first type of cryptographic algorithms to be standardized by ISO. Rather oddly they are classified as irreversible encipherment algorithms by ISO 7498-2 (see Chapter 3). However, this is actually quite a good way of thinking about them. Obviously a hash algorithm must be irreversible as there are far more possible inputs then outputs, but the difficulty in finding two messages that have the same hash code means that a hash code almost uniquely identifies the message it is associated with. This is very similar to the idea that a ciphertext uniquely identifies the message of which it is an encryption.

6.1 Definitions and basic properties

6.1.1 The security of a hash function

Essentially a hash function is just a function that maps an input of any size to a fixed size output. (Here, "an input of any size" means any string of binary digits, and "a fixed size output" means a binary string of a predetermined length.) This output is known as a *hash code* or the *hash of the message*. The key property of a hash function is that its output should look random, and this is where the problem comes. It is very hard to explain in precise mathematical terms what "looks random" means.

The best that it seems we can do is to define a series of properties that a hash function must satisfy. These are described as follows.

> • *Preimage (or first preimage) resistance:* A hash function is preimage-resistant if, given a random hash code, it is computationally infeasible to find an input that the hash function maps to that hash code.

> • *Second preimage resistance:* A hash function is second preimage-resistant if, given an input to the hash function, it is computationally infeasible to find a second input that gives the same hash code.

> • *Collision resistance:* A hash function is collision resistant if it is computational infeasible to find two inputs that give the same hash code.

> • *Indistinguishable from random:* A hash function is indistinguishable from a random function if it is impossible for an attacker to tell the difference between the hash function and a function chosen completely at random from all the functions with the same input/output characteristics as the hash function. A hash function can only be indistinguishable from random if it is keyed.

A hash function that is collision-resistant is necessarily second preimage-resistant, and a hash function that is indistinguishable from random is necessarily collision-resistant and first preimage-resistant. However, a hash function that is second preimage-resistant is not always first preimage-resistant.

A hash function can be keyed or unkeyed. In a keyed hash function the output is partly defined by a secret key K. All the standardized hash functions are unkeyed, but only keyed hash functions can achieve the highest level of security (i.e., be indistinguishable from a random function). Keyed hash functions share a lot of properties with MACs (see Chapter 7), although keyed hash functions have more stringent secure properties. We will not discuss them further here.

A common mistake when thinking about hash functions is to assume they provide a complete message integrity service on their own. The normal argument for this runs as follows: suppose an entity wishes to send a message m to a receiver in an integral way. The sender computes the hash code of the message H and sends both m and H to the receiver. If an attacker alters the message m along the way then they must either (1) find another message that has the same hash code or (2) alter the hash code too. The usual (erroneous) argument is that it is hard for an attacker to do either of these things. While it might be hard for the attacker to find another message that has the same hash code as m, it is not difficult to change the message and find the new hash code. All the attacker need do in order to find this new hash code is evaluate the hash function on the new message (remember that there is nothing secret about the hash function).

6.1.2 Iterative hash functions

All standardized hash functions conform to the same basic model. This model is very similar to that of a CBC mode encryption (see Chapter 5) and to that of a CBC-MAC (see Chapter 7). In order to describe this accurately we will need to introduce some notations that will be consistently used throughout this chapter.

The standardized hash functions are iterative in nature and are computed in a series of rounds. Each round will be defined using a function ϕ. This "round function" takes two inputs: a L_1-bit block of input data and a bit string of length L_2, which is the output of the previous round. The final hash code is a bit string of length $L_H \leq L_2$. There is also an L_2-bit initialization vector IV.

Suppose we wish to find the hash code of a string of data D. All iterative hash functions work in roughly the same way:

1. *Padding:* The data D must be padded so that it contains an integer multiple of L_1 bits, q blocks of L_1 bits each say. The padding method differs depending on the hash function used. We will discuss this further when we discuss the individual hash functions.

2. *Splitting:* The padded message is now divided into a sequence of L_1-bit blocks: $D_1, D_2, \ldots, D_q$. Block D_1 corresponds to the first L_1 bits of the padded message, D_2 to the next L_1 bits, and so on.

3. *Initialization:* A counting variable i is set to 0 and H_0 is set to be IV.

4. *Hashing:* The next intermediate value is computed using the round function, $H_i = \phi(D_i, H_{i-1})$.

5. *Looping:* If $i < q$ then i is increased by one and steps 4 and 5 are repeated.

6. *Output transformation:* The final hash code is given by performing an output transformation on H_q. Typically this will be to truncate H_q so that it is L_H bits long. This is usually done by taking the leftmost L_H bits of H_q, but may be more complicated.

This process is shown in Figure 6.1. This means that to fully describe a hash function we have to specify several different things:

> - The lengths L_1, L_2, and L_H;

> - An L_2-bit initialization vector IV;

> - The padding method;

> - The round function ϕ;

> - The output transformation.

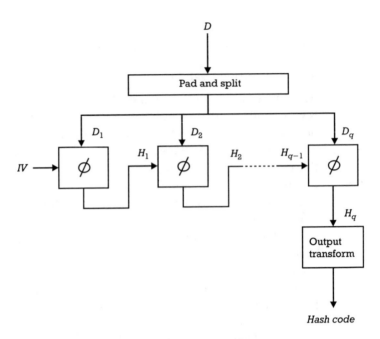

Figure 6.1 The general model for an iterative hash function.

The extensible property of hash functions   Despite the fact that hash functions are meant to behave like random functions, all iterative hash functions share one peculiar and very nonrandom property, known as the extensible property.

Suppose that X is a string of q data blocks that is input to a hash function, and that the output of this hash function is H_q. (For simplicity we assume that the hash function uses a simple padding method such as padding method 1— see Section 6.3.1—and that there is no output transformation or truncation.) If Y_1 is another block of data then it is easy to see that the hash code of the message $X||Y_1$ is $\phi(Y_1, H_q)$. We can repeat this process to extend this to find the hash code of the message $X||Y$ for any Y.

This may not seem to be a very unusual property as we can always compute the hash code of $X||Y$ using the hash function if we know both X and Y. The odd thing about the extensible property is that you do not need to know X in order to compute the hash code of $X||Y$—hence we can still compute this extended hash code even if part of X is secret. It is precisely this property that means we have to be careful in how we define MACs based on hash functions (see Chapter 7).

The situation becomes more difficult if we allow output transformations or truncation. If we truncate the output then we will only recover partial information about H_q from the hash of X and we may be forced to guess some bits. For example, if the hash code of X is the leftmost L_2-1 bits of H_q then it is necessary to guess the final bit before we can compute the hash code of $X||Y$. Naively we would expect to do this with probability $1/2$. Therefore truncation is useful in this sense—the more bits we truncate the more difficult it becomes for an attacker to find an extended hash code. Of course, if we truncate too much (say, down to the point where $L_H = 1$) then it might be easier for the attacker just to guess the hash code for $X||Y$.

While the extensible property of a hash function is not a weakness in the formal sense—it does not allow an attacker to find a pre-image, second pre-image or collision—it does mean that the hash codes produced by an iterative hash function have some very predictable relationships, and it is generally agreed that a hash function should display as little predictability as possible. It is interesting to note that none of the padding methods specified in Section 6.3.1 defeat this "attack," although padding method 3 specified in ISO/IEC 9797-1 (see Chapter 7) does.

6.2   Standards for hash functions

Hash functions have been fairly widely standardized. There seem to be three main bodies that have produced universally respected hash function standards: ISO/IEC JTC1, NIST, and the IETF. Both NIST and IETF have concentrated their efforts on the production of *dedicated hash functions*. A dedicated hash function is a hash function that is not built from any lower level components or designed for any other purpose other than being a hash function.

The NIST secure hash standard (NIST FIPS Pub. 180) was first published in 1993 and has been revised twice since then—the latest version (NIST FIBS Pub. 180-2) was published in 2002. This standard contains the specification of five dedicated hash functions: SHA-1, SHA-224, SHA-256, SHA-384, and SHA-512.

The IETF has standardized the use of hash functions on a more ad hoc basis, and not always without problems. The hash functions it has standardized include the ever popular SHA-1 (IETF RFC 3174), MD2 (IETF RFC 1319), MD4 (IETF RFC 1320), and MD5 (IETF RFC 1321).

The ISO/IEC standard is a lot more general in nature, covering not only dedicated hash functions but also hash functions built up using other primitives and techniques. The ISO/IEC hash function standard (ISO/IEC 10118) has four parts:

- ▸ Part 1: General;

- ▸ Part 2: Hash functions using an n-bit block cipher;

- ▸ Part 3: Dedicated hash functions;

- ▸ Part 4: Hash functions using modular arithmetic.

The first part, ISO/IEC 10118-1, contains general information and terminology that is used in the other three parts. This includes the general model for an iterative hash function given in Section 6.1.2.

6.3   Hash functions based on block ciphers

ISO/IEC 10118-2 specifies how to construct a hash function from a secure block cipher. Since the corresponding ISO standard on block ciphers, ISO 18033-3, has not yet been completed (see Chapter 4) there is no recommendation about which cipher should be used. This means that ISO/IEC 10118-2 does not completely specify any hash function but only a method of creating them—this is similar to the ISO/IEC standard on modes of operation for a block cipher, ISO/IEC 10116 (see Chapter 5). It seems likely, however, that when the ISO/IEC standard on block ciphers is completed, only hash functions created from standardized block ciphers will be approved by ISO.

The notation and terminology associated with a block cipher is described in Section 4.2 but we will briefly review it here. A block cipher is a (reversible) function that maps n-bit blocks of plaintext to n-bit blocks of ciphertext. We will denote e_K to be the encryption function using the key K and d_K to be the decryption function using a key K. Hence if X is an n-bit block then $e_K(X)$ is the encryption of X and $d_K(e_K(X)) = X$.

ISO/IEC actually standardizes four different methods of creating a hash function from an n-bit block cipher, depending on the size of the intermediate "hash variables" H_i. In each case this a multiple of n.

- The first hash function is very simple. It has $L_1 = L_2 = n$, hence both the size of the data blocks D_i and the size of the intermediate hash variables H_i is equal to the block size of the underlying block cipher. This hash function is described in Section 6.3.2.

- The second hash function is a bit more complicated and has $L_2 = 2n$ (although $L_1 = n$ still). This is described in Section 6.3.3.

- The third and fourth hash functions are more complicated again. These work on similar principles to the second hash function but with larger values for L_1 and L_2. We will not describe these hash functions as they do not provide us with any more insight into the workings of block cipher–based hash functions than is given by studying block cipher hash function 2.

6.3.1   Padding methods

Obviously, these hash functions require that the hash function input can be split into input blocks of length L_1. ISO recommends several different ways this can be done. Most of these methods are the same as those that are used to pad data when using a mode of operation of a block cipher (see Chapter 5) or computing a message authentication code (see Chapter 7). The padding methods described in Sections 6.3.1.1–6.3.1.3 are recommended for use with block cipher–based hash functions.

6.3.1.1   Padding method 1

The simplest padding method involves adding as many "0" bits to the end of the data as are required to make the data an exact multiple of L_1 bits long.

As we have noted before and will note again. Any mechanism that uses this padding method is subject to a series of trivial attacks. In this case it is easy to find collisions in a hash function that uses this padding method—if D is the input data and the length of D is not an exact multiple of L_1 then D and $D||0$ will have the same hash code.

6.3.1.2   Padding method 2

The second method involves adding a "1" bit to the end of the data and then as many "0" bits as are required to make the data an exact multiple of L_1 bits long.

This always involves the addition of at least one bit. However, in most cases this will not matter significantly as the addition of one extra bit will not increase the number of data blocks that need to be processed, and hence will not mean that the round function has to be used any more times than is absolutely necessary. However, if the length of the input data is already an exact multiple of L_1 bits then one whole extra block will need to be added. Padding method 2 does not suffer from the same kinds of trivial attacks as padding method 1.

6.3.1.3   Padding method 3

Padding methods 1 and 2 are the same as the padding methods 1 and 2 described in ISO/IEC 9797-1 (see Chapter 7). Padding method 3 is similar in its intent to its counterpart in ISO/IEC 9797-1 but the two methods are slightly different.

The third padding method described in ISO/IEC 10118 involves a new parameter, $r \leq L_1$, which limits the length of the input data. The padding method works as follows:

- A single "1" bit is added to the end of the input data.

- The output of the previous step is concatenated with as many "0" bits as are required to make the data exactly r bits less than an exact multiple of L_1. (Hence the length of the data is $-r$ mod L_1.)

- The length of the original data is encoded into the remaining r bits. This is usually done by setting these remaining r bits to be the (right justified) binary representation of the original length. In this case the padding method can only handle data strings smaller than 2^r.

This final padding method is considered to be the most secure but, since at least $r + 1$ bits need to be added to the original data, it is quite likely that extra data blocks will need to be processed by the round function. Therefore, this padding method is likely to be the slowest of the three recommended.

6.3.2   Block cipher hash function 1

Block cipher hash function 1 is very simple. (We will refer to the first block cipher–based hash function one as "block cipher hash function 1" to uniquely identify it in a way that distinguishes it easily from other hash functions, such as dedicated hash functions.) It processes each data block by encrypting it using the block cipher under a key that is derived from the output of the previous round.

As we have mentioned, a hash function is completed specified by the lengths L_1, L_2, and L_H, the initializion vector IV, the round function ϕ, and the output transformation. For block cipher hash function 1:

- $L_1 = L_2 = n$;

- L_H can be any value less than or equal to L_2;

- IV can be any L_2-bit value.

The final hash code is given by taking the leftmost L_H bits of the final hash variable H_q. It is therefore now only necessary to specify the round function.

Remember that a round function takes as input a data block D_i and the output of round function from the previous round H_{i-1}. The round function for block cipher hash function 1 is very simple:

1. Let $K_i = u(H_{i-1})$. The function u must map n-bit strings to keys that are useable with the block cipher (normally bit strings of some specified length). Obviously the function u must be chosen with some care in order to make sure that the keys used are sufficiently random.

2. Let $B_i = e_{K_i}(D_i)$.

3. Let $H_i = B_i \oplus D_i$.

This process is shown in Figure 6.2.

It is clear that the function u that turns ciphertext blocks into keys must be chosen with a great deal of care. It is somewhat ironic that normally we would use a hash function to provide a suitably random looking function for u. Obviously we cannot do that here! In fact, it is not necessary for u to act randomly just as long as the range of the function is large enough and no outputs are significantly more likely to occur than any other. While we

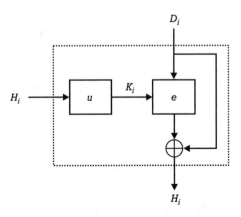

Figure 6.2 The round function for block cipher hash function 1.

do not go into detail here, the standard does give some suggestions for the case when the block cipher is DES (see Section 4.2.1). Their suggestion is a combination of fixing some key bits and setting the other key bits to be equal to the corresponding bits of H_{i-1}.

The reason that the data block D_i is XORed with its encryption also sometimes confuses people. However, this is very important and if it is not done then the hash function becomes weak. This is because it is very easy to figure out the keys K_i. Suppose that we do not perform this final XOR; in other words, the round function becomes

$$\phi(D_i, H_{i-1}) = e_{K_i}(D_i) \quad \text{where } K_i = u(H_{i-1}) \tag{6.1}$$

Note here that $K_0 = u(IV)$. Therefore, if we wish to find an input whose hash code is Y, then we only need to compute

$$X = d_{K_0}(Y) \tag{6.2}$$

as

$$\phi(X, H_0) = Y \tag{6.3}$$

Hence the scheme would not even be first preimage resistant. However, if we include the XOR then the round function is

$$\phi(D_i, H_{i-1}) = e_{K_i}(D_i) \oplus D_i \text{ where } K_i = u(H_{i-1}) \tag{6.4}$$

and so to find a single input block X whose hash code is Y we need to solve

$$e_{K_0}(X) \oplus X = Y \tag{6.5}$$

which is significantly harder.

6.3.3   Block cipher hash function 2

The idea behind block cipher hash function 2 is that it is a more secure version of block cipher hash function 1. It gains this security by using larger intermediate hash variables then, at each round, running two instances of block cipher hash function 1 in parallel and mixing the results. It is this "parallel encryption and mixing" idea that is the basis for hash functions two, three, and four, and it is for this reason that we will only talk about block cipher hash function 2 here.

Block cipher hash function 2 has the following parameters:

- $L_2 = 2n$ and $L_1 = n$;
- L_H can be any value less than or equal to L_2;
- IV can be any L_2-bit value.

The round function for block cipher hash function 2 is described as follows.

1. Split the $2n$-bit block H_{i-1} into two n-bit blocks H_{i-1}^L and H_{i-1}^R. Let H_{i-1}^L be the first n bits of H_{i-1} (the left-hand bits) and let H_{i-1}^R be the remaining n bits (the right-hand bits).

2. Let $K_i^L = u(H_{i-1}^L)$, where u is a function that turns ciphertext blocks into key suitable for use with the block cipher as before.

3. Let $B_i^L = e_{K_i^L}(D_i) \oplus D_i$.

4. Let $K_i^R = u'(H_{i-1}^R)$, where u' is another function that turns ciphertext blocks into block cipher keys. Care must be taken here to make sure that u and u' are sufficiently independent.

5. Let $B_i^R = e_{K_i^R}(D_i) \oplus D_i$.

6. Split the n-bit blocks B_i^L and B_i^R into four $n/2$-bit blocks[1] B_i^{LL}, B_i^{LR}, B_i^{RL} and B_i^{RR}. These are formed so that $B_i^L = B_i^{LL} \| B_i^{LR}$ and $B_i^R = B_i^{RL} \| B_i^{RR}$.

7. Set $H_i = B_i^{LL} \| B_i^{RR} \| B_i^{RL} \| B_i^{LR}$.

This process is shown in Figure 6.3.

Of course, it is very important that the functions u and u' are suitably independent. This will ensure that the keys used every round are (very likely to be) distinct and means that the final output is more likely to look random. If $u(IV) = u'(IV)$ then the scheme is subject to a simple attack. It is recommended that u and u' should be chosen so that $u(H_i) \neq u'(H_i)$ for all possible intermediate values H_i.

The output transformation for block cipher hash function 2 is also slightly different from normal. Remember that the main purpose of an output function is to turn the L_2-bit hash variable H_q into the final L_H-bit hash code. In the case of block cipher hash function 2 this is done by taking the leftmost $L_H/2$ bits of H_q^L and the leftmost $L_H/2$ bits of H_q^R. (If L_H is odd then it is done by taking the leftmost $(L_H+1)/2$ bits of H_q^L and the $(L_H-1)/2$ leftmost bits of H_q^R.)

Block cipher hash function 2 is thought to be significantly more secure than block cipher hash function 1, primarily because it uses larger intermediate hash variables and produces longer hash codes. It is thought that, for a suitably secure n-bit block cipher, finding a collision (two distinct inputs that have the same hash code) would require computing the block cipher $2^{n/2}$ times for block cipher hash function 1 and 2^n times for block cipher hash function 2. This is optimal: We would always expect to find a collision

---

1. For almost every block cipher in existence n is even, hence there will not be a problem in splitting B_i^L and B_i^R in two. However if one does wish to use a block cipher for which n is odd then a similar level of security would be achieved by splitting each of the B_i into two parts: one of length $(n+1)/2$ and one of length $(n-1)/2$.

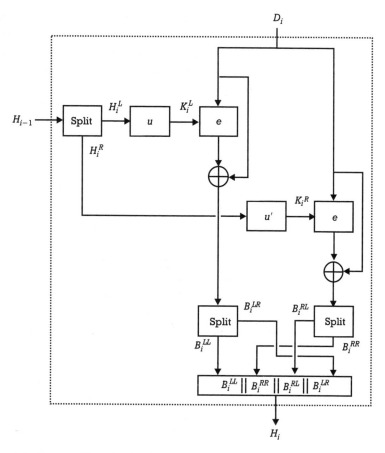

Figure 6.3   The round function for block cipher hash function 2.

in about $2^{L_2/2}$ computations of the round function. This is caused by an odd quirk of probability theory known as the *birthday paradox*. Attacks that make use of this fact are sometimes called *birthday attacks*.

Of course in an actual implementation of a block cipher–based hash function the security depends on many other factors besides the construction, including the security of the block cipher and the functions u and u', which derive the block cipher keys.

6.4   Dedicated hash functions

A dedicated hash function is a hash function that has not been explicitly built from any lower level components, such as a block cipher. These are hash functions that have been built using a round function designed specifically for use as part of a hash function. This can lead to a performance advantage: Dedicated hash functions are generally the fastest type of hash function.

This is partially because they do not have any properties that are not required for a hash function. Block ciphers, for example, need not only to turn inputs into outputs in an unpredictable manner, like hash functions, but they must also use keys and be reversible. Implementing these properties adds complexity to the design, and round functions based on block ciphers are typically slower than round functions for dedicated hash functions.

ISO/IEC 10118-3 specifies seven different dedicated hash functions: Secure Hash Algorithm 1 (SHA-1), SHA-256, SHA-384, SHA-512, RIPEMD-128, RIPEMD-160, and WHIRLPOOL. The SHA hash functions are the same functions that are specified by NIST in NIST FIPS Pub 180-2, although NIST FIPS Pub. 180-2 contains a fifth dedicated hash function that is not included in ISO/IEC 10118-3: SHA-224. SHA-1 is probably the most widely used hash function in use today.

The RIPEMD hash functions were developed in 1992 by several researchers involved in the European Union's RIPE project (see Chapter 2). The newest hash function in the ISO standard is the WHIRLPOOL algorithm. WHIRLPOOL was only developed in 2000 by Paulo Barreto and Vincent Rijmen (the coinventer of the AES algorithm).

Unlike ISO/IEC 10118-2, this part of the standard specifies the hash functions completely. No part of the algorithm is left to be decided by the implementor. This is very useful for interoperability as it means every separate organization using, say, the SHA-1 function can be assured that it is using the same function as the others. Companies that choose to use hash functions based on block ciphers must not only communicate this to the partners but also the type of block cipher being used, the padding method, and the initialization vectors. These are all specified for the dedicated hash functions.

The only class of standardized dedicated hash functions not contained in the ISO/IEC standard are the message digest (MD) family of hash functions. Three MD hash functions are standardized in a series of IETF RFCs (MD2, MD4, and MD5, collectively referred to as MDx). Unfortunately MD4 has been broken and, while MD2 and MD5 have not yet been broken, serious weaknesses have been found in both of their round functions. A long discussion about the inner workings of each of these hash functions would not be productive (as each family of hash functions is very different and, except to the expert, mostly uninteresting). For comparison purposes, the lengths L_1, L_2, and the maximum L_H are given in Table 6.1 (all lengths are given in bits).

Table 6.1 Properties of the Dedicated Hash Functions

Hash Function	L_1	L_2	Maximum L_H
SHA-1	512	160	160
SHA-224	512	256	224
SHA-256	512	256	256
SHA-384	1024	512	384
SHA-512	1024	512	512
RIPEMD-128	512	128	128
RIPEMD-160	512	160	160
WHIRLPOOL	512	512	512
MD2	128	128	128
MD4	512	128	128
MD5	512	128	128

6.5   Hash functions based on modular arithmetic

The last part of the ISO standard, ISO/IEC 10118-4, is based on the use of modular arithmetic. The standard specifies two hash functions, MASH-1 and MASH-2. Like the block cipher–based hash functions standardized in ISO/IEC 10118-2 (see Section 6.3), the MASH algorithms are not completely specified by the standard. The MASH hash functions both have round functions that use algorithms that are somewhat similar to the RSA algorithm (see Section 4.4.1).

Due to the speed of the MASH hash functions (modular arithmetic techniques are extremely slow when compared to block ciphers or dedicated hash functions), the MASH hash functions are rarely used. However, they may be appropriate for use on platforms that have a dedicated hardware chip used to compute RSA encryptions.

6.6   Choosing a hash function

Choosing a hash function is usually fairly simple. First, since speed is such a crucial issue with hash functions, few people even consider using the MASH family of hash functions (see Section 6.5) even when security is of paramount importance. It is generally thought that there are other hash functions that offer a similar security level and much better performance characteristics. Therefore the only decision most users have to make is between using a hash function based on a block cipher and a dedicated hash function.

The security offered by a block cipher–based hash function depends upon the block length of the cipher used. It should be clear from the arguments about the birthday paradox given in Section 6.3.3 that block cipher hash function 1 with a 128-bit block cipher will give about the same security as block cipher hash function 2 with a 64-bit block cipher. It is thought that the security of the block cipher–based hash functions are a little low when they are used with DES. The implementation of block cipher hash function 1 (respectively, block cipher hash function 2) given in the ISO standard estimates that a birthday attack will succeed after only 2^{27} evaluations (respectively 2^{55} evaluations) of the hash function. Most modern applications require hash functions that require at least 2^{80} evaluations to find a collision. This would require the use of a block cipher with at least a 160-bit block length (respectively 80-bit block length) with block cipher hash function 1 (respectively block cipher hash function 2).

In any case, all of the hash functions based on block ciphers are slower than their dedicated counterparts and are thought to have similar security levels. Therefore the only reason one might choose to use a hash function based on a block cipher rather than a dedicated hash function is if the block cipher algorithm is already being used as part of the security system.

For example, if a hash function needs to be implemented on a platform with limited resources (such as a smart card) and the platform already contained an implementation of a block cipher algorithm, then it might be preferable to use a hash function based on that block cipher in order to save space. In such a case the designer would have to make sure that using a block cipher and a hash function based on that block cipher together would not weaken the overall system.

However, most people chose to use dedicated hash functions, and by far the most widely used of these is SHA-1. The only problem with SHA-1 is that it produces comparatively small hash codes—only 160 bits. For longer hash codes it is necessary to choose between using a less popular function, such as SHA-512 or WHIRLPOOL, or using SHA-1 in some (nonstandard) mode of operation.

6.7 Notes

Section 6.1

Many people have tried to define the properties that a hash function must have in order to be secure. These definitions are usually sufficient for most uses of a hash function, but, almost always, the definitions are not sufficient for some small set of anomalous cases. The properties of first and second preimage resistance and collision resistance are the normal benchmark levels of security for a hash function. The notions of first and second preimage resistance was first noted by Merkle [1,2]. Collision resistance was introduced by Damgård [3].

Most hash functions that are second preimage-resistant (or collision-resistant) are also first preimage-resistant, but this is not necessarily the case. A good example of a collision-resistant hash function that is not preimage-resistant can be found in Menezes et al. [4]. Suppose g is a collision resistant hash function that produces outputs of length k (in bits). We can define a new hash function h by setting

$$h(x) = \begin{cases} 1||x & \text{if } |x| = k, \\ 0||g(x) & \text{otherwise} \end{cases}$$

This hash function is clearly not preimage-resistant. However, in order to find a collision in this hash function, we need to find a collision in the hash function g and we have already stated that g is a collision resistant hash function. Hence h is a collision resistant hash function that is not preimage-resistant. The relationship between the different notions of security for a hash function are explored in [5].

In a significantly proportion of cases, however, more is demanded from a hash function than the three standard properties of first preimage resistance, second preimage resistance, and collision resistance. In many cases it is assumed that a hash function will behave like a random function. This is especially true when analyzing the security of asymmetric algorithms where it is known as the random oracle model [6]. The concept that a function could be indistinguishable from a random function was first suggested by Goldreich, Goldwasser, and Micali [7]; however, unkeyed hash functions cannot be indistinguishable from a random function. Nevertheless, where hash functions are used in complex algorithms, it is often assumed that unkeyed hash functions behave randomly in order to simplify the security analysis.

The first examples of an iterative hash function appears in the late 1970s [1,8]. The modern general model is more closely aligned to the "Merkle meta-function" proposed by Merkle [9,10] and Damgård [11]. The construction by Merkle seems to be the first to suggest that some form of length parameter should be included in the input to the round function (see padding method 3 in Section 6.3.1). This helps to prevent certain attacks.

It can be argued that a hash function can provide a certain set of limited security services on its own. For example, the hash of a message can be printed out and stored in a physically secure device, such as a safe. A user can then check the integrity of the message at a later date. Alternatively, a message could be sent over one channel and the hash of the message sent over a second, again to ensure message integrity. In essence, a hash function can reduce the problem of message integrity from the need to protect the integrity of a long data string to the need to just protect the integrity of a short hash code.

As always, descriptions of most of the hash functions discussed in this chapter can be found in Menezes et al. [4].

Section 6.2

The major standards for hash functions are:

- ISO/IEC 10118-1 [12] (general information about hash functions);
- ISO/IEC 10118-2 [13] (hash functions using an n-bit block cipher);
- ISO/IEC 10118-3 [14] (dedicated hash functions);
- ISO/IEC 10118-4 [15] (hash functions using modular arithmetic);
- NIST FIPS Pub. 180-2 [16] (the SHA family of dedicated hash functions);
- IETF RFC 1319 [17] (MD2);
- IETF RFC 1320 [18] (MD4);
- IETF RFC 1321 [19] (MD5);
- IETF RFC 3174 [20] (SHA-1).

Section 6.3

Block cipher hash function 1 was invented by Matyas, Meyer, and Oseas [21] in 1985. Block cipher–based hash functions whose hash code is the same size as the block length have been systematically researched by Preneel, Govaerts, and Vandewalle [22]. Their conclusion is that the Matyas, Meyer, and Oseas hash function is one of a class of only 12 secure hash functions. Block cipher hash function 2, also known as MDC-2, was released by Matyas, Meyer, and

Schilling [23, 24]. It is the subject of an IBM patent (U.S. Patent Number 4,908,861).

For block cipher hash function 1, the function u that derives a block cipher key from an intermediate value is completely specified by the standard for the case when the underlying block cipher is DES. One of the roles of this function in the case when the underlying block cipher is DES is to prevent "weak" DES keys [25] from being used. The use of weak DES keys leads to a trivial attack against the scheme.

The birthday paradox is so named because of the phenomenon that, in a group of only 23 people, it is more likely than not that two people will share the same birthday. The idea behind this seemingly illogical fact can also be applied to hash functions and MACs (see Chapter 7). It turns out that if a hash function has an output of length n then, despite there being 2^n possible outputs for the hash function, we would expect to find two inputs that have the same hash code after trying $\sqrt{2^n} = 2^{n/2}$ different inputs. Therefore, since block cipher hash function 1 and block cipher hash function 2 have maximum outputs of size n and $2n$, respectively, we would expect to find collisions in these hash functions purely by chance after $2^{n/2}$ and 2^n trials, respectively.

In fact, for block cipher hash function 1, there is an even stronger result. It has been shown [22, 26] that if we assume that the underlying block cipher is in some sense "perfect," then the best possible attack against block cipher hash function 1 is the birthday attack given above.

Section 6.4

Most dedicated hash functions seem to be developed as a result of standards initiatives or focused research projects: The SHA family of hash functions were developed for the NIST secure hash standard [16], the RIPEMD family of hash functions was developed by several members of the RIPE project [27], and WHIRLPOOL was developed for evaluation by the NESSIE project [28, 29].

Many of the standardized dedicated hash functions, including four of the five SHA variants and WHIRLPOOL, have recently been analyzed by the NESSIE project. The final security report [28] found no major weaknesses in any of these hash functions. The NESSIE project also conducted extensive performance tests for these hash functions on multiple platforms [29].

All of the MDx algorithms were designed by Rivest [17–19], although the IETF RFC for MD2 was submitted by Kaliski. MD4 was broken outright by Dobbertin [30], who managed to show that the hash function was not collision-resistant. Neither MD2 nor MD5 has been broken outright yet, but in both cases it has been shown that the round functions are not collision-resistant [31–33]. This means that it is possible to find distinct intermediate hash variables H, H' and data input blocks D, D' such that $\phi(D, H) = \phi(D', H')$. This is not the same as being able to find collisions in the complete hash function, but it is a good first step. In fact, the attack against MD2 is even stronger—it has been shown that collisions could be found in the complete MD2 hash function were it not for a checksum block which is added to the input as part of the padding [31].

Section 6.5

The MASH family of hash functions were developed through a long series of papers that broke previous schemes and then proposed repairs. A survey of the early work on the MASH family can be found in [34]. The MASH family of hash functions would probably be of most use in a situation where dedicated hardware for modular arithmetic exists and, in particular, when this dedicated hardware exists but the remaining computing power is limited.

References

[1]   Merkle, R. C., *Secrecy, Authentication, and Public Key Systems,* Technical Report 1979-1, Information Systems Laboratory, Stanford University, 1979.

[2]   Merkle, R. C., *Secrecy, Authentication, and Public Key Systems,* Ann Arbor, MI: UMI Research Press, 1982.

[3]   Damgård, I. B., "Collision Free Hash Functions and Public Key Signature Schemes," in D. Chaum and W. L. Price, (eds.), *Advances in Cryptology–Eurocrypt '87,* Vol. 304, *Lecture Notes in Computer Science,* Springer-Verlag, 1987, pp. 203–216.

[4]   Menezes, A. J., P. C. van Oorschot, and S. A. Vanstone, *Handbook of Applied Cryptography,* Boca Raton, FL: CRC Press, 1997.

[5]   Rogaway, P., and T. Shrimpton, "Cryptographic Hash-Function Basics: Definitions, Implications, and Separations for Preimage Resistance, Second-Preimage Resistance, and Collision Resistance," in R. Bimal and W. Meier, (eds.), *Proceedings of the 11th Workshop on Fast Software Encryption (FSE 2004),* Vol. 3017, *Lecture Notes in Computer Science,* Springer-Verlag, 2004, pp. 373–390.

[6]   Bellare, M., and P. Rogaway, "Random Oracles Are Practical: A Paradigm for Designing Efficient Protocols," *Proc. of the First ACM Conference on Computer and Communications Security,* 1993, pp. 62–73.

[7]   Goldreich, O., S. Goldwasser, and S. Micali, "How to Construct Random Functions," *Journal of the ACM,* Vol. 33(4), 1986, pp. 792–807.

[8]   Rabin, M. O., "Digitalized Signatures," in R. Lipton and R. DeMillo, (ed.), *Foundations of Secure Computation,* New York: Academic Press, 1978, pp. 216–231.

[9]   Merkle, R. C., "One-Way Hash Functions and DES," in G. Brassard, (ed.), *Advances in Cryptology–Crypto '89,* Vol. 435, *Lecture Notes in Computer Science,* Springer-Verlag, 1989, pp. 428–446.

[10] Merkle, R. C., "A Fast Software One-Way Hash Function," *Journal of Cryptology,* Vol. 3, 1990, pp. 43–58.

[11] Damgård, I. B., "A Design Principle for Hash Functions." in G. Brassard, (ed.), *Advances in Cryptology–Crypto '89,* Vol. 435, *Lecture Notes in Computer Science,* Springer-Verlarg, 1989, pp. 416–427.

[12] International Organization for Standardization, *ISO/IEC 10118–1, Information Technology—Security Techniques—Hash-Functions—Part 1: General,* 2nd ed., 2000.

[13] International Organization for Standardization, *ISO/IEC 10118–2, Information Technology—Security Techniques—Hash-Functions—Part 2: Hash-Functions Using an n-Bit Block Cipher,* 2nd ed., 2000.

[14]   International Organization for Standardization, *ISO/IEC 10118–3, Informa-tion Technology—Security Techniques—Hash-Functions—Part 3: Dedicated Hash-Functions*, 2nd ed., 2003.

[15]   International Organization for Standardization, *ISO/IEC 10118–4, Information Technology—Security Techniques—Hash-Functions—Part 4: Hash-Functions Using Modular Arithmetic*, 1998.

[16]   National Institute of Standards and Technology (NIST), *Federal Information Pro-cessing Standards Publication 180-2 (FIPS PUB 180-2): Secure Hash Standard*, August 2002.

[17]   Kaliski, B., *RFC 1319, The MD2 Message-Digest Algorithm*, Internet Engineering Task Force, April 1992.

[18]   Rivest, R. L., *RFC 1320, The MD4 Message-Digest Algorithm*, Internet Engineering Task Force, April 1992.

[19]   Rivest, R. L., *RFC 1321, The MD5 Message-Digest Algorithm*, Internet Engineering Task Force, April 1992.

[20]   Eastlake, D., and P. Jones, *RFC 3174, US Secure Hash Algorithm (SHA-1)*, Internet Engineering Task Force, September 2001.

[21]   Matyas, S. M., C. H. Meyer, and J. Oseas, "Generating Strong One-Way Func-tions with Cryptographic Algorithms," *IBM Technical Disclosure Bulletin*, Vol. 27, 1985, pp. 5658–5659.

[22]   Preneel, B., R. Govaerts, and J. Vandewalle, "Hash Functions Based on Block Ciphers: A Synthetic Approach," D. R. Stinson, (ed.), *Advances in Cryptology–Crypto '93*, Vol. 773, *Lecture Notes in Computer Science*, Springer-Verlag, 1993, pp. 368–378.

[23]   Matyas, S. M, "Key Processing with Control Vectors," *Journal of Cryptology*, Vol. 3, 1991, pp. 113–116.

[24]   Meyer, C. H., and M. Schilling, "Secure Program Load with Manipulation Detection Code," *Proceedings of the 6th Worldwide Congress on Computer and Com-munication Security and Protection (SECURICOM '88)*, 1988, pp. 111–130.

[25]   Davies, D. W., "Some Regular Properties of the 'Data Encryption Standard' Algorithm," in D. Chaum, R. L. Rivest, and A. T. Sherman, (eds.), *Advances in Cryptology–Crypto '82*, Plenum Publishing, 1982, pp. 89–96.

[26]   Black, J., P. Rogaway, and T. Shrimpton, "Black-Box Analysis of the Block-Cipher-Based Hash-Function Constructions Form PGV," in M. Yung, (ed.), *Advances in Cryptology–Crypto 2002*, Vol. 2442, *Lecture Notes in Computer Science*, Springer-Verlag, 2002, pp. 320–335.

[27]   Bosselaers, A., and B. Preneel, (eds.), *Integrity Primitives for Secure Information Systems, Final RIPE Report of the RACE Integrity Primitives Evaluation*, Vol. 1007, *Lecture Notes in Computer Science*, Springer-Verlag, 1995.

[28]   New European Schemes for Signatures, Integrity and Encryption (NESSIE), *NESSIE Security Report*, version 2.0, http://www.cryptonessie.org/, 2003.

[29]   New European Schemes for Signatures, Integrity and Encryption (NESSIE), *Performance of Optimized Implementations of the NESSIE Primitives*, version 2.0, http://www.cryptonessie.org/, 2003.

[30]   Dobbertin, H., "Cryptanalysis of MD4," in D. Gollmann, (ed.), *Fast Software Encryption, Third International Workshop*, Vol. 1039, *Lecture Notes in Computer Science*, Springer-Verlag, 1996, pp. 71–82.

[31] Rogier, N., and P. Chauvaud, "The Compression Function of MD2 Is Not Collision Free," in *2nd Workshop on Selected Areas of Cryptography (SAC '95)*, 1995.

[32] den Boer, B., and A. Bosselaers, "Collisions for the compression function of MD5," in T. Helleseth, (ed.), *Advances in Cryptology–Eurocrypt '93*, Vol. 765, *Lecture Notes in Computer Science*, Springer-Verlag, 1993, pp. 293–304.

[33] Dobbertin, H., "The Status of MD5 After a Recent Attack," *CryptoBytes*, Vol. 2, No. 2, 1996, pp. 1–6.

[34] Girault, M., "Hash-Functions Using Modulo-n Operations," D. Chaum and W. L. Price, (eds.), *Advances in Cryptology–Eurocrypt '87*, Vol. 304 of *Lecture Notes in Computer Science*, Springer-Verlag, 1987, pp. 217–226.

Contents

7.1 Definitions and basic
properties

7.2 Standards for MACs

7.3 CBC-MACs

7.4 MACs based on hash
functions

7.5 Other MAC functions

7.6 Notes

Message Authentication Codes (MACs)

This chapter considers standards for message authentication codes (MACs). MACs are a very widely used cryptographic primitive—in many ways it could be argued that in recent years the MAC has been the most important cryptographic primitive for commercial applications. MACs are used to protect the integrity and guarantee the origin of millions of banking messages exchanged every day, as well as guaranteeing the authenticity of mobile telephones. Without this primitive—or something equally effective—massive fraud against banking and mobile telecommunications systems would be potentially simple.

MACs have been widely used for 20 years or more, and they have been the subject of standards for most of that time. The first standards were country- and industry-specific (U.S. banking standards) but international standards soon followed. The main focus of this chapter is on the general-purpose ISO/IEC international standards for MACs, but other standards, including ANSI and ISO banking standards, NIST FIPS, and Internet RFCs are also briefly discussed.

7.1 Definitions and basic properties

MACs are used to protect the integrity of transmitted or stored data (*data integrity*) and to provide evidence regarding the origin of data (*data origin authentication*). A MAC algorithm takes as input the data string to be protected and a secret key, and gives as output a short, fixed-length string called the MAC. This MAC is then stored or sent with the message to be protected. An entity that receives a transmitted message or recovers a stored message can then check the MAC to determine that it must have been sent by someone who knows the secret key (*origin authentication*) and that it has not been modified (*data integrity*).

MAC checking is performed by using the received or recovered message in conjunction with the same secret key as used to compute the original MAC, to compute a new MAC. This new MAC is then compared with the MAC value sent or stored with the message, and only if the two agree is the message deemed authentic.

Thus, what use of a MAC actually shows about a message is that it must have been constructed by someone with knowledge of the secret key. Hence, if the secret key used to compute a MAC is widely known then the MAC is not much use. Typically, if MACs are used to protect stored data, the secret key will be known only by one party (i.e., the owner of the data) and if MACs are used to protect transmitted messages, then only the sender and receiver will possess the secret key. Of course, this in itself raises important key management issues that are outside the scope of this chapter (see Chapters 11 and 12 on key management and key establishment mechanisms). In particular, if a key is used to protect stored data then the key holder may need to make arrangements to securely back up the secret key, since if it is lost the veracity of the data can no longer be verified; similarly, if two parties are to share a secret key then mechanisms need to be used to agree the key reliably and in a way that protects its secrecy.

Also, it is clear that to be effective the MAC algorithm must possess certain properties. As specified in ISO/IEC 9797-1, the following two properties must hold for a MAC algorithm:

▶ Computing a MAC from a message and a secret key must be straightforward (*usability*).

▶ Finding a MAC for a given message without authorized access to the secret key must be infeasible, even if the attacker has access to the correct MACs for a number of other messages, including some that may be chosen by the attacker (*security*).

The second property also motivates an important class of cryptanalytic attacks against MAC schemes, namely "forgery attacks." A forgery attack is an attack in which an unauthorized party is able to discover the correct MAC for a message of his or her choice without it having been generated by one of the authorized parties. Thus a feasible forgery attack will contravene the second property required of a MAC algorithm, and thus a secure MAC scheme must resist forgery attacks.

Note also that the second property implies in particular that determining the secret key from observation of a number of messages and MACs must be infeasible. This observation motivates the definition of a second class of attacks against MAC algorithms, namely "key recovery attacks." A key recovery attack is an attack in which an unauthorized party is able to determine the key used to compute one or MACs by the authorized parties. Clearly a successful key recovery attack will allow unlimited forgery attacks.

There are two main kinds of MACs in common use, and this is reflected in the schemes that are standardized. Almost certainly the most widely used schemes are the CBC-MACs, discussed in Section 7.3. These schemes require the selection and use of a block cipher (see Chapter 4). The other class consists of schemes based on the use of a hash function (see Chapter 6). These are considered in Section 7.4.

MAC functions may or may not have one or more *one-way* properties. Of particular interest is "known-key one-wayness." A MAC function has this property if, given a MAC and a secret key, it is infeasible to find a message that gives this MAC (with the specified key). In most cases such a property is not required, and, indeed, most widely used MAC functions, including the CBC-MAC schemes, do not possess this property; however the hash function–based schemes do possess this property.

7.2 Standards for MACs

The most comprehensive set of standardized MAC algorithms are those specified in the two-part international standard ISO/IEC 9797. Part 1 specifies six different CBC-MAC variants. A variety of MAC schemes based on the use of hash functions are included in part 2.

However, the oldest MAC standards (apart from a scheme included in an appendix to the NIST modes of operation standard, NIST FIPS 81) are those that were originally published in the 1980s for banking use by ANSI, namely X9.9 (now withdrawn) and X9.19. These standards contain specific CBC-MAC variants and are essentially a subset of the schemes standardized in ISO/IEC 9797-1. Subsequently various international banking standards for MACs were produced by ISO, largely based on the ANSI standards, including ISO 8730, ISO 8731 Parts 1 and 2, and ISO 9807. Apart from ISO 8731-2, the specified algorithms are again a subset of ISO/IEC 9797-1. The exception, ISO 8731-2, contains an algorithm known as the message authentication algorithm (MAA), which is not a CBC-MAC scheme (see also Section 7.5). Although this latter standard has not been withdrawn, the MAA is now to some extent discredited.

Continuing on the theme of standards for CBC-MACs, the 3GPP has standardized a method for generating a CBC-MAC for use in third generation mobile telecommunications networks. This method is different from any method given in ISO/IEC 9797-1 and is discussed briefly in Section 7.3.3.

To complete the discussion of standards for CBC-MACs, there have been recent moves by NIST to standardize a MAC function for use with the block cipher AES. An initial proposal to standardize yet another CBC-MAC variant called RMAC generated a large number of comments suggesting that this was not a good idea and was withdrawn. At the time of writing, NIST appears to be moving toward the adoption of yet another CBC-MAC scheme called OMAC, itself derived from a scheme known as XCBC. The possibility of standardizing OMAC has also been raised within the IRTF Crypto Forum Research Group (CFRG). Another block cipher scheme called PMAC has also been submitted to NIST, although this is not a CBC-MAC scheme (see Section 7.5), and it is not clear whether NIST is likely to adopt it.

There are less standards for MAC algorithms based on the use of a hash function. Apart from ISO/IEC 9797-2, the only standards documents that include a hash function–based MAC are Internet RFC 2104 and ANSI X9.71, which both specify an algorithm called HMAC. This technique is also included in ISO/IEC 9797-2. Internet RFC 2202 provides test vectors for HMAC.

7.3   CBC-MACs

In this section the various CBC-MAC schemes that have been standardized are introduced. Since CBC-MAC schemes are always based on use of a block cipher, we first establish some notation for block ciphers: We write $e_K(X)$ for the block cipher encryption of a plaintext block X using the secret key K; we similarly write $d_K(Y)$ for the decryption of ciphertext block Y using secret key K. Hence, by definition, $d_K[e_K(X)] = X$. We also write n for the length of plaintext and ciphertext blocks handled by the block cipher. For a discussion of standardized block ciphers see Chapter 4.

7.3.1   SMAC—the simplest form of CBC-MAC

To describe the standardized versions of CBC-MAC it is first helpful to consider the most basic form of CBC-MAC, namely, the simple MAC (SMAC). This technique is standardized as MAC algorithm 1 in ISO/IEC 9797-1 and uses a single block cipher key. To compute a SMAC on a message D using the block cipher key K involves the following steps (with the procedure shown diagrammatically in Figure 7.1).

1. *Padding:* The message D must first be "padded" so that it contains an integer multiple of n bits, qn, say. Three different padding methods are standardized in ISO/IEC 9797-1 (see Section 7.3.2), the simplest, albeit not the most secure, of which is to add between 0 and $n-1$ zero bits to the end of the message (this is known as padding method 1).

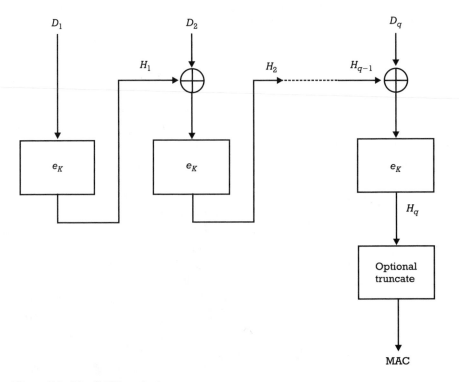

Figure 7.1   The SMAC method.

2. *Splitting:* The padded message is now divided into a sequence of n-bit blocks (i.e., $D_1, D_2, \ldots, D_q$). Block D_1 corresponds to the first n bits of the padded message, D_2 to the next n bits, and so on.

3. *Iteration:* Let $H_0 = 0^n$ (i.e., the n-bit block consisting of all zeros), and for i successively set to $1, 2, \ldots, q$ compute $H_i = e_K(D_i \oplus H_{i-1})$.

4. *Truncation:* The MAC consists of the leftmost m bits of the value H_q, where m is some (fixed) positive integer less than or equal to n. Typical values of m are 16, 32, or 64.

The U.S. banking standard ANSI X9.9 standardizes SMAC with the specific choice for block cipher of DES, using the simple "add zeros" padding method outlined above, and with $m = 32$ (i.e., the MAC consists of the leftmost 32 bits of H_q). The international banking standard ISO 8731-1 adopts precisely the same algorithm. Despite the popularity of this method, it does have two significant security problems leading to possible forgery attacks.

First, the all zeros padding method allows for a trivial forgery attacks in environments where the length of the message is not tightly constrained. This is discussed further in Section 7.3.2.

Second, if $m = n$ (i.e., if the MAC is the same as H_q, the output of the final iteration step), then the following simple "cut and paste" forgery attack is possible given just one known message/MAC pair. Suppose $D_1, D_2, \ldots, D_q$ is a padded message for which the MAC is known to be M. Then the attacker can immediately deduce that the padded message (of twice the length) which has the form:

$$D_1, D_2, \ldots, D_q, M \oplus D_1, D_2, \ldots, D_q \tag{7.1}$$

also has MAC M. Of course, such a message is probably meaningless, and in environments where all messages have length q blocks then this attack will yield an invalid message. However, the existence of such a simple forgery suggests that SMAC is not appropriate for general use. Moreover, the attack just described is only the simplest variant of a family of similar forgery attacks. In fact, any two or more (message, MAC) pairs can be combined in this way to give a MAC forgery, and thus the possibility exists that it will be possible to forge a MAC for a meaningful message. This motivates the design of all the other CBC-MAC schemes, described below.

7.3.2 Padding methods

Before considering alternative forms of CBC-MAC, the standardized padding methods are first discussed. Specifically, padding methods 1, 2, and 3, standardized in ISO/IEC 9797-1, are described. Note that this standard allows any of the three padding methods to be combined with any of the six CBC-MAC algorithms.

As already noted above, padding method 1 is the simplest—it simply involves appending between 0 and $n - 1$ zero bits to the end of a message. The main advantage of this method is that the padded message contains the minimum possible number of blocks after the splitting process (i.e., q is minimal) thus minimizing the number of block cipher encryptions required to compute a MAC.

The main problem with padding method 1 arises because there are up to n different messages that can, after padding, yield the same padded message and hence have the same MAC. An attacker can now substitute one message for another in the knowledge that the MAC will stay unchanged. To give an example, suppose $n = 64$ and consider a message D of 32 bits. Suppose an attacker observes D and the corresponding MAC M. If the attacker knows that padding method 1 is in use, then the attacker can immediately deduce that the 64-bit message D', which consists of D followed by 32 zero bits, also has MAC M. Indeed the same is true of all messages of between 32 and 64 bits that agree with D in their first 32 bits and have all following bits set to zero.

Despite this major issue, padding method 1 is still widely used, largely for legacy reasons, but also because it is efficient (as q is minimal). In fact, in environments where the message length is fixed, this padding method appears sound. However, because of its inherent problems, it cannot be recommended for new applications.

Padding method 2 was designed to avoid the problems with padding method 1, and it has the property that no two distinct messages are the same after the padding process. It operates as follows:

▸ Append a single one bit to the end of the message.

▸ Append the minimal number of zero bits (between 0 and $n - 1$) after the single one bit so as to ensure that the overall padded message length is an integer multiple of n.

It should be clear that if the unpadded message already contains a whole number multiple of n bits, then this padding method will result in the addition of an entire extra block of n bits, consisting of a single one followed by $n - 1$ zeros. This may seem rather inefficient, but it should be pointed out that an extra block will be required only if the original data length is a multiple of n bits. Moreover, even when an extra block is added, this only adds one extra block cipher encryption to the MAC generation process, and has no effect whatever on the amount of data to be stored or sent. This is because it is never necessary to store or send the padding with the message (i.e., the padding is only ever created for the purposes of MAC computation and can thereafter be discarded).

Padding method 3 is an alternative to padding method 2, which, in some cases, makes certain forgery and key recovery attacks more difficult to perform (see Section 7.6). Padding method 3 operates as follows:

▸ Create an n-bit block containing a (right-justified) binary representation of the bit length of the message D. For example, if $n = 64$ and D contains seven bits then this block will consists of 61 zeros followed by three ones. Now prefix the message with this block.

▸ Perform padding method 1 on the message obtained from the previous step.

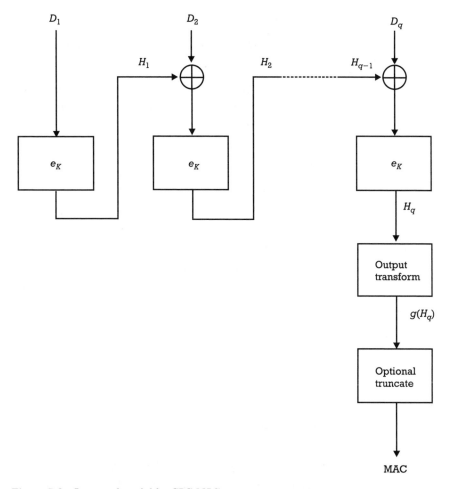

Figure 7.2 A general model for CBC-MACs.

In some sense this last method is the least efficient, since a message padded using method 3 will always contain one more block than a message padded using method 1.

7.3.3 Output transformations

To avoid the forgery problems associated with SMAC, a series of CBC-MAC schemes have been devised, adhering to the general model depicted in Figure 7.2. MACs conforming to this model are computed using the following series of steps, the first three of which are identical to the SMAC computation. The fourth (new) step, consists of the application of an output transformation g, the form of which varies, as discussed below. The presence of this output transformation, if appropriately chosen, prevents the simple forgery attack described in Section 7.3.1:

1. *Padding:* As above;

2. *Splitting:* As above;

3. *Iteration:* As above;

4. *Output transformation:* Apply an output transformation g to H_q to get the n-bit block G; candidates for g are discussed next;

5. *Truncation:* Analogously to above, the MAC consists of the leftmost m bits of the value G, where m is some (fixed) positive integer less than or equal to n.

Using this general model, it is now possible to define a series of different standardized CBC-MAC schemes merely by defining g appropriately.

- *ISO/IEC 9797-1 MAC algorithm 1 (SMAC):* To obtain SMAC it is merely necessary to set g to be the identity function.

- *ISO/IEC 9797-1 MAC algorithm 2 (EMAC):* The output transformation used by EMAC requires a second block cipher key K'. The output transformation g is defined to be block cipher encryption using K'— that is,

$$G = g(H_q) = e_{K'}(H_q) \tag{7.2}$$

It is possible to derive K' from K, without significantly reducing the security of the scheme (as long as steps are taken to ensure that $K' \neq K$). One possibility is to switch certain bits in K. This has the benefit that the creator and verifier of MACs need only share a single block cipher key.

- *ISO/IEC 9797-1 MAC algorithm 3 (ARMAC):* This scheme is also standardized in ANSI X9.19, and hence it is often known as the ANSI retail MAC (ARMAC). Like EMAC, the output transformation for ARMAC requires a second block cipher key K'. However, unlike EMAC, the keys K and K' should be chosen independently. The output transformation g is defined to be a block cipher decryption using the key K' followed by a further block cipher encryption using the key K—that is,

$$G = g(H_q) = e_K[d_{K'}(H_q)] \tag{7.3}$$

As discussed later, ARMAC has certain advantages over EMAC and SMAC in the case where the block cipher has a relatively small key length and block size (e.g., DES).

- *ETSI 3GPP-MAC:* This scheme is unlike the previous schemes in that it has not been standardized for general use—it is a scheme designed specifically for wireless security in a third generation mobile telecommunications network. Again, a second block cipher key K' is required by the output transformation g. The output transformation g is defined as follows:

$$G = g(H_q) = e_{K'}(H_1 \oplus H_2 \oplus \ldots \oplus H_q) \tag{7.4}$$

Table 7.1   Standardized CBC-MAC Algorithms

Name	Standard	Output transformation (g)
SMAC	ISO/IEC 9797-1 #1	Identity
EMAC	ISO/IEC 9797-1 #2	Encryption
ARMAC	ISO/IEC 9797-1 #3	Decryption and encryption
3GPP-MAC	ETSI 3GPP TS 35.201	Encryption of ex-or of H_i
RMAC	NIST draft standard	Encryption using a random key offset

This scheme is thus slightly different in that, while computing the iteration step, it is necessary to maintain a "running accumulated exclusive-or" of all the values H_i; as a result it does not strictly conform to the general model of Figure 7.2.

▸ *RMAC:* Finally, we describe RMAC. Unlike the previous schemes this MAC function has not been standardized; we mention it here because it was recently the subject of a draft standard by NIST, although, because of possible problems with RMAC, NIST is now moving toward the adoption of OMAC instead. Like the three previous schemes, the output transformation requires an additional block cipher key K'. In addition, every time a MAC is generated an n-bit random "salt" R must also be generated. This salt must be sent or stored with the message and MAC. The output transformation is defined as follows:

$$G = g(H_q) = e_{K' \oplus R}(H_q) \tag{7.5}$$

The draft NIST standard specifies padding method 2 must be used for this scheme.

The five schemes discussed so far are summarized in Table 7.1. Of the five schemes fitting the general model, clearly SMAC is the most efficient in that the output transformation (in this case the identity transformation) does not require any additional block cipher encryptions to be performed. Three of the remaining four require one additional encryption operation, while ARMAC requires two additional encryptions.

There are also some differences in the level of resistance to key recovery and forgery attacks offered by these schemes. We summarize these differences in Section 7.3.8.

7.3.4   Other CBC-MAC schemes

Not all the standardized CBC-MAC schemes conform to the general model of Figure 7.2. In Sections 7.3.5 through 7.3.7, such schemes are described. However, we first describe a class of attacks that apply to all MAC schemes adhering to the general model described in Section 7.3.3 and Figure 7.3. These attacks are usually known as "internal collision" attacks. It is the existence of these attacks, which are only of any importance if n is relatively small (say, $n < 100$), as is the case for DES, that motivates the design of some of the alternative CBC-MAC schemes, notably the schemes described in Sections 7.3.5 and 7.3.6.

Suppose a CBC-MAC is to be computed by a method conforming to the general model in Figure 7.2 and that, to simplify this discussion, there is no truncation (i.e., $m = n$). Now consider what occurs if two messages are found which give the same MAC when using the same key; by the birthday paradox calculations (see Section 6.3.3) this is likely given $2^{n/2}$ message/MAC pairs. It is not hard to see that this means that H_q must be the same for the two messages. This observation has two important ramifications:

- If only part of the key is used for computing H_q, as is the case for MAC algorithm 3 (ARMAC), then this will enable an exhaustive search for the key used to compute H_q, independently of the other part of the key.

- If padding method 3 is not used, then the existence of such a collision also enables a simple forgery attack to be conducted. If the same extra n-bit block is appended to the two messages that share the same H_q, then it is not hard to see that these two longer messages will also have the same MAC (i.e., learning the MAC of one of these messages will enable a MAC forgery on the other message).

Thus, when using any of the CBC-MAC schemes conforming to the general model in Figure 7.2, it is necessary to ensure that no single key is used to generate too many MACs; in particular, a key should never be used to generate as many as $2^{n/2}$ MACs (or any number close to this value).

7.3.5 MAC algorithm 4 from ISO/IEC 9797-1

MAC algorithm 4 from ISO/IEC 9797-1 (known as MacDES in the case where DES is the block cipher) uses a slightly modified version of the general model of Figure 7.2, as follows. The only difference is in the iteration step, in which a special initial transformation I is used to compute H_1 from D_1. The revised general model for MAC computation, which includes the previous general model as a special case, is shown in Figure 7.3 and is defined as follows:

1. *Padding:* As above;

2. *Splitting:* As above;

3. *Iteration:* Let $H_1 = I(D_1)$, and for i successively set to $2, 3, \ldots, q$ compute $H_i = e_K(D_i \oplus H_{i-1})$;

4. *Output transformation:* As above;

5. *Truncation:* As above.

ISO/IEC 9797-1 MAC algorithm 4 uses two block cipher keys K' and K'', over and above the key K used in the iteration step. Key K' is used in defining the

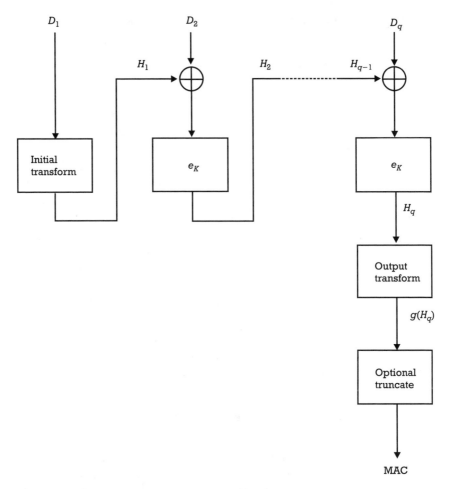

Figure 7.3 Revised general model for CBC-MACs.

output transformation g, which is a single additional encryption, precisely as for MAC algorithm 2. Key K'' is used in the initial transformation, where

$$H_1 = e_{K''}[e_K[(D_1)]] \tag{7.6}$$

This MAC function requires precisely the same number of block cipher encryptions as ARMAC. It also offers certain security advantages over ARMAC, notably the following:

- The simple internal collision-based key recovery attack on ARMAC, outlined in Section 7.3.4, is ruled out (although key recovery attacks more efficient than exhaustive search of the entire key space do exist).

- If padding method 3 is used, then collision-based forgery attacks are more difficult to conduct against this scheme than against ARMAC.

7.3.6   MAC algorithms 5 and 6 from ISO/IEC 9797-1

The final two schemes standardized in ISO/IEC 9797-1 (i.e., MAC algorithms 5 and 6) are both constructed by performing two CBC-MAC computations in parallel.

ISO/IEC 9797-1 MAC algorithm 5 involves two parallel instances of MAC algorithm 1 (i.e., SMAC). The message is padded and split, and SMAC values are computed for two different block cipher keys (K_1 and K_2). These two SMAC values are bit-wise exclusive-ored together, and then truncated to m bits to obtain the MAC value (where $m \leq n$, the block length of the block cipher). Note that the two keys K_1 and K_2 must be derived from a single key K. The method to be used for key derivation is not specified in ISO/IEC 9797-1, although whatever method is used must ensure that the two keys K_1, K_2 are always different.

ISO/IEC 9797-1 MAC algorithm 6 involves two parallel instances of MAC algorithm 4, the results of which are exclusive-ored to obtain the MAC value. The method is analogous to MAC algorithm 5, except that in this case two key pairs are required, since MAC algorithm 4 uses a pair of keys. Again the two key pairs shall be derived from a single key pair by some method, the details of which are not specified in ISO/IEC 9797-1. This derivation method must ensure the two keys in a pair are always different and that the two derived pairs are distinct from one another.

7.3.7   XCBC, TMAC, and OMAC

Finally, we describe XCBC, TMAC, and OMAC, which again do not fit any of the models so far provided. Like RMAC, these schemes are not the subject of standards; however, it would appear that there is a possibility that at least one of these three closely related schemes will be adopted by NIST. We start by describing the operation of XCBC.

First, note that XCBC requires two additional keys K_1 and K_2. However, unlike the schemes described earlier, these keys are not block cipher keys—instead they are both n-bit blocks. Computing a MAC then proceeds as follows.

1. *Padding*: XCBC uses a novel padding method. If the original message length is a multiple of n then no padding is performed. If the original message length is not a multiple of n then padding method 2 is employed. Note that this padding method is not suitable for general use, since if it were used with other CBC-MAC computation methods then trivial forgery attacks would be possible.

2. *Splitting:* As above.

3. *Iteration:* Let $H_0 = 0^n$ (i.e., the n-bit block consisting of all zeros), and for i successively set to $1, 2, \ldots, q-1$ compute $H_i = e_K(D_i \oplus H_{i-1})$. Finally, the computation of H_q depends on the padding process. If no padding was performed then $H_q = e_K(H_{q-1} \oplus D_q \oplus K_1)$. If padding was performed (using padding method 2), then $H_q = e_K(H_{q-1} \oplus D_q \oplus K_2)$.

Table 7.2 ISO/IEC 9797-1 Algorithms

Number	Name	Properties
1	SMAC	No output transform
2	EMAC	Extra final encryption
3	ARMAC	Extra final decryption and encryption
4	MacDES	Extra initial and final encryption
5	Parallel-SMAC	Two parallel instances of SMAC
6	Parallel-MacDES	Two parallel instances of MacDES

4. *Truncation:* The MAC consists of the leftmost m bits of the value H_q, where m is some (fixed) positive integer less than or equal to n. Typical values of m are 16, 32, or 64.

XCBC offers the advantage that, like SMAC, q is minimized by the padding process, and only q block cipher encryptions are required. It is thus as efficient as SMAC and more efficient than any of the other schemes.

TMAC is the same as XCBC, except that K_1 is derived from K_2 using a fixed function (i.e., it requires two instead of three keys). OMAC is like TMAC except that K_1 and K_2 are both derived from K (i.e., it only requires one key).

7.3.8 Choosing a CBC-MAC function

Selecting a CBC-MAC scheme appropriate for a particular application is a nontrivial task. To see this it is only necessary to consider the difficulty NIST is currently having in deciding which (if any) CBC-MAC function to standardize for use with AES. Even if the decision is made to follow the international standard ISO/IEC 9797-1, there are still six choices for the MAC function and three for the padding method (not forgetting the choices with regard to the block cipher[1] and the degree of truncation). These six schemes are summarized in Table 7.2.

The decision needs to be made taking into account many factors derived from the environment in which the MAC function will be used. It is beyond the scope of this book to cover this in detail, although it is worth noting that ISO/IEC 9797-1 contains a series of detailed tables specifying the security of the six standardized MAC functions against both forgery and key recovery attacks. We restrict our attention here to giving general guidance on function choice.

The choice of padding method is relatively easy: Padding method 1 should be avoided, and padding method 3 gives some security advantages over padding method 2. Thus, all else being equal, padding method 3 is probably the method of choice.

To choose appropriate MAC algorithms from the six in ISO/IEC 9797-1 requires the discussion to be divided into a number of cases.

---

1. Of course, for users of NIST standards there is no problem with respect to the block cipher, since AES is the default choice.

▸ *Case I: "Weak" block cipher with a relatively short key and a relatively short block length (e.g., DES).* In this case SMAC and EMAC do not offer sufficient security against key recovery attacks (see Chapter 4). ARMAC and MAC algorithm 4 are probably both appropriate for use, as long as care is taken to limit the number of MACs computed using a single key. MAC algorithm 4 offers certain security advantages, and so, all else being equal, is to be preferred. MAC algorithm 6 may also be attractive in this environment, although it is rather inefficient.

▸ *Case II: Block cipher with a relatively short block length but a long key (e.g., triple DES).* In this case EMAC is probably a sensible choice, although again care should be taken not to compute too many MACs with the same key because of possible internal collision attacks (see Section 7.3.4).

▸ *Case III: Block cipher with a relatively long block length and key (e.g., AES).* Here EMAC again appears appropriate, although the concerns over the number of MACs computed with a single key no longer apply.

Given that it may soon be standardized by NIST, it is important also to consider the usability of OMAC in the above three cases. In case I OMAC would not be appropriate since it would not offer sufficient security against key recovery attacks. In cases II and III, OMAC is a genuine competitor to EMAC. However, in case II it should be observed that the consequences of a successful collision attack on OMAC (arising if too many MACs are computed using a single key) are more serious than with EMAC, since the possibilities for forgery attacks are much greater.

7.4 MACs based on hash functions

In circumstances where the implementation of a hash function is already available, it is potentially attractive to be able to derive a MAC using such a hash function. Such an approach may be particularly attractive because hash functions can sometimes be implemented to have a higher throughput than CBC encryption using a block cipher, resulting in a more efficient MAC computation.

There are three main classes of hash-based MAC functions defined in ISO/IEC 9797-2:

▸ MAC functions that modify the operation of the hash function to incorporate the use of a key;

▸ MAC functions that use the hash function as a black box (i.e., that do not modify the way in which the hash function is computed);

▸ MAC functions specifically designed for short messages.

We consider these in turn.

7.4.1 The MDx-MAC functions

MAC algorithm 1 from ISO/IEC 9797-2 is of the first type (i.e., it involves making modifications to a hash function to incorporate use of a key). These functions are based on a scheme known as MDx-MAC.

ISO/IEC 9797-2 MAC algorithm 1 comes in three versions, based on three different hash functions, namely RIPEMD-128, RIPEMD-160 and SHA-1 (see Chapter 6). In all of these cases the IV and certain constants used within the round function (of the hash function) are altered depending on the key. Apart from this, the round function is applied in the normal way. If the hash code that results from this process is H, then the MAC is $\phi(H, K')$, where K' is some L_2-bit block that depends only on the key. In each case the key used can be of any length up to a maximum of 128 bits.

7.4.2 HMAC

The HMAC scheme, MAC algorithm 2 from ISI/IEC 9797-2, is of the second type (i.e., it uses the hash function as a "black box"). We let h denote the hash function that has been chosen to be used to build the MAC algorithm. Note that ISO/IEC 9797-2 requires that the hash function be chosen from among those standardized in ISO/IEC 10118-3 (see Chapter 6). However, no such restriction is made in RFC 2104.

Like MDx-MAC, the secret key can be of any length, this time up to a maximum of L_1, where L_1 is the length of the data input of the internal round function for h (see Chapter 6). In addition, the minimum length for the key shall be L_2, where L_2 is the bit length of the hash code produced by h.

Computing a MAC involves four steps, described as follows. Suppose the secret key to be used to compute the MAC is K (and that the data string on which the MAC is to be computed is D).

1. *Key expansion:* The secret key is made into a string of L_1 bits, denoted $\bar{K}$ by appending zeros to the right end of K, as necessary. Two different keys $\bar{K}_1$ and $\bar{K}_2$ (both of length L_1) are derived from $\bar{K}$ by bit-wise exclusive-oring two different fixed patterns of zeros and ones to $\bar{K}$.

2. *Hashing:* The value H', which will contain L_2 bits, is obtained as:

$$H' = h(\bar{K}_1 || D) \tag{7.7}$$

where here, as throughout, the vertical bars denote concatenation of data items.

3. *Output transformation:* The value H'', again of L_2 bits, is computed as:

$$H'' = h(\bar{K}_2 || H') \tag{7.8}$$

4. *Truncation:* The MAC (of m bits) is obtained by taking the leftmost m bits of H''.

Note that, although the above scheme uses two iterations of the hash function, this is not as inefficient as it might first appear. The second time that the hash function is computed (in step 3), the input string is very short, and hence this should be a fast computation, regardless of the length of the data string D.

7.4.3   MDx-MAC variant for short messages

Finally, MAC algorithm 3 from ISO/IEC 9797-1 is of the third type listed above (i.e., it is specifically designed to be efficient for short messages, namely messages containing at most 256 bits). Like MAC algorithm 1, it involves modifying the hash function to make use of a key. Again like MAC algorithm 1, it comes in three versions, based on three different hash functions, namely RIPEMD-128, RIPEMD-160, and SHA-1 (see Chapter 6). In each case, specific modifications are recommended to the hash functions to incorporate use of a key, and in each case the key used can be of any length up to a maximum of 128 bits.

7.4.4   Choosing a hash-based MAC function

The first factor in deciding which MAC function to use (from among those based on hash functions) is whether the implementor has access to the internals of the implementation of the hash function. In some cases the implementor will only have access to a series of function calls giving access to a cryptographic library (i.e., the implementor will have no choice but to use the hash function as a "black box.") In other cases the implementor will have access to the details of the implementation of the hash function, or will be in a position to produce his or her own implementation of the hash function.

In the first case there is no alternative but to use HMAC. In the second case, one of MAC algorithms 1 (MDx-MAC) and 3 should be used—the choice between them should be made on the basis of the lengths of the messages to be input to the MAC algorithm. If MACs are to be computed for messages of at most 256 bits then MAC algorithm 3 will be significantly more efficient. Otherwise MAC algorithm 1 is the preferred choice.

7.5   Other MAC functions

We conclude the main part of this chapter by briefly discussing two MAC algorithms that do not fit into the two categories covered in Sections 7.3 and 7.4.

MAA is almost unique in being designed specifically for the purpose of computing a MAC (i.e., it does not rely on a separate block cipher or hash function). The operation of MAA is based on a combination of common logical and arithmetical functions, and it has been designed to be readily implementable in software. As mentioned above, although ISO 8731-2, which standardizes MAA, has not been withdrawn, the MAA is now to some extent discredited, since attacks on this scheme have been published. These attacks mean that a single key should only be used to compute a relatively limited number of messages.

The other scheme we mention here is PMAC, a much more recent scheme that has been submitted as a candidate for adoption by NIST. PMAC is based on the use of a block cipher, although it is not a CBC-MAC scheme. The unique property of PMAC is that it has been designed to be arbitrarily parallelizable, by contrast with CBC-MAC schemes that are inherently serial.

When computing PMAC, it is first necessary to divide the message into n-bit blocks, $M_1, M_2, \ldots, M_q$ (just as in a CBC-MAC scheme). However, the key difference is that each block M_i is then processed independently of every other block, by first ex-oring it with an n-bit block dependent only on the key K and the value of i, and then encrypting it using the block cipher. The MAC value is then derived by ex-oring the outputs of all the individual block encryptions, before performing a further block cipher encryption.

7.6 Notes

Section 7.1

For a more general treatment of MACs, the reader is encouraged to refer to Section 9.5 of [1]. Properties required of a MAC algorithm are specified in ISO/IEC 9797-1 [2]. The known-key one-wayness property is required in some applications of MAC functions; see, for example, ISO 15764 [3].

Section 7.2

The idea of computing a CBC-MAC using DES as the block cipher is now more than over 25 years old [4]. The first standardized MAC technique is SMAC, discussed in Appendix F of the 1980 U.S. federal standard FIPS Pub. 81 [5]. This was followed in the early 1980s by two U.S. banking standards, ANSI X9.9 [6] and ANSI X9.19 [7] (the first of which was withdrawn in 1999 [8]). The subsequent ISO banking standards include ISO 8730 [9], ISO 8731 Parts 1 and 2 [10, 11], and ISO 9807 [12]. ISO/IEC 9797-1 [2] is in fact the third version of the ISO/IEC CBC-MAC standard—previous editions were published in 1989 [13] and 1994 [14]. Work started on another revision of ISO/IEC 9797-1 in late 2003; the new version will exclude MAC algorithms 5 and 6 and will include OMAC.

Other CBC-MAC schemes include the 3GPP-MAC scheme [15]. RMAC was proposed in 2002 by Jaulmes, Joux, and Valette [16] and was then included in a NIST draft [17]. TMAC and OMAC were proposed by Iwata and Kurosawa [18, 19], and are derived from a scheme known as XCBC [20].

HMAC was originally proposed by Bellare, Canetti, and Krawczyk [21], before its adoption by the IETF in 1997 [22]. To assist implementors, a set of test vectors for HMAC when used with the hash functions MD5 and SHA-1 was published in RFC 2202 [23]. ISO/IEC 9797-2, which also incorporates HMAC, was first published in 2000 [24] (like ISO/IEC 9797-1, it includes test vectors for all the standardized MAC algorithms). The U.S. banking standard ANSI X9.71 [25] also adopts HMAC.

Section 7.3

Internal collision-based attacks against ARMAC were described by Preneel and van Oorschot [26] and Knudsen and Preneel [27]. These attacks motivated the design of MacDES, which was proposed by Knudsen and Preneel [27] as a superior alternative to ARMAC for use with "weak" block ciphers such as DES. Subsequently, Coppersmith, Knudsen, and Mitchell [28, 29] found attacks which, while not breaking the scheme in practice, showed that the advantages of MacDES over ARMAC are not as great as previously thought, although they are still significant.

The 3GPP-MAC scheme was designed specifically for use with the 3GPP 64-bit block cipher KASUMI (see Chapter 4). The best known attacks on this scheme are given in [30], although these attacks do not seriously threaten the security of the scheme.

The RMAC scheme was proposed in by Jaulmes, Joux, and Valette [16]. Its inclusion in a draft standard published by NIST in 2002 [17] attracted a large number of negative comments, and it no longer appears to be a candidate for standardization. A series of attacks against RMAC have been proposed (see, for example, [31, 32]) which, while not invalidating it, raised doubts as to its claimed superiority to other schemes.

The XCBC scheme was originally proposed by Black and Rogaway [20]. Subsequently, Kurosawa and Iwata proposed a two-key version TMAC [19], and the same authors then proposed a one-key version OMAC [18]. While these schemes are provably secure, some anomalies in the design of TMAC and OMAC have recently been identified [33].

An attack on ISO/IEC 9797-1 MAC algorithm 5 was described in 2003 by Joux, Poupard, and Stern [34]. As a result, MAC algorithms 5 and 6 are likely to be omitted from the next edition of ISO/IEC 9797-1, since they do not appear to offer significant advantages over other standardized CBC-MAC schemes (and they are much less efficient).

A series of tables in Annex B of ISO/IEC 9797-1 provide a detailed guide to the best known attacks on all the standardized CBC-MAC schemes.

In recent years considerable progress has been achieved in developing mathematical proofs of the security of CBC-MAC schemes. While details of these proofs are beyond the scope of this book, we briefly review the main known results. The first main result regarding provably secure CBC-MAC schemes was achieved in 1984 by Bellare, Kilian, and Rogaway [35], who showed that SMAC is secure for fixed-length messages. In 2000, Petrank and Rackhoff [36] proved that EMAC is secure if the message length is a multiple of n, and hence is also secure as long as the padding method is 1-1 (i.e., Padding Method 2 or 3 is used). Proofs of security also exist for all the recently proposed schemes, including RMAC [16], XCBC [20, 37], TMAC [19, 37], and OMAC [18, 37]. While ARMAC and MacDES do not possess proofs of security, heuristically one would expect them to be at least as secure as EMAC, since they involve adding one encryption operation to the EMAC construction. A proof of security for 3GPP-MAC was published in 2003 [38], but the proof was shown to be flawed later in the same year [39];

indeed, it was shown that a proof of security for 3GPP-MAC in the "standard" framework is impossible to achieve. However, by making a slightly stronger, albeit reasonable, assumption about the security of the block cipher, Iwata and Kohno [40] have provided a proof of security for 3GPP-MAC.

Section 7.4

MDx-MAC was proposed by Preneel and van Oorschot [41] in 1995. HMAC was proposed in 1996 by Bellare, Canetti, and Krawczyk [21], as a solution to problems with simpler, flawed hash-based MAC constructions involving simply concatenating a key with the data and then applying a hash function. Such MAC schemes are susceptible to forgery attacks arising from the extensible property of hash functions (see Chapter 6). HMAC was first standardized in Internet RFC 2104 [22], before its adoption in ISO/IEC 9797-2 [24]. It has since also been adopted as a U.S. Federal Standard in NIST FIPS PUB 198 [42].

Section 7.5

MAA was originally proposed in 1984 by Davies [43]. The best known attack on MAA is due to Preneel, Rijmen and van Oorschot [44]. PMAC was proposed in 2001 by Black and Rogaway, who submitted it for consideration by NIST. The scheme was not formally published until 2002 [45].

References

[1]   Menezes, A. J., P. C. van Oorschot, and S. A. Vanstone, *Handbook of Applied Cryptography*, Boca Raton, FL: CRC Press, 1997.

[2]   International Organization for Standardization, *ISO/IEC 9797–1, Information Technology—Security Techniques—Message Authentication Codes (MACs)—Part 1: Mechanisms Using a Block Cipher*, 1999.

[3]   International Organization for Standardization, *ISO 15764:2004, Road Vehicles—Extended Data Link Security*, 2004.

[4]   Campbell, C. M., Jr., "Design and Specification of Cryptographic Capabilities," in D. K. Branstad, (ed.), *NBS Special Publication 500-27: Computer Security and the Data Encryption Standard*, U.S. Department of Commerce, National Bureau of Standards, 1977, pp. 54–66.

[5]   National Institute of Standards and Technology (NIST), *Federal Information Processing Standards Publication 81 (FIPS PUB 81): DES Modes of Operation*, December 1980.

[6]   Accredited Standards Committee X9—Financial Services, *ANSI X9.9–1986 (Revised), Financial Institution Message Authentication (Wholesale)*, April 1986.

[7]   Accredited Standards Committee X9—Financial Services, *ANSI X9.19, Financial Institution Retail Message Authentication*, August 1986.

[8]   American Bankers Association, *ANSI X9 TG–24–1999, Technical Guideline: Managing Risk and Migration Planning: Withdrawal of ANSI X9.9, Financial Iinstitution Message Authentication Codes (MAC) Wholesale*, 1999.

[9]   International Organization for Standardization, *ISO 8730: 1986, Banking—Requirements for Message Authentication (Wholesale)*, 2nd ed., 1990.

[10]   International Organization for Standardization, *ISO 8731–1: 1987, Banking—Approved Algorithm for Message Authentication—Part 1: DEA*, 1987.

[11]   International Organization for Standardization, *ISO 8731–2: 1992, Banking—Approved algorithm for Message Authentication—Part 2: Message Authenticator Algorithm*, 2nd ed., 1992.

[12]   International Organization for Standardization, *ISO 9807, Banking and Related Financial Services—Requirements for Message Authentication (Retail)*, 1991.

[13]   International Organization for Standardization, *ISO/IEC 9797: 1989, Data Cryptographic Techniques—Data Integrity Mechanism Using a Cryptographic Check Function Employing a Block Cipher Algorithm*, December 1989.

[14]   International Organization for Standardization, *ISO/IEC 9797: 1994, Information-Technology—Security Techniques—Data Integrity Mechanism Using a Cryptographic Check Function Employing a Block Cipher Algorithm*, 2nd ed., 1994.

[15]   European Telecommunications Standards Institute (ETSI), *3GPP TS 35.201, 3rd Generation Partnership Project; Technical Specification Group Services and System Aspects; 3G Security; Specification of the 3GPP Confidentiality and Integrity Algorithms; Document 1: f8 and f9 Specification*, June 2002.

[16]   Jaulmes E., A. Joux, and F. Valette, "On the Security of Randomized CBC-MAC Beyond the Birthday Paradox Limit: A New Construction," in J. Daemen and V. Rijmen, (eds.), *Proceedings of the 9th International Workshop on Fast Software Encryption (FSE 2002)*, Vol. 2365, *Lecture Notes in Computer Science*, Springer-Verlag, 2002, pp. 237–251.

[17]   National Institute of Standards and Technology (NIST), *NIST Special Publication 800-38B, Draft Recommendation for Block Cipher Modes of Operation: The RMAC Authentication Mode*, October 2002.

[18]   Iwata, T., and K. Kurosawa, "OMAC: One-Key CBC MAC," in T. Johansson, (ed.), *Fast Software Encryption, 10th International Workshop, FSE 2003*, Vol. 2887, *Lecture Notes in Computer Science*, Springer-Verlag, 2003, pp. 129–153.

[19]   Kurosawa, K., and T. Iwata., "TMAC: Two-Key CBC MAC," in M. Joye, (ed.), *Topics in Cryptology—CT-RSA 2003*, Vol. 2612, *Lecture Notes in Computer Science*, Springer-Verlag, 2003, pp. 33–49.

[20]   Black, J., and P. Rogaway, "CBC-MACs for Arbitrary Length Messages: The Three-Key constructions," in M. Bellare, (ed.), *Advances in Cryptology—Crypto 2000*, Vol. 1880, *Lecture Notes in Computer Science*, Springer-Verlag, 2000, pp. 197–215.

[21]   Bellare, M., R. Canetti, and H. Krawczyk, "Keyed Hash Functions and Message Authentication," in N. Koblitz, (ed.), *Advances in Cryptology—Crypto '96*, Vol. 1109 of *Lecture Notes in Computer Science*, Springer-Verlag, 1996, pp. 1–15.

[22]   Krawczyk, H., M. Bellare, and R. Canetti, *RFC 2104, HMAC: Keyed-Hashing for Message Authentication*, Internet Engineering Task Force, February 1997.

[23]   Cheng, P., and R. Glenn, *RFC 2202, Test Cases for HMAC-MD5 and HMAC-SHA-1*, Internet Engineering Task Force, September 1997.

[24]   International Organization for Standardization, *ISO/IEC 9797-2, Information Technology—Security Techniques—Message Authentication Codes (MACs)—Part 2: Mechanisms Using a Hash-Function*, 2000.

[25] Accredited Standards Committee X9—Financial Services, *ANSI X9.71–2000, Keyed Hash Message Authentication Code*, 2000.

[26] Preneel, B., and P. C. van Oorschot, "A Key Recovery Attack on the ANSI X9.19 Retail MAC," *Electronics Letters*, Vol. 32, 1996, pp. 1568–1569.

[27] Knudsen, L. R., and B. Preneel, "MacDES: MAC Algorithm Based on DES," *Electronics Letters*, Vol. 34, 1998, pp. 871–873.

[28] Coppersmith, D., L. R. Knudsen, and C. J. Mitchell, "Key Recovery and Forgery Attacks on the MacDES MAC Algorithm," in M. Bellare, (ed.), *Advances in Cryptology—Crypto 2000*, Vol. 1880, *Lecture Notes in Computer Science*, Springer-Verlag, 2000, 184–196.

[29] Coppersmith, D., and C. J. Mitchell, "Attacks on MacDES MAC Algorithm," *Electronics Letters*, Vol. 35, 1999, pp. 1626–1627.

[30] Knudsen, L. R., and C. J. Mitchell, "Analysis of 3GPP-MAC and Two-Key 3GPP-MAC," *Discrete Applied Mathematics*, Vol. 128, 2003, pp. 181–191.

[31] Knudsen, L. R., and T. Kohno., "Analysis of RMAC," in T. Johansson, (ed.), *Fast Software Encryption, 10th International Workshop, FSE 2003*, Vol. 2887, *Lecture Notes in Computer Science*, Springer-Verlag, 2003, pp. 182–191.

[32] Knudsen, L. R., and C. J. Mitchell, "Partial Key Recovery Attack Against RMAC," *Journal of Cryptology*, to appear.

[33] Mitchell, C. J., *On the Security of XCBC, TMAC and OMAC*, Technical Report RHUL-MA-2003-4, Mathematics Department, Royal Holloway, University of London, August 2003.

[34] Joux, A., G. Poupard, and J. Stern, "New Attacks Against Standardized MACs," T. Johansson, (ed.), *Fast Software Encryption, 10th International Workshop, FSE 2003*, Vol. 2887, *Lecture Notes in Computer Science*, Springer-Verlag, 2003, pp. 170–181.

[35] Bellare, M., J. Kilian, and P. Rogaway, "The Security of the Cipher Block Chaining Message Authentication Code," in Y. G. Desmedt, (ed.), *Advances in Cryptology—Crypto '94*, Vol. 839, *Lecture Notes in Computer Science*, Springer-Verlag, 1994, pp. 341–358.

[36] Petrank, E., and C. Rackoff, "CBC MAC for Real-Time Data Sources," *Journal of Cryptology*, Vol. 13, 2000, pp. 315–338.

[37] Iwata, T., and K. Kurosawa, "Stronger Security Bounds for OMAC, TMAC and XCBC," in T. Johansson and S. Maitra, (eds.), *Progress in Cryptology–Indocrypt 2003*, Vol. 2904, *Lecture Notes in Computer Science*, Springer-Verlag, 2003, pp. 402–415.

[38] Hong, D., "A Concrete Security Analysis for 3GPP-MAC," in T. Johansson, (ed.), *Fast Software Encryption, 10th International Workshop, FSE 2003*, Vol. 2887, *Lecture Notes in Computer Science*, Springer-Verlag, 2003, pp. 154–169.

[39] Iwata, T., and K. Kurosawa, "On the Correctness of Security Proofs for the 3GPP Confidentiality and Integrity Algorithms," in K. G. Paterson, (ed.), *Cryptography and Coding, 9th IMA International Conference*, Vol. 2898, *Lecture Notes in Computer Science*, Springer-Verlag, 2003, pp. 306–318.

[40] Iwata, T., and T. Kohno, "New Security Proofs for the 3GPP Confidentiality and Integrity Algorithms," in W. Meier and B. Roy, (eds.), *Proceedings of FSE 2004*, Vol. 3017, *Lecture Notes in Computer Science*, Springer-Verlag, 2004, pp. 427–444.

[41]   Preneel, B., and P. C. van Oorschot, "MDx-MAC and Building Fast MACs from Hash Functions," in D. Coppersmith, (ed.), *Advances in Cryptology—Crypto '95*, Vol. 963, *Lecture Notes in Computer Science*, Springer-Verlag, 1995, pp. 1–14.

[42]   National Institute of Standards and Technology (NIST), *Federal Information Processing Standards Publication 198 (FIPS PUB 198): The Keyed-Hash Message Authentication Code (HMAC)*, March 2002.

[43]   Davies, D. W., "A Message Authenticator Algorithm Suitable for a Mainframe Computer," in G. R. Blakley and D. Chaum, (eds.), *Advances in Cryptology—Crypto '84*, Vol. 196, *Lecture Notes in Computer Science*, Springer-Verlag, 1985, pp. 393–400.

[44]   Preneel, B., V. Rijmen, and P. C. van Oorschot, "A Security Analysis of the Message Authenticator Algorithm (MAA)," *European Transactions on Telecommunications*, Vol. 8, 1997, pp. 455–470.

[45]   Black, J., and P. Rogaway, "A Block-Cipher Mode of Operation for Parallelizable Message Authentication," in L. R. Knudsen, (ed.), *Advances in Cryptology—Eurocrypt 2002*, Vol. 2332, *Lecture Notes in Computer Science*, Springer-Verlag, 2002, pp. 384–397.

CHAPTER

8

Contents

8.1 Definitions and basic properties

8.2 Standards for digital signatures

8.3 The Digital Signal Algorithm (DSA)

8.4 RSA-based signature schemes

8.5 Digital signatures and the law

8.6 Choosing a digital signature scheme

8.7 Notes

Digital Signatures

Digital signatures were first envisaged in the late 1970s as a possible use for asymmetric cryptography. They are designed to provide all the advantages of real-life contract signatures in a digital setting, allowing people to negotiate contracts over vast distances and very quickly. Previously, contracts could only be signed by hand and so paper copies of these contracts often needed to be sent between signatories several times; now, contracts can be digitally signed at the touch of a button.

A digital signature must mimic several properties of a handwritten signature if it is to be effective. In particular, a digital signature should ensure that the data or contract is not changed after it has been signed and that the signer cannot later on repudiate his or her signing. (Non-repudiation is discussed in detail in Chapter 9.) These properties make digital signature schemes useful in a more general setting, not just for negotiating contracts, and at all levels of the security architecture (see Chapter 3).

8.1 Definitions and basic properties

A digital signature scheme is actually a set of three algorithms:

- A key generation algorithm. Since all digital signature schemes are asymmetric, the key generation algorithm actually produces two keys: a private signing key and a public verification key. The public verification key should be distributed to everyone who may wish to verify a digital signature, whereas the private signing key should be kept secret. In this respect, the private signing key is similar to the private decryption key, and the public verification key is similar to the public encryption key, of an asymmetric encryption scheme (see Chapter 4).

- A signing algorithm. The signing algorithm takes as input the private signing key and the data or message that needs to be signed. It outputs a digital signature of that data.

> ▸ A verification algorithm. The verification algorithm takes as input the public signing key, a digital signature and, possibly, the data that was signed. It either outputs *valid*, which indicates that the given digital signature is a correct signature for that data, or *invalid*, which indicates that the given digital signature is not a correct signature for that data. Optionally, if the given signature is valid, the verification may also output some or all of the message (see Section 8.1.2).

The idea behind a digital signature is that it should be computationally infeasible for any party to compute a correct digital signature without knowing the signing key. This means that a digital signature provides integrity protection for the signed data—as any attacker that alters the data will also need to compute the digital signature for the altered message.

In this way, digital signatures are very similar to message authentication codes (see Chapter 7). In fact, it is often helpful to think of digital signatures as asymmetric MAC schemes.

Just as with MAC algorithms, the inability of an attacker to forge a digital signature means that the signature identifies the source of the message. Since a valid digital signature can only be produced by someone who has access to the signing key, and assuming that only one person has access to that key, a valid digital signature provides data origin authentication. Unlike a MAC algorithm (where, for the scheme to provide a useful authentication method, the secret symmetric key has to be shared between two or more people), a digital signature uniquely identifies the source of the signature and it is possible to prove this fact to a third party. Hence, digital signatures also provide a non-repudiation service.

Just as it is a common mistake to assume that a encryption scheme provides some kind of integrity protection (see Chapter 4), it is often mistakenly thought that a digital signature scheme provides some kind of confidentiality service. Although some signature schemes do protect the confidentiality of the data, many do not, and it is perfectly possible that an attacker who has access to a digital signature may be able to deduce some information about the message that has been signed. The problems associated with sending data in both a confidential and integral manner are briefly discussed in Chapter 16. Reversible signature schemes do not protect the confidentiality of the data, while, generally speaking, nonreversible signature schemes do protect the confidentiality of the data.

Attacks against digital signature schemes   The different types of possible attacks against a digital signature scheme are similar to those possible against a MAC scheme (see Chapter 7). The main security objective of a digital signature scheme is to guarantee that the signature was produced by someone who knew both the message and the private signing key. Hence, it should be infeasible for an attacker to find a correct signature for a message without authorised access to the signing key.

This motivates two different types of attacks against digital signature schemes: *forgery attacks* and *key recovery attacks*. In a forgery attack, an attacker attempts to find a valid signature σ for a message m that has not previously been signed. A good digital signature scheme should be able to resist this kind of attack even if the attacker has access to the public verification key and the correct signatures for a number of other messages, including some that may have been chosen by the attacker themselves.

Some security experts have suggested that good signature schemes should be able to resist an even stronger class of forgery attacks where the attacker is deemed to have broken the scheme if he or she can find either a correct signature for a new message or a new signature for a previously signed message. It is unclear how useful this stronger notion of security is. After all, all the attacker is actually doing is reaffirming the original signer's commitment to a message.

The second type of attack is a key recovery attack, where an attacker tries to determine the private signing key from a series of messages and their signatures and the public verification key. Obviously, if an attacker can successfully perform a key recovery attack then he or she can use the private key to forge messages and so perform a successful forgery attack.

In practice, there have been very few successful key recovery attacks. Most successful attacks against digital signature schemes have been forgery attacks.

The relationship between digital signature schemes and asymmetric encryption schemes
When considering asymmetric cryptography it is often said that digital signature schemes and asymmetric encryption schemes are in some way opposites of each other. In an asymmetric encryption scheme one uses the public key for encryption (i.e., to produce the ciphertext) and the private key for decryption. In an digital signature scheme one uses the private key to produce the "ciphertext" (the digital signature) and the public key to verify it.

This leads people to believe that, in order to construct a digital signature scheme, it is only necessary to run an asymmetric encryption scheme "backwards" (i.e., to keep the encryption key secret and make the decryption key public). The (erroneous) line of thinking is that this makes a good signature scheme because only the holder of the encryption key can encrypt messages and therefore produce signatures. This is a very dangerous way of thinking.

First, asymmetric encryption schemes are designed so that it is infeasible to compute the decryption key from the encryption key. It is often fairly easy to compute the encryption key from the decryption key, hence making the decryption key public (as we would have to do in order to use an asymmetric encryption scheme to produce digital signatures) would invalidate the security of the whole scheme.

Second, an attacker against a digital signature scheme is trying to do something subtly different from an attacker against an asymmetric encryption scheme. In an asymmetric encryption scheme, the attacker is trying to discover some information about the decryption of a *given* ciphertext. In a digital signature scheme, the attacker is trying to produce a new signature for *any* message. This slight difference means that some schemes that are perfectly secure when used for encryption need to be modified to make good digital signature schemes.

A good example of this is the RSA encryption scheme discussed in Chapter 4. Suppose that we use RSA to sign messages using an encryption exponent e (that is kept secret) and a decryption exponent d (that is made public) for a modulus n. If we naively sign messages using RSA "backwards" (i.e., sign message m by computing the signature $\sigma = m^e \bmod n$) then the resulting signature scheme is easily broken by a forgery attack. It is an easy task for an attacker to find a message α and a valid signature β by choosing β to be a random number between 1 and n and computing $\alpha = \beta^d \bmod n$. (This produces a valid message/signature pair because $\alpha^e = \beta \bmod n$ if and only if $\alpha = \beta^d \bmod n$.) Hence, running the RSA encryption scheme "backwards" does not give a secure signature scheme, despite the fact that RSA is (in some sense) a secure encryption scheme.

8.1.1   Deterministic and probabilistic signature schemes

We briefly met the concepts of deterministic and probabilistic schemes when talking about asymmetric encryption schemes in Chapter 4. A deterministic encryption scheme is one in which there is only one valid encryption of any message; a probabilistic encryption scheme is one in which there are lots of ciphertexts that correspond to a message. Hence, the ECB mode of a block cipher (see Chapter 5) is a deterministic encryption schemes, but asymmetric ciphers have to be probabilistic if they are to achieve the high levels of security demanded of them.

A similar situation arises with signature schemes: Signature schemes can be either deterministic or probabilistic. A deterministic signature scheme is one in which there is only one valid signature for each message; a probabilistic signature scheme is one where each message has lots of valid signatures. (although it should still be infeasible to find any of those signatures without knowing the signing key).

Unlike asymmetric encryption schemes, however, there is nothing to say that a deterministic digital signature scheme cannot be secure. Indeed, there are several examples of standardized digital signature schemes that are deterministic. In general, however, it seems to be simpler to construct probabilistic schemes, although these have the drawback of needing to have access to a good source of random bits (see Chapter 16).

At this point it is convenient to introduce some notation that will be used throughout the rest of the book. (As we shall see, digital signature schemes are widely used in building more complex protocols such as entity authentication protocols and key establishment protocols.) Since digital signature schemes are necessarily asymmetric, we need to introduce two keys. We let s_X denote the private (signing) key belonging to the entity X and P_X be the corresponding public (verification) key for X. The authenticity of these keys will need to be established before they can be used (see Chapter 13). We will let $\mathcal{S}$ denote the signing algorithm of the digital signature scheme and $\mathcal{V}$ denote the verification algorithm. Hence, $\mathcal{S}$ is an algorithm that takes a message m and a signing key s_X as input, and outputs a signature σ, whereas

V is an algorithm that takes (at least) a verification key P_X and a signature σ as input and outputs either *valid* or *invalid*. This notation is summarized in Table 8.1.

8.1.2   Reversible and nonreversible signature schemes

It is possible to categorize digital signature schemes in many different ways. We have already seen that it is possible to separate them into schemes that always produce the same signature for any given message (deterministic signature schemes) and those that are likely to produce different signatures if a message is signed more than once (probabilistic signature schemes). Another way to categorize signature schemes is based on whether they are reversible or not.

As the name implies, a reversible digital signature scheme is one in which it is possible to reconstruct a message from a valid signature. In this case, the verification algorithm does more than merely decide whether a given signature is valid: it must first decide if is valid and, if it is valid, it must then recompute the signed message. This means that the verification algorithm of a reversible digital signature scheme only takes a signature σ and a public verification key P_X as input; they do not need to be given a copy of the message m.

It is important to remember, at this stage, that digital signature schemes do not always provide confidentiality. Any message that is signed using a reversible signature scheme will be easily readable by any entity who has access to the public key (and possibly even by those that do not!). It is therefore important to make sure that the use of a reversible signature scheme does not compromise the security objectives of the overall system.

Nonreversible signature schemes are digital signature schemes in which no part of the message can be recovered from the signature. Here the verification algorithm has to do nothing more than decide if the given signature is valid or not. Typically, the verification algorithm of a nonreversible digital signature scheme will take three inputs: the signature σ, the verification key P_X, and the message m of which σ claims to be a signature.

One can argue that is it possible to build a reversible signature scheme from a nonreversible scheme. If S and V are the signing and verification algorithms for a nonreversible signature scheme then it is possible to construct

Table 8.1   Notation for Digital Signature Schemes

Variable	Definition
s_X	The private signing key belonging to entity X
P_X	The public verification key belonging to entity X
S	The signing algorithm
$S(m, s_X)$	A signature produced by signing a message m using the secret key s_X
V	The verification algorithm
$V(\sigma, P_X)$	The result of verifying a signature σ using a public key P_X
$V(m, \sigma, P_X)$	The result of verifying the signature σ of a message m using a public key P_X

reversible signing and verification algorithms $\mathcal{S}'$ and $\mathcal{V}'$ by setting

$$\mathcal{S}'(m, s_X) = m \| \mathcal{S}(m, s_X) \tag{8.1}$$

and

$$\mathcal{V}'(m\|\sigma, P_X) = \begin{cases} \text{invalid} & \text{if } \mathcal{V}(m, \sigma, P_X) = \text{invalid} \\ m & \text{if } \mathcal{V}(m, \sigma, P_X) = \text{valid} \end{cases} \tag{8.2}$$

This demonstrates an important point. Nonreversible signature schemes usually produce signatures that are shorter than the messages they are signing, while reversible signature schemes *must* produce signatures that are longer than the associated message. This is because the signature must also contain an encoding of the message. Since nonreversible signature schemes produce shorter signatures, it may be thought that they are more efficient—this is not necessarily true. While the signature produced by a nonreversible signature scheme is shorter, it is also necessary to send the message along with the signature. When using a reversible signature scheme, only the signature need ever be transmitted.

One problem with reversible signature schemes is that they usually only work for short messages. Longer messages can be sent using partial message recovery. Here the message is split into two parts: a short recoverable part and the remaining nonrecoverable part. The signature is computed using both parts of the message but only the nonrecoverable part need be sent along with the signature. The verification algorithm checks whether the signature is valid and, if it is, outputs the recoverable part of the message.

Last, it should not be thought that the terms "reversible signature scheme" and "nonreversible signature scheme" are consistently used. The ISO/IEC JTC1 committee prefer to use the term "signature scheme with message recovery" for "reversible signature scheme," and "signature scheme with appendix" for "nonreversible signature scheme." The latter term is used because nonreversible signatures are often sent as an appendix to a message.

8.1.3 Identity-based and certificate-based signature schemes

Another way to categorize digital signature algorithms is based on the way in which the public key P_X used to verify a signature is defined. As was mentioned in Chapter 4, the main problem with asymmetric key management is being sure that the public key you have obtained is the correct public key for the entity with which you are attempting to communicate.

Normally, a public key (such as the public verification key used in a digital signature algorithm) is vouched for by a trusted third party, known as a certification authority or CA, which supplies a certificate which attests to the fact that the public key in question does, in fact, belong to the correct entity. This is known as a public-key infrastructure (PKI) and is discussed in detail in Chapter 13. The use of trusted third parties is discussed in Chapter 14.

The alternative to using a PKI is to use an identity-based system. Here the public key can be directly derived from the identity of the person (for example, from his or her e-mail address). This removes the need for certificates, as the public key is directly related to the identity of the entity with whom you wish to communicate, and therefore the public key could *only* belong to that entity. If certificates are not needed then neither are certification authorities, and this removes a expensive component of the overall system.

However, the use of an identity-based system places constraints on the public key. If an entity with a certain identity is going to use the system then its public key *must* be the one that is related to its identity. This means that the public key is fixed beforehand, and only the private key needs to be computed by the key generation algorithm.

Signature schemes that are based on the use of a traditional PKI and certificates are known as *certificate-based signature schemes,* whereas signature schemes based on the use of identities are, unsurprisingly, known as *identity-based signature schemes*. It appears to be more difficult to construct identity-based signature schemes than certificate-based schemes, and they are not commonly used. We will therefore focus our attention on certificate-based signature schemes.

8.2 Standards for digital signatures

The most important standard for digital signatures is, without doubt, NIST FIPS Pub. 186. This standard, known as the Digital Signature Standard (DSS), contains a scheme called the Digital Signature Algorithm (DSA). This is a probabilistic, nonreversible, certificate-based signature scheme that is heavily used within the financial sector. It is currently on its second edition.

As well as NIST, all of the other major standardization bodies have produced digital signature standards. The financial sector has produced several international standards that standardize DSA including ANSI X9.30.1 and ANSI X9.62. DSA is also standardized by the IEEE 1363 group.

The ANSI X9 standardization group has standardized one other signature scheme: a nonreversible signature scheme known as rDSA. This scheme is based on the RSA encryption algorithm (see Chapter 4) and is very similar to the reversible signature scheme that we will be discussing in Section 8.4. The scheme is specified in ANSI X9.31.

The ISO/IEC JTC1 committee has standardized a more diverse portfolio of signature schemes: 11 digital signature schemes in total, split over two multipart standards. The two standards categorize signature schemes according to whether they are reversible or not. ISO/IEC 9796 deals with reversible signature schemes, which it terms "digital signature schemes giving message recovery," whereas ISO/IEC 14888 deals with nonreversible signature schemes, termed "digital signature schemes with appendix."

ISO/IEC 9796 was introduced in 1991 and originally only contained a scheme based on the RSA encryption algorithm (see Chapter 4). This standard was withdrawn in 1999 after the scheme was successfully broken by Coppersmith, Halevi, and Jutla, and, independently, by Grieu. However, at the time that the standard was withdrawn, work had already started in a second and third part of the standard. These parts were published in 1997 and 2000 respectively, with a second edition of ISO/IEC 9796-2 being published in 2002. The withdrawal of the original part means that there is no ISO/IEC 9796-1!

Work started on the ISO/IEC JTC1 standard on nonreversible digital signatures, ISO/IEC 14888, in the mid 1990s. This is a three-part standard. Part 1 contains a general model for nonreversible digital signature schemes and some terms and definitions that are relevant to the other parts, but does not actually standardize any specific signature algorithms. Part 2 standardizes identity-based signature schemes. Part 3 standardizes certificate-based signature schemes. Both the DSA and a variant of the rDSA schemes are standardized in ISO/IEC 14888-3.

Technically, ISO/IEC JTC1 has produced three standards on signature schemes: ISO/IEC 9796, ISO/IEC 14888, and ISO/IEC 15946. The latter standard, ISO/IEC 15946, contains variants of the schemes contained in ISO/IEC 9796 and ISO/IEC 14888 but designed to work on elliptic curve groups. Since we do not consider elliptic curves in this book, we will not discuss these schemes further. It has recently been decided that having such a large number of standards on signature schemes is confusing, and work has begun on integrating the schemes of ISO/IEC 15946 into the other two standards. It is not yet clear whether this will eventually mean that the two other standards, ISO/IEC 9796 and ISO/IEC 14888, will also be merged.

The IETF has endorsed DSA for use within the Internet community. The standards that the IETF has produced on signature schemes (such as the IETF RFC 3075 on the use of signatures in XML documents) all seem to reference NIST FIPS Pub. 186-2 for the technical details of the DSA. These documents concentrate more on the encoding and use of signature schemes than the technical details of a how a signature scheme works.

8.3 The Digital Signal Algorithm (DSA)

DSA is probably the most popular of all of the digital signature schemes. It was first proposed by Kravitz in 1991 and has since been adopted by all the major standardization bodies. It is a certificate-based, nonreversible, probabilistic digital signature scheme.

In almost all nonreversible digital signature schemes, the technical mechanism that produces the signature is not applied to the message itself but to a hashcode computed by applying a hash function to the message. This serves two purposes: First, it produces a short, fixed-length string that is easy to manipulate, and second, it mixes up the messages before they are signed. Hence, two similar messages will have completely different hash codes and so are unlikely to produce similar signatures. The DSA is no exception to this rule; indeed, some standardized versions of the DSA go further, insisting that the SHA-1 hash function be used to compute the hash code. More information about hash functions can be found in Chapter 6.

As we have mentioned, a digital signature scheme is defined by three algorithms: the key generation algorithm, the signing algorithm, and the verification algorithm. We will now describe these algorithms in detail.

Key generation   The DSA key generation algorithm needs to produce both a random public verification key and a private signing key. (The verification key can be chosen using random methods because the signature scheme is certificate based.) Key generation is an important part of the key life cycle (see Chapter 11) and should only be performed by an authorized entity, such as a system's administrator.

A pair of DSA keys are produced as follows:

1. Randomly generate a large prime number p, known as the *modulus*. The modulus p should be at least 512 bits long. The random generation of primes should be done very carefully—see Chapter 16.

2. Randomly generate a large prime q such that q divides into $p - 1$. The prime q is known as the *order* and should be at least 160 bits long.

3. Randomly generate an integer g that has order q modulo p (i.e., an integer between 2 and $p - 1$ for which the smallest number n for which $g^n \equiv 1 \bmod p$ is q). This is known as the *base*. A base can be easily computed by picking any integer h between 2 and $p - 1$ and computing $g = h^{(p-1)/q}$. If $g \neq 1$, then g is a good base.

4. Randomly pick an integer x between 1 and $q - 1$. Set $y = g^x \bmod p$.

5. The public key consists of the modulus p, the order q, the base g and y.

6. The private key consists of the integer x (along with all the elements of the public key).

Note that p, q, and g are sometimes referred to as the public parameters of the scheme because they can be made public and are necessary for both signing and verification. The value y is only needed for verification and so it is sometimes referred to as the public key on its own.

Signing   The signing algorithm works on a message m of arbitrary length. We consider how to sign the message m using a secret key x and a modulus p, an order q, and a base g. To sign a message the following steps are performed.

1. Apply a hash function *hash* to the message m to gain a hash code *hash(m)*. It is important that all parties have previously agreed upon the use of this hash function. For this reason, some standards include picking an appropriate hash function as part of the key generation algorithm.

2. Randomly pick a random value k between 1 and $q - 1$.

3. Compute

$$R = (g^k \bmod p) \bmod q \qquad (8.3)$$
$$S = k^{-1}(hash(m) + xR) \bmod q \qquad (8.4)$$

k^{-1} is the inverse of k modulo q (i.e., the unique value between 1 and q such that $k \cdot k^{-1} \equiv 1 \bmod q$).

4. Output the two parts of the signature: R and S.

Verification   In order to verify a signature, the verification algorithm needs to have access to three things: the message m, the complete signature (R, S), and the public key (which consists of a modulus p, an order q, a base g, and the integer value y). The verification algorithm then performs the following steps:

1. Compute $W = S^{-1} \bmod q$. Hence, W is the unique integer between 1 and q such that $S \cdot W \equiv 1 \bmod q$.

2. Compute $U_1 = W \cdot hash(m) \bmod q$.

3. Compute $U_2 = W \cdot R \bmod q$.

4. Compute $V = (g^{U_1} \cdot y^{U_2} \bmod p) \bmod q$.

The verification algorithm outputs *valid* if $V = R$ and *invalid* otherwise.

From our point of view, it is not very important to understand *why* a valid signature is accepted by the verification algorithm whereas it is thought to be infeasible to forge a signature that the verification algorithm will accept.

The main advantage of the DSA algorithm, apart from its widespread acceptance, is the speed in which signatures can be computed. Since the hash code of the message is only used in computing S, many parts of the signature can be precomputed and stored until they are needed. After a suitably random value k is chosen, the signing algorithm can precompute R, xR and $k^{-1} \bmod q$. This significantly speeds up the signature calculation.

8.4   RSA-based signature schemes

Many of the reversible digital signature schemes are based on the use of the RSA encryption algorithm. In this section we will describe a reversible signature scheme given in ISO/IEC 9796-2. All of the schemes in ISO/IEC 9796-2 are based on similar principles. Nonreversible versions of this scheme are also standardized in ISO/IEC 14888-3 and ANSI X9.31.

Before attempting to understand the material in this section, the reader should be familiar with terminology and notation associated with the RSA encryption scheme (see Chapter 4). When using RSA to produce digital signature schemes, the public verification key will consist of the modulus n and the decryption exponent d. The private signing key will be the encryption exponent e.

In Section 8.1, we discussed the problems with using the RSA encryption scheme to produce digital signatures. The main problem occurs because it easy to find pairs (α, β) such that $\alpha^e = \beta \bmod n$ using only the decryption exponent d. We can do this by choosing a value for the signature β and computing the message $\alpha = \beta^d \bmod n$ associated with that signature.

It is important to note that, in this attack, the attacker can choose the signature β but has little control over the value of α. The security of RSA-based signature schemes comes from the way that α is constructed. Generally, the value α is not the message that needs to be signed but some special encoding of that message known as a *message representative*. The security of an RSA-based signature scheme comes from the fact that it is hard for an attacker to find a signature β such that the associated message representative α is a valid encoding of any message m.

We will describe a simplified version of an ISO/IEC 9796-2 signature scheme. The standardized version of the signature scheme has been generalized so that the public decryption exponent d (the exponent used to verify a signature) can be even. While this results in a slightly more efficient scheme, especially when the public decryption exponent $d = 2$ is used, understanding the (slightly more complicated) mathematics of this improvement will not help explain the methodology of the signature scheme, hence we have omitted it.

The signature scheme we will describe is a certificate-based, deterministic, reversible digital signature scheme. It should be noted that ISO/IEC 9796-2 also contains probabilistic versions of this scheme.

Key generation   Key generation for the RSA-based signature scheme is exactly the same as for the RSA encryption scheme, except that the public verification key comprises the modulus n and the decryption exponent d, and the private signing key comprises the encryption exponent e.

Signing   Suppose m is an a short message. To sign this message using a public key consisting of a modulus n and a decryption exponent d, the following steps are performed.

1. First, construct the message representative α. The message representative consists of five sections:

$$\alpha = header \, \| padding \, \| m \| hash \, \| trailer \tag{8.5}$$

where each of the different sections has a specific purpose:

- The variable *header* consists of a small set of bits that identifies the signature scheme being used.

- The variable *padding* consists of a set of preagreed padding values, used to make sure that the message representative α is the same length as the modulus n.

> • m is the message.

> • The variable *hash* is the hash code of the message computed using a preagreed hash function (see Chapter 6).

> • The variable *trailer* consists of a small sequence of bits that may (optionally) identify the hash function used in computing the hash code.

2. Set $\sigma = \alpha^d \bmod n$.

3. Output the signature σ.

Verification   To verify a signature σ using a modulus n and a private key consisting of an encryption exponent e, the following steps are computed.

1. Compute the message representative $\alpha = \sigma^e \bmod n$.

2. Split the message representative up into the five sections: *header, padding, m, hash,* and *trailer.*

3. Check that the *header, padding,* and *trailer* sections are correct. The format of these sections is specified by the standard; if these sections are not correctly formatted then the signature is declared *invalid.*

4. Optionally, the identity of the hash function can be recovered from the *trailer.*

5. Check that the received hash code *hash* is the same as the hash code computed by applying the hash function to the recovered message m. If the hash code is not the same then the signature is declared *invalid.*

6. Declare that the signature is *valid* and output m.

The idea behind this algorithm is that if an attacker chooses the signature σ in advance then the corresponding message representative α (which is computable using the public key) is unlikely to have the correct format and so the signature will be declared invalid. Alternatively, if the attacker chooses the message representative in advance then he or she will not be able to compute the correct signature σ as he or she does not have access to the private signing key e.

All of the reversible signature schemes in ISO/IEC 9796-2 are similar to this algorithm but, in each case, the message representative is formatted slightly differently. The nonreversible signature scheme known as rDSA (which is standardized in ANSI X9.31 and ISO/IEC 14888-3) is also similar to this scheme but the message m is not included in the message representative.

The advantage of schemes of these forms is that they can be constructed in such a way that their verification algorithm is very fast (unlike the DSA scheme, which has a fast signing algorithm but a slower verification algorithm).

8.5   Digital signatures and the law

The technical specifications are not the only important standardized document that relate to digital signatures. Digital signatures seek a way to mimic handwritten signatures, and, if they are to be effective, this means that they need to be legally binding. It is therefore not surprising that many legal bodies have started examining the effect of digital signatures in law.

Obviously, it is not the intention of this book to describe the intricacies of contract law (nor do we believe we could do the subject justice!) but it is useful for any party interested in digital signatures to be aware of their legal status.

A contract can be defined as a promise that the law will enforce, or the performance of which it in some way recognizes as a duty. A signature is any kind of marking that has been made for the purposes of authenticating a document, including handwritten signatures, typed signatures, and any other kind of mark. The American Bar Association (ABA) notes that signatures can be applied to documents for many different reasons, including the following:

- Evidence. A signature identifies a document with the signer.

- Ceremony. The signing procedure calls the signer's attention to the legal significance of the signer's act.

- Approval. The signer may be approving or authorizing an action by signing a document.

A key criterion in signature law is the signer's intent to sign the document. Signers must be aware that they are about to sign a document, and intend to do so, for a signature to be valid.

8.5.1   U.S. legislation

One of the first pieces of legislation to recognize a digital signature as a valid legal signature was the Utah Digital Signature Act of 1995 (revised in 1996). The publication of this act largely coincided with the publication (and subsequent revision) of the ABA guidelines on digital signatures and their use within electronic commerce. More recently, the United States passed a nationwide bill on the use of digital signatures: the Electronic Signatures in Global and National Commerce Act of 2000, commonly known as the ESIGN legislation.

The ESIGN act is only relevant on interstate and foreign transactions, with local state legislation (such as the Utah Digital Signature Act) taking precedence for intrastate transactions. However, the ESIGN act does note that state legislation can only supersede the ESIGN Act if the alternative procedures or requirements for the "use or acceptance of . . . electronic signatures . . . do not require, or accord greater legal status or effect to" the technical specification for electronic signatures described in the ESIGN act, or if the legislation is an enactment of the Uniform Electronic Transactions Act (UETA).

This essentially means that the intrastate legislation must recognize the level of trust and the legal status of electronic signatures as set down by the ESIGN Act.

The ESIGN Act defines an electronic signature as

> . . . an electronic sound, symbol, or process, attached to or logically associated with, a contract or other record and executed and adopted by a person with the intent to sign the record.

This is vastly different to the concept of a digital signature as we have discussed it up until now! It does not require any mathematical method of binding the document to the signature, and it does not provide an integrity, origin authentication, or non-repudiation service. An electronic signature can be as simple as a typed signature on the bottom of an e-mail or a digital recording of a person agreeing to the contact.

This does not mean that all types electronic signatures are equal under the law. The intent of the ESIGN Act is not to define what constitutes a binding electronic signature—digital signatures as we have discussed them are not even mentioned in the act—but to allow electronic signatures of any kind to be presented as evidence in court. It is the responsibility of the court to decide if a given electronic signature is legally equivalent to a handwritten signature.

The term "digital signature" is not defined in the ESIGN act but is defined by both the Utah Digital Signature Act and the ABA digital signature guidelines. The ABA guidelines define a digital signature as follows.

> A transformation of a message using an asymmetric cryptosystem and a hash function such that a person having the initial message and the signer's public key can accurately determine:
>
> 1. Whether the transformation was created using the private key that corresponds to the signer's public key;
>
> 2. Whether the initial message has been altered since the transformation was made.

This, and other parts of the guidelines, strongly suggests that at the time the guidelines were published, the ABA considered a digital signature to be the result of using an irreversible digital signature scheme. This is not surprising—the idea of a irreversible digital signature being appended to a document is the natural extension of the use of a handwritten signature. The Utah Digital Signature Act defines a digital signature in exactly the same way except that the requirement that a hash function be involved is removed.

The advantage of the ABA guidelines over the ESIGN act is that the ABA guidelines specifically state that a digitally signed message, along with an appropriately certified public verification key—see Chapter 13—is "as valid, effective, and enforceable as if the message had been written on paper." Furthermore, a digital signature constitutes a legal signature provided that it has been "(1) affixed by the signer with the intention of signing the message, and (2) verified by reference to the public key listed in a valid certificate." Essentially, this affords a digital signature and a digital contract the same status in law as a paper contract and a handwritten signature.

8.5.2 Certification authorities

A public key infrastructure (PKI) and the use of a certification authority (CA) in particular are the methods whereby a public verification key can be associated with a single person. Standards for PKIs and certification authorities will be discussed in detail in Chapter 13, and we do not intend to preempt that discussion here; however, it is useful to note that a CA must accept certain responsibilities if a signature is to be considered binding in a court of law.

A digital signature cannot be linked to a person unless the public verification key for that signature can also be linked to that person. A CA often provides that link and, if a digital signature is to be given weight in a court of law, it must do so within a certain legal framework. For example, for a certificate (which is an electronic document that states that a particular public verification key belongs to a particular individual) to be valid in court, it must be signed by the CA using an electronic signature that is recognized by that court.

Both the U.S. legislation (discussed in Section 8.5.1) and the EU legislation (discussed in Section 8.5.3) describe the responsibilities and requirements of a certification authority in some depth.

8.5.3 EU legislation

The European Union has chosen to follow a similar path to the United States when dealing with digital signatures. Enforced by a European Union directive (Directive 1999/93/EC), each of the EU member states must enact legislation that recognizes electronic signatures as legally admissible in court. Just as in the U.S. ESIGN act, the EU directive states that an electronic signature cannot be denied legal effectiveness and admissibility just because it is in electronic form.

The EU definition of an electronic signature is similar to the U.S. definition. It reads:

> "Electronic signature" means data in electronic form which are attached to or logically associated with other electronic data and which serve as a method of authentication.

The EU directive, however, goes further than the ESIGN act and defines an "advanced electronic signature" as

> ... an electronic signature which meets the following requirements:
>
> 1. It is uniquely linked to the signatory;
>
> 2. It is capable of identifying the signatory;

3. It is created using means that the signatory can maintain under his or her sole control;

4. It is linked to the data to which it relates in such a manner that any subsequent change of the data is detectable.

Hence, a digital signature counts as more than just an electronic signature under EU law—it counts as an advanced electronic signature. An advanced electronic signature that has been created using a secure signature creation device and that is based upon a qualified (valid and secure) certificate shall

> satisfy the legal requirements of a signature in relation to data in electronic form in the same manner as a handwritten signature satisfies those requirements in relation to paper-based data.

This means that, under EU law, a sufficiently secure digital signature is equivalent to a handwritten signature.

The United Kingdom has enacted the EU directive in the Electronic Communications Act 2000. The act recognizes the admissibility of electronic signatures in U.K. courts but leaves it to the court to decide whether an electronic signature has been correctly used, and what weight it should be given, in a particular case. It is interesting to note that the Electronic Communications Act makes no mention of advanced electronic signatures, nor their legal standing.

The Electronic Communications Act also mandates that the government should keep a record of all "approved providers of cryptography support services," including certification authorities. The approval of the government will only be provided if the company is willing to comply with any requirements that the government chooses to impose on these support services, although the act specifically states that the government may not impose a "key escrow" requirement. Note that this arrangement does not prohibit a company from offering a cryptographic support service without approval from the U.K. government; it merely acts a register for service providers that have been "independently assessed against particular standards of quality."

8.6 Choosing a digital signature scheme

There are, as always, several issues to consider when choosing a digital signature scheme. The first is the level of interoperability required. If the system is expected to interact with external systems then it is sensible to use a signature scheme compatible with those systems. In particular, if the system is to be used within the financial sector then it makes sense to use one of the two ANSI-standardized schemes: DSA and rDSA.

The choice between DSA and rDSA will depend heavily on the purpose for which the scheme will be use. DSA, like most discrete logarithm–based schemes, is useful in a multiuser environment and may allow for the quick signing of messages. The integer factorization–based schemes, such as rDSA, do not adapt as well to the multiuser setting but tend to allow for the quick verification of signed messages.

If interoperability is not required, or does not significantly restrict the choices available to you, then the next point to consider is whether message recovery is required. Many uses of digital signature schemes, particularly those that use the scheme as part of a protocol for some other security purpose, do not require message recovery. In this case it is far more bandwidth efficient to use a nonreversible signature scheme (such as DSA or rDSA). Of course, even if message recovery is required then it still may be convenient to use a nonreversible signature scheme and to simply append the signature to the message.

Should a reversible signature scheme be desired then one is forced to select a scheme from ISO/IEC 9796. The arguments for and against choosing a discrete logarithm–based scheme or an integer factorization–based scheme are similar to the arguments for choosing DSA or rDSA. Nonreversible schemes can be selected from ISO/IEC 14888 or any of the standards from the financial sector. Identity-based signature schemes are rarely used (although, due to recent research, this attitude may be changing).

The last point to consider is legal obligation. If the signature is being used in a situation where legal non-repudiation is required (i.e., in a situation where forging a signature will result in a contract being contested in a court of law) then the signature scheme must conform to the legal restrictions discussed in Section 8.5.

8.7 Notes

Section 8.1

The idea that a digital signature could replace a handwritten signature was first proposed in the seminal paper by Diffie and Hellman [1]. This was also the paper that first introduced the notion of asymmetric cryptography. While this paper introduced the idea of a digital signature, it wasn't until about a decade later that the security requirements for a digital signature scheme that we now accept as being correct were introduced.

The notion of forgery that we have used in Section 8.1 was first introduced by Goldwasser, Micali, and Rivest in a paper published in 1988 [2]. Before this time it was considered impossible to find a signature scheme that was unforgeable in this sense.

The stronger notion of forgery, where an attack is deemed successful if the attacker forges a signature for a new message or finds a new signatures for a previously signed message, was introduced later; see, for example, [3].

It is, as was stated in the main body of the text, unclear how useful the stronger notion of forgery is. It is possible to imagine a situation where finding such a forgery would break the intent of the system: Consider, for example, a situation where Alice orders drinks from Bob on-line. Alice may repeatedly send in the same order, and hence the same message, and so Bob might be concerned about making sure that a new message he receives is genuine and not just an old message being resent by an attacker. (This property is called message freshness and is quite a common problem in designing security protocols; see Chapter 10.) In order to convince himself that a message is genuine, he requires Alice to digitally sign the message and only believes that the message is genuine if it contains a new signature that he has not seen before.

Such a system would require that the signature scheme used satisfied the stronger notion of unforgeability in order to work. Such a system would also be unwieldy and is unlikely to be used in practice, as more elegant solutions to the freshness problem exist (see Chapter 10).

For deterministic schemes, where each message has only one possible signature, the two notions of unforgeability are equivalent.

By now it should not come as much of a surprise for the reader to discover that descriptions of many popular digital signature schemes can be found in Menezes et al. [4]. A more mathematical treatment of the field of digital signatures can be found in Stinson [5].

The example of how to construct a reversible signature scheme from a nonreversible signature scheme demonstrates how it is necessary to send the message along with signature when using a nonreversible scheme. So, in practice, the reversible signature scheme that we constructed is often the scheme that is actually used.

We did not show that it is possible to construct a nonreversible signature scheme from a reversible signature scheme. If S and V are the signing and verification algorithms of a reversible signature scheme, then it is possible to construct a nonreversible signature scheme by setting the signing and verification algorithms, S' and V', to be

$$S'(m, s_X) = S(m, s_X)$$

and

$$V'(m, \sigma, P_X) = \begin{cases} \text{valid} & \text{if } m = V(\sigma, P_X) \\ \text{invalid} & \text{otherwise} \end{cases}$$

Unlike the previous example, where a reversible scheme was constructed from a nonreversible scheme, this scheme is of little use and is very unlikely to be used in practice.

Identity-based cryptography, that is, asymmetric cryptography where the public key can be derived from the recipients identity, has huge advantages. Because the public key is intrinsically bound to the identity of the entity to whom the key belongs, there is no need to install an expensive public key infrastructure to authenticate that key. While we have not explicitly stated it, it is important to know to which "domain" a user belongs before attempting to derive his or her public key. This domain will define exactly how to derive the public key from a user's identity.

However, there are also some problems that are intrinsically associated with using identity-based cryptography. Since a user's public key is defined by his or her identity, the key generation algorithm can no longer be a random process but must be deterministic. In order to make this process secure, private keys must be generated by a trusted third party that has some extra, secret knowledge about the signature scheme. This means that the trusted third party has complete control over the key generation process and has access to the private key of all the other entities in the system.

There is also a problem with revocation. Once a private key has been issued for an identity by the trusted third party, that private key will be valid forever. Hence there must be some extra mechanism in place to inform users if a public key is revoked. On-line key status discovery protocols, as discussed in Section 13.6 of Chapter 13, are particularly useful in this respect. Another interesting solution is to derive a public key from a combination of the user's identity and the current date. The user will only be able to obtain the associated private key if the TTP that controls key generation will issue that private key to the user; hence, the TTP can revoke a user simply by refusing to issue it with the correct private keys for a particular date. The key revocation problem will be discussed in more detail, along with certificate-based public-key infrastructures, in Chapter 13.

Section 8.2

The Digital Signature Algorithm, contained in the Digital Signature Standard [6], is also contained in several other important standards, including ANSI X9.30.1 [7], ISO/IEC 14888-3 [8], and IEEE 1363 [9].

There is also a standardized elliptic curve version of the DSA (known as ECDSA) [6, 9–11]. Elliptic curves are complex mathematical structures that appear to have some useful cryptographic properties. A good introduction to elliptic curve cryptography, including information on the ECDSA, is given by Hankerson, Menezes, and Vanstone [12]. More technical information on the use of elliptic curves in cryptography can be found in Blake et al. [13], and the security of ECDSA is discussed in detail in [14].

The DSA and ECDSA signature schemes have also be recently evaluated by the NESSIE project in terms of its security and performance [15, 16]. It was evaluated against several other signature schemes, some of which have also been standardized, and judged to be one of the best of the proposed schemes.

The other signature scheme endorsed by the financial sector is known as rDSA and is specified in ANSI X9.31 [17].

The original signature scheme contained in ISO/IEC 9796 [18] was attacked by Coron, Naccache, and Stern [19], although they do not manage to completely break the scheme. The scheme was eventually broken by Coppersmith et al. [20] and by Grieu [21]. There are no known attacks against the schemes contained in either ISO/IEC 9796-2 [22] or ISO/IEC 9796-3 [23].

The general-purpose ISO/IEC standard on nonreversible signature schemes is ISO/IEC 14888. It consists of three parts: a general introduction [24], a series of identity-based mechanisms [25], and a series of certificate-based mechanisms [8]. Many of the schemes contained in ISO/IEC 14888-3 can also be implemented using elliptic curve techniques. These schemes are standardized in ISO/IEC 15946 [11].

As we have mentioned, IETF RFCs have tended to endorse other signature standards, such as the Digital Signature Algorithm, rather than standardize new signature schemes of their own. IETF documents and standards, such as IETF RFC 3075 [26], tend to concentrate on describing the practical uses of signature schemes.

Section 8.3

The Digital Signature Algorithm was first introduced by Kravitz as a proposed NIST FIPS standard in 1991 and was officially declared a standard in 1994 [6]. It is also the subject of a U.S. patent (U.S. patent number 5,231,668), although no license is required for its use.

For a proof of the correctness of the DSA algorithm, see Stinson [5]. A short proof is also contained in an appendix of NIST FIPS 186-2 [6].

It should be noted that there is a small chance that the DSA algorithm will fail to verify a valid signature. This happens if $S \equiv 0 \bmod q$. In this case it is impossible to invert S modulo q, that is, there is no integer value W such that $S \cdot W \equiv 1 \bmod q$. Hence, the verification algorithm fails at step 1.

Also, if the DSA is to be used by more than one entity in a system, it is not necessary for each entity to generate a complete new public key. The public parameters of the system (p, q, and g) can be used by every participant. This means that each entity only has to generate a secret key x between 1 and $q - 1$, and a public value $y = g^x \bmod p$.

It is easy to show that the DSA signature scheme is insecure whenever the same value k is used to sign two different messages. Suppose (R, S) and (R, S') are signatures for two different messages m and m', but that both of these signatures have been computed using the same value of k. It is easy to see that

$$S - S' = k^{-1}(\text{hash}(m) - \text{hash}(m')) \bmod q$$

and so

$$k = \frac{\text{hash}(m) - \text{hash}(m')}{S - S'} \bmod q$$

From here it is easy to recover the private key x as

$$x = \frac{Sk - \text{hash}(m)}{R}$$

It should be clear that attack can also be used if an attacker can find out the value k used to create a signature (R, S) for a message m. Nguyen and Shparlinski [27] have gone further and shown that it is possible to recover the private key if only a fraction of the bits of k are known to the attacker. Bleichenbacher [28] also proposed an attack against DSA by noting that, in the original specification of the algorithm, small values of $k \bmod q$ were more likely to occur than larger ones. The DSS was subsequently changed to make sure that k is chosen randomly out of all possible values.

Section 8.4

The use of RSA as a signature scheme was first proposed in the initial paper on the RSA scheme by Rivest, Shamir, and Adleman [29]. The method they proposed is very similar to the methods used today—to prove the integrity of a message by supplying an encrypted version of that message or a hash code of that message. Since that paper, the main efforts in this area have been to find efficient ways of securely formatting the message representative before encryption.

More details on the improved RSA signing function can be found in ISO/IEC 9796-2 [22].

It is possible to adapt the given scheme to provide partial message recovery. It should be noted that the current scheme can only sign messages that are at most the size of the modulus less the size of the *hash*, *header*, and *trailer* fields. The scheme can be extended to sign messages of any length. Here we split a message m into two parts: a recoverable part m_1 and a nonrecoverable part m_2. The recoverable part of the message m_1 must be short enough that it can be included in the message representative. The message representative is constructed as before but only the recoverable part of the message is included, that is, the message representative has the form:

$$\alpha = header \, \| padding \, \| m_1 \| hash \, \| trailer$$

It is important that the hash code is still computed by applying the hash function to the whole message m.

Signature verification is given in the obvious way. The verification algorithm recomputes the message representative from the signature and checks that the hash code is valid using both the recoverable part of the message contained in the message representative and the nonrecoverable part which must be sent along with the signature. If the signature is valid (i.e., the hash codes match), then the recoverable part of the signature is released.

Unlike the DSA scheme, RSA-based signature schemes cannot be used by more than one user. If two users wish to use RSA based signature schemes, then they must both compute completely separate public and private keys, and no parameters can be shared or the entire scheme is compromised.

Section 8.5

There are several technical (i.e., nonlegal) books that discuss the status of digital signatures in law, including Adams and Lloyd [30] and Ford and Baum [31]. Rosenoer [32] is, by now, a little out of date but does contain material on earlier developments, such as the Utah Digital Signature Act. The definitions of "contract" and "signature" in Section 8.5 are adapted from this latter source.

Electronic signatures are given legal status in the United States by the ESIGN Act [33]. This follows certain state-wide legislation such as the Utah Digital Signature Act [34] and the advice of the American Bar Association [35].

It is interesting to note that there are some unusual definitions and seemingly paradoxical results of the U.S. legislation. For example, the ESIGN Act specifically notes that a recording of an oral communication shall not qualify as an electronic record but that a recorded sound may act as an electronic signature. It is also interesting to note that the Utah Digital Signature Act defines an "asymmetric cryptosystem" as "an algorithm or series of algorithms which provide a secure key pair." This somewhat contradicts the definitions we have been using in this book!

EU directive 1999/93/EC [36] mandates that all European Union member states should enact legislation that allows electronic signatures to be presented as evidence in court. It also notes that the EU has the right to recommend digital signature schemes by publishing references to well-defined standards. Such a recommendation has been published as ETSI SR 002176 [37] and includes references to ISO/IEC 14888-3 [8], IEEE 1363 [9], and FIPS 186-2 [6].

The United Kingdom has enacted this EU directive in the Electronic Communications Act [38]. Advice on interpreting this act can be found in the explanatory notes provided by the U.K. government [39] and the Law Commission Report [40].

Both the U.S. and the EU legislations recognize the need for a digital signature to be verified using a public key that has been correctly validated (see Chapter 13), and both the ESIGN Act and the EU directive 1999/93/EC state the requirements that a certificate authority (CA) must satisfy in order to be considered secure. The IETF has produced a profile for qualified certificates (the EU notion of a secure certificate) for use on the Internet. This profile is contained in IETF RFC 3039 [41].

References

[1]   Diffie, W., and M. E. Hellman, "New Directions in Cryptography," *IEEE Transactions on Information Theory*, Vol. 22, 1976, pp. 644–654.

[2]   Goldwasser, S., S. Micali, and R. L. Rivest, "A Digital Signature Scheme Secure Against Adaptive Chosen Message Attacks," *SIAM Journal of Computing*, Vol. 17, No. 2, April 1988, pp. 281–308.

[3]   Goldreich, O., *Foundations of Cryptography: Basic Applications*, Cambridge, England: Cambridge University Press, 2004.

[4]   Menezes, A. J., P. C. van Oorschot, and S. A. Vanstone, *Handbook of Applied Cryptography*, Boca Raton, FL: CRC Press, 1997.

[5]   Stinson, D. R., *Cryptography: Theory and Practice*, Boca Raton, FL: CRC Press, 1995.

[6]   National Institute of Standards and Technology (NIST), *Federal Information Processing Standards Publication 186-2 (FIPS PUB 186-2): Digital Signature Standard (DSS)*, January 2000.

[7]   Accredited Standards Committee X9—Financial Services, *ANSI X9.30.1, Public Key Cryptography for the Financial Services Industry—Part 1: The Digital Signature Algorithm (DSA)*, 1997.

[8] International Organization for Standardization, *ISO/IEC 14888-3: 1998, Information Technology—Security Techniques—Digital Signatures with Appendix—Part 3: Certificate-Based Mechanisms*, 1998.

[9] Institute of Electrical and Electronics Engineers, *IEEE Standard Specifications for Public-Key Cryptography*, 2000.

[10] Accredited Standards Committee X9—Financial Services, *ANSI X9.62, Public Key Cryptography for the Financial Services Industry: The Elliptic Curve Digital Signature Algorithm (ECDSA)*, 1998.

[11] International Organization for Standardization, *ISO/IEC 15946, Information Technology—Security Techniques—Cryptographic Techniques Based on Elliptic Curves*, 2002.

[12] Hankerson, D., A. J. Menezes, and S. Vanstone, *Guide to Elliptic Curve Cryptography*, New York: Springer-Verlag, 2004.

[13] Blake, I., G. Seroussi, and N. Smart, *Elliptic Curves in Cryptography*, Cambridge, England: Cambridge Univeristy Press, 1999.

[14] Blake, I., G. Seroussi, and N. Smart, *Elliptic Curves in Cryptography II: Further Topics*, Cambridge, England: Cambridge University Press, 2004.

[15] New European Schemes for Signatures, Integrity and Encryption (NESSIE), *NESSIE Security Report*, version 2.0, http://www.cryptonessie.org/, 2003.

[16] New European Schemes for Signatures, Integrity and Encryption (NESSIE), *Performance of Optimized Implementations of the NESSIE Primitives*, version 2.0, http://www.cryptonessie.org/, 2003.

[17] Accredited Standards Committee X9—Financial Services, *ANSI X9.31, Digital Signatures Using Reversible Publis Key Cryptography for the Financial Services Industry (rDSA)*, 1998.

[18] International Organization for Standardization, *ISO/IEC 9796, Information Technology—Security Techniques—Digital Signature Scheme Giving Message Recovery*, September 1991.

[19] Coron, J. S., D. Naccache, and J. P. Stern, "On the Security of RSA Padding," in M. Weiner, (ed.), *Advances in Cryptology—Crypto '99*, Vol. 1666, *Lecture Notes in Computer Science*, Springer-Verlag, 1999, pp. 1–18.

[20] Coppersmith, D., S. Halevi, and C. Jutla, "ISO 9796-1 and the New Forgery Strategy," http://grouper.ieee.org/groups/1363/Research/Cryptanalysis.html, 1999.

[21] Grieu, F., "A Chosen Message Attack on the ISO/IEC 9796-1 Signature Scheme," in B. Preneel, (ed.), *Advances in Cryptology—Eurocrypt 2000*, Vol. 1233, *Lecture Notes in Computer Science*, Springer-Verlag, 2000, pp. 70–80.

[22] International Organization for Standardization, *ISO/IEC 9796-2: 2002, Information Technology—Security Techniques—Digital Signature Schemes Giving Message Recovery—Part 2: Integer Factorization Based Mechanisms*, 2nd ed., 2002.

[23] International Organization for Standardization, *ISO/IEC 9796-3: 2000, Information Technology—Security Techniques—Digital Signature Schemes Giving Message Recovery—Part 3: Discrete Logarithm Based Mechanisms*, 2000.

[24] International Organization for Standardization, *ISO/IEC 14888-1: 1998, Information Technology—Security Techniques—Digital Signatures with Appendix—Part 1: General*, 1998.

[25]   International Organization for Standardization, *ISO/IEC 14888-2: 1999, Information Technology—Security Techniques—Digital Signatures with Appendix—Part 2: Identity-Based Mechanisms*, 1999.

[26]   Eastlake, D., J. Reagle, and D. Solo, *RFC 3075, XML-Signature Syntax and Processing*, Internet Engineering Task Force, March 2001.

[27]   Nguyen, P. Q., and I. E. Shparlinski, "The Insecurity of the Digital Signature Algorithm with Partially Known Nonces," *Journal of Cryptology*, Vol. 15, No. 3, 2002, pp. 151–176.

[28]   Bleichenbacher, D., "On the Generation of DSA One-Time Keys," *6th Workshop on Elliptic Curve Cryptography (ECC 2002)*, 2002.

[29]   Rivest, R. L., A. Shamir, and L. Adleman. "A Method for Obtaining Digital Signatures and Public-Key Cryptosystems, *Communications of the ACM*, Vol. 21, 1978, pp. 120–126.

[30]   Adams, C., and S. Lloyd, *Understanding PKI: Concepts, Standards, and Deployment Considerations*, 2nd ed., Reading, MA: Addison-Wesley, 2003.

[31]   Ford, W., and M. S. Baum, *Secure Electronic Commerce*, 2nd ed., Upper Saddle River, NJ: Prentice Hall, 2001.

[32]   Rosenoer, J., *Cyberlaw: The Law of the Internet*, New York: Springer-Verlag, 1997.

[33]   Government of the United States of America, *Electronic Signatures in Global and National Commerce Act*, 2000, http://frwebgate.access.gpo.gov/cgi-bin/getdoc.cgi?dbname=106_cong_bills&docid=f:s761enr.txt.pdf.

[34]   Utah State Legislature, *Utah Digital Signature Act*, 1996, http://www.le.state.ut.us/~code/TITLE46/TITLE46.htm.

[35]   American Bar Association, *Digital Signature Guidelines: Legal Infrastructure for Certification Authorities and Secure Electronic Commerce*, 1996, http://www.abanet.org/scitech/ec/isc/dsg.pdf.

[36]   European Parliament and the Council of the European Union, *Directive 1999/93/EC of the European Parliament and of the Council on a Community Framework for Electronic Signatures*, 1999, http://europa.eu.int/eur-lex/pri/en/oj/dat/2000/l_013/l_01320000119en00120020.pdf.

[37]   European Telecommunications Standards Institute (ETSI), *ETSI SR 002176, Electronic Signatures and Infrastructures (ESI); Algorithms and Parameters for Secure Electronic Signatures*, March 2003.

[38]   Government of the United Kingdom, *Electronic Communications Act 2000*, 2000, http://www.hmso.gov.uk/acts/acts2000/20000007.htm.

[39]   Government of the United Kingdom, *Explanatory Notes to Electronic Communications Act 2000*, 2000, http://www.hmso.gov.uk/acts/en/2000en07.htm.

[40]   Law Commission, *Electronic Commerce: Formal Requirements in Commercial Transactions*, 2001.

[41]   Santesson, S., et al., *RFC 3039, Internet X.509 Public Key Infrastructure: Qualified Certificates Profile*. Internet Engineering Task Force, January 2001.

CHAPTER

9

Contents

9.1 Introduction

9.2 Standards for non-repudiation

9.3 Non-repudiation model and services

9.4 Non-repudiation using symmetric cryptography

9.5 Non-repudiation using asymmetric cryptography

9.6 Time-stamping and non-repudiation

9.7 Notes

Non-Repudiation Mechanisms

Non-repudiation is one of the five main classes of security services defined in the OSI security architecture (see Chapter 3). A non-repudiation service enables the participant in a communications session to prevent another party in the session from denying having taken a particular action (e.g., having sent or received a message). In this chapter we consider ways in which this service may be provided, all of which relate to the generation of evidence of an event or action, that, when necessary, can be used later to help resolve any dispute as to what actually occurred.

9.1 Introduction

The OSI security architecture defines two main types of non-repudiation. The first, and probably most fundamental, is *non-repudiation of origin,* in which the recipient of a message is provided with the means to prevent the originator of the message from denying having sent it. In paper-based communications, such a service is conventionally provided by the use of a handwritten signature, where the signed document constitutes the *non-repudiation evidence*. Of course, not only can a handwritten signature be forged, but it also only applies to the piece of paper on which it is written. Thus, to provide evidence of the origin of a multipage document, it is necessary to manually sign (or at least initial) each page of the document, as is commonly required for legally binding documents.

The other service defined in the OSI security architecture is *non-repudiation of delivery,* in which the sender of the message is provided with the means to prevent the recipient of the message from denying having received it and having recognized its content. In paper-based communications such a service is typically provided by requiring the recipient of a message to manually sign a receipt for the document. Here, as in systems based on cryptography, a fundamental problem arises if the recipient takes the document but refuses to sign a receipt (i.e., refuses to provide the evidence needed to resolve a subsequent dispute

159

about whether or not the document was received). Of course, in a conventional environment the damage can be limited because the delivery agent will have witnessed the refusal of the recipient to provide a receipt; however, in an electronic environment (e.g., where the message is an e-mail) there will typically be no witnesses to the act of receipt and refusal to generate a receipt. This is an issue we return to later in the chapter.

Fundamental to practical use of a non-repudiation mechanism is the means to resolve disputes. That is, a mechanism provides evidence that can be used to resolve disputes, but such evidence will be of little or no value in the absence of a *non-repudiation policy* specifying how evidence should be generated and managed and how the evidence should be used in the event of a dispute.

The remainder of this chapter is structured as follows. Section 9.2 contains a review of the main standards for non-repudiation mechanisms. Section 9.3 reviews a model for the provision of non-repudiation and definitions of the various types of non-repudiation service. Sections 9.4 and 9.5 then provide descriptions of possible non-repudiation mechanisms based on symmetric and asymmetric cryptography respectively. Finally, Section 9.6 considers the use of a time-stamping service in the context of non-repudiation.

9.2 Standards for non-repudiation

The only standard for non-repudiation mechanisms is ISO/IEC 13888. This multipart ISO/IEC standard specifies techniques for the provision of non-repudiation services. It overlaps to some extent with standards on digital signatures (see Chapter 8), since digital signatures can also be used to provide non-repudiation services.

However, ISO/IEC 13888 is not just concerned with digital signatures. Part 1 gives a general model for the provision of non-repudiation, including a discussion of the role of trusted third parties, and describes at a high-level how non-repudiation services can be provided. The use of tokens is also discussed. Finally, several non-repudiation services are defined, as discussed in Section 9.3.3.

Part 2 discusses the provision of non-repudiation services using symmetric cryptographic techniques. Such schemes require the on-line involvement of a TTP or *notary*. Part 3, covering asymmetric cryptography, is concerned with how digital signature techniques can be used to provide these types of services.

9.3 Non-repudiation model and services

ISO/IEC 13888 Part 1 provides a framework for the description of specific non-repudiation mechanisms, as given in Parts 2 and 3. We first describe the underlying model, and then consider the non-repudiation services in the context of this model.

9.3.1   A model for non-repudiation

ISO/IEC 13888-1 defines a detailed model for the provision of non-repudiation services, identifying for each type of non-repudiation the entity (or entities) that provide the service, and the entity that benefits from the service. In every case, "providing the service" means providing evidence that the event in question took place. In fact, as far as ISO/IEC 13888 is concerned, events regarding which non-repudiation services are provided are always connected to the delivery of a message from its originator to the intended recipient.

The model is shown in Figure 9.1, in which the solid arrows represent the transport of a message, and the dotted arrows represent the possible provision of non-repudiation services. In the latter case the direction of the arrow is from the provider of the evidence to the user of the evidence (i.e., the entity to which the service is being provided).

The main entities in the model are described as follows.

▸ The *originator* (i.e., the entity that originates the message with respect to which non-repudiation of services are to be provided);

▸ The *recipient* (i.e., the entity to which the message is being sent by the originator);

▸ One or more *delivery authorities* (i.e., the entities responsible for transferring the message from the originator to the recipient).

Note that, in some cases, there may be no delivery authorities (i.e., the message is transferred directly from the originator to the recipient). In such a case, some of the non-repudiation services (e.g., non-repudiation of submission and transport) are undefined.

Finally note that there are other important entities not shown in the model. Specifically, a TTP (the *evidence verification authority*) will be required to validate evidence at some time after its generation in order to resolve disputes.

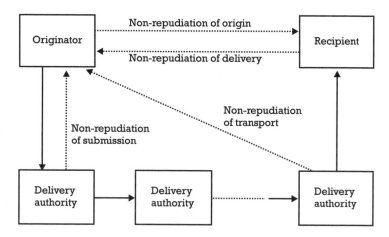

Figure 9.1   Non-repudiation model.

Other TTPs, including notaries and *observers* (otherwise known as *monitoring authorities*), may also be involved in evidence generation.

9.3.2 Types of evidence

ISO/IEC 13888–1 identifies two main types of evidence, namely that provided using MACs, as described in Chapter 7, and that provided using digital signatures (see Chapter 8).

ISO/IEC 13888-1 actually defines the notion of a *secure envelope*, which essentially consists of data whose integrity and origin is to be guaranteed, concatenated with a MAC computed on that data using a secret key—that is,

$$\text{SENV}_K(D) = D\|\text{MAC}_K(D) \tag{9.1}$$

where K is the secret key, D is the data being protected, and "SENV" denotes the secure envelope function. The use of MACs to provide non-repudiation services requires the active involvement of a TTP in the generation as well as the validation of non-repudiation evidence. Non-repudiation mechanisms based on MACs are the main focus of ISO/IEC 13888-2.

By contrast, the use of digital signatures only requires active TTP involvement in evidence validation. Non-repudiation mechanisms using digital signatures are the focus of ISO/IEC 13888-3.

9.3.3 Non-repudiation services

A total of eight non-repudiation services are defined in ISO/IEC 13888-1. Among them are the following four services, which are likely to be the most important. In fact, parts 2 and 3 of ISO/IEC 13888 only define mechanisms to provide these four services (although modified versions of these mechanisms can be used to provide the other four services). Each of these services is provided by giving evidence to the party being given protection.

- *Non-repudiation of origin*, which protects against the message originator falsely denying having originated the message. As shown in Figure 9.1, this service is provided by the originator to the recipient.

- *Non-repudiation of submission*, which protects against a message delivery authority falsely denying acceptance of the message from the originator. As shown in Figure 9.1, this service is provided by the delivery authority that initially receives the message from the originator to the originator.

- *Non-repudiation of transport*, which protects against a message delivery authority falsely denying delivery of the message to the recipient. As shown in Figure 9.1, this service is provided by one of the delivery authorities to the originator.

- *Non-repudiation of delivery*, which protects against the message recipient falsely denying the receipt and initial processing of the message. As shown in Figure 9.1, this service is provided by the recipient to the originator.

The other four services defined in ISO/IEC 13888-1 are described as follows:

- *Non-repudiation of creation,* which protects against a message creator denying having created all or part of the content of a message;

- *Non-repudiation of knowledge,* which protects against the recipient falsely denying having read or otherwise having taken notice of the content of a message (e.g., executing a program);

- *Non-repudiation of receipt,* which protects against the false denial of the recipient that he or she has received the message;

- *Non-repudiation of sending,* which protects against the false denial of the originator having actually sent the message (as opposed to having originated it).

Given that no specific mechanisms to provide these latter four services have been defined, we do not discuss them further here, except to note that the differences between non-repudiation of origin, creation, and sending are very small, as are the differences between non-repudiation of delivery, receipt, and knowledge.

9.3.4 Non-repudiation tokens

ISO/IEC 13888-1 defines three different types of *non-repudiation tokens* (i.e., pieces of cryptographically protected evidence). The classification is based on the type of entity that generates the token. Note that all tokens will either contain a secure envelope based on a MAC, or a digital signature, as well as the message (or a function of the message) with respect to which non-repudiation services are being provided.

- A *generic non-repudiation token* is generated by an originator, a recipient, or a delivery authority.

- A *time-stamping token* is generated by a special TTP known as a *time-stamping authority* (TSA). A time-stamping token can be used to provide evidence as to the time prior to which a piece of evidence was generated. Time-stamping authorities are discussed in detail in Chapter 14.

- A *notarization token* is generated by a notary TTP and provides evidence that the notary has been passed certain data by a specified entity. Thus such a token is evidence that the specified entity has indeed seen the data at the time the token is generated.

Apart from cryptographic values and the message, the token will typically contain a variety of other information, including entity and policy identifiers and one or more time-stamps (i.e., date/time values indicating when an event occurred).

9.4 Non-repudiation using symmetric cryptography

ISO/IEC 13888-2 describes a set of four mechanisms providing non-repudiation services using a combination of symmetric cryptography (i.e., MACs) and a trusted third party. The four non-repudiation services covered by these mechanisms are non-repudiation of origin, delivery, submission, and transport. We describe two of these four mechanisms in detail and then briefly summarize the other two mechanisms.

Note that ISO/IEC 13888-2 also describes examples of how the basic set of four mechanisms can be combined in practice to provide more than one non-repudiation mechanism, although we do not consider these examples here.

In both the mechanisms we describe we suppose that the originator (entity A) is to send a message m to the recipient (entity B), and suppose also that A and B both trust a trusted third party T. We suppose also the following.

- "MAC" and h are a MAC function and a cryptographic hash function agreed by all the parties (see Chapters 6 and 7, respectively).

- A and T share a secret key K_A.

- B and T share a secret key K_B.

- T possesses a secret key K_T.

9.4.1 Non-repudiation of origin using MACs

We first describe the mechanism for providing non-repudiation of origin. This mechanism is actually an exchange of messages (a *non-repudiation exchange*), which we refer to here as a *protocol* for simplicity.

As shown in Figure 9.2, the mechanism operates as follows:

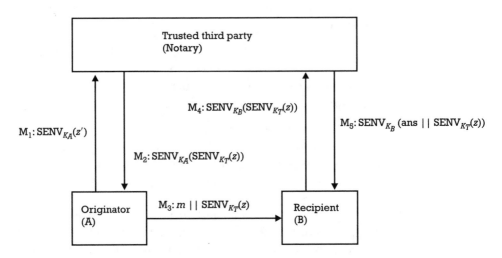

Figure 9.2 Non-repudiation of origin using MACs.

$M_1 : A \rightarrow T : \text{SENV}_{K_A}(z')$

   where $z' = P||i_A||i_B||i_T||[i_O]||[Q]||h(m)$;

$M_2 : T \rightarrow A : \text{SENV}_{K_A}(\text{SENV}_{K_T}(z))$

   where $z = P||i_A||i_B||i_T||[i_O]||t_T||[Q]||h(m)$;

$M_3 : A \rightarrow B : m \, || \, \text{SENV}_{K_T}(z)$;

$M_4 : B \rightarrow T : \text{SENV}_{K_B}(\text{SENV}_{K_T}(z))$;

$M_5 : T \rightarrow B : \text{SENV}_{K_B}(\text{ans}||\text{SENV}_{K_T}(z))$.

where

  ‣ i_A, i_B, and i_T are identifiers for A, B, and T, respectively, and (optionally) i_O is an identifier for an observer, if present.

  ‣ $\text{SENV}_K(D)$ is a secure envelope computed using the secret key K on data D such that

$$\text{SENV}_K(D) = D||\text{MAC}_K(D) \tag{9.2}$$

  ‣ P denotes an identifier for the non-repudiation policy (or policies) in force.

  ‣ (Optional) Q is any other data to be protected.

  ‣ t_T is a time-stamp generated by the TTP T (indicating the time at which the evidence was generated).

  ‣ "ans" is one bit indicating whether or not the non-repudiation evidence is valid.

The following processing is associated with the protocol. A first generates message M_1 using the key K_A shared with T. On receipt of M_1, T verifies the MAC inside the secure envelope and checks that the fields in the data part of the secure envelope are as expected. If the checks succeed, T generates a time-stamp t_T, and generates $\text{SENV}_{K_T}(z)$, as evidence to be provided to B. T then creates M_2 and sends it to A.

On receipt of M_2, A verifies the MAC in the secure envelope using K_A. A also checks that the fields contained in z match those sent to T in message M_1, and that the time-stamp t_T contained in z is current. If the checks succeed, A now sends message m and the evidence $\text{SENV}_{K_T}(z)$ to B as message M_3.

When B receives M_3, B needs to obtain assurance from T that the evidence is current and valid. B first computes $h(m)$ using the received message m and compares it with the value in $\text{SENV}_{K_T}(z)$. If this check fails then B knows that the evidence is invalid and terminates the protocol. Otherwise B assembles M_4, using the key K_B shared with T, and sends it to T. On receipt of M_4, T verifies the MAC inside the secure envelope and checks that the fields in the data part of the secure envelope are as expected, and that the time-stamp t_T is current. Depending on the results of the checks, T sets "ans" accordingly, and then generates and sends message M_5.

When B receives M_5, B verifies the MAC in the secure envelope, checks the value of "ans," and checks that $\text{SENV}_{K_T}(z)$ is as expected. After verifying M_5, B retains $\text{SENV}_{K_T}(z)$ as evidence that A really did send message m to B.

It is important to note that, during the protocol, T does not see message m. In the event of a dispute, B can provide the message M and the evidence $\text{SENV}_{K_T}(z)$ to an adjudicating party. This party can then contact the TTP T and provide it with $\text{SENV}_{K_T}(z)$. The TTP can check whether or not this evidence is valid and indicate the result of the check to the adjudicator.

9.4.2 Non-repudiation of delivery using MACs

We next describe the mechanism for providing non-repudiation of delivery. As above, we suppose that the originator (entity A) sends a message m to the recipient (entity B), and suppose also that A and B both trust a trusted third party T.

As shown in Figure 9.3, the mechanism operates as follows.

$M_1 : A \rightarrow B : m$;

$M_2 : B \rightarrow T : \text{SENV}_{K_B}(z')$

   where $z' = P||i_A||i_B||i_T||[i_O]||t_B||[Q]||h(m)$;

$M_3 : T \rightarrow B : \text{SENV}_{K_B}(\text{SENV}_{K_T}(z))$

   where $z = P||i_A||i_B||i_T||[i_O]||t_T||t_B||[Q]||h(m)$;

$M_4 : B \rightarrow A : \text{SENV}_{K_T}(z)$;

$M_5 : A \rightarrow T : \text{SENV}_{K_A}(\text{SENV}_{K_T}(z))$;

$M_6 : T \rightarrow A : \text{SENV}_{K_A}(\text{ans}||\text{SENV}_{K_T}(z))$.

where

- i_A, i_B, and i_T are identifiers for A, B, and T, respectively, and (optionally) i_O is an identifier for an observer, if present.

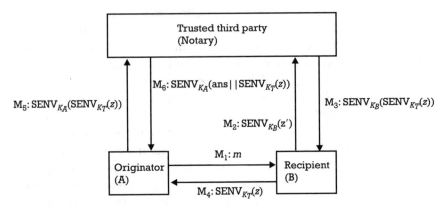

Figure 9.3 Non-repudiation of delivery using MACs.

- $\text{SENV}_K(D)$ is a secure envelope computed using the secret key K on data D, as above:

$$\text{SENV}_K(D) = D\|\text{MAC}_K(D) \tag{9.3}$$

- P denotes an identifier for the non-repudiation policy (or policies) in force.

- (Optional) Q is any other data to be protected.

- t_B is a time-stamp generated by the recipient (indicating the time at which m was received).

- t_T is a time-stamp generated by the TTP T (indicating the time at which the evidence was generated).

- "ans" is a bit indicating whether or not the non-repudiation evidence is valid.

The following processing is associated with the protocol. A first sends the message m to B. When B receives the message, B generates a time-stamp t_B, and then generates message M_2 using the key K_B shared with T. On receipt of M_2, T verifies the MAC inside the secure envelope and checks that the fields in the data part of the secure envelope are as expected. If the checks succeed, T generates a time-stamp t_T and generates $\text{SENV}_{K_T}(z)$ as evidence to be provided to A. T then creates M_3 and sends it to B.

On receipt of M_3, B verifies the MAC in the secure envelope using K_B. B also checks that the field z matches that sent to T in message M_2 and that the time-stamp t_T contained in z is current. If the checks succeed, B now sends the evidence $\text{SENV}_{K_T}(z)$ to A as message M_4.

When A receives M_4, A needs to obtain assurance from T that the evidence is current and valid. A first computes $h(m)$ using the message m and compares it with the value in $\text{SENV}_{K_T}(z)$. If this check fails then A knows that the evidence is invalid and terminates the protocol. A also checks that the time-stamps t_B and t_T are acceptably current for subsequent use as evidence. If these checks succeed, A assembles M_5, using the key K_A shared with T, and sends it to T. On receipt of M_5, T verifies the MAC inside the secure envelope and checks that the fields in the data part of the secure envelope are as expected and that the time-stamp t_T is current. Depending on the results of the checks, T sets "ans" accordingly and then generates and sends message M_6.

When A receives M_6, A verifies the MAC in the secure envelope, checks the value of "ans," and checks that $\text{SENV}_{K_T}(z)$ is as expected. After verifying M_6, A retains $\text{SENV}_{K_T}(z)$ as evidence that B has indeed received the message m.

As for the previous protocol, T does not see message m. In the event of a dispute, A can provide the message m and the evidence $\text{SENV}_{K_T}(z)$ to an adjudicating party. This party can then contact the TTP T, and provide it with $\text{SENV}_{K_T}(z)$. The TTP can check whether or not the evidence is valid, and indicate the result of the check to the adjudicator.

Note that problems can arise if the recipient refuses to provide evidence of successful delivery. There are a number of ways this problem can be addressed. For example, the originator could also require delivery authorities to provide non-repudiation of transport, so that the originator has evidence that the message reached the recipient. Alternatively, in the context of an ongoing communications relationship, the originator could terminate all dealings with the recipient on the first occasion that the recipient refuses to provide evidence of message receipt.

9.4.3 Other mechanisms

ISO/IEC 13888-2 does contain two other mechanisms, one providing non-repudiation of submission and the other non-repudiation of transport. These two mechanisms operate in a very similar way to the non-repudiation of delivery mechanism described immediately above. That is, the delivery authority obtains the evidence from the TTP and passes it to the originator, who then asks the TTP to verify the evidence.

9.5 Non-repudiation using asymmetric cryptography

Part 3 of ISO/IEC 13888 describes how to construct and use digitally signed tokens to provide non-repudiation services. More specifically, it defines four types of tokens:

- A *non-repudiation of origin (NRO) token* is sent from the originator to the recipient and provides the recipient with non-repudiation of origin.

- A *non-repudiation of delivery (NRD) token* is sent from the recipient to the originator and provides the originator with non-repudiation of delivery.

- A *non-repudiation of submission (NRS) token* is sent from the delivery authority that first receives the message from the originator back to the originator and provides the originator with non-repudiation of submission.

- A *non-repudiation of transport (NRT) token* is sent from a delivery authority to the originator and provides the originator with non-repudiation of transport.

Sections 9.5.1 and 9.5.2 describe the format of NRO and NRD tokens.

9.5.1 Non-repudiation of origin using signatures

Suppose originator A wishes to send a message m to recipient B, and that A wishes to provide B with non-repudiation of origin using signatures.

The originator will be required to possess a signature key pair, and the recipient will need to have a trusted copy of the originator's public key. This could be achieved using a public key certificate (see Chapter 13) or by some other means. The originator then sends the message m in an NRO token, where an NRO token is defined to have the following format:

$$z||S_A(z) \tag{9.4}$$

where

$$z = P||f||i_A||i_B||[i_T]||t_A||[t'_A]||[Q]||h(m) \tag{9.5}$$

and $S_A(X)$ denotes the signature of A on data string X, f is a flag indicating that this is an NRO token, i_T is an (optional) identifier for a TTP, t_A is the time when the token was generated, t'_A is (optionally) the time at which the message was sent, and P, i_A, i_B, Q and h are as defined in Section 9.4. Note that here and in Section 9.5.2, $S_A(X)$ is used as a convenient shorthand for $\mathcal{S}(X, s_A)$, as defined in Chapter 8.

On receipt of the token, the recipient verifies the signature using the trusted copy of A's public signature verification key. If it is valid then the token is retained as evidence of the origin of the message.

9.5.2   Non-repudiation of delivery using signatures

Suppose originator A sends a message m to recipient B, and that B wishes to provide non-repudiation of delivery to A using signatures. The recipient will be required to possess a signature key pair, and the originator will need to have a trusted copy of the recipient's public key. As previously, this could be achieved using a public key certificate (see Chapter 13) or by some other means.

After A has sent the message m to B, B responds by sending A an NRD token, where an NRD token is defined to have the following format:

$$z||S_B(z) \tag{9.6}$$

where

$$z = P||f'||i_A||i_B||[i_T]||t_B||[t'_B]||[Q]||h(m) \tag{9.7}$$

and $S_B(X)$ denotes the signature of B on data string X, f' is a flag indicating that this is an NRD token, i_T is an (optional) identifier for a TTP, t_B is the time when the token was generated, t'_B is (optionally) the time at which the message was received, and P, i_A, i_B, Q, and h are as defined in Section 9.4.

On receipt of the token, the originator verifies the signature using the trusted copy of B's public signature verification key. If it is valid then the token is retained as evidence of delivery of the message.

Just as for mechanisms based on MACs, problems can arise if the recipient refuses to provide evidence of successful delivery. There are a number of ways this problem can be addressed. Similar solutions to those proposed in Section 9.4.2 apply.

9.5.3   Other mechanisms

The formats of NRS and NRT tokens are very similar to those of NRO and NRD tokens, and we do not discuss them further here.

9.6   Time-stamping and non-repudiation

An informative annex to ISO/IEC 13888-3 describes the use of a TTP to provide a time-stamping service. Such a service involves a TTP adding a time-stamp and its signature to data provided by a requester. This data could be a previously signed non-repudiation token. As discussed in Chapter 14, the use of such a time-stamping service is vital if signatures, and hence non-repudiation tokens, are to have long term validity. The addition of a trusted third party time-stamp protects against subsequent revocation or expiry of the private key used to sign the non-repudiation token.

9.7   Notes

Section 9.1

Zhou's book on non-repudiation [1] provides a very detailed analysis of the topic. Earlier works of note on the topic include the 1997 Ph.D. theses of Roe [2] and Zhou [3]. A discussion of the concept of repudiation in law can be found in Appendix I of [4].

Section 9.2

ISO/IEC 13888 Parts 1–3 were published in 1997 and 1998 [5–7]. Part 1 is currently being revised, and the FDIS text was published in 2003 [8].

Section 9.3

A detailed discussion of non-repudiation services and mechanisms for the provision of such services can be found in Chapter 9 of [4].

Section 9.4

A number of authors have proposed more complex non-repudiation protocols designed to force message recipients to provide the evidence necessary to provide non-repudiation of delivery. For example, Zhou and Gollmann [9] proposed the use of a TTP which does not release the key necessary to decrypt a message until it receives a signed receipt (essentially an NRD token); to prevent denial of service attacks where messages from the TTP are blocked, the TTP is required to post the decryption key for the message on a public Web site. This and other solutions are also discussed in [10] (see also [1]).

Section 9.5

The use of digital signatures to provide non-repudiation services is in most cases inextricably linked with the use of public key infrastructures (discussed in Chapter 13) and TTP services, especially time-stamping services (discussed in Chapter 14).

References

[1]   Zhou, J., *Non-Repudiation in Electronic Commerce*, Norwood, MA: Artech House, 2001.

[2]   Roe, M., "Non-Repudiation and Evidence," Ph.D. thesis, University of Cambridge, 1997.

[3]   Zhou, J., "Non-Repudiation," Ph.D. thesis, Royal Holloway, University of London, 1997.

[4]   Ford, W., and M. S. Baum, *Secure Electronic Commerce*, 2nd ed., Upper Saddle River, NJ: Prentice Hall, 2001.

[5]   International Organization for Standardization, *ISO/IEC 13888–1: 1997, Information Technology—Security Techniques—Non-Repudiation—Part 1: General*, 1997.

[6]   International Organization for Standardization, *ISO/IEC 13888–3: 1997, Information Technology—Security Techniques—Non-Repudiation—Part 3: Mechanisms Using Asymmetric Techniques*, 1997.

[7]   International Organization for Standardization, *ISO/IEC 13888–2: 1998, Information Technology—Security Techniques—Non-Repudiation—Part 2: Mechanisms Using Symmetric Techniques*, 1998.

[8]   International Organization for Standardization, *ISO/IEC FDIS 13888–1: 2003, Information Technology—Security Techniques—Non-Repudiation—Part 1: General*, 2nd ed., 2003.

[9]   Zhou, J., and D. Gollmann, "A Fair Non-Repudiation Protocol," *Proceedings: 1996 IEEE Symposium on Security and Privacy*, IEEE Computer Society Press, 1996, pp. 55–61.

[10] Zhou, J., R. Deng, and F. Bao, "Evolution of Fair Non-Repudiation with TTP," in J. Pieprzyk, R. Safavi-Naini, and J. Seberry, (ed.), *Information Security and Privacy, 4th Australasian Conference, ACISP '99*, Vol. 1587, *Lecture Notes in Computer Science*, Springer-Verlag, 1999, pp. 258–269.

Contents

10.1 Introduction

10.2 Standards for entity authentication protocols

10.3 Cryptographic mechanisms

10.4 Timeliness checking mechanisms

10.5 Authentication using symmetric cryptography

10.6 Authentication using asymmetric cryptography

10.7 Manual authentication protocols

10.8 Choosing an authentication protocol

10.9 Notes

Authentication Protocols

While data origin authentication and data integrity are almost inevitably provided together, entity authentication is a completely different matter. As discussed in Chapter 3, entity authentication is concerned with verifying the identity of a party with whom communications are taking place. As a result, the provision of this service almost inevitably involves a series of messages being exchanged between the parties concerned, each transfer of a message being known as a *pass* of the protocol.

Such a sequence of messages is normally called an *entity authentication protocol*, or simply an authentication protocol (we use this shorter term throughout). For historical reasons, the term "authentication mechanism" is instead used throughout ISO/IEC 9798. However, the term authentication protocol is used almost universally elsewhere.

Entity authentication can only be achieved for a single instant in time. Typically, an authentication protocol is used at the start of a connection between a pair of communicating entities. If security (e.g., confidentiality and integrity) is required for information subsequently exchanged during the life of the connection, then other cryptographic mechanisms will need to be used (e.g., encryption and the use of MACs) to protect that data. The keys needed for these cryptographic operations can be agreed or exchanged as part of the authentication protocol—this is covered further in Chapter 12 on key establishment mechanisms.

Thus, one application of entity authentication is "authenticated session key establishment." Other applications exist that are not directly related to session key exchange. Examples of such applications include the following:

▸ Secure clock synchronization;

▸ Secure RPC (remote procedure call);

▸ Secure transactions.

However, details of applications of authentication protocols are outside the scope of this book.

10.1 Introduction

ISO 7498-2 (see Chapter 3) defines entity authentication as "the corroboration that an entity is the one claimed." It is also possible to distinguish
between protocols providing unilateral authentication and those providing
mutual authentication. *Unilateral authentication* is defined as "entity authentication that provides one entity with assurance of the other's identity but
not vice versa" and *mutual authentication* is defined as "entity authentication
that provides both entities with assurance of each other's identity."

Throughout this chapter we will refer to the two entities who are involved
in an authentication protocol as A and B—if you prefer you can think of
them as Alice and Bob, although explicit references to gender are avoided
here. After all, A and B will almost inevitably be computers or dedicated
electronics rather than people, although they may be acting on behalf of
individuals.

We also use notation in line with that employed in earlier chapters, specifically:

- [...]: the inclusion of fields within square brackets indicates they are
  optional.

- Cert_X denotes the public key certificate of entity X.

- $e_K(X)$ denotes the ciphertext resulting from the symmetric encryption
  of data string X using the secret key K.

- $e_A(X)$ denotes the ciphertext resulting from the asymmetric encryption of data string X using the public encryption key of entity A (this
  is used as a convenient shorthand for the notation $\mathcal{E}(X, e_A)$, defined
  in Chapter 12).

- i_X denotes an identifier (name) for any entity X.

- K_{AB} denotes a secret key shared by A and B.

- $\text{MAC}_K(X)$ denotes the MAC computed on data string X using the
  secret key K.

- $S_A(X)$ denotes the digital signature on data string X computed using
  the private key of entity A (this is used as a convenient alternative to
  the notation $\mathcal{S}(X, s_A)$, defined in Chapter 8).

- $X\|Y$ denotes the concatenation of blocks of bits X and Y.

- $X \oplus Y$ denotes the bit-wise exclusive-or (exor) of blocks of bits X and
  Y (of the same length).

The remainder of this chapter is structured as follows. Section 10.2 summarizes relevant standards documents. Sections 10.3 and 10.4 review the
cryptographic and noncryptographic mechanisms that can be used as part
of an authentication protocol. The protocols themselves are described in the
next three sections: Section 10.5 is concerned with protocols using symmetric

cryptography, Section 10.6 with protocols using asymmetric cryptography, and Section 10.7 with manual authentication protocols (i.e., protocols involving manual intervention at the authenticating devices). Finally, Section 10.8 describes the factors that need to be considered when choosing an authentication protocol.

10.2   Standards for entity authentication protocols

ISO/IEC has published a multipart standard, ISO/IEC 9798, specifying a general-purpose set of authentication protocols. The five parts published so far have the following coverage:

- ISO/IEC 9798-1—a general part, containing definitions of terms and notation, and a simple model of an authentication protocol;

- ISO/IEC 9798-2—specifying protocols based on the use of symmetric encryption;

- ISO/IEC 9798-3—specifying protocols based on the use of digital signatures;

- ISO/IEC 9798-4—specifying protocols based on the use of MACs;

- ISO/IEC 9798-5—specifying a range of *zero knowledge* protocols (see Section 10.3.4 for a brief introduction to zero knowledge protocols).

A further part (Part 6), which is under development, contains a series of "manual authentication" protocols. These protocols are designed to enable two personal devices that share an insecure communications channel to authenticate one another with the assistance of their owners, who are required to manually transfer data between the devices.

The protocols specified in ISO/IEC 9798 are intended for use in a variety of application domains. As such they have been designed to be as "robust" as possible [i.e., they have been specifically engineered to resist all known attacks (as long as they are used in the way specified)].

Three other bodies have produced entity authentication standards, namely ITU-T (formerly CCITT), NIST, and the IETF. ITU-T X.509 (better known for its specifications for public key and attribute certificates) contains three authentication protocols based on the use of digital signatures. NIST FIPS Pub. 196 also contains a set of authentication protocols based on the use of digital signatures; however, these are a subset of those standardized in ISO/IEC 9798-3.

Internet RFC 1510 contains a specification of version 5 of the Kerberos authentication protocol, based on the use of symmetric cryptography. Because of the widespread use of this protocol, we discuss this protocol in more detail in Section 10.5. A further authentication protocol known as S/KEY, designed specifically for authentication of users to a remote server, is specified in RFC 1760. This is based on use of a cryptographic hash function (see Chapter 6). An authentication protocol (DASS) based on the use of digital signatures is given in RFC 1507. Finally, note that a discussion of the particular authentication requirements of the Internet can be found in RFC 1704.

10.3 Cryptographic mechanisms

Authentication protocols require the use of a combination of either shared secrets (keys or passwords) or signature/verification key pairs. These are used to ensure that the recipient of a protocol message knows the following:

> ▸ Where it has come from (origin authentication);

> ▸ That it has not been interfered with (data integrity).

A variety of different types of cryptographic mechanism can be used to provide integrity and origin authentication for individual protocol messages. We consider five main possibilities, which form the basis of the mechanisms standardized in ISO/IEC 9798.

> ▸ Symmetric encryption;

> ▸ Use of a MAC function (or cryptographic check function);

> ▸ Use of a digital signature;

> ▸ Use of asymmetric encryption;

> ▸ Use of other asymmetric cryptographic techniques.

We next consider each of these options in a little more detail. However, it is important to note that cryptographic mechanisms by themselves cannot provide all the functions making up an authentication protocol. Most importantly, they do not guarantee freshness (i.e., the verification that a protocol message is not simply a replay of a previously transmitted (valid) protocol message, protected using a currently valid key). This is a topic we return to in Section 10.4.

10.3.1 Using symmetric encryption

Symmetric encryption algorithms form the basis of all the mechanisms standardized in ISO/IEC 9798-2, and encryption is also the main cryptographic technique used in the Kerberos scheme. To use symmetric encryption to protect a message in a protocol, the sender enciphers it with a secret key known only to the sender and recipient. The recipient can then verify the origin of the message by first deciphering the message and then checking that it "makes sense" (i.e., that its structure is in accordance with rules implicitly or explicitly agreed between the two parties). If the message does make sense, then the recipient can deduce that it must therefore have been encrypted using the correct secret key, and since only the genuine sender knows this key, it must therefore have been sent by the claimed originator.

This reasoning makes a number of assumptions about the nature of the encryption algorithm and the capabilities of the recipient. First and foremost, if this process is to be performed automatically by a computer (as we would expect), then we need to define what "makes sense" means for a computer, especially as the contents of the message might include random session keys and random *challenges*. We also assume that an interceptor cannot manipulate an enciphered message (without knowledge of the key used to encipher it) in such a way that it still "makes sense" after decipherment. This constrains the type of encryption algorithm that is suitable for use in this application; for example, stream ciphers are usually unsuitable for use as part of an authentication protocol.

The usual solution to this problem is the addition of deliberate *redundancy* (according to some agreed formula) to the message prior to encryption. The presence of this redundancy can then be automatically checked by the recipient of the message (after decipherment). One common method of adding redundancy to a message is to calculate a manipulation detection code (MDC), a sort of checksum dependent on the entire message, and append it to the message prior to encryption. The MDC calculation function will typically be a public function, and could, for example, be instantiated using a hash function (see Chapter 6).

Of course, for this latter approach to work, the methods for adding redundancy and encryption must not allow an attacker (without knowledge of the secret encryption key) to construct an enciphered message for which there is a non negligible probability that the deciphered version will possess "correct" redundancy. This must hold even if the attacker has access to large numbers of intercepted encrypted messages. The selection of appropriate combinations of redundancy and encryption mechanisms is a non trivial task, which makes this approach a somewhat problematic one. Of course, the problem can be solved by replacing the (public) MDC function with a keyed MAC; however, the obvious solution is then to adopt protocols based purely on MACs. Probably the best solution is simply to implement encryption using an authenticated encryption mechanism—see Chapters 5 and 16.

10.3.2 Using MACs

MAC functions are used in the mechanisms standardized in ISO/IEC 9798-4 and ISO/IEC 9798-6 (although ISO/IEC 9798-4 refers to them as *cryptographic check functions*). A MAC function takes as input a secret key and a message and gives as output a MAC (i.e., a fixed length value). There are a variety of possible types of MAC functions, as described in detail in Chapter 7. We only remark here that, by appending it to the message upon which it is computed, a MAC can be used to provide data origin authentication. The recipient of the message can recompute the MAC using the received version of the message and a copy of the shared secret key—if the recomputed value agrees with the received value then the recipient can be confident that the message originates from a possessor of the secret key.

10.3.3 Using digital signatures

Digital signatures form the basis of mechanisms standardized in ISO/IEC 9798-3, ITU-T X.509, and NIST FIPS Pub. 196. As discussed in Chapter 8, a digital signature function is an example of a public key scheme (i.e., an asymmetric cryptographic technique). A fundamental property of asymmetric schemes is that keys come in matching pairs made up of a public key and a private key and that knowledge of the public key of a pair does not reveal knowledge of the private key. The pair of keys for a digital signature algorithm are the following.

▸ A private *signing key*, which defines the signature transformation and which is known only to the key pair owner;

▸ A public *verification key*, which defines the verification transformation and which can be made available to any party needing to verify signatures originating from the owner of the private key.

A signature will typically function somewhat like a MAC; that is, the possessor of the private key uses it to derive the digital signature of a message, which is then appended to the message. As discussed in Chapter 8, this is known as a nonreversible signature scheme. The recipient then uses the public verification key to check the signature. If the signature verifies correctly, then the recipient can be sure of the origin and integrity of a message, since a fundamental property of a digital signature scheme is that the creation of a valid digital signature requires knowledge of the private key.

When we present protocols based on digital signatures we implicitly assume that a nonreversible signature scheme is used. That is, when one party sends another a signed data string, the protocol message includes all the data to be signed as well as the signature on the data. If the protocol is implemented using a reversible signature scheme (i.e., one in which part or all of the data string can be recovered from the signature), then the data that can be recovered from the signature does not actually need to be sent.

10.3.4 Zero-knowledge protocols

The (draft) second edition of ISO/IEC 9798-5 contains a total of six zero-knowledge protocols, based on the use of a variety of different asymmetric cryptographic techniques. In any authentication protocol, the party being authenticated proves its identity by demonstrating knowledge of a secret or private key—in that respect, zero-knowledge protocols are no different from other authentication protocols. However, zero knowledge protocols have the additional property that there is a mathematical proof that an observer (including the other legitimate party in the protocol) learns absolutely nothing about the secret or private key as a result of executing the protocol.

10.3.5 Using asymmetric encryption

Two of the six zero-knowledge protocols are based on the use of asymmetric encryption. These protocols operate rather differently from those based on symmetric encryption, since in an asymmetric setting anyone can encrypt using a public key, but only the owner of the matching private key can decrypt. Thus a party can authenticate itself using asymmetric encryption by proving it can decrypt an encrypted data string. That is, if one party (e.g., *A*) sends the other party (e.g., *B*) a data string encrypted using *B*'s public key, then *B* can authenticate itself to *A* by sending back a message that is a function of the plaintext data string.

10.3.6   Using other asymmetric cryptographic techniques

The other four zero-knowledge protocols in ISO/IEC 9798-5 are rather different from all the other standardized protocols in that they do not use general-purpose cryptographic primitives (such as encryption or signature schemes); instead they use primitives specifically designed for the protocol.

10.4   Timeliness checking mechanisms

As we have already briefly noted, providing origin and integrity checking for protocol messages is not all that is required. We also need a means of checking the "freshness" of protocol messages to protect against replays of messages from previous valid exchanges. There are two main methods of providing freshness checking:

▸ The use of time-stamps (either clock-based or "logical" time-stamps);

▸ The use of nonces or challenges (as in the challenge-response protocols employed for user authentication).

We consider these two approaches in turn.

10.4.1   Time-stamps

Clearly the inclusion of a date/time-stamp in a message enables the recipient of a message to check it for freshness, as long as the time-stamp is protected by cryptographic means. However, in order for this to operate successfully all entities must be equipped with securely synchronized clocks. Providing these clocks is a nontrivial task (the clock drift of a typical PC can be 1–2 seconds/day).

Every entity receiving protocol messages will need to define a time acceptance "window" on either side of their current clock value. A received message will then be accepted as "fresh" if and only if its time-stamp falls within this window. This acceptance window is needed for two main reasons:

▸ Clocks vary continuously, and hence no two clocks will be precisely synchronized, except perhaps at some instant in time.

▸ Messages take time to propagate from one machine to another, and this time will vary unpredictably.

The use of an acceptance window is itself a possible security weakness, since it allows for the undetectable replays of messages for a period of time up to the length of the window. To avert this threat, each entity is required to store a "log" of all recently received messages, specifically all messages received within the last t seconds, where t is the length of the acceptance window. Any newly received message is then compared with all the entries in the log and if it is the same as any of them then it is rejected as a replay. Note that, in the discussions of example protocols using time-stamps, this message log checking is not explicitly mentioned.

As discussed previously, a fundamental problem associated with the use of time-stamps is the question of how synchronized clocks should be provided. One solution is to use a cryptographically protected secure clock service. This can be implemented by building it upon an authentication protocol not based on time-stamps (e.g., one based on nonces—see the following) that is employed at regular intervals to distribute a master clock value; the value is then used to update each entity's individual clock. Another solution is for all entities to have reliable access to an accurate time source (e.g. a national radio broadcast time such as the U.K. Rugby time signal).

One alternative to the use of clocks is for every pair of communicating entities to store a pair of sequence numbers, which are used only in communications between that pair. For example, for communications between A and B, A must maintain two counters: n_{AB} and n_{BA} (B will also need to maintain two counters for A). Every time A sends B a message, the value of n_{AB} is included in the message, and at the same time n_{AB} is incremented by A.

Every time A receives a message from B, then the sequence number contained in the message from B (n say) is compared with n_{BA} (as stored by A), and the following apply:

> ‣ If $n > n_{BA}$, then the message is accepted as fresh, and n_{BA} is reset to equal n.

> ‣ If $n \leq n_{BA}$, then the message is rejected as an "old" message.

These sequence numbers are sometimes known as logical time-stamps, after the well-known concept in the theory of distributed systems. Before proceeding, note that, unlike protocols using nonces (described next), time-stamp protocols, both clock-based and logical time-stamp–based, do not automatically provide linking between the different messages of an authentication protocol. That is, if there are two instances of the same protocol running concurrently between the same two parties and using the same key or keys, then there is no property inherent within the protocol that enables the recipient of a message to know which protocol instance it belongs to. This is an issue we explore in more detail in Section 10.5.2.

10.4.2 Nonces

The inclusion of a *nonce* (i.e., a randomly chosen value that acts as a "challenge" to the entity being authenticated) in protocol messages is a completely different method of establishing message freshness. Protocols based on the use of nonces are also known as challenge-response protocols, since the inclusion of the nonce in a response proves that the message must have been created after the nonce was chosen, and hence establishes its freshness.

More specifically, one party (e.g., A) sends the other party (e.g., B) a nonce (Number used ONCE); B then includes this nonce in the response to A. Then, as long as the nonce has never been used before, at least within the lifetime of the current key, A can verify the freshness of B's response (given that message integrity is provided by some cryptographic mechanism). Note that it is always up to A, the nonce provider, to ensure that the choice of nonce is appropriate (i.e., that it has not been used before).

The main property required of a nonce is the *one-time* property (i.e., the property that it has never been used before). If this property is all that is ever required, then A could ensure it by maintaining a single counter; whenever a nonce is required for use with any other party, the current counter value is used as the nonce, and the counter is incremented. However, in order to prevent a certain type of attack, sometimes known as a *preplay* attack, many protocols also need nonces to be unpredictable to any third party.

Hence nonces are typically chosen at random from a set sufficiently large to mean that the probability of the same nonce being used twice is effectively zero. If nonces are randomly chosen, then the necessary size of the set of possible nonces is a function of the 'birthday paradox' calculation (see also Section 6.3.3 of Chapter 6). That is, if the maximum number of nonces ever to be used with a single key is 2^n, then the size of the set from which random nonces are drawn should be significantly greater than 2^{2n}.

10.5 Authentication using symmetric cryptography

ISO/IEC 9798-2 and 9798-4 both contain authentication protocols based on the use of symmetric cryptography. We describe examples of these protocols, along with S/KEY and Kerberos, both of which also use symmetric cryptography. The protocols are divided into three categories, namely unilateral authentication protocols, mutual authentication protocols, and TTP-aided authentication protocols.

10.5.1 Unilateral authentication protocols

ISO/IEC 9798-2 and 9798-4 both contain two protocols providing unilateral authentication. In both cases one protocol uses time-stamps and requires only one message to be passed, whereas the other protocol uses nonces and involves two messages. The protocols of this type are summarized in Table 10.1. As examples, we describe two of the four protocols; the other two are very similar.

Unilateral authentication using time-stamps and encryption   The first example can be found in ISO/IEC 9798-2. It is based on the use of time-stamps to guarantee message freshness and encryption for origin and integrity checking of protocol messages. Since it provides unilateral authentication, B can check

Table 10.1   Unilateral Authentication Protocols Using Symmetric Crypto

Source	Description
ISO/IEC 9798-2 clause 5.1.1	One-pass protocol using encryption and a time-stamp; see Figure 10.1
ISO/IEC 9798-2 clause 5.1.2	Two-pass protocol using encryption and a nonce
ISO/IEC 9798-4 clause 5.1.1	One-pass protocol using a MAC and a time-stamp
ISO/IEC 9798-4 clause 5.1.2	Two-pass protocol using a MAC and a nonce; see Figure 10.2
RFC 1760 (S/KEY)	Two-pass protocol using a nonce; see Figure 10.3

A's identity, but not vice versa. Prior to use of the protocol A and B must share a secret key K_{AB}, must also agree on a method of encryption (and associated redundancy), and must share synchronized clocks.

As shown in Figure 10.1, the single message in the protocol is:

$$M_1 : A \rightarrow B : \text{Text}_2 || e_{K_{AB}}(t_A || [i_B] || \text{Text}_1)$$

where:

- Text$_1$ and Text$_2$ are data strings, whose use will depend on the application of the protocol (Text$_1$ could include an MDC, as used to provide the desired redundancy prior to encryption).

- t_A denotes a time-stamp generated by A—note that t_A could be replaced by a sequence number (i.e., a logical time-stamp).

When B receives the message from A, B deciphers the encrypted part. B then checks three things: that the deciphered message "makes sense" (has the appropriate redundancy), that the time-stamp is fresh, and that B's name is correctly included. If, and only if, all three checks are correct, then B accepts A as valid.

The reason that B's identifier i_B is included in the encrypted part of M_1 is to protect against "reflection" attacks, where a malicious party masquerades as A by sending B a message B previously sent to A to authenticate itself to A in a separate invocation of the protocol. In circumstances where the protocol is only ever used in one direction, (e.g., where B is a server and A is a client and it is only ever necessary for A to authenticate itself to B),

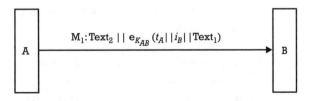

Figure 10.1   Unilateral authentication using encryption and a time-stamp.

reflection attacks are not a threat. In such a circumstance the standard allows i_B to be omitted.

As mentioned above, use of the data strings "Text$_1$" and "Text$_2$" will depend on the application domain. For example, Text$_1$ might be used for session key transfer and might also include an MDC. Either or both of these strings may be omitted.

Unilateral authentication using nonces and MACs   The second example is taken from ISO/IEC 9798-4. It is based on the use of nonces (for freshness) and a MAC for origin and integrity checking. Analogous to the previous example, B can check A's identity, but not vice versa. Prior to use of the protocol A and B must share a secret key K_{AB} and must also agree on a MAC algorithm.

The two messages in the protocol, shown in Figure 10.2, are listed as follows:

$M_1: B \rightarrow A : r_B \| \text{Text}_1$

$M_2: A \rightarrow B : \text{Text}_3 \| \text{MAC}_{K_{AB}}(r_B \| [i_B] \| \text{Text}_2)$

where:

- Text$_1$–Text$_3$ are data strings, as above.

- r_B denotes a random nonce chosen by B.

When B sends the message M_1, B stores the nonce r_B. When A receives message M_1, A assembles the string $r_B \| i_B \| \text{Text}_2$ and computes $\text{MAC}_{K_{AB}}$ $(r_B \| i_B \| \text{Text}_2)$, using the shared secret K_{AB}. When B receives message M_2, B first assembles the string $r_B \| i_B \| \text{Text}_2$ and then computes $\text{MAC}_{K_{AB}}(r_B \| i_B \| \text{Text}_2)$, using the shared secret K_{AB}. B then checks that the newly computed MAC agrees with the one in message M_2; if the check succeeds, then B accepts A as valid. Note that, in order for B to perform the checking, B must have the means to obtain the data string "Text$_2$." One possibility is that Text$_3$ contains a copy of Text$_2$, perhaps in an enciphered form. Another possibility is that B can predict what this string looks like in advance.

Note that, as previously, i_B is included within the scope of the MAC in message M_2 to prevent reflection attacks. As before, its inclusion is optional.

The S/KEY user authentication protocol   We now consider one other unilateral authentication protocol, namely the S/KEY scheme, as specified in RFC 1760.

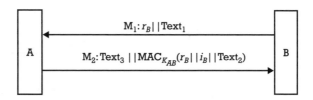

Figure 10.2 Unilateral authentication using a MAC and a nonce.

This protocol is designed to enable a host computer, B, to authenticate a remote user A. It is designed so that the information that needs to be stored by the host computer does not need to be kept secret, although maintaining its integrity is fundamentally important. It is assumed that the user has access to some kind of computing device with both an input and an output device (e.g., a keyboard and screen) that can be used to perform certain calculations.

User A must possess a k-bit secret key K (RFC 1760 specifies $k = 64$, although this appears a little short given current cryptanalytic techniques). This key is derived from a "pass-phrase" of arbitrary length, thus avoiding the need for it to be stored by the user's hardware. The user and host must also agree on a one-way function h, which takes a k-bit input and gives a k-bit output. The function built into the public domain implementation of S/KEY is based on the MD4 hash function (see Chapter 6), although it could be based on any other suitable function (e.g., SHA–1 or RIPEMD–160).

The key is used to generate a sequence of "one-time passwords" in the following way. Each host that the user wishes to access is assigned a k-bit seed value D and a "count" value c, which will initially be set to some fixed value (e.g., 1,000). For each user wishing to gain access, the host retains three things:

- A copy of the seed D for that user, which is fixed for a number of uses of the protocol, this number being determined by the initial count value c;

- The current count value c for that user, which is decreased by one every time the protocol is used;

- The previous one-time password for that user.

When user A wishes to gain access to host B, the following procedure is followed (see Figure 10.3):

1. The host decrements its stored counter for that user and sends the value of this decremented counter (e.g., c) to the user in conjunction with the seed value (e.g., D) such that

    $M_1 : B \rightarrow A : c||D$

2. On receipt of M_1, the user takes D and bit-wise exors it with its 64-bit key to obtain a 64-bit value $S = K \oplus D$. The one-way function h is

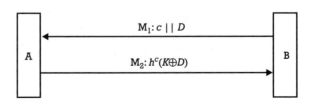

Figure 10.3 The S/KEY unilateral authentication protocol.

then recursively applied to S a total of c times to obtain the 64-bit one-time password P. The value P is then sent back to the host as follows:

$$M_2 : A \rightarrow B : P = h^c(K \oplus D)$$

3. On receipt of M_2, the host applies the one-way function to P once and compares the result with its stored "old password" P' [where $P' = h^{c+1}(K \oplus D) = h(P)$]. If the two values agree then the user is authenticated, and the "old" stored password P' is replaced with P. Otherwise the user is rejected.

Setting the system up will require the user to enter his or her pass-phrase into the host, where the initial count c can be chosen and the initial password computed and stored. It is important to note that the host does not need to retain any secrets, since it only keeps the "old" password, from which the new password cannot be derived. Finally note that, when c reaches its minimum value (typically $c = 1$), the host and user will need to set up the system again, using a new value of the seed D and setting the counter c back to its maximum value.

The scheme can be thought of as a special case of the nonce/MAC example from ISO/IEC 9798-4 given above. We can make S/KEY fit this example by omitting i_B (it is unnecessary since the protocol is only ever used in one direction), and letting $r_B = c||D$ and $\text{MAC}_K(r_B) = h^c(K \oplus D)$.

Note, however, that it is a requirement for use of any of the ISO/IEC 9798 nonce-based protocols that the nonces (r_B, in this case) should be unpredictable by any third party. However, in the S/KEY scheme $r_B = c||D$ is not unpredictable, since successive nonces from a particular host to a particular user will consist of an identical seed concatenated with a count value that decreases by one every time. This leads to a possible problem, namely that, if a malicious third party knows D (e.g., by having overheard one use of the protocol) and can impersonate the host to the remote user, then the scheme can be broken using a "preplay attack."

This attack involves the malicious third party, who is impersonating the legitimate host, sending the user the seed D together with a minimal value of c (say, $c = 1$). The malicious third party receives $h(K \oplus D)$ in response, and can then use this to compute $h^c(K \oplus D)$ for any value of $c > 1$. Thus, he or she can potentially impersonate the user many times to the genuine host. Hence S/KEY should only be used in circumstances where the remote user can be sure of the identity of the host to which he or she is authenticating.

10.5.2 Mutual authentication protocols

As in the unilateral authentication case, ISO/IEC 9798-2 and 9798-4 both contain two protocols providing mutual authentication, one using time-stamps and requiring two messages to be passed, and the other protocol using nonces and involving three messages. As examples, we describe two of the four protocols; the other two are very similar. We also describe a third

Table 10.2 Mutual Authentication Protocols Using Symmetric Crypto

Source	Description
ISO/IEC 9798-2 clause 5.2.1	Two-pass protocol using encryption and time-stamps
ISO/IEC 9798-2 clause 5.2.2	Three-pass protocol using encryption and nonces; see Figure 10.4
ISO/IEC 9798-4 clause 5.2.1	Two-pass protocol using MACs and time-stamps; see Figure 10.5
ISO/IEC 9798-4 clause 5.2.2	Three-pass protocol using MACs and nonces
Internet Draft cat-sskm-01 (AKEP2)	Three-pass protocol using MACs and nonces; see Figure 10.6

protocol, known as AKEP2, which is similar to, but not quite the same as, one of the protocols in ISO/IEC 9798-4; it is important because it possesses a proof of security. It is also contained in an Internet draft (albeit one that has now expired).

The protocols of this type are summarized in Table 10.2.

Mutual authentication using nonces and encryption   The first example comes from ISO/IEC 9798-2. It is based on the use of nonces for freshness and encryption for origin and integrity checking. Since it provides mutual authentication, B can check A's identity and vice versa. Prior to use of the protocol A and B must share a secret key K_{AB} and must also agree on a method of encryption (and associated redundancy).

As shown in Figure 10.4, the three messages in the protocol are:

$M_1 : B \rightarrow A : r_B || \text{Text}_1$

$M_2 : A \rightarrow B : \text{Text}_3 || e_{K_{AB}}(r_A || r_B || [i_B]) || \text{Text}_2)$

$M_3 : B \rightarrow A : \text{Text}_5 || e_{K_{AB}}(r_B || r_A || \text{Text}_4)$

where:

- Text$_1$–Text$_5$ are data strings, as above (Text$_2$ and Text$_4$ may contain MDCs).

- r_A and r_B denote random nonces generated by A and B, respectively.

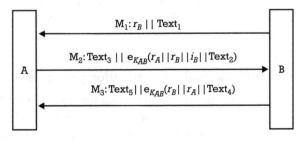

Figure 10.4 Mutual authentication using encryption and nonces.

When B sends message M_1, B stores the nonce r_B. When A sends message M_2, A stores the nonces r_A and r_B. When B receives M_2, B deciphers the enciphered string and checks that the deciphered message "makes sense" (has the appropriate redundancy), that the nonce it includes is the one B sent in message M_1, and that B's name is correctly included. If all three checks succeed, then B accepts A as valid, and sends M_3. When A receives M_3, A deciphers the encrypted part and checks that the deciphered message "makes sense" (has the appropriate redundancy), and that the nonces it includes are the expected ones. If both checks succeed, then A accepts B as valid.

Before proceeding observe that the inclusion of i_B in message M_2 is, as before, to prevent reflection attacks, and may be omitted in cases where such attacks cannot occur. It is also interesting to note that i_A is not included in the encrypted part of message M_3. This is not accidental; it is simply that the inclusion of the identifier is unnecessary (i.e., its omission does not enable any attacks to be performed).

Mutual authentication using time-stamps and MACs   The second mutual authentication example is taken from ISO/IEC 9798-4. It is based on the use of time-stamps (for freshness) and MACs for origin and integrity checking. Prior to use of the protocol A and B must share a secret key K_{AB}, must also agree on a MAC algorithm, and must share synchronized clocks.

As shown in Figure 10.5, the two messages in the protocol are:

$M_1\text{: } A \rightarrow B : t_A||\text{Text}_2||\text{MAC}_{K_{AB}}(t_A||[i_B]||\text{Text}_1)$
$M_2\text{: } B \rightarrow A : t_B||\text{Text}_4||\text{MAC}_{K_{AB}}(t_B||[i_A]||\text{Text}_3)$

where:

▪ Text$_1$–Text$_4$ are data strings, as previously.

▪ t_A and t_B denote time-stamps generated by A and B respectively [note that t_A and t_B could be replaced by sequence numbers, (i.e., logical time-stamps)].

When B receives M_1, B first assembles the string $t_A||i_B||\text{Text}_1$, and then computes $\text{MAC}_{K_{AB}}(t_A||i_B||\text{Text}_1)$, using the shared secret K_{AB}. B then checks that the time-stamp t_A is fresh and that the newly computed check value agrees with the one in message M_1. If the checks succeed, then B accepts

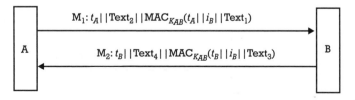

Figure 10.5   Mutual authentication using MACs and time-stamps.

A as valid and sends message M_2. When A receives M_2, A first assembles the string $t_B||i_A||\text{Text}_3$ and then computes $\text{MAC}_{K_{AB}}(t_B||i_A||\text{Text}_3)$, using the shared secret K_{AB}. A then checks that the time-stamp t_B is fresh, and that the newly computed check value agrees with the one in message M_2. If the checks succeed, then A accepts B as valid. Note that, in order for A and B to perform their checks, they must have the means to obtain the data strings "Text$_3$" and "Text$_1$" respectively. One possibility is that Text$_4$ (Text$_2$) contains a copy of Text$_3$ (Text$_1$), perhaps in enciphered form. Another possibility is that A and B can predict what the strings look like in advance.

Note that there is nothing to link the two messages of the protocol together (i.e., if two invocations of the protocol are running simultaneously, then there is nothing explicit in the protocol description to enable A, the recipient of message M_2, to deduce to which copy of message M_1 this corresponds). This could be a problem for some applications; however, it is simple to solve.

If A wishes to be sure that M_2 is a response to M_1, then A can include an "exchange identifier" in message M_1 (in the data string Text$_1$) and then require B to insert the same identifier in message M_2 (in the data string Text$_3$).

Finally observe that, just as before, the inclusion of i_B and i_A in messages M_1 and M_2 is to prevent reflection attacks, and where such attacks are not a threat these identifiers may be omitted.

Mutual authentication using nonces and MACs   The third mutual authentication example is known as AKEP2 and was originally proposed by Bellare and Rogaway. It is very similar to a protocol standardized in ISO/IEC 9798-4. It is based on the use of nonces (for freshness) and MACs for origin and integrity checking. Prior to use of the protocol A and B must share a secret key K_{AB} and must agree on a MAC algorithm.

As shown in Figure 10.6, the two messages in the protocol are:

$M_1 : B \to A : r_B$

$M_2 : A \to B : i_A||i_B||r_B||r_A||\text{MAC}_{K_{AB}}(i_A||i_B||r_B||r_A)$

$M_3 : B \to A : i_B||r_A||\text{MAC}_{K_{AB}}(i_B||r_A)$

where r_A and r_B denote random nonces generated by A and B, respectively.

When B sends message M_1, B stores the nonce r_B. When A sends message M_2, A stores the nonces r_A and r_B. When B receives M_2, B verifies that the

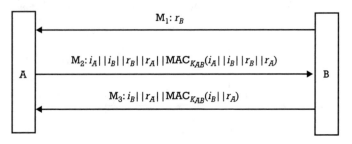

Figure 10.6 Mutual authentication using MACs and nonces.

received value r_B is the same as the one sent in M_1 and that the identifiers are correct, and then recomputes the MAC and compares it with the received value. If all the checks succeed, then B accepts A as valid, and computes and sends M_3. When A receives M_3, A checks that the received value r_A is the same as the one sent in M_2 and that i_B is correct, and then recomputes the MAC and compares it with the received value. If all the checks succeed then A accepts B as valid.

The main difference between this protocol and the mechanism specified in ISO/IEC 9798-4 is that the MAC in message M_3 of the latter protocol is computed over r_B and r_A, instead of i_B and r_A. In practice this difference does not appear to make any difference to the level of security achieved.

10.5.3 Third party–aided mechanisms

In order to use any of the authentication protocols based on the use of symmetric cryptography, entities A and B need to share a secret key. The mechanisms so far described all assume that A and B already share a secret key.

However, if such a key is not in place then a more elaborate mechanism must be used. One way of providing the required shared secret key is through the use of a mutually trusted third party (TTP) with whom both A and B share a secret. The (on-line) TTP cooperates to enable A and B to authenticate one another. A number of such TTP-based mutual authentication protocols have been standardized, including two in ISO/IEC 9798-2, and one (known as Kerberos) in Internet RFC 1510. We now describe both the ISO/IEC protocols, together with Kerberos. The protocols of this type are summarised in Table 10.3.

It could reasonably be argued that all these protocols are in fact key establishment techniques, the focus of Chapter 12, since, as well as enabling A and B to authenticate one another, the protocols also provide them with a mutually trusted (authenticated) secret key. In fact, using the terminology of Chapter 12, in all these protocols the TTP is acting as a key distribution center (KDC) since the protocols provide A and B with a secret key chosen by the TTP. However, we consider these protocols in this chapter rather than Chapter 12 for two main reasons. First, the standards documents in which the protocols are specified describe them as authentication protocols. Second, the protocols may be used in circumstances where the initial authentication between A and B is the only matter of importance, and the key that is established is never subsequently used—in fact, this is a common mode of use for Kerberos.

Table 10.3 TTP-Aided Mutual Authentication Protocols

Source	Description
ISO/IEC 9798-2 clause 6.1	Four-pass protocol using encryption and time-stamps; see Figure 10.7
ISO/IEC 9798-2 clause 6.2	Five-pass protocol using encryption and nonces; see Figure 10.8
RFC 1510 (Kerberos)	Six-pass protocol using encryption and time-stamps; see Figure 10.9

TTP-aided authentication using time-stamps   The first protocol we consider is given in ISO/IEC 9798-2, and uses time-stamps to guarantee freshness, and encryption for origin and integrity checking. We assume that, prior to use of the protocol, A and B share secret keys K_{AT} and K_{BT} respectively with the TTP, T, and that all parties have agreed on an encryption algorithm (and a method of adding redundancy prior to encryption). It is also necessary for all parties to share synchronized clocks (or to have pair-wise synchronized counters as required to support the use of "logical time-stamps").

As shown in Figure 10.7, the four messages in the protocol are the following:

M_1: $A \rightarrow T$: $p_A||i_B||\text{Text}_1$

M_2: $T \rightarrow A$: $\text{Text}_4 || e_{K_{AT}}(p_A||K_{AB}||i_B||\text{Text}_3) ||$
$\qquad\qquad\qquad e_{K_{BT}}(t_T||K_{AB}||i_A||\text{Text}_2)$

M_3: $A \rightarrow B$: $\text{Text}_6 || e_{K_{BT}}(t_T||K_{AB}||i_A||\text{Text}_2) || e_{K_{AB}}(t_A||i_B||\text{Text}_5)$

M_4: $B \rightarrow A$: $\text{Text}_8 || e_{K_{AB}}(t_B||i_A||\text{Text}_7)$

where the following are true:

▸ p_A is a "time variant parameter" generated by A, that allows A to verify that M_2 is a response to M_1 (p_A needs to be nonrepeating, but does not need to be unpredictable).

▸ t_T, t_A, and t_B are time-stamps generated by T, A, and B respectively; these values could be replaced by sequence numbers (i.e., logical time-stamps).

The logical procedure associated with the message flows is as follows. After receiving M_1, the TTP T first chooses a new session key K_{AB} for use by A and B. The TTP T then generates a new time-stamp t_T, and uses it,

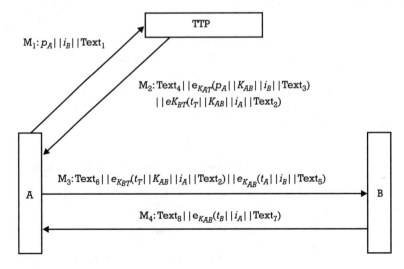

Figure 10.7 TTP-aided authentication using time-stamps.

together with the session key K_{AB} and the received time-variant parameter p_A, to generate the message M_2.

When A receives M_2, A first decrypts the part encrypted using K_{AT}. A then checks that the deciphered string contains the appropriate redundancy, and that the values p_A and i_B are correctly included. If the checks succeed, then A retrieves the new session key K_{AB}, generates a new time-stamp t_A, and uses them, in conjunction with the second part of M_2, to construct M_3.

When B receives M_3, B first deciphers the part enciphered using K_{BT}. B then checks that the deciphered string contains the appropriate redundancy, that the time-stamp t_T is fresh, and that i_A is correctly included. If the checks succeed, then B retrieves the new session key K_{AB} and deciphers the other part of message M_3. B then checks that the deciphered string contains the appropriate redundancy, that the time-stamp t_A is fresh, and that i_B is correctly included. If these checks succeed, then B accepts A as valid and sends message M_4.

When A receives M_4, A deciphers it and checks that the deciphered string contains the appropriate redundancy, that the time-stamp t_B is fresh, and that i_A is correctly included. If the checks succeed, then A accepts B as valid.

TTP-aided authentication using nonces   The next protocol we describe is also from ISO/IEC 9798-2 and uses nonces to guarantee freshness. We assume that, prior to use of the protocol, A and B share secret keys K_{AT} and K_{BT} respectively with the TTP T and that all parties have agreed on an encryption algorithm (and a method of adding redundancy prior to encryption).

The five messages in the protocol, shown in Figure 10.8, are listed as follows:

M_1: $B \rightarrow A : r_B || \text{Text}_1$

M_2: $A \rightarrow T : r'_A || r_B || i_B || \text{Text}_2$

M_3: $T \rightarrow A : \text{Text}_5 || e_{K_{AT}}(r'_A || K_{AB} || i_B || \text{Text}_4) || e_{K_{BT}}(r_B || K_{AB} || i_A || \text{Text}_3)$

M_4: $A \rightarrow B : \text{Text}_7 || e_{K_{BT}}(r_B || K_{AB} || i_A || \text{Text}_3) || e_{K_{AB}}(r_A || r_B || \text{Text}_6)$

M_5: $B \rightarrow A : \text{Text}_9 || e_{K_{AB}}(r_B || r_A || \text{Text}_8)$

where r_A, r'_A, and r_B are nonces, the first two generated by A and the latter generated by B.

The logical procedure associated with the message flows is as follows. B first generates and stores a nonce r_B, and sends M_1 to A. Upon receiving M_1, A stores r_B, generates and stores a nonce r'_A, and sends M_2 to T.

After receiving M_2, the TTP T first chooses a new session key K_{AB} for use by A and B. The TTP T then uses the session key K_{AB}, the received nonces r'_A and r_B, and the stored secret keys K_{AT} and K_{BT} to generate message M_3.

When A receives M_3, A first decrypts the part encrypted using K_{AT}. A then checks that the deciphered string contains the appropriate redundancy, and that the values r'_A and i_B are correctly included. If the checks succeed, then A

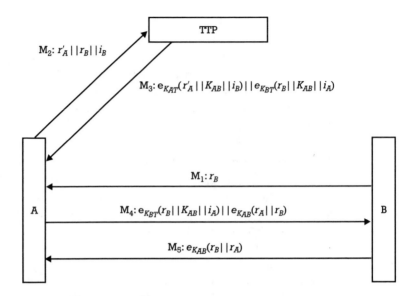

Figure 10.8 TTP-aided authentication using nonces.

retrieves the new session key K_{AB}, generates and stores a second nonce r_A, and uses them, in conjunction with the second part of M_3, to construct M_4.

When B receives M_4, B first deciphers the part encrypted using K_{BT}. B then checks that the deciphered string contains the appropriate redundancy, and that r_B and i_A are correctly included. If the checks succeed, then B retrieves the new session key K_{AB} and decrypts the other part of message M_4. B then checks that the deciphered string contains the appropriate redundancy, and that r_B is correctly included. If these checks succeed, then B accepts A as valid and sends message M_5.

When A receives M_5, A deciphers it and checks that the deciphered string contains the appropriate redundancy, and that r_A and r_B are correctly included. If the checks succeed, then A accepts B as valid.

TTP-aided authentication: Kerberos   The Kerberos authentication protocol was originally devised as part of Project Athena at MIT. It was designed to provide a means for workstation users (clients) and servers (and vice versa) to authenticate one another. A number of versions of Kerberos have been produced; we concentrate on the latest version, known as Version 5. It is important to note that the previous version of Kerberos (Version 4) has been widely used and is significantly different from Version 5. A complete specification of Kerberos Version 5 is given in Internet RFC 1510. Kerberos is widely integrated into versions of the Unix operating system and is also supported by recent versions of Microsoft Windows.

Kerberos Version 5 is based on the combined use of symmetric encryption and a hash function (acting as an MDC) for integrity and origin checking, and time-stamps for freshness checking. The data to be encrypted is first input to the hash function, and the resulting hash code is concatenated with the data prior to encryption. Kerberos Version 5 uses the DES block cipher for encryption (see Chapter 4) combined with one of MD4, MD5, or a cyclic redundancy check (CRC) as the MDC (see Chapter 6). The use of a CRC, although permitted, is not recommended. Given that the DES block cipher can no longer be regarded as secure, Release 1.2 of Kerberos Version 5 implements triple DES (3DES), as described in Chapter 4.

Kerberos makes use of two different types of TTP:

- An authentication server (AS);

- A ticket-granting server (TGS).

The client C has a long-term shared secret key with the AS, which is used to set up a short-term shared secret key with the TGS. The TGS is then involved in setting up shared session keys between the client and server.

The idea behind having two TTPs is that a user only needs to load his or her long-term secret key (typically a password of some kind), as shared with the AS, into the workstation for the minimum amount of time. Once the short-term secret key is established (with the TGS), the long-term secret key can be erased from the workstation. This minimizes the risk of exposure of the long-term secret key.

As shown in Figure 10.9, the Kerberos protocol involves a total of six messages M_1–M_6.

- Messages M_1 and M_2 are exchanged between the client and the AS; this typically happens only once per "log in."

- Messages M_3 and M_4 are exchanged between the client and the TGS (using a key provided by the AS). Such an exchange happens whenever the client wants to communicate with a new server. After an initial exchange of messages M_1 and M_2, and until the expiry of the

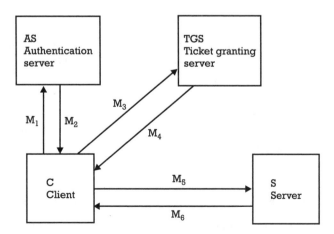

Figure 10.9 Kerberos messages.

key set up between the client and the TGS, new exchanges of messages M_3 and M_4 can occur without repeating messages M_1 and M_2.

> ▸ Messages M_5 and M_6 are exchanged between the client and server (using a key provided by the TGS). Messages M_5 and M_6 can be repeated any number of times during the lifetime of the key set up between the client and the server, without repeating messages M_3 and M_4.

The contents of each of the six Kerberos messages are as follows:

M_1: $C \to$ AS : $i_C||i_T||$from$||$to$||n_C$

M_2: AS $\to C$: $i_C \parallel e_{K_{AST}}(K_{CT}||i_C||$from$||to) \parallel e_{K_{ASC}}(K_{CT}||n_C||$from$||to||i_T)$

M_3: $C \to$ TGS : $i_S||$from$||$to$||n'_C \parallel e_{K_{AST}}(K_{CT}||i_C||$from$||to) \parallel e_{K_{CT}}(i_C||t_1)$

M_4: TGS $\to C$: $i_C \parallel e_{K_{TS}}(K_{CS}||i_C||$from$||to) \parallel e_{K_{CT}}(K_{CS}||n'_C||$from$||to||i_S)$

M_5: $C \to S$: $e_{K_{TS}}(K_{CS}||i_C||$from$||$to$) \parallel e_{K_{CS}}(i_C||t_2)$

M_6: $S \to C$: $e_{K_{CS}}(t_2)$

where the following are true:

> ▸ i_C, i_S, and i_T are identifiers for the client C, the sever S, and the TGS, respectively.

> ▸ n_C and n'_C are nonces generated by the client C.

> ▸ K_{AST} is a long-term secret key shared by the AS and the TGS.

> ▸ K_{ASC} is a long-term secret key shared by the AS and the client C.

> ▸ K_{TS} is a long-term secret key shared by the TGS and the server S.

> ▸ K_{CT} is a secret key shared by the client C and the TGS (established by messages M_1 and M_2).

> ▸ K_{CS} is a secret key shared by the client C and the server S (established by messages M_3 and M_4).

> ▸ t_1 and t_2 are time-stamps.

> ▸ "from" and "to" indicate a specified time interval (start time and end time)—it is used to limit the validity of a key. The "from" value is optional.

In message M_2, $e_{K_{AST}}(K_{CT}||i_C||$from$||to)$ is called the ticket for the TGS. In message M_4, $e_{K_{TS}}(K_{CS}||i_C||$from$||$to$)$ is called the ticket for the server S. Note that message M_6 is optional.

10.6 Authentication using asymmetric cryptography

ISO/IEC 9798-3 and 9798-5 both contain authentication protocols based on the use of asymmetric cryptography. We now describe examples of these protocols. Similar to the symmetric case, the protocols are divided into two categories, namely, unilateral authentication protocols and mutual authentication protocols.

10.6.1   Unilateral authentication mechanisms

ISO/IEC 9798-3 contains two unilateral authentication protocols based on the use of digital signatures. One is based on time-stamps and the other on nonces (the one based on nonces is also specified in NIST FIPS Pub. 196). We do not present them here—they are very similar to the corresponding protocols contained in ISO/IEC 9798-2 and ISO/IEC 9798-4. For a similar reason we do not describe the one-pass unilateral authentication mechanism in ISO/IEC 9594-8 (i.e., ITU-T X.509), which is also based on digital signatures. In addition, ISO/IEC 9798-5 contains a further five unilateral authentication protocols based on zero-knowledge techniques. The example of a unilateral authentication protocol that we present is taken from the current committee draft version of the second edition of this latter standard.

The protocols of this type are summarized in Table 10.4. Note that the clause numbers specified for ISO/IEC 9798-5 are taken from the current committee draft of the second edition of this standard and not from the 1999 first edition.

A mechanism based on discrete logarithms   This example is specified in clause 6 of the first edition of ISO/IEC 9798-5 and in clause 7 of the current draft of the second edition. The security of this scheme is based on the difficulty of the "discrete logarithm problem" (as is the DSA digital signature scheme

Table 10.4   Unilateral Authentication Protocols Using Asymmetric Crypto

Source	Description
ISO/IEC 9594-8 clause 18.2.2.1	One-pass protocol using a signature and a time-stamp
ISO/IEC 9798-3 clause 5.1.1	One-pass protocol using a signature and a time-stamp
ISO/IEC 9798-3 clause 5.1.2	Two-pass protocol using a signature and a nonce
ISO/IEC 9798-5 clause 5 (Fiat-Shamir)	Three-pass protocol using ID-based cryptography
ISO/IEC 9798-5 clause 6 (GQ2)	Three-pass protocol based on difficulty of integer factorization
ISO/IEC 9798-5 clause 7 (Schnorr)	Three-pass protocol based on difficulty of discrete logarithms; see Figure 10.10
ISO/IEC 9798-5 clause 8 (GPS1/2/3)	Three-pass protocol based on difficulty of discrete logarithms
ISO/IEC 9798-5 clause 9.3 (Brandt et al.)	Two-pass protocol based on asymmetric encryption
FIPS Pub. 196 clause 3.3	Two-pass protocol using a signature and a nonce (derived from ISO/IEC 9798-3 clause 5.1.2)

discussed in Chapter 8). Since this is a unilateral authentication mechanism, B can check A's identity, but not vice versa.

Requirements   Prior to use of the protocol A and B must agree on three public parameters p, q, and g, where the following are true:

- p is a large prime (e.g., with a binary representation containing 1,024 bits).

- q is a large prime that is a factor of $p - 1$.

- g is a positive integer less than p with the property that g has multiplicative order q modulo p; in other words, $g^q \bmod p = 1$ and $g^i \bmod p \neq 1$ for all i satisfying $1 \leq i < q$.

These values could be agreed and shared by a large community of users.

Furthermore, A must have a key pair (y_A, z_A) where z_A, the private key, shall be a random positive integer less than q and $y_A = g^{z_A} \bmod p$. B must possess a trusted copy of y_A; if necessary this could be achieved by having A send B a copy of a public key certificate for A's public key in either the first or the third message of the protocol (for details on the construction and use of public key certificates, see Chapter 13).

The protocol   As shown in Figure 10.10, the three messages in the protocol are as follows:

M_1: $A \rightarrow B$: $g^r \bmod p$

M_2: $B \rightarrow A$: d

M_3: $A \rightarrow B$: $r - dz_A \bmod q$

where the following are true:

- r denotes a random value chosen by A ($1 < r < q$).

- d denotes a random value chosen by B ($1 < d < q$).

A first chooses a random value r and stores it for use later in the protocol. A then computes $g^r \bmod p$ and sends it as message M_1 to B. When B receives

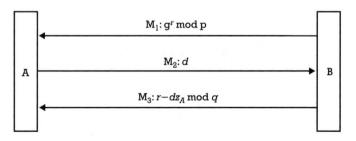

Figure 10.10   Unilateral authentication using discrete logs.

M_1, B stores the value in the message and also generates (and stores) a random value d, which is sent back to A in message M_2. On receipt of M_2, A computes the value $r - dz_A \bmod q$, using the stored secret r, the received value d, and A's long-term private key z_A. A then sends this value to B in message M_3.

When B receives message M_3, B first checks that the value in the message, D say, satisfies $0 < D < q$. If not then B must reject A. Otherwise B computes the value

$$(y_A)^d g^D \bmod p$$

using B's trusted copy of A's public key, the received value D, and the stored value d. B then compares this value to the value received in M_1; if (and only if) the check succeeds, then B accepts A as valid.

A variant of the scheme exists where A sends $h(g^r \bmod p)$ in message M_1, where h is a hash function agreed by A and B (see Chapter 6 for examples of suitable hash functions). The mechanism is otherwise identical except that B's checking at the end of the protocol also involves a hash computation. Such a process increases the computational load slightly, but reduces the number of bits that need to be transmitted from A to B.

10.6.2 Mutual authentication mechanisms

We present two different mutual authentication mechanisms based on asymmetric cryptography—one of the three mutual authentication protocols contained in ISO/IEC 9798-3, and the only mutual authentication protocol contained in the revised version of ISO/IEC 9798-5. One of the three mutual authentication protocols in ISO/IEC 9798-3 is also specified in NIST FIPS Pub. 196. Two of the three authentication protocols in ITU-T X.509 can be used to provide mutual authentication; like the schemes in ISO/IEC 9798-3 they are based on the use of digital signatures, and since they are rather similar to the 9798-3 schemes we do not describe them here.

The protocols of this type are summarized in Table 10.5. As previously, the clause number specified for ISO/IEC 9798-5 is taken from the current committee draft of the second edition of this standard, and not from the 1999 first edition.

Authentication using time-stamps and signatures The mutual authentication scheme from ISO/IEC 9798-3 is based on the use of time-stamps to guarantee freshness (the other mutual authentication protocol from ISO/IEC 9798-3, which is not presented here, is based on nonces and contains three messages). Since it provides mutual authentication, B can check A's identity and vice versa. Prior to use of the protocol the two parties must agree on a signature scheme and must both have signature key pairs. Also, A and B must be equipped with certificates for their public keys (see Chapter 13); alternatively A and B must have obtained reliable copies of each other's public keys by some other means.

Table 10.5 Mutual Authentication Protocols Using Asymmetric Crypto

Source	Description
ISO/IEC 9594-8 clause 18.2.2.2	Two-pass protocol using signatures and time-stamps
ISO/IEC 9594-8 clause 18.2.2.3	Three-pass protocol using signatures and nonces
ISO/IEC 9798-3 clause 5.2.1	Two-pass protocol using signatures and time-stamps; see Figure 10.11
ISO/IEC 9798-3 clause 5.2.2	Three-pass protocol using signatures and nonces
ISO/IEC 9798-3 clause 5.2.3	Four-pass (parallelizable) protocol using signatures and nonces
ISO/IEC 9798-5 clause 9.3 (Helsinki)	Three-pass protocol based on asymmetric encryption; see Figure 10.12
FIPS Pub. 196 clause 3.3	Three-pass protocol using signatures and nonces (derived from ISO/IEC 9798-3 clause 5.2.2)

As shown in Figure 10.11, the two messages in the protocol are:

$M_1: A \rightarrow B : [\text{Cert}_A]||t_A||i_B||\text{Text}_2||S_A(t_A||i_B||\text{Text}_1)$

$M_2: B \rightarrow A : [\text{Cert}_B]||t_B||i_A||\text{Text}_4||S_B(t_B||i_A||\text{Text}_3)$

The logical procedure associated with the message flows is as follows. When B receives M_1, B first verifies the certificate Cert_A (if present), and thereby obtains a trusted copy of A's public key; if the certificate is not present B needs to have reliably obtained a copy of A's public key by some other means. B then checks that the time-stamp t_A is fresh and that (using a copy of A's public verification key) the signature in M_1 is a valid signature on the string $t_A||i_B||\text{Text}_1$. If the checks succeed, then B accepts A as valid and sends message M_2.

When A receives M_2, A first verifies the certificate Cert_B (if present), and thereby obtains a trusted copy of B's public key; if the certificate is not present A needs to have reliably obtained a copy of B's public key by some other means. A then checks that the time-stamp t_B is fresh and that the signature in M_2 is a valid signature on the string $t_B||i_A||\text{Text}_3$. If the checks succeed, then A accepts B as valid.

Note that, in order for A and B to perform their checks, they must have the means to obtain the data strings Text_3 and Text_1, respectively. One possibility is that Text_4 (Text_2) contains a copy of Text_3 (Text_1), perhaps in enciphered

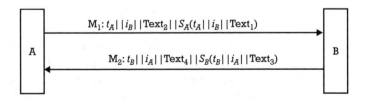

Figure 10.11 Mutual authentication using signatures and time-stamps.

form. Another possibility is that A and B can predict what the strings look like in advance.

Note also that, just as in the mutual authentication protocol based on MACs and time-stamps, presented in Section 10.5, there is nothing to link the two messages of the protocol together. Thus, if A wishes to be sure that M_2 is a response to M_1, then A can include an "exchange identifier" in message M_1 (in the data string Text$_1$) and then require B to insert the same identifier in message M_2 (in the data string Text$_3$).

Authentication using asymmetric encryption   The second mutual authentication scheme we describe here uses asymmetric encryption and is taken from ISO/IEC 9798-5; this protocol is sometimes known as the *Helsinki protocol*. This scheme is, in fact, the only mutual authentication protocol in this part of ISO/IEC 9798.

Prior to use of the protocol the two parties must agree on a hash function h and an asymmetric encryption scheme and must both have encryption key pairs. Also, A and B must also be equipped with reliable copies of each other's public keys; this could be achieved through the prior exchange of public key certificates (see Chapter 13), or by some other means.

As shown in Figure 10.12, the two messages in the protocol are:

M_1: $B \rightarrow A$: $e_A(i_B||r_B||h(i_B||r_B))$
M_2: $A \rightarrow B$: $e_B(i_A||r_B||r_A||h(i_A||r_B||r_A))$
M_3: $B \rightarrow A$: r_A

The logical procedure associated with the message flows is as follows. When B sends M_1, B stores r_B. When A receives M_1, A first decrypts the entire message using A's private decryption key. A next verifies the internal structure of the decrypted string by first recovering i_B, r_B, and $h(i_B||r_B)$, then recomputing the hash code from i_B and r_B, and finally comparing the computed value with the recovered hash code. A also checks that i_B is the identifier for the party with whom A believes itself to be communicating. If both checks succeed, then A stores r_B, generates and stores r_A, and prepares and sends message M_2.

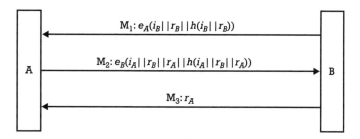

Figure 10.12 Mutual authentication using asymmetric encryption.

When B receives M_2, B first decrypts the entire message using B's private decryption key. B next verifies the internal structure of the decrypted string by first recovering i_A, r_B, r_A and $h(i_A||r_B||r_A)$, then recomputing the hash-code from i_A, r_B, and r_A, and finally comparing the computed value with the recovered hash code. B also checks that i_A is the identifier for the party with whom B believes itself to be communicating and checks that the recovered value r_B is the same as the value sent in M_1. If all the checks succeed, then B accepts A as valid and sends message M_3.

When A receives M_3, A checks that the received value is the same as the value sent in M_2. If so, then A accepts B as valid.

Note that the inclusion of hash codes within the encrypted strings in messages M_1 and M_2 could be regarded as the explicit inclusion of MDCs in messages. This compares with the descriptions of protocols based on symmetric encryption, where we have made the use of such MDCs an implicit option.

10.7 Manual authentication protocols

Manual authentication techniques have been designed to enable wireless devices to authenticate one another via an insecure wireless channel with the aid of a manual transfer of data between the devices. Manual transfer refers to the human operator of the devices copying data output from one device into the other device, comparing the output of the two devices, or entering the same data into the two devices.

Using the terminology of Stajano, the problem is that of the "secure imprinting" of a personal device. That is, suppose a user has two wireless-enabled devices (e.g., a mobile phone and a personal digital assistant (PDA) and that he or she wishes the two devices to establish a secure association for their wireless intercommunications. This will, for example, enable the two devices to securely share personal data. Solving the problem requires the two devices to mutually authenticate one another and, where necessary, to establish a shared secret key, all using a wireless communications link. A shared secret key can be used as the basis for future secure communications between the two devices, including further mutual authentications.

The main threat to the process is via a so-called man-in-the-middle attack on the wireless link. Because the link uses radio, a third party with a receiver and a powerful transmitter could manipulate the communications between the devices, in a way that will not be evident to the user. Thus, the attacker could masquerade as the first device to the second device and as the second device to the first device and set up separate keys with each. To prevent this, it will be necessary for the device operator to input and output data via the devices' user interfaces (i.e., perform a manual data transfer) to enable the devices to verify each other's identifies.

This is the context of use for the manual authentication protocols contained in the draft standard ISO/IEC 9798-6. The standard makes the following assumptions about the devices conducting the protocol.

- The two devices have access to a wireless communications channel, which can be used to exchange as much data as required; however, no assumptions are made about the security of this channel—for example, it may be prone to manipulation by an active attacker.

- The two devices are both under the control of either a single human user, or a pair of users who trust one another and who share a communications channel whose integrity is protected by some means (e.g., using handwritten notes or a voice channel). Both devices have a means to input or output a sequence of digits (i.e., they have at least a numeric keypad or a multidigit display, but not necessarily both).

- If a device does not have a keypad, then it must at least have an input (e.g., a button) allowing the successful conclusion of a procedure to be indicated to the device. Similarly, if a device lacks a multicharacter display, then it must at least have an output capable of indicating the success or failure of a procedure (e.g., red and green lights or a sound output).

We do not assume that the devices have any prior keying relationship (e.g., shared secret keys) or are equipped with any keys by their manufacturers. Of course, the problem would become dramatically easier if every device had a unique signature key pair and a certificate for its public key signed by a widely trusted CA. However the overhead of personalizing every device in this way is likely to be prohibitive, particularly for low-cost devices.

Similarly, we do not assume that the two devices share a trusted communications link (e.g., as might be provided by a hard-wired connection). Such a link, even if it only guaranteed data integrity and data origin authentication (and not confidentiality), would again make the problem simple, since it could be used to support a Diffie-Hellman exchange (as described in Chapter 12). However, it would be unreasonable to always expect such a link to exist, since many simple wireless devices are likely to possess no wired communications interfaces.

The standardized manual authentication protocols are summarized in Table 10.6. The clause number specified for ISO/IEC 9798-6 is taken from the current committee draft of this standard. We now describe two of the schemes from the current draft of ISO/IEC 9798-6.

Table 10.6   Manual Authentication Protocols

Source	Description
ISO/IEC 9798-6 clause 6.1	Uses a short check-value; suitable for use where one device has a display and the other a keypad; see Figure 10.13
ISO/IEC 9798-6 clause 6.2	Uses a short check-value; suitable for use where both devices have a display
ISO/IEC 9798-6 clause 7.1	Uses a MAC; suitable for use where both devices have a keypad; see Figure 10.14
ISO/IEC 9798-6 clause 7.2	Uses a MAC; suitable for use where one device has a display and the other a keypad

10.7.1 Manual authentication using a short check-value

We first describe a scheme which uses keyed check-functions having short check-values (e.g., of around 16–20 bits) and using short keys (again of 16–20 bits). These check-functions are essentially MAC functions producing short outputs. In practice, use of a conventional MAC function (see Chapter 7) will probably provide acceptable results; in such a case the short key could be padded with a fixed string to construct a block cipher key.

The scheme we describe is designed for use in the situation where one device (A) has a display and the other (B) has a keypad, although a simple variant exists for the case where both devices have a display. We also assume that the two devices wish to agree on the value of a public data string D, the possible uses of which are discussed below. The scheme operates as follows (see also Figure 10.13).

1. A data string D is agreed between A and B using the wireless channel.

2. Device A generates a random key K of length appropriate for use with the check-function (i.e., of 16–20 bits); A also generates the check-value $\text{MAC}_K(D)$. The key and check-value are then output to the display by device A.

3. The user enters the check-value and the key K, read from the display of device A, into device B (using the keypad).

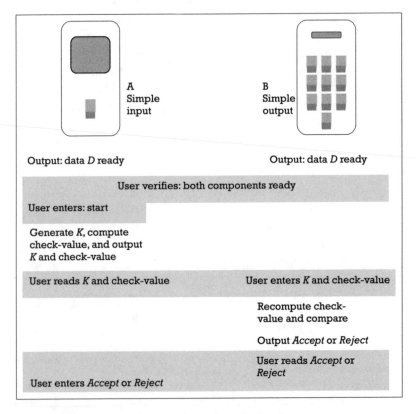

Figure 10.13 Manual authentication using a short check-value.

4.   Device B uses the key K provided by the user to recompute $\text{MAC}_K(D)$, and compares this with the value entered by the user. The device outputs an indication of success or failure, depending on whether or not the check-values agree.

5.   The user copies this success/failure indication back into device A.

The probability of a successful attack on this scheme (where A and B agree on different data values) is less than 2^{-13} (i.e., 1 in 8,000) for 16-bit keys and check-values and less than 2^{-17} (i.e., 1 in 130,000) for 20-bit keys and hash codes.

It should be clear that the data D could be the concatenation of A's and B's public keys, for some asymmetric cryptosystem. This could support the registration process for a small-scale PKI, or could simply be used as the basis for subsequent secure communications. In particular the public keys could be used (e.g., as Diffie-Hellman public keys) to provide the basis for an authenticated secret key establishment protocol, requiring no further intervention by the user.

As previously mentioned, a variant of the above mechanism can be devised to cover the situation where both devices A and B have a display, but neither of them has a keypad (although they must both possess a means of indicating successful completion of the protocol). Briefly, in this case, the first two steps are as above. However, in addition to displaying the key and check-value, device A sends the key to device B via the wireless channel (and hence in this case the key is available to an attacker). Device B uses the received key to recompute the check-value on its version of the data string, and finally displays the key received from A together with the check value it has computed. The user completes the process by comparing the values displayed by the two devices. Only if the key and check-value agree completely does the user give a "success" indication to both devices.

10.7.2   Manual authentication using a full-length MAC function

A different class of manual authentication protocols can be constructed using a conventional MAC function (again, see Chapter 7). The scheme we describe is designed for use in the situation where both devices have a keypad, although a simple variant exists for the case where one device has a display (see below). As previously, we assume that the two devices wish to agree on the value of a public data string D. The scheme operates as follows (see also Figure 10.14).

1.   A data string D is agreed between A and B using the wireless channel.

2.   The user generates a short random bit-string R, (e.g., of 16–20 bits) and enters it into both devices.

3.   Device A generates a random MAC key K_1 and computes the MAC value $M_1 = \text{MAC}_{K_1}(i_A||D||R)$, where i_A is an identifier for A. Device A sends M_1 to B via the wireless link.

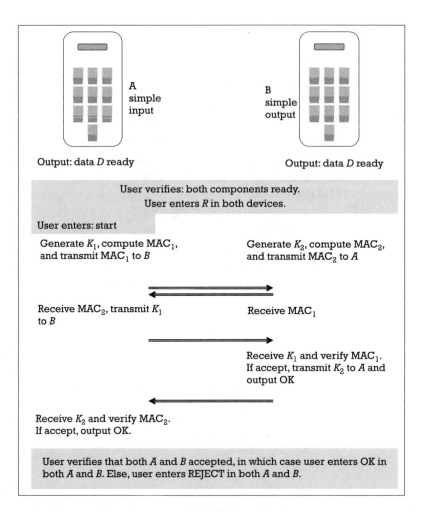

Figure 10.14 Manual authentication using a MAC.

4. Device B generates a random MAC key K_2 and computes the MAC value $M_2 = \text{MAC}_{K_2}(i_B\|D\|R)$, where i_B is an identifier for B. Device B sends M_2 to A via the wireless link.

5. When device A receives M_2 from B (and not before), A sends B the key K_1.

6. When device B receives M_1 from A (and not before), B sends A the key K_2.

7. On receipt of K_2, A uses it to recompute M_2, where the data employed in the computation consists of its stored value of D, the expected identifier i_B, and the random value R input by the user. If the recomputed M_2 agrees with the value received from B then A indicates success.

8. On receipt of K_1, B uses it to recompute M_1, where the data employed in the computation consists of its stored value of D, the expected identifier i_A, and the random value R input by the user.

If the recomputed M_1 agrees with the value received from A then B indicates success.

9. If (and only if) both devices indicate success, the user indicates success to both devices.

Finally note that steps 2/3 and also 4/5 may be conducted in parallel.

The likelihood of a successful attack against the above scheme is 2^{-r}, for an r-bit value R (i.e., the odds against a successful attack are 1 in 70,000 or 1 in a million for a 16- or 20-bit random value R).

Two variants of the scheme exist, both of which are included in the draft standard. The first variant involves a total of r "rounds," where r is the number of bits in R. In each round, one bit of R is used, and the devices exchange MACs and keys as in the scheme described above. While this increases significantly the amount of data exchanged between the devices, it removes the need for the user to give success indications to the devices at the end of the protocol.

The second variant applies to the case where one device has a display and the other has a keypad. In this case, step 2 is modified so that the device with the display generates the random value R and displays it to the user, who then enters it into the other device. All other steps of the scheme remain unchanged.

10.8 Choosing an authentication protocol

Choosing an authentication protocol appropriate for a particular application is a nontrivial task. The protocols discussed in this chapter cover a wide range of different situations with respect to resources of the two entities, including their keying relationship, the types of cryptographic scheme used, the requirements for stored state information, and the possible requirement for securely synchronized clocks. Moreover, some protocols provide mutual authentication whereas others only provide unilateral authentication. Finally, if it is also necessary to establish a shared secret key as a result of an authentication protocol, then other issues come into play, as discussed in Chapter 12.

First observe that manual authentication protocols, as discussed in Section 10.7, must be treated separately from other authentication protocols, since these are designed for a completely different type of environment. We therefore exclude these protocols from our discussion.

When choosing a protocol it is necessary to take into account the following factors in making a choice between protocols.

▸ Regardless of the operational environment, probably the most fundamental choice is between a unilateral or a mutual authentication protocol.

▸ If the parties involved in the protocols have access to securely synchronized clocks then the protocol used will typically involve one less message than where such clocks are not available. A similar saving can also be made if the parties involved share a pair of sequence numbers to be used for detecting replays of messages. However, managing such sequence numbers adds complexity and requires both parties to store state—indeed, if state is lost, then the result can be a catastrophic loss of the ability to authenticate other entities.

▸ Some protocols require the entities involved to generate random values [e.g., for random nonces or other random values used in the protocol (as in the zero-knowledge authentication protocols)]. In some cases, it may be nontrivial for a device to generate such a value, especially if the protocol is implemented within a very constrained environment such as a smart card. The failure to generate random values so that they are unpredictable to external observers may cause major vulnerabilities to arise.

▸ The nature of the keying relationship necessary to support the protocol should also be considered in the context of the operational environment. For example, if the two parties have an existing shared secret key, then one of the protocols specified in ISO/IEC 9798-4 may be most appropriate. However, if such a key does not exist, but the users will have access to a PKI, then a protocol using asymmetric cryptography (e.g., one of those specified in ISO/IEC 9798-3 or ISO/IEC 9798-5) may be more appropriate.

▸ Some cryptographic algorithms, notably most asymmetric algorithms, are considerably more complex to perform than others. This difference can play a major role in deciding which types of protocol to employ, particularly if the devices involved either have limiting processing resources or must conduct many instances of the protocol in parallel.

▸ Certain cryptographic techniques, notably digital signatures and MACs, are inherently more suited to providing integrity and origin protection for protocol messages than others, notably symmetric and asymmetric encryption. As we have seen, the use of encryption requires the deployment of additional techniques such as MDCs to ensure the integrity and origin authenticity of protocol messages. In general it is probably safer to restrict use of protocols based on encryption to legacy applications.

▸ Some protocols are more prone than others to denial of service (DoS) attacks, where one or more malicious parties attempts to disable a computer by causing it to perform large numbers of complex cryptographic computations (e.g., generating verifying signatures). This clearly relates to the previous issue, namely the computational complexity of the cryptographic algorithms in use. Some protocols have been designed to reduce the threat of such attacks by requiring the attacking parties to engage in at least as much computational effort as the potential victims (see also Chapter 12).

> The communications complexity of a protocol, (i.e., the number of messages) and the lengths of individual messages need to be considered. In some environments (e.g., those with restricted communications capabilities), the communications complexity will need to be minimized. In general, minimizing communications loads will tend to favor protocols using symmetric rather than asymmetric cryptography, as well as favoring those based on time-stamps rather than nonces.

> Finally, the protocol user may well wish to consider whether or not a protocol possesses a proof of security. A proof of security is not a guarantee that an attack cannot be found, since a provably secure protocol will only be guaranteed to combat threats within the scope of the mathematical model within which the proof has been constructed. Moreover, the proof itself may be incorrect. However, all else being equal, it is reasonable to argue that a protocol with a proof is to be preferred to one without.

10.9 Notes

Section 10.1

Chapter 10 of Menezes, van Oorschot, and Vanstone [1] provides a more detailed discussion of authentication protocols. A more recent comprehensive discussion of authentication protocols can be found in Boyd and Mathuria's book [2].

The first discussion of authentication protocols is contained in the landmark 1979 paper of Needham and Schroeder [3]. This paper contains a series of protocols based on different cryptographic primitives and has set the context for the now large literature on authentication protocols.

Section 10.2

The first published standard for authentication protocols was the 1988 edition of X.509 [4]. One section of this CCITT Recommendation contains a series of three authentication protocols based on the use of digital signatures (under the heading of "strong authentication"). Unfortunately, one of the three protocols contained a flaw, as discovered by Burrows, Abadi, and Needham [5–8] (see also [9]). This flaw was rectified in the second and subsequent editions of the recommendation [10–12] (see also the parallel ISO/IEC standard, ISO/IEC 9594-8 [13]).

ISO work on standards for authentication protocols started in the late 1980s, culminating in the publication in the early to mid-1990s of the first editions of Parts 1–3 of ISO/IEC 9798 [14–16]. Work on Part 4 commenced as the first three parts neared completion, with the first edition appearing in 1995 [17]. All of these four parts were then revised, essentially for editorial reasons (no changes were made to the mechanisms), and the revised standards appeared in the late 1990s [18–21]. The original motivation for ISO/IEC 9798 Parts 2 and 3 was provided by Needham and Schroeder [3].

Work on ISO/IEC 9798-5 started somewhat later, and the standard was finally published in 1999 [22]. A revised version, containing a larger selection of mechanisms, is now nearing publication [23]. ISO/IEC 9798-6 [24] is of much more recent origin, work only starting in early 2003. The standard adopts techniques previously proposed for Bluetooth and designed to enable mobile devices owned by a single individual to set up secure links.

NIST FIPS Pub. 196 [25] is based on ISO/IEC 9798-3 and was published in 1997.

The Kerberos protocol [26, 27] was developed as part of the Athena project at MIT, quite independently from the ISO/IEC work. The Kerberos protocol has evolved over time, so that the version specified in RFC 1510 [28] is actually Version 5 of the scheme. The S/KEY protocol (specified in RFC 1760 [29]) is closely based on an original idea of Lamport published in 1981 [30]. RFC 1704 [31], dating back to 1994, gives a lot of useful general advice on authentication methods for use across the Internet. The *Distributed Authentication Security Service* (DASS) protocol is specified in RFC 1507 [32].

Section 10.3

Using a combination of symmetric encryption and an MDC to provide origin authentication and integrity protection for a message is not a recommended approach. Both the method for encryption and the MDC technique need to be selected with considerable care. Some versions of Kerberos possess vulnerabilities arising from the use of an inappropriate MDC (see [33]). For a more detailed discussion of these issues, see Section 9.6.5 of [1].

There is a large literature on zero knowledge protocols. Section 10.4 of [1] contains a useful overview.

Section 10.4

The classic 1978 paper of Lamport [34] provides a detailed discussion of the use of various types of time stamps in a general distributed systems setting. The need to keep a log of recently received messages to prevent replays of messages within the "window" of time stamp checking was first discussed by Lam [35].

There are a number of other possible issues with the use of time stamps. Gong [36] has pointed out that if an authentication protocol is executed when one party has an incorrectly synchronized clock, the messages sent in that protocol may be used later to impersonate one of the entities even after all clocks have been correctly synchronized. Bellovin and Merritt [33, 37] also provide a discussion of the risks of using time stamps.

One important scheme for providing securely synchronized clocks is the Network Time Protocol (NTP), Version 3 of which is specified in RFC 1305 [38]. A simplified version of NTP for Internet use, known as the Simple Network Time Protocol (SNTP), is specified in RFC 2030 [39]. The NTP protocol uses symmetric cryptographic techniques, and ongoing work within the IETF

Secure Time Working Group is aimed at specifying how public key cryptography can be used to support NTP [40].

The possibility of preplay attacks on protocols using predictable nonces was first pointed out by Gong [41].

Section 10.5

The existence of reflection attacks, the motive for including the identifier for the recipient within the scope of encryption and MAC computations in symmetric cryptography–based protocols were first pointed out in [42]. An alternative to the use of identifiers (also pointed out in ISO/IEC 9798-2 and 9798-4) is to employ unidirectional keys, that is, separate keys for protecting messages sent from A to B and from B to A.

The limitations of S/KEY in the case where the host can be impersonated appear to have been observed by a number of authors in the mid-1990s—see, for example, [43] or Note 10.7 of [1].

AKEP2 was first proposed by Bellare and Rogaway in 1993 [44], and is given as Protocol 12.20 in [1]. A version of this protocol is included in a 1999 Internet draft [45], although this draft has now expired.

Note that neither of the TTP protocols standardized in ISO/IEC 9798-2 are quite the same as the Needham-Schroeder protocol because of the need to address the problem identified by Denning and Sacco [46].

If Kerberos is used with a guessable password as the long-term secret shared by the client and the authentication server, then password-guessing attacks may be possible. This and other possible security issues with Kerberos are discussed by Bellovin and Merritt in [33, 37], who also propose possible solutions to the password guessing problem. For details of the current version of Kerberos, see http://web.mit.edu/kerberos/www.

Section 10.6

The ID-based unilateral authentication protocol specified in clause 5 of ISO/IEC 9798-5 is a generalization of the Fiat-Shamir protocol [47] due to Guillou and Quisquater [48]. The integer-factorization–based unilateral authentication protocol given in clause 6 of ISO/IEC 9798-5 is the QG2 protocol of Guillou and Quisquater [49]. The unilateral authentication protocol based on discrete logarithms in ISO/IEC 9798-5 clause 7 is due to Schnorr [50]. The GPS1/GPS2/GPS3 unilateral authentication mechanisms, specified in clause 8 of ISO/IEC 9798-5, are attributed to Girault, Paillès, Poupard, and Stern [51–53]. Finally, the unilateral authentication protocol based on asymmetric encryption given in clause 9.3 of ISO/IEC 9798-5 is attributed to Brandt et al. [54].

Early versions of the ISO/IEC 9798-3 three-pass mutual authentication protocol using signatures and nonces were subject to interleaving attacks; see, for example, [55].

The mutual authentication mechanism based on asymmetric encryption is known as the Helsinki protocol. An earlier version of this protocol was shown to be flawed by Horng and Hsu [56] and subsequently fixed in [57].

Interestingly, the flaw and the fix mirror the changes proposed after similar problems were identified in a Needham and Schroeder protocol by Lowe [58, 59]. If the asymmetric encryption function in use has the nonmalleability property (see, for example, [60]), then the hash codes do not need to be included in messages M_1 and M_2 of the Helsinki protocol.

Section 10.7

The problem of initializing personal devices is discussed by Stajano and Anderson in [61, 62]. For a general guide to manual authentication, see [63, 64]. The current version of ISO/IEC 9798-6 (the first CD [24]) contains a total of four different manual authentication mechanisms. Two of these mechanisms derive from work of Gehrmann and Nyberg [65]. The other two mechanisms are from Larsson [66] and Jakobsson [67].

Some of the ISO/IEC 9798-6 schemes may also be included in a future version of the Bluetooth standards. The existing Bluetooth specifications already contain a solution to device imprinting, but this solution has well-known security shortcomings if the initial exchange between devices can be wiretapped [63, 68].

The first protocol of this type was proposed by Maher [69], who proposed using manual techniques to authenticate a standard Diffie-Hellman key establishment process (see Chapter 12). However, the techniques contained in ISO/IEC 9798-6 reduce the work involved for the human operator of the devices.

Section 10.8

The Bellare and Rogaway AKEP2 protocol possesses a proof of security [44]. Blake-Wilson, Johnson, and Menezes [70, 71] examined signature-based authentication protocols and have, amongst other things, shown that the the three-pass signature-based protocol from ISO/IEC 9798-3 is secure.

For further details about proofs of security for authentication protocols, the reader is referred to Ryan et al. [72] and Boyd and Mathuria [2].

References

[1]   Menezes, A. J., P. C. van Oorschot, and S. A. Vanstone, *Handbook of Applied Cryptography*, Boca Raton, FL: CRC Press, 1997.

[2]   Boyd, C. A., and A. Mathuria, *Protocols for Key Establishment and Authentication*, New York: Springer-Verlag, 2003.

[3]   Needham, R. M., and M. D. Schroeder, "Using Encryption for Authentication in Large Networks of Computers," *Communications of the ACM*, Vol. 21, 1978, pp. 993–999.

[4]   Comité Consultatif International de Télégraphique et Téléphonique, *CCITT Recommendation X.509 (1988), The Directory—Authentication Framework*, 1988.

[5]   Burrows, M., M. Abadi, and R. Needham, "Authentication: A Practical Study in Belief and Action," in M. Vardi, (ed.), *Proceedings of the Second Conference on*

Theoretical Aspects of Reasoning and Knowledge, Morgan Kaufmann, 1988, pp. 325–342.

[6] Burrows, M., M. Abadi, and R. Needham, "A Logic of Authentication," *ACM Operating Systems Review,* Vol. 23, No. 5, 1989, pp. 1–13.

[7] Burrows, M., M. Abadi, and R. Needham, "A Logic of Authentication," *Proceedings of the Royal Society of London, Series A,* Vol. 426, 1989, pp. 233–271.

[8] Burrows, M., M. Abadi, and R. Needham, *A Logic of Authentication,* Technical Report 39, Digital Equipment Corporation Systems Research Center, February 1990, revised version.

[9] I'Anson, C., and C. J. Mitchell. "Security Defects in CCITT Recommendation X.509—The Directory Authentication Framework," *ACM Computer Communication Review,* Vol. 20, No. 2, 1990, pp. 30–34.

[10] International Telecommunication Union, *ITU-T Recommendation X.509 (1993), The Directory—Authentication Framework,* 2nd ed., 1993.

[11] International Telecommunication Union, *ITU-T Recommendation X.509 (08/97), The Directory—Authentication Framework,* 3rd ed., 1997.

[12] International Telecommunication Union. *ITU-T Recommendation X.509 (03/2000), The Directory—Public-Key and Attribute Certificate Frameworks,* 4th ed., 2000.

[13] International Organization for Standardization, *ISO/IEC 9594–8: 2001, Information Technology—Open Systems Interconnection—The Directory: Part 8: Public-Key and Attribute Certificate Frameworks,* 4th ed., 2001.

[14] International Organization for Standardization, *ISO/IEC 9798–1: 1991, Information Technology—Security Techniques—Entity Authentication Mechanisms—Part 1: General Model,* 1991.

[15] International Organization for Standardization, *ISO/IEC 9798–2: 1994, Information Technology—Security Techniques—Entity Authentication Mechanisms—Part 2: Entity Authentication Using Symmetric Techniques,* 1994.

[16] International Organization for Standardization, *ISO/IEC 9798–3: 1994, Information Technology—Security Techniques—Entity Authentication Mechanisms—Part 3: Entity Authentication Using a Public Key Algorithm,* 1994.

[17] International Organization for Standardization, *ISO/IEC 9798–4: 1995, Information Technology—Security Techniques—Entity Authentication—Part 4: Mechanisms Using a Cryptographic Check Function,* 1995.

[18] International Organization for Standardization, *ISO/IEC 9798–1: 1997, Information Technology—Security Techniques—Entity Authentication—Part 1: General,* 2nd ed., 1997.

[19] International Organization for Standardization, *ISO/IEC 9798–2: 1999, Information Technology—Security Techniques—Entity Authentication—Part 2: Mechanisms Using Symmetric Encipherment Algorithms,* 2nd ed., 1999.

[20] International Organization for Standardization, *ISO/IEC 9798–3: 1998, Information Technology—Security Techniques—Entity Authentication—Part 3: Mechanisms Using Digital Signature Techniques,* 2nd ed., 1998.

[21] International Organization for Standardization, *ISO/IEC 9798–4: 1999, Information Technology—Security Techniques—Entity Authentication—Part 4: Mechanisms Using a Cryptographic Check Function,* 2nd ed., 1999.

[22]   International Organization for Standardization, *ISO/IEC 9798-5: 1999, Information Technology—Security Techniques—Entity Authentication—Part 5: Mechanisms Using Zero Knowledge Techniques*, 1999.

[23]   International Organization for Standardization, *ISO/IEC FCD 9798–5, Information Technology—Security Techniques—Entity Authentication—Part 5: Mechanisms Using Zero Knowledge Techniques*, 2003.

[24]   International Organization for Standardization, *ISO/IEC CD 9798–6, Information Technology—Security Techniques—Entity Authentication—Part 6: Mechanisms Using Manual Data Transfer*, December 2003.

[25]   National Institute of Standards and Technology (NIST), *Federal Information Processing Standards Publication 196 (FIPS PUB 196): Entity Authentication Using Public Key Cryptography*, February 1997.

[26]   Steiner, J. G., C. Neuman, and J. I. Schiller, "Kerberos: An Authentication Service for Open Network Systems," *Proceedings: Usenix Association, Winter Conference 1988*, Berkeley, CA, February 1988, pp. 191–202.

[27]   Neuman, B. C., and T. Ts'o, "Kerberos: An Authentication Service for Computer Networks," *IEEE Communications Magazine*, Vol. 32, No. 9, September 1994, pp. 33–38.

[28]   Kohl, J., and C. Neuman, *RFC 1510, The Kerberos Network Authentication Service (V5)*, Internet Engineering Task Force, September 1993.

[29]   Haller, N., *RFC 1760, The S/KEY One-Time Password System*, Internet Engineering Task Force, February 1995.

[30]   Lamport, L., "Password Authentication with Insecure Communication," *Communications of the ACM*, Vol. 24, 1981, pp. 770–772.

[31]   Haller, N., and R. Atkinson, *RFC 1704, On Internet Authentication*, Internet Engineering Task Force, October 1994.

[32]   Kaufman, C., *RFC 1507, DASS: Distributed Authentication Security Service*, Internet Engineering Task Force, September 1993.

[33]   Bellovin, S. M., and M. Merritt, "Limitations of the Kerberos Authentication System," *Proceedings of the Usenix Winter 1991 Conference*, 1991, pp. 253–267.

[34]   Lamport, L., "Time, Clocks, and the Ordering of Events in a Distributed System," *Communications of the ACM*, Vol. 21, 1978, pp. 558–565.

[35]   Lam, K.-Y., "Building an Authentication Service for Distributed Systems," *Journal of Computer Security*, Vol. 1, 1993, pp. 73–84.

[36]   Gong, L., "A Security Risk of Depending on Synchronized Clocks," *ACM Operating Systems Review*, Vol. 26, No. 1 January 1992, pp. 49–53.

[37]   Bellovin, S. M., and M. Merritt, "Limitations of the Kerberos Authentication System," *ACM Computer Communication Review*, Vol. 20, No. 5, October 1990, pp. 119–132.

[38]   Mills, D. L., *RFC 1305, Network Time Protocol (Version 3): Specification, Implementation and Analysis*, Internet Engineering Task Force, March 1992.

[39]   Mills, D. L., *RFC 2030, Simple Network Time Protocol (SNTP) Version 4 for IPv4, IPv6 and OSI*, Internet Engineering Task Force, October 1996.

[40]   Mills, D. L., *Internet Draft draft-ietf-stime-ntpauth-04, Public Key Cryptography for the Network Time Protocol: Version 2*, Internet Engineering Task Force, November 2002.

[41] Gong, L., "Variations on the Themes of Message Freshness and Re-play," *Proceedings: Computer Security Foundations Workshop VI*, June 1993, pp. 131–136.

[42] Mitchell, C. J., "Limitations of Challenge-Response Entity Authentication," *Electronics Letters*, Vol. 25, 1989, pp. 1195–1196.

[43] Mitchell, C. J., and L. Chen, "Comments on the S/KEY User Authentica-tion Scheme," *ACM Operating Systems Review*, Vol. 30, No. 4, October 1996, pp. 12–16.

[44] Bellare, M., and P. Rogaway, "Entity Authentication and Key Distribution," in D. R. Stinson, (ed.), *Advances in Cryptology—Crypto '93*, Vol. 773, *Lecture Notes in Computer Science*, Springer-Verlag, 1994, pp. 232–249.

[45] Doonan, W., *Internet Draft draft-ietf-cat-sskm-01, SPKM with Shared Secret Keys (SSKM)*, Internet Engineering Task Force, 1999.

[46] Denning, D. E., and G. M. Sacco, "Timestamps in Key Distribution Protocols," *Communications of the ACM*, Vol. 24 1981, pp. 533–536.

[47] Fiat, A., and A. Shamir, "How to Prove Yourself: Practical Solutions to Iden-tification and Signature Problems," in A. M. Odlyzko, (ed.), *Advances in Cryptology—Crypto '86*, Vol. 263, *Lecture Notes in Computer Science*, Springer-Verlag, 1987, pp. 186–194.

[48] Guillou, L. C., and J.-J. Quisquater, "A Practical Zero-Knowledge Protocol Fit-ted to Security Microprocessor Minimizing Both Trasmission and Memory," in C. G. Günther, (ed.), *Advances in Cryptology—Eurocrypt '88*, Vol. 330, *Lecture Notes in Computer Science*, Springer-Verlag, 1988, pp. 123–128.

[49] Guillou, L. C., M. Ugon, and J.-J. Quisquater, "Cryptographic Authentication Protocols for Smart Cards," *Computer Networks*, Vol. 36, 2001, pp. 437–451.

[50] Schnorr, C. P., "Efficient Identification and Signatures for Smart Cards," in G. Brassard, (ed.), *Advances in Cryptology—Crypto '89*, Vol. 435, *Lecture Notes in Computer Science*, Springer-Verlag, 1990, pp. 239–252.

[51] Girault, M., "Self-Certified Public Keys," in D. W. Davies, (ed.), *Advances in Cryptology—Eurocrypt '91*, Vol. 547, *Lecture Notes in Computer Science*, Springer-Verlag, 1992, pp. 490–497.

[52] Girault, M., and J.-C. Pailles, "On-Line/Off-Line RSA-Like," *Proceedings of WCC 2003*, 2003.

[53] Poupard, G., and J. Stern, "Security Analysis of a Practical On the Fly Authenti-cation and Signature Generation," in K. Nyberg, (ed.), *Advances in Cryptology—Eurocrypt '98*, Vol. 1403, *Lecture Notes in Computer Science*, Springer-Verlag, 1998, pp. 422–436.

[54] Brandt, J., et al., "Zero-Knowledge Authentication Scheme with Secret Key Exchange (Extended Abstract)," in S. Goldwasser, (ed.), *Advances in Cryptology—Crypto '88*, Vol. 403 of *Lecture Notes in Computer Science*, Springer-Verlag, 1990, pp. 583–588.

[55] Gollmann, D., "What Do We Mean by Entity Authentication?" *Proceedings: 1996 IEEE Symposium on Security and Privacy*, 1996, pp. 46–54.

[56] Horng, G., and C.-K. Hsu, "Weakness in the Helsinki Protocol," *Electronics Let-ters*, Vol. 34, 1998, pp. 354–355.

[57] Mitchell, C. J., and C. Y. Yeun, "Fixing a Problem in the Helsinki Protocol," *ACM Operating Systems Review*, Vol. 32, No. 4, October 1998, pp. 21–24.

[58]   Lowe, G., "An Attack on the Needham-Schroeder Public-Key Authentication Protocol," *Information Processing Letters*, Vol. 56, 1995, pp. 131–133.

[59]   Lowe, G., "Breaking and Fixing the Needham-Schroeder Public-Key Protocol Using FDR," in T. Margaria and B. Steffen, (eds.), *Tools and Algorithms for Construction and Analysis of Systems, Second International Workshop, TACAS '96*, Vol. 1055, *Lecture Notes in Computer Science*, Springer-Verlag, 1996, pp. 147–166.

[60]   Bellare, M., et al., "Relations Among Notions of Security for Public-Key Encryption Schemes," in H. Krawczyk, (ed.), *Advances in Cryptology–Crypto '98*, Vol. 1462, *Lecture Notes in Computer Science*, Springer-Verlag, 1998, pp. 26–45.

[61]   Stajano, F., *Security for Ubiquitous Computing*, New York: John Wiley and Sons, 2002.

[62]   Stajano, F., and R. Anderson, "The Resurrecting Duckling: Security Issues for Ad-Hoc Wireless Networks," in B. Christianson et al., (eds.), *Security Protocols, 7th International Workshop*, Vol. 1976, *Lecture Notes in Computer Science*, Springer-Verlag, 2000, pp. 172–194.

[63]   Gehrmann, C., C. J. Mitchell, and K. Nyberg, "Manual Authentication for Wireless Devices," *Cryptobytes*, Vol. 7, No. 1, 2004, pp. 29–37.

[64]   Gehrmann, C., and K. Nyberg, "Security in Personal Area Networks," in C. J. Mitchell, (ed.), *Security for Mobility*, Ch. 9, New York: IEE, 2004, pp. 191–230.

[65]   Gehrmann, C., and K. Nyberg, "Enhancements to Bluetooth Baseband Security," *Proceedings of Nordsec 2001*, November 2001.

[66]   Larsson, J.-O., "Higher Layer Key Exchange Techniques for Bluetooth Security," *Open Group Conference*, Amsterdam, October 2001.

[67]   Jakobsson, M., "Method and Apparatus for Immunizing Against Offline Dictionary Attacks," U.S. Patent Application 60/283,996, filed on April 16, 2001.

[68]   Jakobsson, M., and S. Wetzel, "Security Weaknesses in Bluetooth," in D. Naccache, (ed.), *Topics in Cryptology—CT-RSA 2001*, Vol. 2020, *Lecture Notes in Computer Science*, Springer-Verlag, 2001, pp. 176–191.

[69]   Maher, D. P., "Secure Communication Method and Apparatus," U.S. Patent Number 5,450,493, September 1995.

[70]   Blake-Wilson, S., D. Johnson, and A. Menezes, "Key Agreement Protocols and their Security Analysis," in M. Darnell, (ed.), *Cryptography and Coding, 6th IMA International Conference*, Vol. 1355, *Lecture Notes in Computer Science*, Springer-Verlag, 1997, pp. 30–45.

[71]   Blake-Wilson, S., and A. Menezes, "Entity Authentication and Authenticated Key Transport Protocols Employing Asymmetric Techniques," in B. Christianson et al., (eds.), *Security Protocols, 5th International Workshop*, Vol. 1361, *Lecture Notes in Computer Science*, Springer-Verlag, 1998, pp. 137–158.

[72]   Ryan, P., et al., *The Modeling and Analysis of Security Protocols: The CSP Approach*, Reading, MA: Addison-Wesley, 2000.

Key Management Frameworks

Contents

11.1 Standards for key management

11.2 Definitions and basic properties

11.3 The general framework

11.4 The ANSI X9.24 framework

11.5 Notes

The evolution of key management has been somewhat different to the evolution of specific cryptographic mechanisms. Mechanisms have usually developed through a series of theoretical and practical discoveries, obtained by proposing and breaking schemes. Key management has evolved as a series of best practices, obtained from practical experience.

The fact that the security of any cryptographic system depends on the security of its keys means that these keys must be given the highest levels of protection. However every operation using a key potentially leaks some information about its value. For example, if we are dealing with an encryption key, then every ciphertext that an attacker observes tells the attacker that the secret key must be one in which that ciphertext could be produced by encrypting a message under that key. The more the attacker knows about the properties of the message, the more information he or she gains about the key from the observed ciphertext.

Of course, this information still needs to be processed in order to be able to find a useful method of attacking a scheme. From a purely practical point of view it is easy to see that the longer a key is in use, the more time an attacker will have to launch a meaningful attack against the scheme. Moreover, if a key is compromised for any reason, the damage will potentially last for the period that the key remains in use—another good reason for frequent key updates.

All of this leads us to the motivating observation of key management: that keys must have a usage lifetime, known as a key *life cycle*. This life cycle must deal with the creation, distribution, usage, archiving, and destruction of keys.

This chapter will only deal with general frameworks for key management. Specific mechanisms (in particular, mechanisms for key distribution) will be discussed in later chapters.

11.1 Standards for key management

Three bodies have worked extensively on key management issues: ANSI X9, ISO TC68, and ISO/IEC JTC1. ISO/IEC JTC1 have

published a three-part general purpose standard on key management: ISO/
IEC 11770. The first part of this standard is of particular relevance to this
chapter. This part is dedicated purely to developing a key management framework, and many of the concepts of key management we will be discussing
are taken from it.

As has been discussed several times in previous chapters, the financial
sector was one of the first major industries to heavily adopt the use of cryptography. It was particularly quick to recognize the importance of standardized key management techniques. As early as 1985 ANSI published its first
standards on this subject: ANSI X9.17 (first published in 1985) and ANSI
X9.24 (first published in 1992). Both deal with key management issues for
financial institutions; ANSI X9.17 deals with key management issues between banking establishments, and ANSI X9.24 deals with key management
issues between retail devices, such as between point-of-sale devices and the
banking establishments that control them.

However, ANSI X9.17 specifically targeted the use of single-length DES
keys and the financial institutions eventually recognized that this would not
give them the levels of protection they require (see Section 4.2.1 for more
details about DES). As a result, ANSI X9.17 was withdrawn in 1999. On the
other hand, the third edition of ANSI X9.24 was recently published. This
latter standard deals exclusively with symmetric key management and only
standardizes those techniques that utilize symmetric cryptography. It does
not explicitly develop a key management framework but rather implies one
by placing strict rules on the way keys can be used and manipulated.

Both of these standards have played an influential role in development
of the key management standards published by the ISO banking technical
committee, TC68. This committee has published several standards that include (mostly implicit) key management frameworks for banking. The most
relevant of these are ISO 8732 (which is based on ANSI X9.17) and ISO
11568 (which is a multipart standard based on ANSI X9.24). The implied
framework of these standards is essentially the same as the framework for
ANSI X9.24 described in Section 11.4.

11.2   Definitions and basic properties

Key management is concerned with all operations to do with keys *except*
their actual use by a cryptographic algorithm. This includes their generation,
distribution, storage, and destruction.

11.2.1   Threats and protection

Unlike security mechanisms such as encryption schemes or digital signatures, it is quite difficult to make precise mathematical statements about
what constitutes an attack against a key management system. However, it
is easy to make some informal statements about possible threats to security

concerning keys. The main threats against a key management system include the following.

> • The unauthorized disclosure of keys;

> • The unauthorized modification of keys;

> • The misuse of keys. This could mean either the use of a key by some party without authorization or for some unauthorized purpose, or the use of a key whose usage period has expired.

The realization of any of these threats may compromise a security service, although this depends on the nature of the security service offered. It is important that a security policy specifies which threats the key management system needs to address.

It is important to note that it is not always necessary to find a cryptographic solution to a key management problem. Indeed ISO/IEC 11770 identifies three noncryptographic methods for providing key security.

The first is the use of physical security. If a key is kept physically secure [e.g., by storing it in a tamper-resistant security module (TRSM) that is carried around by the user (sometimes called a "token")] then many key management problems are removed. For example, it would be very difficult for an attacker to find out the value of the key or to modify it remotely. Standards for security modules are briefly discussed in Chapter 16.

Alternatively, keys can be protected by noncryptographic means. For example, the freshness and validity of keys can be ensured by associating them with time-stamps or sequence numbers. These mechanisms may not provide a complete security solution and may need to be combined with other (possibly cryptographic) mechanisms.

Last, it is possible to approach key management from an organizational or hierarchial point of view. Here levels of importance are attached to keys, and lower level keys are derived from higher level ones. This will be discussed in Section 11.2.4.

11.2.2   Basic definitions

The first important task that the ISO/IEC 11770 standard undertakes is to give some precise definitions about keys and key management techniques. The three basic definitions are listed as follows.

> • *Key:*   A sequence of symbols that controls the operation of a cryptographic transformation (e.g., encipherment, decipherment, cryptographic check function, signature generation, or signature verification).

> • *Keying material:*   The data (e.g., keys and initialization values) necessary to establish and maintain cryptographic keying relationships. Keying material is usually transmitted between entities who wish to set up a key. It could be that the keying material is a key that one party

has generated and is securely transmitting to another, or it could be that the keying material is only some partial information about that key and that this keying material needs to be combined with other keying material at a later stage to form a key. This leads naturally to the concept of key control.

▶ *Key control:* The ability to choose the key, or the parameters used in key computation. Therefore, if one party was to generate a secret key and then distribute it to other parties, then that party would be said to have key control as they have the ability to choose the key that is distributed. This is a very simple example; deciding which party has key control in a protocol can be a very difficult issue. This issue is discussed in more detail in Chapter 12.

11.2.3 Key separation

One important principle of key management is key separation. Simply stated, key separation is the idea that a key should only ever be used for one purpose. For example, an encryption key should only be ever used in conjunction with a encryption algorithm and not, for example, also be used with a MAC algorithm (even if that MAC algorithm uses the same block cipher as the encryption scheme).

Key separation is enforced because it can be very difficult to determine if a system is secure if the keys in that system are used to do two different things. The entire system could be insecure even though the individual components of the system are secure.

The principle of key separation does not just apply to algorithms (e.g., one key for a MAC algorithm and one for an encryption algorithm) but also to the purposes that these algorithms are put to. Consider, as a simple example, a MAC scheme; the scheme is secure only if each MAC key is only shared between two entities; hence it is important that no one key is used to compute the MAC of messages intended for different recipients.

11.2.4 Key hierarchies

A key hierarchy is a way of adding structure to a set of keys and provides a convenient way of defining the scope of use of each key, and hence helps manage key separation. In a key hierarchy keys are classified in terms of levels of importance and, except for the keys at the lowest level, keys at one level are only used to protect keys at the level direct below. (This is an example of key separation.) This organizational approach has two major advantages. First, it becomes easier to change the lower level keys more frequently without having to use complex key distribution methods. Second, it limits the use of the higher level, long-term keys, thus reducing the opportunities an attacker has to discover information about them.

The main disadvantage of key hierarchies is that the compromise of a high-level key may mean that all of the keys below it are compromised too. If the master key, the key at the very top of the hierarchy, is compromised then every key in the system may be compromised.

Often a new key is formed from a higher level key by "derivation." This involves combining the (secret) higher level key with some nonsecret data to obtain the new lower level key. For example, one could form a series of new keys for the employees of a department by applying a hash function (see Chapter 6) to a concatenation of the employee's name and the secret departmental key. The employees can then derive session keys from the combination of their own secret key and, for example, the date and/or time. It would be these session keys that are actually used to perform cryptographic operations.

Derived keys must be generated using a special security process. The process must be nonreversible and unpredictable. It must be nonreversible so that it is impossible for any number of holders of the derived keys to be able to find out any information about higher level keys, even if these key holders share information about their own keys. It must be unpredictable so that nobody can predict the value of a key unless he or she holds the higher level keys used to derive it.

If keys are derived in this manner, then obviously each key would be a function of the higher level key that created it. Thus, if a higher level key is compromised, all of that key's "children" (and their children, etc.) will be compromised too. Key hierarchies are usually only associated with the use of symmetric schemes.

11.2.5   Registration authorities

A key management system will often include the use of many trusted third parties (TTPs) (see Chapter 14). These TTPs may be involved in such areas as key generation, key distribution (see Chapter 12), or the certification of public keys (see Chapter 13).

One important entity that is often overlooked is the *registration authority*. A registration authority is a TTP responsible for verifying a user's identity when issuing a key to that user and for storing management information regarding users and their keys.

The focus of the registration authority differs slightly in asymmetric and symmetric schemes. In a symmetric scheme the registration authority's primary responsibility is to maintain a register of the keys and related information (such as the owner of the key). In an asymmetric scheme, where the focus is on authenticating a user's public key to another user, the main purpose of a registration authority is to check a user's identity.

11.3   The general framework

ISO/IEC 11770-1 standardizes a general model for the key life cycle. In this model, keys exist in one of three different *key states* (shown in Figure 11.1). These states are described as follows.

▸ *Pending active:*   The key exists but has not yet been activated for use. A key becomes pending active after it has been generated and remains so throughout any distribution and storage that occurs before the key is actually made available for use.

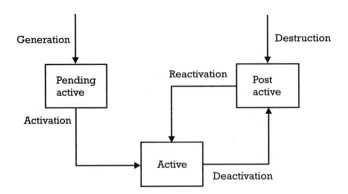

Figure 11.1   The key life cycle.

> *Active:*   In this state the key is actually in use.

> *Post active:*   In this state the key has been retired from active use but has not yet been destroyed. This does not mean that the key cannot ever be used again. Indeed it is often quite important that the key be available for certain specific uses such as verification of digital signatures or decryption of previously encrypted messages.

A key moves between key states by *key transitions*. In broad terms these are the following.

> *Generation:*   The key is generated by some party (who would have key control) or some collection of parties. The key then becomes pending active. As a pending active key it can be archived, registered, and distributed to users.

> *Activation:*   A key becomes active by being activated. This may involve some authority publicly declaring that a key is valid (e.g., by issuing a certificate).

> *Deactivation:*   Similarly a key becomes post active by being deactivated. This can occur, for example, if the key's initially agreed usage period has expired or if some authority declares that the key should no longer be in use (e.g., by revoking its certificate).

> *Reactivation:*   A key that has been deactivated (i.e., is now post active) can be reactivated and become active again. This may occur if, for example, the key's usage period is extended or if the relevant authority withdraws its revocation.

> *Destruction:*   If the key never needs to be used again then the key should be securely destroyed. This might not be as easy as it sounds! The key must be destroyed in a way that means in cannot be recovered (in accordance with the security policy). Furthermore, the destruction key transition is not the same as the destruction of a single copy of a key. The destruction key transition involves destroying all of the

copies of a key, except (possibly) those keys that have been deliberately archived, and deregistering the key.

This model provides a general working framework to talk about the different states that a key may be in, and what happens when a key moves between states. This is somewhat similar to the security framework developed in ISO 7498-2 (see Chapter 3). It provides a framework for discussing key management principles without actually providing any details about the services necessary to implement this framework.

Just as in ISO 7498-2, ISO/IEC 11770-1 also describes the services that would need to be in place in order to implement this framework. It is quite a long list! We will cover these by discussing each of the different possible key transitions. The complete list of services is summarized in Table 11.1.

Of course, even when a user has established which services are required to implement a security policy, the user still has to find specific mechanisms for making those services available. Mechanisms for distributing secret keys are discussed in Chapter 12. Mechanisms for making public keys available are discussed in Chapter 13.

11.3.1 Key generation

The key generation transition creates a key out of nothing, or rather it creates a key based only on the specifications of the key required and a good source of random bits (see Chapter 16). There are many services that can be offered when a key is generated but only the following service is mandatory.

Table 11.1   The Relationship Between Services and Transitions

Transition	Service	Applicability
Generation	Generate Key	Mandatory
	Register Key	Optional
	Create key certificate	Optional
	Distribute key	Optional
	Store key	Optional
Activation	Install key	Mandatory
	Create key certificate	Optional
	Derive key	Optional
	Distribute key	Optional
	Register key	Optional
	Store key	Optional
Deactivation	Archive key	Optional
	Revoke key	Optional
	Store key	Optional
Reactivation	Install key	Mandatory
	Create key certificate	Optional
	Derive key	Optional
	Distribute key	Optional
	Store key	Optional
Destruction	Destroy key	Mandatory
	Deregister key	Mandatory (if registered)
	Archive key	Optional

Generate key   This is the service that actually generates the key. The exact form the service takes depends very much on the nature of the key that needs to produced. If a secret (symmetric) key needs to be produced then the key generation process will typically involve generating a random bit string of a specified length. If an asymmetric key pair needs to be produced, then this will typically be a lot more complicated and computationally demanding. In either case a good source of random bits will be required (see Chapter 16).

Key generation is considered quite different from key derivation (see Section 11.3.2). Although both produce a key, the generate key service produces this key using a random (probabilistic) process and should be considered the start of a key's life cycle. To contrast, the derive key service is deterministic and gains its security from taking secret inputs (the higher level keys in the key hierarchy), rather than by generating a new key randomly.

A key that has just been generated may not be ready for immediate use; there may be a lot that needs to be done before that key can be used. For example, the key may have been generated on behalf of a user by a TTP and will need to be distributed to that user, or it might be registered as belonging to that user and placed into storage. Hence the following services can optionally be offered before a key becomes pending active.

Register key   As discussed in Section 11.2.5, a key can be registered with a registration authority. The registration authority may have various different duties depending on the security policy. In an asymmetric scheme the main duty of a registration authority is usually to verify the identity of the owner of the public key. In a symmetric scheme the main duty of a registration authority is to maintain a register of keys and related information. Key registration is one of two operations provided by the registration authority (the other being key deregistration).

Create key certificate   This operation only applies to public key schemes and involves a certification authority creating a digital certificate that guarantees the correctness of a public key. This can only be done after a public key has been registered. Certification will be discussed further in Chapter 13.

Distribute key   Generally speaking a key will be generated by one of two parties: Either the user will generate his or her own keys or the key will be generated by a TTP on behalf of the user. If the key is not generated by the user then the key will need to be securely transported to the user. In asymmetric schemes the public key will always need to be distributed to potential users in some way.

Mechanisms for the transport of both secret keys for symmetric schemes and private keys for asymmetric schemes will be discussed in Chapter 12. Mechanisms for distributing public keys will be discussed in Chapter 13.

Secret keys for symmetric schemes and private keys should only be distributed before they become active if the user has a secure method of storing these keys. Public keys should only be distributed before they become active if it is clear when they will be activated.

Store key If a key is not to be used immediately then it must securely stored until it is ready for use. This can be done either by a user or by a TTP (usually either the key generation party or some dedicated key storage facility). Obviously, the security protecting the key while it is in storage must be at least equal to the protection that the key will require when it is in use.

Keys stored by this service are expected to be retrieved in the short or medium term, or kept for backup purposes. It is expected that any attempted compromise of the storage facility should be detectable (e.g., via an intrusion detection system).

11.3.2 Key activation

Key activation occurs when a key actually becomes available for use in the cryptographic application for which it was generated. Again there is only one mandatory service that must be used during key activation, and that is key installation.

Install key This service takes a key that has previously been generated and makes it available to the cryptographic applications that intend to use it.

Many of the services that can optionally be used during the key generation transition can also optionally be used during the activation transition. These include register key, create key certificate, distribute key, and store key. Only one new optional service is offered in the activation transition: derivation.

Derive key This is the service that derives a key from a higher level key in a key hierarchy (see Section 11.2.4). It is slightly odd that this service is only available during the activation transition and not during the generation transition—after all, it does mean the creation of a new key! Presumably this is because a key can be derived at any time and so need not be derived before it is needed. However, it is not clear that this is a useful assumption, and there may be a case for allowing key derivation in the key generation transition.

11.3.3 Key deactivation

This is the first of the negative transitions, in the sense that the previous two transitions were about enabling a key to be used, whereas key deactivation is about restricting a key's use. The most important part of this transition is the revoke key service.

Revoke key The revoke key service removes a key from use; hence it can be considered the opposite of the install key service. However the revoke key service would only be used if the key needs to be "deactivated" before its expires (i.e., before the end of a keys agreed usage period). A key would need to be prematurely revoked if it is thought to have been compromised, the cryptographic algorithm has been compromised, or the user has been deauthorized. A revoked key is not necessarily destroyed but may now only be used for decipherment and verification purposes.

Other optional services at this transition include store key (see Section 11.3.1) and archive key.

Archive key   The archive key service is similar to the store key service in that it provides a way of storing an unused key. However, whereas the store key service is only used to store keys for the short to medium term, the archive key service is used to provide long-term storage of keys. Keys should only be archived if their immediate use is unlikely, but the possibility exists that they may need to be retrieved at some future date to settle disputes. The problems associated with archiving digital data are discussed in more detail in Chapter 14.

11.3.4 Key reactivation

There are many reasons why a key could be reactivated: It could be that a key's usage period has been extended, that an investigation of a suspected key compromise reveals that the key remains safe for use, or that an employee who has been absent for an extended period returns to the company and his or her key needs to be reinstated.

   In this case the key needs to be placed back into active use. In order to do this it may be necessary to use some of the following services: install key, derive key (see Section 11.3.2), create key certificate, distribute key, or store key (see Section 11.3.1). Of these, only the install key service is mandatory.

   Obviously we will not need to reregister the key as it has not yet been deregistered.

11.3.5 Key destruction

Key destruction is the final phase of the key life cycle. It should destroy all copies of the key that exist in an organization (with the possible exception of those keys that have been archived for long-term storage). There are two services that are mandatory during this transition: destroy key and deregister key.

Destroy key   This service securely destroys all keys that are in use or in short- to medium-term storage. This is not always as easy as sounds. The deletion function on most computer file systems may not be sufficient, as information about the key will still be available on the hard disk of the machine. There are programs that go further and make sure that the key is overwritten with random data, but even this may not be sufficient to defeat a computer forensics expert. To ensure complete destruction it may be necessary to physically destroy the device that contained the key. This is a decision that will have to be made as part of the security policy.

Deregister key   This service is only mandatory if the key is registered. It updates the information held by the registration authority by removing any active associations between the key and a user (or users). This does not necessarily mean that the complete record held by the registration authority is deleted—only that it should be noted that the key has been destroyed. Of course the destroy key service may need to contact the registration authority and request that any copies of the key that are held in its records are also destroyed.

If the complete destruction of keys is unacceptable then the standard does allow for some keys to be kept in long-term storage. Hence, the archive key service is also offered during this transition (see Section 11.3.3).

11.4   The ANSI X9.24 framework

The ANSI X9.24 key management standard does not contain an explicit framework, but rather it implicitly implies a framework by mandating the way keys can be used, stored, and transmitted. It is meant for use by all financial institutions and therefore has a clear idea of the threats it needs to address and the services it needs to provide. This means that it is far more specific than ISO/IEC 11770-1, which is left deliberately vague to accommodate many different business models.

Technically, ANSI X9.24 is a multipart standard on symmetric key management but currently only one part actually exists: symmetric key management using symmetric techniques [the management of secret (symmetric) keys using symmetric algorithms]. This allows ANSI to add new parts (for example, on asymmetric techniques) at some point in the future. The standard is actually even more specific than this title suggests. Since the financial world almost exclusively uses the Triple-DES block cipher (see Chapter 4), all of the details of ANSI X9.24 are geared toward the management of DES keys.

The key management framework implied in ANSI X9.24 is similar to that of ISO/IEC 11770-1 (and to all other standardized key management frameworks). It basically consists of the following series of key transitions: key generation, key distribution, key utilization, key replacement, and key destruction and archival. Beyond this the standard mandates a few global requirements relating to auditing and storage.

It is worth noting that the ANSI model does differ slightly from the ISO/IEC 11770 model. The ISO/IEC framework, for example, explicitly defines the service that activates the key for use, and this service is a mandatory part of the key activation transition. In the ANSI framework, a key that has been distributed (an optional service in the ISO/IEC framework) is immediately available for utilization. Presumably keys can be stored before they enter the key utilization phase, but this is never stated. Other differences include the lack of a key reactivation transition in the ANSI model and the lack of a specific revoke key service. We now consider the ANSI framework in detail.

11.4.1   General requirements

ANSI makes demands about both the auditing procedures for, and the storage of, cryptographic keys. The auditing demands are very simple: All instances when a cryptographic key is used (including any key transitions) must be recorded. The storage requirements are a little bit more complicated.

Obviously a key feature of any key management framework must be to ensure that secret keys are never available to an attacker without some kind of confidentiality protection. The ANSI framework insists that keys may only exist in one of three forms:

- Inside a tamper resistant security module (TRSM);
- Encrypted under some kind of "key encrypting key";
- Protected by a dual control method such as key splitting.

A TRSM is a specific piece of hardware designed to provide secure storage and computing power. In order to do this it must have two layers of protection. It must protect against attackers who wish to discover the secret information it contains either by asking it to perform certain functions or by physically attacking it, or both. For example, an attacker may do one of the following.

- Try to convince the TRSM that it is a high-level user and alter the key it contains;
- Attempt to break into the TSRM and read its memory using another device;
- Convince the device to perform some legitimate operations while measuring certain characteristics of the device (such as the amount of power it consumes or the time it takes) and derive the key from that information.

A TRSM must resist all these types of attacks. Standards for security modules are briefly considered in Chapter 16.

The use of a key encrypting key implies a key hierarchy. Here a low-level key, known as a *transaction key*, is encrypted by a key in the level above, called the *key encrypting key*. The encrypted transaction key can then be securely distributed provided that the key encrypting key is kept secret. Of course, when the transaction key arrives at its destination, it will need to be decrypted before it can be used, and so the receiver will need a copy of the key encrypting key too. The key encrypting key could be transported by encrypting it under a higher level key or it could be the master key. Obviously the master key cannot be distributed in an encrypted form. The only alternative to the use of encryption and TRSMs is to use dual control. In this case, the key is split into one or more components. The only way to recover the key, or any information about the key, is to gather together all of these key fragments and combine them in some way. Dual control is discussed in more detail in Chapter 12.

These restrictions means that a key is cryptographically useless unless it is contained within a TRSM. (Obviously we cannot use an encrypted or split key as a basis for any cryptographic operation.) This means that all cryptographic operations must take place *inside* a TRSM and hence the ANSI framework requires all cryptographic operations to take place within specialist hardware. This is a cost burden that may be unacceptable outside of the financial sector.

11.4.2 Key generation

The key generation transition in the ANSI framework is essentially the same as the generate key service that needs to be used during the key generation transition of the ISO/IEC framework. The only difference is that the ANSI framework recommends that check values are generated with any new keys. These check values need to be generated using a (keyed) cryptographic process.

11.4.3 Key distribution

Specific key distribution mechanisms will be discussed in the next chapter. One feature of the ANSI framework is that it mandates that any unauthorized attempt to install, modify, or reuse a key must be prevented or, at least, detected. Of course, it would be nice if any unauthorized attacks against a key could be prevented but this is not always possible. For example, consider the case where an encrypted key is distributed over an insecure channel, an attacker can always attempt to modify the key. In such cases it might not be possible to prevent this modification (and recover the proper key) but such modification should always be detectable.

It should be remembered that the ANSI X9.24 framework only supports symmetric key distribution techniques (key distribution techniques using symmetric algorithms), even though several ANSI standards exist on asymmetric key distribution techniques (see Chapter 12).

11.4.4 Key utilization

The ANSI X9.24 standard enforces some of the ideas behind key separation (see Section 11.2.3). All keys used within an ANSI framework must be different (or rather the same key can only be used twice if the situation arises purely by chance) and no key can be used for more than one purpose. However, and this is, strictly speaking, contrary to the idea of key separation, ANSI X9.24 allows a key derived from another key to be used for a different purpose; for example, an entity's MAC key could be derived from its encryption key. This would create a simple key hierarchy.

The ANSI standard also insists that the compromise of any one key shared between two entities must not compromise keys shared with any other entity. Technically this means that it *could* compromise other keys shared with the same entity (for example, if two keys were used for different purposes but related). Hence great care must be taken when one is using a derived key if it is to be used with in conjunction with a different entity to its parent key; for example, if one is using an encryption key to produce a second encryption key for use with a different entity then one must be sure that the compromise of the first key does not compromise the second. In practice most keys will be independently generated and so this will not be an issue.

11.4.5   Key replacement

Keys must be replaced in one of two circumstances:

- If the key is known or suspected to have been compromised, then it must be replaced immediately. Obviously the replacement key must not be related in any way to the compromised key.

- All cryptographic keys must be replaced within the time it takes to determine a key by exhaustive search.

The latter of these two circumstances is heavily skewed toward the fact that we are dealing with secret (symmetric) keys. Private (asymmetric) keys can almost always be found using a method quicker than exhaustive search. On the other hand symmetric schemes whose keys can be found significantly faster than by exhaustive search are generally considered weak. Of course, in practice, if a method of determining a key faster than exhaustive search was known, then all that would be required is to replace the key within the time it takes to determine the key by that method (as the possibility exists that the key will be compromised after that time). The standard does not specify the mechanisms that need to be used to replace the key.

11.4.6   Key destruction and archival

Except for archival purposes, the standard insists that all keys that are no longer in use (including keys whose usage period has expired and keys that have been compromised) must be destroyed, where "destroyed" means that it is impossible to recover the keys by any physical or electronic means. As one may expect, archived keys need to kept in a manner that preserves their security.

11.5   Notes

This chapter covered the key management frameworks of three separate bodies. The general details were taken from ISO/IEC 11770-1 [1]. The remaining two parts [2, 3] of this standard will be dealt with in Chapter 12. This part of the standard is almost unique in that it concentrates solely on the key management framework and provides no details of mechanisms that might be used to implement this framework.

The approach of ANSI X9.24 [4] and ANSI X9.17 [5], now withdrawn [6], is very different. These standards approach the subject in terms of rules and requirements that must be satisfied. These rules and requirements imply a key management framework but do not explicitly give one. To a certain extent this means that the framework is open to interpretation by the developer but, in reality, the requirements are so strict that it would be difficult to misinterpret them.

The withdrawal of ANSI X9.17 has left something of a void in the ANSI standards portfolio. The document that officially withdrew the standard, ANSI X9 TG26 [6], is more than a simple statement: It details an entire strategy describing how the techniques of ANSI X9.17 could be replaced with newer techniques with minimum risk. However, while it cites newer ANSI standards as replacements for the key establishment mechanisms contained in ANSI X9.17, it does not appear to specify a new framework for wholesale key management within the financial sector. It is unclear whether the revised version of ANSI X9.24 is meant to fill this role, or whether ANSI X9.17 has been superseded by the the corresponding ISO standard, ISO 8732 [7].

Soon after the ANSI X9 standards were originally published, the ISO technical committee on banking (ISO TC68) began work on producing corresponding international standards. The results were ISO 8732 [7], which is based on ANSI X9.17, and ISO 11568 [8–13], which is based on ANSI X9.24. Of particular relevance to this chapter is ISO 11568-1 [8], which introduces the concept of key management; ISO 11568-2 [9], which introduces many of the general ideas contained in Section 11.2; and ISO 11568-3 [10], which specifies the key life cycle for secret (symmetric) keys. The framework that these documents establish is almost identical to that of ANSI X9.24.

Of the remaining parts of ISO 11568, parts 4 and 5 [11, 12] discuss the public key life cycle and will be discussed in Chapter 13. The last part, ISO 11568-6 [13], contains descriptions of key management schemes that are approved for use in retail situations. As this does little to enlighten the reader as to the technical reasons for implementing a key management scheme in a particular way, it will not be discussed further.

There are several good introductory texts available on key management. Chapter 12 of Menezes et al. [14] serves as a good, if somewhat technical, introduction. Other good sources include Kou [15] and Davies and Price [16].

References

[1]   International Organization for Standardization, *ISO/IEC 11770–1, Information Technology—Security Techniques—Key Management—Part 1: Framework*, 1996.

[2]   International Organization for Standardization, *ISO/IEC 11770–2, Information Technology—Security Techniques—Key Management—Part 2: Mechanisms Using Symmetric Techniques*, 1996.

[3]   International Organization for Standardization, *ISO/IEC 11770–3, Information Technology—Security Techniques—Key Management—Part 3: Mechanisms Using Asymmetric Techniques*, 1999.

[4]   American Bankers Association, *ANSI X9.24–2002, Retail Financial Services—Symmetric Key Management—Part 1: Using Symmetric Techniques*, 2002.

[5]   Accredited Standards Committee X9—Financial Services, *ANSI X9.17, Financial Institution Key Management (Wholesale)*, 1995.

[6]   Accredited Standards Committee X9—Financial Services, *ANSI X9 TG–26–1999, Technical Guideline: Managing Risk and Mitigation Planning: Withdrawl of ANSI X9.17, Financial Institution Key Management (Wholesale)*, 1999.

[7]   International Organization for Standardization, *ISO/IEC 8732, Banking—Key Management (Wholesale)*, 1988.

[8]   International Organization for Standardization, *ISO/IEC 11568–1, Banking—Key Management (Retail)—Part 1: Introduction to Key Management*, 1994.

[9]   International Organization for Standardization, *ISO/IEC 11568–2, Banking—Key Management (Retail)—Part 2: Key Management Techniques for Symmetric Ciphers*, 1994.

[10]   International Organization for Standardization, *ISO/IEC 11568–3, Banking—Key Management (Retail)—Part 3: Key Life Cycle for Symmetric Ciphers*, 1994.

[11]   International Organization for Standardization, *ISO/IEC 11568–4, Banking—Key Management (Retail)—Part 4: Key Management Techniques for Public Key Cryptosystems*, 1998.

[12]   International Organization for Standardization, *ISO/IEC 11568–5, Banking—Key Management (Retail)—Part 5: Key Life Cycle for Public Key Cryptosystems*, 1998.

[13]   International Organization for Standardization, *ISO/IEC 11568–6, Banking—Key Management (Retail)—Part 6: Key Management Schemes*, 1999.

[14]   Menezes, A. J., P. C. van Oorschot, and S. A. Vanstone, *Handbook of Applied Cryptography*, Boca Raton, FL: CRC Press, 1997.

[15]   Kou, W., *Networking Security and Standards*, Boston, MA: Kluwer Academic Press, 1997.

[16]   Davies, D. W., and W. L. Price, *Security for Computer Networks*, 2nd ed., New York: John Wiley and Sons, 1989.

CHAPTER

12

Contents

12.1 Definitions and basic properties

12.2 Standards for key establishment

12.3 Physical mechanisms

12.4 Mechanisms using symmetric cryptography

12.5 Mechanisms using asymmetric cryptography

12.6 Key establishment based on weak secrets

12.7 Key establishment for mobile networks

12.8 Choosing a key establishment scheme

12.9 Notes

Key Establishment Mechanisms

Building on the key management framework discussed in Chapter 11, we now examine key establishment mechanisms. These are mechanisms that enable two parties to establish some kind of secret between them. Our main focus in this chapter will be on how two parties can agree on a secret value (typically a secret key for a symmetric algorithm).

Key establishment mechanisms can be classified into two categories: key transport mechanisms and key agreement mechanisms. Key transport mechanisms are ways in which an existing secret key can be securely transferred from one entity to another. Key agreement mechanisms are methods whereby two parties can derive a key between them without one party having complete control over the key generation process.

Although, as we have said, key establishment standards tend to concentrate on establishing shared secret keys, many of the key transport techniques are also applicable to the distribution of private keys for asymmetric algorithms. The problem of distributing a private asymmetric key from the entity who performed key generation to the user of the key is often overlooked but potentially suffers from the same problems as the distribution of shared secret keys. Key transport mechanisms are particularly relevant for private key distribution; key agreement mechanisms typically establish a shared random or pseudorandom bit string and thus are less suited to providing the complicated mathematical structures required in asymmetric keys.

12.1 Definitions and basic properties

For our purposes, a key establishment mechanism will be a way of establishing a shared secret (symmetric) key between two entities. Formally, the ISO/IEC key management standard, ISO/IEC 11770, defines key establishment as follows.

› *Key establishment:* The process of making available a shared secret key to one or more entities. Key establishment includes key agreement and key transport.

This in turns begs the question: what are key agreement and key transport? These are defined as follows.

> ‣ *Key agreement:*   The process of establishing a shared secret key between entities in such a way that neither of them can predetermine the value of the key.

> ‣ *Key transport:*   The process of transferring a key from one entity to another entity, suitably protected.

Generally speaking, key transport mechanisms are used when one entity generates a key on its own and wishes to distribute it to other entities. This means that any entity that receives a key via a key transport mechanism needs to be able to trust not only the mechanism that delivered the key but also that the entity who generated the key did it in a suitable secure way. On the other hand, key agreement mechanisms are generally used when two parties wish to generate a shared key but do not trust each other sufficiently to allow one party to be in complete control of the key generation process, or when one party wishes to compute a key for use with another party when that party is offline.

Whilst key agreement mechanisms may be seen as being superior to key transport mechanisms as they have more desirable properties, the differences between the two are similar to the differences between symmetric and asymmetric cryptography. Like asymmetric cryptography, the desirable properties of key agreement protocols (such as shared control of the key generation process and the ability to compute keys off-line) are balanced against a performance disadvantage: Key agreement protocols tend to be slower than key transport mechanisms and/or require more messages to be passed between the communicating entities. One of the prime applications of asymmetric cryptography is in developing key agreement protocols.

In terms of their role within the general key management framework proposed in Chapter 11, key establishment mechanisms may be used as part of several different services. The most obvious service that would make use of a key establishment mechanism is the *distribute key* service. This service would most likely make use of some kind of key transport mechanism. A key transport mechanism would also be needed whenever keying material is being transported over insecure channels, and hence could also be used to securely deliver a key to a third party as part of a *store key*, *archive key*, or *register key* service.

Key agreement mechanisms, on the other hand, are not likely to be used to provide a *distribute key* service but are more likely to be part of a *generate key* or *derive key* service. If the key agreement mechanism is used to produce long-term keys from scratch then it would be considered to be providing part of a *generate key* service. If the key agreement mechanism is used to produce session keys from existent keys then it would more likely be considered to be providing part of a *derive key* service.

12.1.1 Key establishment mechanisms and authentication protocols

No matter which service the key establishment mechanism is providing, the threats are the same. The mechanism must guard against the unauthorized disclosure of the key, the unauthorized modification of the key, or the use of a key whose usage period has expired. Hence a key establishment mechanism must protect against all of the possible threats given in Section 11.2.1 of Chapter 11.

It is easy to see that a key establishment mechanism must keep all keying material confidential and must prevent attackers from being able to alter the key material (and hence the resultant key) in transit. It is therefore tempting to think that key establishment mechanisms are just combinations of an encryption algorithm and some kind of integrity protection algorithm, such as a MAC or a digital signature. In fact, key establishment algorithms are more closely related to authentication protocols than any specific type of confidentiality or integrity protection mechanism.

The word that suggests this in the discussion of the threats against key establishment mechanisms in Section 11.2.1 is "unauthorized." This means that an entity that receives any information as part of a key establishment mechanism must be sure that the sender is authorized to establish a new key, and this means that senders need to authenticate themselves. Any message that is passed between entities as part of a key establishment protocol should have its origin authenticated and its freshness guaranteed (and not just be a replay of some earlier execution of the protocol).

One reason that the messages need to be fresh is because a key establishment mechanism must protect against the threat of a key being used after its usage period has expired. If an attacker can replay all the messages used in an earlier execution of the protocol then he or she may be able to force an entity to use an expired key—a key that the attacker has had time to attack.

This is particularly a problem for key transport mechanisms. Key agreement mechanisms generally require input from both entities and so, even if an attacker were to replay old messages, it is unlikely that the secret key the two entities "agree" on would be the same as any previously used key. An entity receiving a key via a key transport mechanism, however, is likely to have had no control over the key generation process and must guard against false or old keys.

Chapter 10 discusses mechanisms that can be used to provide the necessary data origin authentication and guarantee message freshness. Of the three mechanisms that can be used to provide data origin authentication (encryption algorithms, MACs, and digital signatures) encryption seems to be the most obvious choice for use within a key establishment algorithm as we will generally require some form of encryption to protect the confidentiality of the keying material anyway. Thus encryption is generally used to provide data origin authentication for symmetric key transport protocols (in combination with some other technique, such as an MDC—see Chapter 10).

A message encrypted using an asymmetric encryption scheme provides no form of data origin authentication, even when combined with an MDC.

Therefore when using asymmetric techniques, digital signatures become the most obvious choice for providing the necessary authentication. (An asymmetric encryption scheme can provide origin authentication if a party demonstrates that it can successfully decrypt a random string chosen by the other party. This requires an extra message being passed though.)

The mechanisms used to prove timeliness (freshness) in a key establishment mechanism are the same as those used in an authentication protocol (i.e., time-stamps and nonces). These techniques are discussed in detail in Chapter 10.

12.1.2 Properties of key establishment mechanisms

There are several concepts that are unique to key establishment and deserve to be discussed in detail. In this section we will discuss the role of key authentication, key confirmation, and key control.

Key authentication   Key authentication is the property of a key establishment mechanism that guarantees the mechanism's security. Key authentication properties can be subdivided into *implicit key authentication* and *explicit key authentication*. The two properties are subtly different.

Implicit key authentication from A to B is the assurance for entity B that entity A is the only other entity that can possibly be in possession of the correct key (i.e., the shared key that they are trying to establish). It is therefore essential that a key establishment mechanism has implicit key authentication, or at least only concedes knowledge of the key to the intended recipient and some known TTPs.

Explicit key authentication from A to B is slightly stronger. It is the assurance for entity B that entity A *is* the only other entity in possession of the correct key. The difference between implicit and explicit key authentication is that in explicit key authentication B must be convinced not only that A is the only entity that *could* have received the correct key but also that A *has* received it. This leads nicely onto the concept of *key confirmation*.

Key confirmation   Key confirmation from A to B is the assurance for entity B that entity A is in possession of the correct key.

Key confirmation can be achieved in a number of ways, ranging from simply using the key (if, for example, entity A uses the key to compute the MAC of a known data string correctly then entity B can have a certain amount of confidence that entity A must be in possession of the correct key) to complex zero-knowledge protocols that allow an entity to demonstrate knowledge of a secret without revealing any information about it. Hence explicit key authentication guarantees key confirmation; indeed, explicit key authentication is the combination of implicit key authentication and key confirmation.

Key control   Key control is related to key confirmation. Whereas key confirmation is about one entity demonstrating to another that he or she knows the established key, key control is concerned with who gets to choose the key in the first place. Put simply, an entity has key control if that entity has the ability to choose the shared key that is being established. This is not to say that either of the two communicating entities must have key control in a key establishment protocol. It is possible that neither of the two entities has key control but rather some TTP does. Of course, it is also possible that no entity has key control.

In key transport mechanisms, one entity generally does have key control. In a key transport mechanism, one entity generates a key and forwards it securely to another entity. In this case the first entity clearly has key control. From the definition of a key agreement mechanism it would appear as if neither entity should have key control. However, we shall see that it is possible that one entity may gain some measure of key control if he or she "cheats" a little.

It is sometimes more difficult to establish which entity has key control when there are TTPs involved, especially when we are dealing with key agreement mechanisms. As we shall see it is possible for a key agreement mechanism to involve a third party with complete key control (see Section 12.4.2). This is a somewhat controversial statement—many sources would describe these kinds of mechanisms as three-party key transport mechanisms rather than key agreement mechanisms and firmly state that no entity can possibly have key control in a key agreement mechanism. In the end, it is not the way that one chooses to classify different mechanisms that is important, but that the implementor has a sound understanding of the properties of the individual mechanisms and how they will work within a security system

12.2 Standards for key establishment

There are many more standards that discuss key establishment than provide a complete key management framework. However, unlike, say, encryption, there is a lot of overlap between standards, and mechanisms that appear in one standard are likely to appear in other standards too. Like most of the standards we study, we separate key establishment mechanisms into two classes: mechanisms that use symmetric techniques and mechanisms that use asymmetric techniques.

12.2.1 Standards using symmetric techniques

Most of the major methods for key establishment using symmetric techniques are covered by ISO/IEC 11770-2. These include the use of key translation centers (KTCs) and key distribution centers (KDCs). These techniques are mirrored in the ISO banking standard ISO 8732. The main difference between the general ISO/IEC standards and the ISO banking standards is in the level of detail. ISO/IEC 11770-2 only standardizes the cryptographic techniques in a rather abstract way, whereas the ISO banking standards are very specific—they specify the mechanism details right down to the way in which the messages passed between entities should be formatted.

The mobile telephone industry has also developed a voluntary series of standards to allow key establishment between mobile handsets and supporting telecommunications networks. These standards were developed by 3GPP to address the particular problems that occur with mobile phones, especially when mobile phones are *roaming* (i.e., not directly connected to their home networks but routing communications through some third-party network). The key establishment procedure for a 3GPP phone is described in 3GPP TS 33.102.

The Kerberos entity authentication/key establishment protocol, described in Chapter 10 and standardized in IETF RFC 1510, is another good example of a symmetric key establishment protocol. Other, less well used, symmetric key establishment mechanisms are described in IETF RFCs including several more experimental schemes, such as the Photuris session-key management protocol, which contains a simple mechanism design to prevent denial of service (DoS) attacks.

12.2.2 Standards using asymmetric techniques

Key establishment is probably the most widely used application of public key cryptography. Indeed the very first example of a public key cryptographic scheme was a key agreement protocol, invented by Diffie and Hellman in 1976. This is now one of the most widely standardized protocols based on asymmetric techniques and has motivated the invention of numerous encryption schemes, digital signature schemes, and more complex key agreement protocols. We shall return to the Diffie-Hellman protocol in Section 12.5.1. Again, we find that ISO/IEC 11770, and in particular ISO/IEC 11770-3, is a good source for high-level descriptions of asymmetric key establishment protocols. This standard gives a high-level description of how key establishment protocols can be constructed from an asymmetric scheme with certain properties. The main body of the standard makes no suggestion as to what these asymmetric schemes should be, although some appropriate schemes are given in an informative annex.

Other standards are more specific. The banking community has developed several national and international standards on this subject, including ANSI X9.42 and ISO 11166 (which has two parts). The IEEE 1363 group has standardized asymmetric key establishment techniques, and there is an RSA PKCS standard (RSA PKCS # 3) that deals explicitly with key establishment using the Diffie-Hellman protocol. The Diffie-Hellman protocol is also specified in IETF RFC 2631.

Furthermore, variants of many of the mechanisms described in ISO/IEC 11770-3 are suitable for use with elliptic curve groups. These protocols are standardized in ISO/IEC 15946-3, ANSI X9.63 and in the IEEE 1363 standard. Elliptic curves are complex mathematical constructions that are sometimes used in cryptography but are far beyond the scope of this book.

All of these standards on key establishment using asymmetric techniques concentrate on standardizing key agreement protocols. This is not to say that there are no key transport mechanisms that use asymmetric techniques; indeed, key transport using asymmetric cryptography is standardized in ISO/IEC 11770-3 and ISO 11166. However, the main focus of research in the area of key establishment using asymmetric techniques tends to be on the development of key agreement protocols.

The Internet also has a series of standards for key establishment. The two most widely used protocols on the internet are the transport layer security (TLS) protocol described in RFC 2246, and the Internet key exchange (IKE) protocol described in RFC 2409. Both of these primarily rely on the use of asymmetric key establishment techniques, although an extension to the TLS protocol that uses the Kerberos authentication/key establishment protocol is described in RFC 2712. The Kerberos protocol is itself described in RFC 1510.

12.3 Physical mechanisms

Physical methods of key establishment are mechanisms in which keying material is placed into a physical device [for example, it could be printed on a piece of paper or loaded into a small tamper-resistant security module (TRSM)] and physically transported between entities. Here cryptographic security is often replaced with physical and procedural security: The data could be transported in a locked safe or by a trusted individual. Sometimes the data is protected by both physical and cryptographic security; for example, the keying material could be encrypted and loaded into a TRSM, and then transported by a trusted individual. In all cases the physical security component must be responsible for providing some security service. If this was not the case then the entire service could be offered electronically—a method that would probably be a lot cheaper. Standards for security modules, including TRSMs used for key distribution, will be discussed in Chapter 16.

Almost all physical methods for key establishment are simple key transport mechanisms where a trusted person delivers a key securely to a recipient. This minimizes the number of physical trips that have to be made (and thus the expense). However there is no theoretical reason why more complex protocols cannot be realized using physical data transfer; indeed some authentication protocols rely on the manual transfer of data by a trusted human controller (see Chapter 10).

Most security standards do not encourage the use of physical mechanisms for key establishment—perhaps because security administrators tend to prefer to base their security systems on predictable things like computers rather than unpredictable things like human beings! ISO/IEC 11770 briefly mentions the possibility of delivering keys physically but does not dwell on it. The only set of standards that deals with the subject in depth are the banking standards; in particular ANSI X9.24 and ISO 8732.

The ANSI X9.24 standard (see Chapter 11) only allows keys to exist in one of three protected states:

‣ Inside a TRSM;

‣ Encrypted with some kind of key encrypting key;

‣ Protected by some kind of dual control method (see Section 12.3.1).

In the latter two cases, the keying material can be physically written down and transported. Under these circumstances it is considered best practice to seal the data inside two envelopes (an *inner envelope* and *outer envelope*). Whilst the outer envelope may show signs of wear due to the rigours of travel, the inner envelope is only likely to show signs of damage if an attacker has attempted to gain access to the data inside it. In this case the data should not be trusted.

If the data is loaded onto a TRSM then it is necessary to physically carry the TRSM from one place to another. Such a TRSM is often known as a *key loading device*.

12.3.1 Dual control

Dual control is the idea that every important decision and piece of important data is under the control of two or more individuals. Hence, no single individual can access that information or force the system to do something that it should not. This is a form of protection against insider attacks—attacks from individuals who already have some kind of legitimate access to the system. It also helps protect individuals against blackmail or coercion attacks, in exactly the same way as using multiple keys for a bank safe.

When applied to cryptographic keys, the classic method of dual control is called key splitting. Here a key K is split into two seemingly random strings k_1 and k_2 such that $K = k_1 \oplus k_2$. Knowledge of one of the key fragments k_i does not give an attacker any clue about the actual value of the key K. Only when an attacker has both of the fragments (i.e., k_1 and k_2) can he or she find out any information about the key. This can be easily generalized to cover the case where three or more components are combined to form the key.

Obviously when a key is subjected to some form of dual control, each of the key fragments must be kept secret and only be kept apart for the shortest period of time necessary to distribute the key (or to perform whatever function caused the key to be split in the first place). Afterward the key fragments will need to be securely destroyed. More information about key splitting can be found in ANSI X9.69.

12.4 Mechanisms using symmetric cryptography

ISO/IEC 11770-2 describes 13 different key establishment mechanisms based on symmetric cryptography, each making use of a different security technique or possessing different security properties:

- Six are based on direct communication between the entities (with no support from a third party).

- Four are based on the use of a KDC.

- Three are based on the use of a KTC.

All these mechanisms tend to rely on encryption as the basis for entity authentication. A different approach is taken by ISO 8732, which uses encryption only to protect the confidentiality of the key and uses a MAC to provide entity authentication.

Here, as elsewhere in the book, we will adopt the following notation for symmetric algorithms:

- $e_K(X)$ denotes the encryption of the n-bit plaintext block X using the secret key K.

- $\text{MAC}_K(X)$ denotes the MAC computed on the data string X using the secret key K.

- K_{AB} denotes a secret key shared by the entities A and B.

- i_X denotes an identifier (name) for an entity X.

- t_X denotes a time-stamp computed by, or intended for, entity X.

- r_X denotes a nonce produced by entity X.

- F (or F_X) denotes some keying material (produced by entity X).

In all cases we will be concerned with the establishment of keying material between two entities A and B (if preferred, these entities can be thought of as two users, Alice and Bob). The method by which A and B derive a key from the keying material F will need to be agreed before the protocol is executed. If only one entity produces the keying material then it is convenient to think of F as an encoding of the key to be used, but it is possible that F will have to be processed—for example, be input to a hash function in conjunction with some publicly available data—and that the hash code, or part of it, will be used as the key. The process of turning the keying material F into an useable key is known as *key extraction*.

12.4.1   Direct communication

Key establishment mechanisms based on direct communication are mechanisms that allow two entities to establish a new shared secret key provided they already share a secret key K_{AB}. The six methods contained in ISO/IEC 11770-2 range from the absurdly simple (for example, A sends an encrypted version of F to B but does not include any form of freshness checking or identification) to more complicated procedures based on time-stamps or nonces.

As these protocols are so similar to those discussed in Section 10.5 of Chapter 10 we will only discuss two examples: a key transport mechanism based on the use of time-stamps and a key agreement mechanism based on the use of nonces.

Key transport using time-stamps   The first technique is key establishment mechanism 3 from ISO/IEC 11770-2. As with all authentication and key establishment protocols based on the use of an encryption algorithm and time-stamps we must assume that A and B have secure synchronized clocks and have agreed on a method of redundancy for the encryption algorithm. More details about these issues can be found in Chapter 10.

The protocol consists of a single message, namely:

$$M_1: A \rightarrow B : e_{K_{AB}}(t_A||i_B||F||\text{Text}_1)$$

where Text_1 is an application-dependent data string (including possibly an MDC to provide integrity checking—see Chapter 10). A constructs M_1 using the key K_{AB} it shares with B, its time-stamp, and B's identifier, and sends this to B.

On receipt of M_1, B decrypts it and checks three things: (1) that it "makes sense" (i.e., has the correct redundancy), (2) that the time-stamp is valid, and (3) that B's name i_B is correctly included. If all of these are correct then B can be assured that A is the sender of the message and can derive the shared key from the keying material F.

This protocol gives implicit key authentication from B to A and from A to B as both can be sure that no other person can discover the keying material F (as no other person knows K_{AB}). B has key confirmation, as B can be assured that A must have known the keying material F before sending the message. Therefore B has explicit key authentication. A cannot be sure that B has received the message and so does not have key confirmation; however, A does have key control, as A generates the keying material F.

Key agreement using nonces   The second technique is key establishment mechanism 6 from ISO/IEC 11770-2—the most complicated of all the direct key establishment mechanisms. Again we will assume that A and B have agreed on a method of redundancy for the encryption algorithm.

The protocol consists of three messages:

$$M_1 : B \rightarrow A : r_B$$

$$M_2 : A \rightarrow B : e_{K_{AB}}(r_A||r_B||i_B||F_A||\text{Text}_1)$$

$$M_3 : B \rightarrow A : e_{K_{AB}}(r_B||r_A||F_B||\text{Text}_2)$$

where Text_1 and Text_2 are application-dependent data strings, as above.

The protocol runs in four stages. First B generates and stores a nonce r_B. B sends this nonce to A as message M_1.

When A receives M_1, A responds by generating (and storing) a nonce r_A of its own and some keying material F_A. A encrypts and sends both nonces and the keying material back to B, along with B's identifier i_B to prevent reflection attacks.

On receipt of message M_2, B decrypts it and checks that (1) it makes sense (has the appropriate redundancy), (2) its nonce r_B is correctly included, and (3) its identifier i_B is correctly included. If these checks are correct then B extracts A's keying material F_A and generates some keying material of its own, F_B. B sends a final message M_3 to A that contains an encrypted version of both nonces and B's keying material.

When A receives the final message, A decrypts it and checks that (1) it makes sense and (2) both nonces are correctly included. If these checks are correct, then A extracts B's keying material F_B. Now both entities have both sets of keying material, F_A and F_B, and can derive a key by combining them.

In this mechanism both parties have implicit key authentication (as no other party knows the shared key K_{AB}) but neither has key confirmation, so neither party has explicit key authentication. On the surface it seems as if no party has key control either, but if the method of combining the two sets of keying material is weak (for example, if we derive a key by computing the exclusive-or of F_A and F_B) then it is possible that B will be able to choose F_B in such a way that it has control over the value of the key.

ISO 8732   ISO 8732 only standardizes one method of establishing a key from direct communication, and it is very similar to the mechanism using time-stamps described above. However, ISO 8732 demands the following.

  ‣ The encryption algorithm that is used is DES or Triple-DES.

  ‣ Logical time-stamps (counters) are used for freshness, thus avoiding the problem of synchronized clocks.

  ‣ Text$_1$ does not contain an MDC but a MAC is sent along with the encrypted material. This MAC is computed using the secret key K that the two entities are attempting to establish. Since B knows that the only other entity that can know K is A, this provides entity authentication.

The drawbacks of direct communication   There are two major drawbacks to establishing keys using direct communication methods. The first is obvious: The two entities who wish to establish a shared key must already share a key. This key must have been established via some other method. This apparent contradiction does not mean that these mechanisms are useless. Direct communication is a very useful way of, for example, establishing short-term session keys from long-term shared secrets.

The second problem is more subtle. If direct communication is to be used as the primary method of key establishment in an organization then every member of that organization must share a secret key with every other member of that organization. This means that an organization with n members will have to securely store approximately $n^2/2$ keys, and these keys will have to be stored in many different places. This could present a huge security challenge. As an example, consider what happens if a new member joins the organization: That user needs to generate a new key for use with every other member of the organization. These keys then have to be securely distributed to every other member of the organization.

12.4.2   Key distribution centers

To alleviate some of the problems associated with direct communication, especially the large numbers of keys that have to be stored, TTPs can be used. This approach is not without drawbacks of its own—most notably a high level of trust will need to be placed in the third party as it will have unfettered access to all of the keys in the system. Thus an malicious third party would have the ability to do anything or impersonate anyone. The use of TTPs is discussed in detail in Chapter 14.

A key distribution center (KDC) is a TTP that generates and distribute keys on behalf of other entities. Generally speaking, if A wishes to establish a key with B then A makes a request to the KDC T who generates a suitable key K and securely distributes this to both A and B. In all cases we will assume that entity A (respectively entity B) shares a secret key K_{AT} (resp. K_{BT}) with the KDC T.

If A requests a KDC to establish a shared key with an entity B then the KDC must inform B of the request and the new key. There are two ways in which the KDC can do this: it can either send the information directly to B, or it can send the information back to A and let A forward it on to B. This latter technique is called *key forwarding*. Key forwarding is used by almost all the standardized key establishment mechanisms involving third parties.

The advantage of key forwarding is that it prevents the KDC from having to set up a new communication session with B—the only entity with which the KDC has to communicate is A and, since A contacted the KDC initially, there already exists a session between these two entities.

It is quite difficult to decide whether mechanisms involving a KDC are key transport or key agreement mechanisms. Certainly the problems associated with a KDC are all problems associated with key transport mechanisms: how to securely transport a key to some other entities via an untrusted network. However, since neither A or nor B can predetermine any information about the key it intends to establish, we choose to classify KDC-based key establishment mechanisms as key agreement mechanisms. This does not mean that no entity has key control though: A KDC invariably has key control itself. We will only give one example of a key agreement mechanism using a KDC.

Key agreement using time-stamps and a KDC   We now describe a generalized version of the key establishment mechanism using a KDC described in ISO 8732. Use of this mechanism requires A, B, and T to have securely synchronized clocks. Strictly speaking, A and B do not need to have synchronized clocks, but only need to have clocks synchronized with the KDC. Of course, if the time-stamps are based on a real-time clock then A and B will have synchronized clocks anyway. However, if logical time-stamps are used then the protocol does not require A and B to maintain sequence numbers for each other.

For this particular algorithm (only!) we do not require A and B to have agreed a method of redundancy for use with the encryption algorithm.

The protocol consists of three messages:

$M_1 : A \to T : i_B || \text{Text}_1$

$M_2 : T \to A : i_B || t_A || t_B || e_{K_{AT}}(F) || e_{K_{BT}}(F) || \text{Text}_2 ||$
$\qquad\qquad \text{MAC}_K(i_B || t_A || t_B || e_{K_{AT}}(F) || e_{K_{BT}}(F) || \text{Text}_2)$

$M_3 : A \to B : i_T || t_B || e_{K_{BT}}(F) || \text{Text}_3 ||$
$\qquad\qquad \text{MAC}_K(i_T || t_B || e_{K_{BT}}(F) || \text{Text}_3)$

where Text$_1$–Text$_3$ are application-dependent data strings, and K is the shared key that A and B are trying to establish (i.e., K is the key that is derived from the keying material F). This process is shown pictorially in Figure 12.1.

The protocol works as follows. First A sends a message to the KDC specifying the entity with which it wishes to establish a shared key. The KDC responds with message M_2. At this point A checks that (1) the time-stamp t_A is valid and (2) B's identifier i_B is correctly included. If so, A recovers the new shared key K from the keying material encrypted under the long-term key it shares with the KDC. Last, A checks the integrity and authenticity of the message by checking that the MAC given in the message is correct. If all of these checks are correct then A accepts the new key and constructs message M_3 from the remaining parts of M_2 and i_T and sends this to B.

B's actions are similar to A's. First B checks that the time-stamp t_B is valid and recovers the key K from the keying material encrypted under the long-term secret key it shares with the KDC. Next it checks the integrity and authenticity of the message by checking that the MAC given in the message is correct. If all of these checks are correct then B accepts the new key. The KDC's identifier i_T is included so that B can identify which KDC encrypted the keying material and therefore which key B needs to use to decrypt it.

This mechanism gives implicit key authentication to both entities, as no other entity knows the secret keys they share with the KDC. Since A has to compute a MAC on the data in message M_3 using the new shared key K, B can have some measure of confidence that A has the correct key. Hence B has key confirmation from A and hence has explicit key authentication. A does not have any kind of key confirmation and so does not have explicit key authentication. As always the KDC has key control.

One potential problem with the scheme occurs if the key K is ever compromised (i.e., if an attacker learns the value of K). In such a case, and assuming that the attacker observed the value $e_{K_{BT}}(F)$ when the scheme was originally executed, the attacker can always convince the entity B to

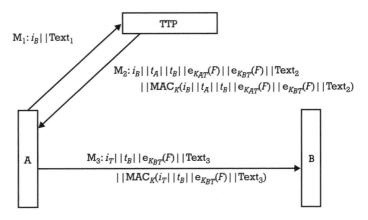

Figure 12.1   A key transport method using time-stamps and a KDC.

reuse K by resending message M_3 with a new time-stamp and new MAC computed using K. Hence, in this protocol, it is very important that either there is a mechanism in place to prevent an entity reusing an old key or that extra security is put in place to make sure that established keys are never compromised.

This mechanism is quite different to the mechanisms described in ISO/IEC 11770-2. This is because its security relies on the use of a MAC algorithm and only uses symmetric encryption to protect the confidentiality of the keying material (rather than to provide any kind of authentication itself). The mechanisms contained in ISO/IEC 11770-2 all use encryption algorithms to provide data origin authentication (although the ISO/IEC 11770-2 mechanisms may implicitly involve the use of a MAC as a method of providing redundancy—see Chapter 10).

Kerberos   It should be noted that the Kerberos authentication protocol discussed in Chapter 10 is also based on the use of a KDC. Since the Kerberos protocol is discussed in detail in Chapter 10 we will not discuss it further here except to note that it provides explicit key authentication to the client C and that the ticket granting server (TGS) has key control.

12.4.3 Key translation centers (KTCs)

A key translation center (KTC) is a TTP that facilitates the transport of user-generated keying material from one entity to another. Generally speaking, if A wishes to transport a key to B using a KTC then A encrypts it under the key it shares with the KTC T and passes this ciphertext to T; the KTC then decrypts and re-encrypts it using the key that it shares with B. Either A or the KTC can then forward the keying material to B. As before we will assume that entity A (respectively entity B) shares a secret key K_{AT} (resp. K_{BT}) with the KTC T.

We now give an example from ISO/IEC 11770-2. A protocol based on the use of a KTC is also standardized in ISO 8732, but we will not discuss that here. The astute reader will be able to determine roughly how this protocol works from the previous examples.

Key transport using nonces and a KTC   The protocol described here is key establishment mechanism 13 from ISO/IEC 11770-2. As with all of the protocols from this standard, we assume that all parties have agreed on a method of adding redundancy to a message prior to application of the encryption algorithm.

The protocol involves five messages:

$$M_1 : B \rightarrow A : r_B$$

$$M_2 : A \rightarrow T : e_{K_{AT}}(r_A||r_B||i_B||F||\text{Text}_1)$$

$$M_3 : T \rightarrow A : e_{K_{AT}}(r_A||i_B||\text{Text}_2)||e_{K_{BT}}(r_B||F||i_A||\text{Text}_3)$$

$$M_4 : A \rightarrow B : e_{K_{BT}}(r_B||F||i_A||\text{Text}_3)||e_K(r_A'||r_B||\text{Text}_4)$$

$$M_5 : B \rightarrow A : e_K(r_B||r_A'||\text{Text}_5)$$

where Text_1–Text_5 are application-dependent data strings. These data strings may also contain MDCs. This process is shown pictorially in Figure 12.2.

This may look complicated but it is not difficult to understand if you consider it in two stages. The first three-and-a-half messages are designed to get a copy of the keying material F to B and are similar to the direct communication method using nonces that is discussed in Section 12.4.1. The remaining messages are designed to confirm that the key K has been correctly computed by both A and B.

The large number of different nonces that this protocol uses can also sometimes be confusing if their purposes are not clear. The nonce r_B is designed to enable B to check that the message it receives from the KTC is fresh. The nonce r_A is present to allow A to check that the message it receives from the KTC is fresh. Finally, the nonce r'_A is designed to provide assurance that the key confirmation exchange between A and B is fresh.

B starts the protocol by sending a nonce r_B to A. A responds by generating some keying material F. A then sends this keying material to the KTC (encrypted, of course) along with B's nonce r_B, a new nonce r_A, and B's identifier so that the KTC knows which key to use to re-encrypt the keying material. The KTC recovers the keying material, constructs the message M_3, and returns this to A.

At this point•A decrypts the section of M_3 encrypted under the key K_{AT} and checks that (1) it has the correct redundancy, (2) it includes the nonce r_A, and (3) it contains B's identifier i_B. If these checks are correct then A generates a new nonce r'_A and constructs the message M_4 from the remaining portion of M_3 (encrypted under the key K_{BT}) and by encrypting the nonce r_B and the new nonce r'_A under the new shared key K derived from the keying material F.

When B receives message M_4, B's actions are similar to A's. It first decrypts and checks that (1) it has the correct redundancy, (2) it contains B's nonce r_B, and (3) it correctly includes A's identifier i_A. If these checks are correct,

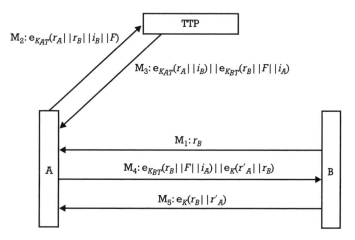

Figure 12.2 A key transport mechanism using nonces and a KTC.

then B recovers the new shared key K from the keying material F. B uses this key to decrypt the second part of the message M_4 and checks that it has the correct redundancy and that it contains the nonce r_B. At this point B is convinced that A must have correctly computed the key K.

B now constructs the message M_5 and sends this back to A. A decrypts this message and checks that it has the correct redundancy and that it contains the nonces r_B and r'_A. If these checks are correct then A is convinced that B must also have computed the key K.

This mechanism gives both parties explicit key authentication. Since A generates the keying material F, A has key control.

12.4.4 Key establishment between different security domains

Key distribution protocols based on KTCs and KDCs are only useful if there is some third party that both entities A and B trust. This is easy if A and B belong to the same security domain: As they are both under the control of the same security administrator, the administrator can set up a TTP service that both entities trust. However things become a little more complicated when A and B do not belong to the same security domain, and therefore do not both trust a single third party. (For more information about security domains and security administrators see Chapter 3).

One general approach to solving this problem is as follows. Suppose that A trusts a third party T_A, and B trusts a distinct third party T_B. If A wishes to transport a key to entity B then A securely passes the key to T_A (since A and T_A share a secret key, the two entities can use a direct communication technique to transport the key). T_A can then employ a key transport mechanism to share that key with T_B, and T_B can employ some further (direct) key transport mechanism to share that key with B.

This effectively moves the key transport problem from between A and B to between T_A and T_B. This may seem a little meaningless as the key transport problem still exists, but now it has been passed to entities that may have greater resources to deal with it. Obviously T_A and T_B still need to have some way of establishing a secret shared key between them. They may negotiate shared keys directly between them, or they may employ the services of some higher level trusted party to act as a KTC (or KDC) for them.

The situation is similar if the entities A and B wish to use a key agreement protocol. Either T_A and T_B can forward messages from A to B and allow them to negotiate the key between them, or T_A and T_B can agree on a key between them and forward the results on to A and B (in a manner similar to a KDC).

These techniques are similar to those used when an entity wishes to obtain a public-key certificate for an entity that belongs to a different security domain. For more information about public-key infrastructures see Chapter 13.

12.5 Mechanisms using asymmetric cryptography

Asymmetric cryptography has many features that are extremely useful in key establishment. Using asymmetric techniques, key establishment can be done noninteractively, digital signatures can be used to provide non-repudiation, and, generally, asymmetric techniques do not require entities to share keys beforehand. Of course, there is a price to pay for these advantages. The two biggest downsides are probably that asymmetric techniques tend to be more computationally complex than symmetric techniques and therefore slower, and that, in order to use an asymmetric key establishment technique, the entities will probably need a supporting public-key infrastructure (PKI). PKIs are discussed in detail in Chapter 13.

The earliest example of an asymmetric key establishment technique is the Diffie-Hellman key agreement protocol, invented in 1976. In fact, this is the first published example of any asymmetric technique! While the basic form of the protocol is not really recommended for use (it has no freshness mechanism and can only be used once for each pair of entities), the basic idea of the protocol is still considered sound, and it is the basis for many different applications besides key management. We discuss this protocol in Sections 12.5.1 and 12.5.2.

ISO/IEC 11770-3 describes 13 key establishment techniques and three public key transport mechanisms. Of the 13 key establishment techniques, seven are key agreement mechanisms, and six are key transport mechanisms.

We use the following notation for asymmetric algorithms:

- P_X denotes the public key of entity X (in an encryption scheme P_X will be used for encryption, whereas P_X will be used for verification in a signature scheme).

- s_X denotes the private key of entity X (in an encryption scheme s_X will be used for decryption, whereas s_X will be used for signing in a signature scheme).

- $\mathcal{E}\,(m, P_X)$ denotes the encryption of the message m using the public key P_X.

- $\mathcal{D}\,(C, s_X)$ denotes the decryption of the ciphertext C using the private key s_X.

- $\mathcal{S}\,(m, s_X)$ denotes the signature of the message m using the private key s_X.

- $\mathcal{V}\,(m, \sigma, P_X)$ denotes the result of the verification of the signature σ for the message m using the public key P_X.

- i_X denotes an identifier for entity X.

- t_X denotes a time-stamp produced by entity X.

- F (or F_X) denotes the keying material (produced by entity X).

When we use a digital signature scheme, we will implicitly use a nonreversible scheme; however it should be easy to see that a reversible scheme will work just as well. Obviously, if a key establishment mechanism employs a reversible digital signature algorithm then only the nonrecoverable part of the message needs be transmitted with the signature. For more information about digital signature schemes, see Chapter 8.

12.5.1   The Diffie-Hellman function

All of the key agreement techniques described ISO/IEC 11770-3 are presented in full generality. In other words, just as ISO/IEC 11770-2 describes mechanisms for key establishment based on some unspecified block cipher, ISO/IEC 11770-3 describes how to build key agreement mechanisms using an unspecified asymmetric primitive.

This asymmetric primitive is not an encryption algorithm, but is instead a special function P with the following properties:

1. P takes two inputs: an input h from the set H, and an input g from the set G.

2. For any two inputs $h \in H$ and $g \in G$, it must be easy to compute the output $P(h, g)$.

3. For any two inputs $h \in H$, and $g \in G$, the output $P(h, g)$ must be a member of the set G.

4. For any inputs $h_1, h_2 \in H$, and $g \in G$ we must have that

$$P(h_1, P(h_2, g)) = P(h_2, P(h_1, g)). \tag{12.1}$$

5. For any inputs it should be computationally infeasible for an attacker to work out $P(h_1, P(h_2, g))$ from $P(h_1, g)$, $P(h_2, g)$, and g.

While using this special function P allows us to describe key establishment mechanisms that do not explicitly depend upon any one mechanism, P is almost always implemented in the same way. In almost all cases P is based on the exponentiation function in a specific (large) cyclic group, (i.e., the same function as is used in the original version of the Diffie-Hellman protocol).

The most basic version of this "Diffie-Hellman function" works as follows. First choose a large prime p. The function P is then described as

$$P(h, g) = g^h \bmod p \tag{12.2}$$

where $1 \leq g \leq p - 1$ and $1 \leq h \leq p - 2$. Hence $G = \{1, 2, \ldots, p - 1\}$ and $H = \{1, 2, \ldots, p - 2\}$.

This function satisfies most of the properties that we require of P. It is certainly easy to compute and has the correct input and output sets. Furthermore it satisfies condition 4 because

$$P(h_1, P(h_2, g)) = (g^{h_2})^{h_1} = g^{h_2 h_1} = g^{h_1 h_2} = (g^{h_1})^{h_2} = P(h_2, P(h_1, g)) \tag{12.3}$$

We therefore only have to worry about condition 5—the security condition—and it is here that we run into a problem. Unfortunately, if we just use the basic version of the Diffie-Hellman function then we cannot guarantee that the condition 5 will hold. In order to to meet condition 5, we need to "tweak" the Diffie-Hellman function slightly.

Along with p we need to choose a number α ($1 < \alpha \le p - 1$) such that $\alpha^q \equiv 1 \pmod{p}$ for some large prime number q (although it can be shown that q cannot be too large as q must divide into $p - 1$). We now insist that P can only be fed inputs h and g if $1 \le h \le q - 1$ and g is a power of α, (i.e., $g = \alpha^k \bmod p$ for some value of k). Therefore the two input sets are now the following:

- G is the set of numbers $1, \alpha \bmod p, \alpha^2 \bmod p, \alpha^3 \bmod p, \dots, \alpha^{q-1} \bmod p$.

- H is the set of numbers $1, 2, 3, \dots, q - 1$.

The actual definition of P remains the same [i.e., $P(h, g) = g^h \bmod p$]. It is widely believed that with these input restrictions, and provided p and q are large enough, condition 5 will hold for P.

The only other choice for P that is in common use is also based on the Diffie-Hellman protocol but, in this case, the group G is an elliptic curve group and the function P is given by a scalar multiplication function in that group. Key establishment algorithms based on elliptic curve groups are not standardized in ISO/IEC 11770 but are included in ISO/IEC 15946, ANSI X9.63, and IEEE 1363.

12.5.2 Key agreement mechanisms

We now give three examples of key agreement mechanisms. The first two are taken from ISO/IEC 11770-3 and are described in terms of the "special function" P described above. It may be helpful to think of P as the Diffie-Hellman function. The last example is the station-to-station (STS) protocol that forms the basis for several of the IETF key agreement mechanisms. While this protocol is usually described using the Diffie-Hellman function, we will adapt it to use the ISO/IEC special function P.

In all cases the mechanisms are designed to establish a shared key between two entities A and B. For both of the ISO/IEC protocols, both A and B will need to have a public and private key based on the function P. In order to do this they must first agree on a "base" value $\alpha \in G$. They can do this publicly because knowing α will not help an attacker to discover the key that A and B are going to establish, but it is important that both entities have access to a correct value for α. In fact α will typically be a "global parameter" used by a community of users. A then picks a private key s_A at random from H and computes public key $P_A = P(s_A, \alpha)$. B does the same, and obtains a secret key s_B and a public key P_B. It is vitally important that A has an authentic copy of B's public key P_B and vice versa. Distributing authentic public keys is the main function of a PKI (see Chapter 13).

The STS protocol is slightly different. While it makes use of the special function P, it does not require A or B to produce static public keys in quite the same way that the ISO/IEC mechanisms do. Instead, the security of the STS protocol is based on the use of digital signature schemes for entity authentication and data integrity. Hence, it is important for both A and B to have authentic copies of each other's public verification keys for use with some agreed digital signature scheme. Again, these authentic public keys will normally be distributed by a PKI (see Chapter 13). The confidentiality of the newly agreed key is protected by the use of the special function P.

It is interesting to note that, while ISO/IEC 11770-3 seeks to be as general as possible by defining key agreement schemes in terms of the "special function" P, it does not contain all the standardized asymmetric key agreement protocols. The most notable exception is probably the MQV key agreement protocol, which is standardized in the IEEE 1363, the ANSI X9.42, and the ANSI X9.63 standards. This key agreement protocol is still based on the Diffie-Hellman key agreement protocol but is difficult to write down in terms of the "special function" P, as it requires P to have more than the five stated properties of Section 12.5.1. The MQV protocol is slightly more complex than the other protocols in this section and will not be discussed further.

The Diffie-Hellman key agreement protocol   We will now describe a generalized version of the original key agreement protocol described by Diffie and Hellman in 1976, using the special function P described in Section 12.5.1. This protocol is standardized as key agreement mechanism 1 in ISO/IEC 11770-3. If the function P is the Diffie-Hellman function then the resulting key agreement scheme is also standardized in IEEE 1363, RSA PKCS #3, ANSI X9.42, and IETF RFC 2631.

The protocol works as follows. A computes the shared key $K_A = P(s_A, P_B)$, and B computes the shared key $K_B = P(s_B, P_A)$. These two keys are identical because:

$$
\begin{aligned}
K_A &= P(s_A, P_B) \\
    &= P(s_A, P(s_B, \alpha)) \quad \text{[because } P_B = P(s_B, \alpha)] \\
    &= P(s_B, P(s_A, \alpha)) \quad \text{[because of the properties of } P] \\
    &= P(s_B, P_A) \quad \text{[because } P_A = P(s_A, \alpha)] \\
    &= K_B
\end{aligned}
$$

The first thing to notice about this protocol is that no messages are passed between A and B. This means that if A wishes to establish a shared key with B then A does not need to interact with B in any way (and, in particular, it means that B does not have to be on-line). All A needs to do is obtain an authentic copy of B's public key and make sure that an authentic copy of its own public key is available to B. It also means that no matter how often A and B execute this protocol, the resulting key they establish will always be the same. This means that if A and B wish to update their shared key then they will have to do this via some other technique.

It should also be noted that the key that they derive is a member of the set G and not, as is typically required, a bit string of some predetermined length. The easiest way to derive a secret bit string from the keys K_A and K_B is to apply a hash function to these keys (see Chapter 6).

This mechanism gives implicit key authentication to both parties provided that the public keys are authentic. So, providing that A has an authentic copy of B's public key P_B, then A has implicit key authentication as A knows that only B has the private key needed to compute the key (and vice versa). Neither party has key confirmation, so neither party has explicit key authentication.

It is difficult to establish who has key control in this mechanism. It is likely that no entity has key control—certainly no entity can manipulate the protocol so that the shared key is some predetermined value. However, if entity A knows entity B's public key before A chooses its own private key, then entity A is in a position to compute the shared key K before deciding whether or not to select a particular private key. If A does not like the shared key K resulting from a particular candidate private key then A can choose a new private key and try again. Hence entity A would have a certain measure of control over the key value.

In practice, however, it is unlikely that this measure of control would be significant. Obviously, the problem is completely avoided if A does not generate its own private key or if A cannot obtain a copy of B's public key until after A has chosen its own.

Key agreement using nonces   The fact that A and B can only produce one key using the Diffie-Hellman protocol described above (unless either A or B changes their public key) is a major drawback. To remove this problem we now describe a mechanism based on the same principles as the Diffie-Hellman protocol, but using nonces to ensure that a fresh key is constructed every time the protocol is run. The protocol is key establishment mechanism 5 from ISO/IEC 11770-3.

The protocol involves the exchange of two messages between A and B:

$$M_1 : A \rightarrow B : P(r_A, \alpha)\|\text{Text}_1$$

$$M_2 : B \rightarrow A : P(r_B, \alpha)\|\text{Text}_2$$

where Text_1 and Text_2 are application-dependent data strings.

The protocol proceeds as follows. First, A generates a random nonce r_A from the set H of input values for P and sends $P(r_A, \alpha)$ to B. This value is sometimes referred to as A's *ephemeral* public key (as opposed to P_A which is known as A's *static* public key). On receipt of M_1, B also generates a random nonce r_B from H and sends $P(r_B, \alpha)$ to A. Again, this value is sometimes referred to as B's ephemeral public key. It should be noted that M_1 and M_2 could actually be sent in parallel (i.e., B does not need to process M_1 before generating M_2).

Now each party computes the shared key. A does this by computing

$$P(r_A, P_B)\|P(s_A, P(r_B, \alpha)) \tag{12.4}$$

and B determines the same value by computing

$$P(s_B, P(r_A, \alpha))\|P(r_B, P_A) \tag{12.5}$$

These values are the same because of the properties of the function P. The shared key is the hash code of these shared values (see Chapter 6).

The mechanism provides implicit key authentication to both parties but provides key confirmation to neither. However, if B includes the MAC of a known data string in Text_2, computed using the newly agreed secret key, then B can provide key confirmation to A. Neither party has key control, although, as above, since B receives $P(r_A, \alpha)$ before generating its own nonce r_B, B can influence the value of the key by choosing the value of the nonce r_B carefully. This will not give B complete key control but may allow it to select the shared key from a range of values (computed using different values of r_B).

A similar mechanism appears in ANSI X9.42, but in this case the shared values are computed slightly differently. Here A computes the secret key as

$$P(r_A, P(r_B, \alpha))||P(s_A, P_B) \tag{12.6}$$

and B computes the secret key as

$$P(r_B, P(r_A, \alpha))||P(s_B, P_A) \tag{12.7}$$

Once again a shared key can be computed by computing the hash code of these shared values. However ANSI X9.42 is more specific than ISO/IEC 11770-3 and requires that the function P is the Diffie-Hellman function described in Section 12.5.1. This mechanism is known as dhHybrid1.

The station-to-station (STS) protocol   The STS protocol is based on the use of the special function P for confidentiality and digital signatures for entity authentication and data integrity. Freshness is provided by using different random values in each execution of the protocol, in a manner similar to the use of nonces. While the basic version of the STS protocol is not standardized, it is the basis for several of the IETF-standardized key agreement protocols, including the Internet key exchange (IKE) protocol defined in IETF RFC 2409.

The protocol involves the exchange of three messages between A and B:

$$M_1 : A \rightarrow B : P(r_A, \alpha)$$

$$M_2 : B \rightarrow A : P(r_B, \alpha)||\ S(P(r_B, \alpha)||P(r_A, \alpha)||i_A, s_B)$$

$$M_3 : A \rightarrow B : S(P(r_A, \alpha)||P(r_B, \alpha)||i_B, s_A)$$

Again, it is useful to think about the protocol in two parts: The first message and the first half of the second message allow A and B to agree a key, the remaining messages provide entity authentication.

The protocol runs as follows. First, A generates a random element r_A from the set H, stores a copy of it and sends the value $P(r_A, \alpha)$ to B. B then chooses another random value r_B from the set H, and computes the secret key K by applying a hash function to the value

$$P(r_B, P(r_A, \alpha)) = P(r_A, P(r_B, \alpha)) \tag{12.8}$$

B sends the value $P(r_B, \alpha)$ to A so that A can compute the same key value. Hence, A and B can compute a secret shared key with each other but, at this point, they have no kind of entity authentication assurance from the other. Therefore, along with $P(r_B, \alpha)$, B sends some authentication information. B computes this authentication by taking the two random values $P(r_A, \alpha)$ and $P(r_B, \alpha)$ (along with A's identifier) and signing them.

On receipt of message M_2, A first computes the secret shared key K from the received value $P(r_B, \alpha)$ and the stored value r_A. A then verifies that B has provided a correct signature on the two values they have exchanged (and A's identifier). At this point A has authenticated B and can be confident that B has recovered the correct key K as B must have received the correct value $P(r_A, \alpha)$ to have included it in the signature. Hence, it only remains for A to authenticate itself to B. This it does in a similar way, by sending B a signed version of the two random values that A and B have exchanged (along with B's identifier).

B authenticates A in the obvious way (i.e., B verifies that A's signature is indeed a correct signature on the two exchanged values and B's identifier). This mechanism provides both parties with explicit key confirmation, and neither party has key control.

12.5.3   Key transport mechanisms

The asymmetric mechanisms for key transport are similar to those using symmetric cryptography: Both use encryption for confidentiality and a further mechanism to provide integrity. In symmetric cryptography that integrity mechanism is usually either an MDC or a MAC. In asymmetric cryptography the integrity mechanism is usually a signature scheme. Due to the similarities between symmetric and asymmetric key transport mechanisms, we only give one example of an asymmetric key transport mechanism here.

Key transport using time-stamps and signatures   We now describe key transport mechanism 2 from ISO/IEC 11770-3. Use of this mechanism requires that entity A has obtained an authentic copy of entity B's public encryption key (for an asymmetric encryption scheme) and that entity B has obtain an authentic copy of entity A's public verification key (for a digital signature scheme). The protocol consists of just one message:

$$M_1 : A \rightarrow B : \mathcal{E}(i_A || F || \text{Text}_1, P_B) || i_B || t_A ||$$
$$\mathcal{S}(i_B || t_A || X || \text{Text}_2, s_A) || \text{Text}_3$$

where Text_1–Text_3 are application-dependent data strings, and X is the ciphertext produced by the encryption operation, that is,

$$X = \mathcal{E}(i_B || F || \text{Text}_1, P_B) \tag{12.9}$$

The mechanism operates as follows. A first generates some keying material F and encrypts it, along with A's identifier i_A, using B's public encryption key.

This will protect the confidentiality of the keying material and ensure that only B can recover the key. Next A produces a digital signature on B's identifier i_B, a time-stamp and the ciphertext that has just been computed. A sends both the ciphertext and the signature to B.

On receipt of message M_1, B first decrypts the encrypted block and recovers both A's identifier i_A and the keying material F. To ensure that the message is authentic B checks that (1) the time-stamp is fresh, (2) the message includes B's identifier i_B, and (3) the signature on the message is authentic. If all of these checks are correct then B accepts the keying material.

This mechanism provides implicit key authentication to both parties provided that each entity has access to an authentic copy of the other's public key. A needs to have an authentic copy of B's public key to be sure that only B can recover the keying material. B needs to have an authentic copy of A's public key to be sure that A sent the message. Since A generated the keying material, B can have some measure of confidence that A must know F. Hence B has explicit key authentication. A has no key confirmation from B and so does not receive explicit key authentication but does have key control.

This mechanism is similar to that described in the banking standard ISO 11166-2. The main differences are that the banking standard specifies that the encryption and signing operations are specific schemes based on the RSA algorithm (see Chapter 4), and A only signs the encrypted message block X.

12.6 Key establishment based on weak secrets

One problem with almost all the mechanisms that we have discussed up to now is that they involve computers holding some kind of secret information: either a secret key shared with a third party or a private key for an asymmetric algorithm. This is perfectly satisfactory when the entity in question is a computer, or a human user that only ever uses one machine. It is not so satisfactory when we consider a human user who wants to be able to use several different machines.

If this is necessary then there are a few options. The first would be to store the key in a portable TRSM (e.g., a smart card) and allow users to physically carry the key around with them. This would certain comply with the security restrictions laid down by ANSI X9.24 (see Chapter 11). The second option would be not to store the key on the host computer, but to allow the user to enter it manually.

Of course, this has the disadvantage that the user has to remember the key and, since keys are likely to be long complicated binary strings with little or no logic to them, this could be quite a task for the user! One solution to this problem is to ask the user to remember passwords from which keys can be derived instead of forcing the user to remember the keys themselves. These passwords are sometimes known as *weak* or *low entropy* secrets.

Only one of the currently standardized key establishment schemes is designed to work with weak secrets, namely the Kerberos scheme. This scheme was briefly discussed in Section 12.4.2 and described in detail in Chapter 10. However, two further standards are currently being developed to address the problem of key establishment via weak secrets. These are a new, fourth part of ISO/IEC 11770 and the IEEE P1363.2 standard being developed by the IEEE 1363 group.

A key feature of all the schemes in these new standards is that they are designed to protect against password-guessing attacks. That is, even if an attacker successfully eavesdrops on a protocol in which a key is established using a password, it is not possible for the attacker to determine either party's password (or discover the established key) using an exhaustive search.

12.7   Key establishment for mobile networks

The problem of key establishment between mobile phones and mobile networks is slightly different to the generic key establishment problem we have been considering up to now. This is because we know a lot more about the relationship between the two entities that need to establish a shared key, and we can take advantage of this knowledge to construct more efficient key establishment schemes. We will only consider one specific example of a key establishment scheme for a mobile network, namely the scheme standardized by the in 3GPP in TS 33.102.

The network architecture for mobile phones is fairly simple. Each mobile phone (or *handset*) is associated with one particular mobile network, known as the handset's *home environment*. However, owing to the mobile nature of handsets, a handset may not always be in range of a transmitter that belongs to its home environment. In this case a handset will connect to a third-party *serving network* that will act as an intermediary between the handset and its home environment. This is known as *roaming*.

The handset will connect to the serving network wirelessly, (i.e., through the use of radio signals). This means that anyone with a correctly tuned receiver can eavesdrop on any information passing back and forth between the handset and the serving network. In order to preserve the confidentiality and integrity of this information, the 3GPP standard describes a method to establish a series of shared secret keys between the handset and the serving network. It is assumed that the information that passes between the serving network and the home environment is secure (see Figure 12.3).

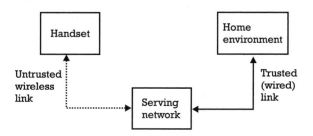

Figure 12.3   The 3GPP network architecture.

The problem with establishing a shared secret key between the handset and the serving network is that they do not share any long-term secret key. This is a fundamental property of the network. As a business, the serving network would not wish to waste resources storing a long-term secret key for a different network's customer. Similarly, the owner of the handset would not want a long-term secret key (which could be used for eavesdropping) to be in the hands of a third party who may use it unscrupulously.

It is instead assumed that the handset and the home environment share a long-term secret key K and that there is a method whereby the home environment and the serving network can communicate securely.

The key establishment scheme uses five different algorithms:

- A MAC function $f1$;

- A response function $f2$;

- A cipher key generation function $f3$;

- An integrity key generation function $f4$;

- An anonymity key generation function $f5$.

Each of these algorithms takes the long-term secret key shared by the handset and the home environment as input; hence, none of the outputs can be predicted by anyone who does not have access to that key, including the serving network.

The key establishment protocol runs as follows. We will let SN denote the serving network and HE denote the home environment.

1. $SN \rightarrow HE:$ $i_{Handset}$
   Since the serving network does not share a long-term secret key with the handset, the serving network is forced to request some data from the home environment to authenticate the handset. These are known as *authentication vectors*.

2. $HE \rightarrow SN:$ $RAND||XRES||CK||IK||AUTN$
   The home environment responds by passing a series of authentication vectors back to the serving network. These vectors consist of five data values:

   - The value $RAND$ is a randomly generated number. It is used as a challenge and allows the handset to authenticate itself to the serving network.

   - The value $XRES = f2(RAND, K)$ is the expected response that the serving network will receive from the handset if the handset is authentic.

   - The value $CK = f3(RAND, K)$ is the cipher key that the serving network will use to encrypt data passing over the insecure wireless link to the handset.

- Similarly, the value $IK = f4(RAND, K)$ is the integrity key that the serving network will use to compute MACs.

▸ The last value, $AUTN$, is more complicated. It is the information that the handset will use to authenticate the serving network. (Obviously, since $AUTN$ is actually generated by the home environment, the best that the handset can do is authenticate the fact that the serving network is in contact with the home environment and trust that the home environment has successfully authenticated the serving network.) The authentication method makes use of a MAC for entity authentication and a logical time-stamp (sequence number) for freshness. The value of $AUTN$ is computed as

$$AUTN = SQN \oplus AK||MAC \tag{12.10}$$

where SQN is the a sequence number (logical time-stamp), $AK = f5(RAND, K)$ is the anonymity key, and the MAC is computed as $MAC = f1(SQN||RAND, K)$.

Typically the home environment will pass more than one of these authentication vectors to the serving network at a time, so that the serving network may challenge the handset to identify itself more than once without needing to request more data from the home environment.

3. $SN \rightarrow Handset:$ $RAND||AUTN$
   The serving network passes the random challenge $RAND$ and the authentication information $AUTN$ to the handset.

4. $Handset \rightarrow SN:$ RES
   The handset now has two jobs to do: First it must authenticate the serving network using $AUTN$, and then it must authenticate itself to the serving network by computing the correct response RES to the random challenge $RAND$ that it has been sent. First, the handset computes the anonymity key $AK = f5(RAND, K)$ and recovers the sequence number SQN from $AUTN$. Next the handset authenticates the serving network by checking that the sequence number SQN is correct (i.e., greater than the stored value) and that the MAC value received is equal to $f1(SQN||RAND, K)$. If both of these checks are correct then the handset has authenticated the network, so it computes the new shared keys $CK = f3(RAND, K)$ and $IK = f4(RAND, K)$ and updates the sequence number SQN. Last, the handset authenticates itself to the network by computing the response $RES = f2(RAND, K)$ to the challenge $RAND$ and sending this back to the serving network.

5. SN authenticates $Handset$
   The serving network now only has to authenticate the handset. It does this by checking that the response RES it has received from the handset is the same as the expected response $XRES$.

If we assume that the home environment has authenticated the serving network before releasing the authentication vectors to it, then this mechanism gives implicit authentication to both parties. There is no key confirmation for the keys that are going to be used (i.e., *CK* and *IK*).

It is interesting to note that, while this mechanism is standardized, the functions involved, $f1 - f5$, are not. This is because there is no need for these functions to be the same for every network. Since the only two parties that evaluate these functions are the home environment and the handset (which has been programmed with software issued by the home environment), there is no need for anyone else to know what these functions are. 3GPP does provide a set of example functions, known as the MILENAGE algorithm set, but their use is not mandatory.

12.8 Choosing a key establishment scheme

Choosing a key establishment mechanism is a complicated and subtle business. Just as keys are at the very heart of cryptography, so key management is at the very heart of an organization's security policy—the choice of key establishment mechanism will influence many other aspects of security management, and different solutions to the key establishment problems are likely to lead to radically different overall security solutions.

In deciding on a key establishment mechanism, there are several factors that should be taken into consideration. The first is the level of interoperability the system needs to have with other, independently developed, systems. If the system needs to be highly interoperable with other systems then it will be necessary to use the same key management techniques as all the other systems. For example, a key management system for a mobile phone company needs to be interoperable with other mobile phone systems, hence the implementor has no choice but to follow the 3GPP standards.

If interoperability is less important, then an organization may choose to develop its own, tailored, key establishment system, and the choice of mechanism will depend on a series of other factors. The relative importance of these factors depends very heavily on the nature of the environment in which the key establishment mechanism will be used. Certainly the following need to be considered:

- The size of the organization (both now and in the future). For a small organization simple solutions may be practical—for example, users could establish keys using the direct communication methods of Section 12.4.1 and the initial keys could be distributed physically (see Section 12.3). For larger organizations, or organizations that are physically separated, more complex solutions will be required.

- The available computing power and bandwidth. It may be impractical to use some of the more complex key establishment techniques, such as those based on asymmetric cryptography (see Section 12.5), on some devices. Similarly, if the network to which these devices are connected only has limited bandwidth, then it may be prudent to select a mechanism that involves the transfer of a smaller number of protocol messages.

‣ The requirements of other parts of the security system. Other parts of the system may already use security techniques that could be adapted to handle key establishment. For example, if the security requirements necessitate the use of some kind of non-repudiation framework (see Chapter 9) then it might be cost-efficient to set up a PKI (see Chapter 13) to handle both non-repudiation and key establishment. Alternatively, if the authentication framework (see Section 10) required the use of a TTP then it might also be cost-efficient to have that third party act as a KDC or KTC (see Sections 12.4.2 and 12.4.3).

‣ The needs of the users. If a user does not have a machine of his or her own, or wishes to be able to work on any of a multitude of machines, then it will be necessary for that user to access his or her keys from a large number of (possibly untrustworthy) machines. This may require the use of a key establishment mechanism based on weak secrets (see Section 12.6) or keys stored physically on a TRSM (see Section 12.3).

‣ Legacy systems and migration issues. If a key management system is being introduced to replace an existing operational solution, then it might be highly desirable to choose a solution that is sufficiently similar to the system that is currently deployed in order to ease migration. For example, the 3GPP key establishment scheme described in Section 12.7 is very similar to the key establishment scheme designed for use in second generation GSM mobile networks. This similarity has eased the transition between the use of GSM networks and 3GPP networks.

12.9 Notes

Section 12.1

Owing to the peculiar evolution of key management systems—an evolution based on best practices in industry rather than by academic research—it is difficult to track down the origin of many of the important concepts in key management. Crucial concepts such as key authentication, key confirmation, and key control have grown up from the use of keys rather than from academic discussion, and the development of key management standards by informed professionals has played an important role in the evolution of these ideas.

This chapter only introduces some of the many possible mechanisms that can be used to established shared secret keys. For more information on this subject, the reader is referred to Boyd and Mathuria [1]. The basic principles of key establishment using symmetric and asymmetric techniques are also discussed in Stallings [2]. There is also a nice summary of the ISO 8732 standard for key establishment in the wholesale banking sector in Davies and Price [3].

It should be noted that, while standard key agreement protocols are less suited to generating the complex keys required by asymmetric applications, key agreement protocols can still be used to generate these keys. A key agreement protocol will typically ensure that both parties can establish a suitably random binary string of some predetermined length in a confidential manner. If this random string is used as the random bits that a key generation algorithm (see Chapters 4 and 8) uses, then both parties can generate the same asymmetric keys by running the same key generation algorithm.

Section 12.2

Four main standard bodies have produced standards for key establishment using symmetric techniques. Two of these are applicable only to specific sectors: the ISO 8732 standard [4], which is applicable to the financial sector, and the 3GPP TS 33.102 standard [5], which is only applicable to the mobile phone sector. A general key establishment standard has been produced by the ISO/IEC JTC1 committee, of which ISO/IEC 11770-2 [6] deals with key establishment using symmetric techniques.

The Kerberos protocol is standardized in IETF RFC 1510 [7]. Other IETF standards include the Photuris session-key management protocol, which is contained in IETF RFC 2522 [8].

There are two main approaches to key establishment using asymmetric techniques. The general ISO/IEC JTC1 standard, ISO/IEC 11770-3 [9], defines several key establishment mechanisms based on a general function that satisfies certain security properties. Hence the standard does not, strictly speaking, define any complete protocols. However, there is a tacit understanding that these protocols should be instantiated using the Diffie-Hellman function (see Section 12.5.1).

Other standards are more specific. Almost all the standardized key agreement protocols are based on the Diffie-Hellman protocol and this is standardized in ANSI X9.42 [10], IETF RFC 2631 [11], IEEE 1363 [12, 13], and RSA PKCS #3 (see Chapter 4 for more information about the RSA PKCS series of standards). There are also several standardized elliptic curve versions of the Diffie-Hellman protocol; see ISO/IEC 15946 [14], ANSI X9.63 [15], and IEEE 1363 [12, 13].

The second class of techniques, namely, asymmetric key transport techniques, is usually based on asymmetric encryption and digital signature schemes. Asymmetric key transport schemes are standardized in ISO/IEC 11770-3 [9] and ISO 11166 [16, 17].

The IETF schemes are standardized in RFC 2246 [18] (the TLS protocol) and RFC 2409 [19] (the IKE protocol). These are fairly high-level descriptions concerned more with the describing the messages that need to be passed between two computers to facilitate establishing a key, rather than concentrating on the key establishment technique itself. An extension of the TLS protocol that uses the Kerberos authentication/key establishment protocol is described in RFC 2712 [20].

Section 12.3

The most common situation in which keys are distributed physically is in the distribution of PINs for ATM cards. Here the "key" is distributed using several sealed packages: the outer letter which contains the address of the recipient, and the sealed inner letter which contains the actual PIN.

The idea of key splitting can be extended so that the key is split between more than two parties. The simplest way to split a key K between n users is to generate n key fragments $k_1, \ldots, k_n$ such that

$$K = k_1 \oplus k_2 \oplus \ldots \oplus k_n$$

This has the disadvantage that the key cannot be legitimately recovered unless all the key fragments are correctly received. More complex schemes exist in which the key is split between n users but the key can be recovered provided that some smaller (threshold) number of key fragments are correctly received. These schemes are known as *secret sharing schemes*, the first examples of which were independently given by Blakley [21] and Shamir [22] in the late 1970s.

Section 12.4

The ISO/IEC 11770-2 key establishment mechanisms that use direct communication are strongly based on the ISO/IEC 9798-2 entity authentication schemes [23] (see Chapter 10).

The idea of using a trusted third party to facilitate key establishment was first introduced by Needham and Schroeder [24] in 1978. While their protocol was subsequently broken [25, 26], the idea remained.

All of the ISO/IEC 11770-2 key establishment mechanisms that make use of a key distribution center are based on the Bauer, Berson, and Feiertag correction [25] to the Needham and Schroeder protocol. The ISO 8732 protocol, described in Section 12.4.2, is similar to the key establishment protocol proposed by Boyd [27] (although the Boyd protocol uses nonces for freshness instead of time stamps, and was published about a decade after the ISO 8732 protocol was released). The Kerberos key distribution protocol [28, 29] was discussed in detail in Chapter 10.

The attack against the ISO 8732 protocol described in Section 12.4.2 was noted by Boyd (Colin Boyd, personal communication, April 2004).

Section 12.5

The Diffie-Hellman protocol was introduced in the famous paper by Diffie and Hellman [30]. This paper introduced both the Diffie-Hellman "special function" described in Section 12.5.1 and the Diffie-Hellman key agreement protocol described in Section 12.5.2. The tweaked version of the Diffie-Hellman function, in which small subgroups are avoided, has been attributed by Boyd and Mathuria [1] to Vanstone, but no original paper seems to exist on the subject.

It should be noted that special function P defined in Section 12.5.1 is denoted by F in ISO/IEC 11770-3. We have changed this designation to avoid confusing this function with the keying material.

The more complicated key agreement protocol using nonces, discussed in Section 12.5.2, is actually the MTI A(0) protocol developed by Matsumoto,

Takashima, and Imai [31]. There have been several proposed attacks against this scheme that suggest it can be broken if it is not implemented carefully—see, for example, [32]. One of the more interesting attacks [33] demonstrates that an attacker can successfully impersonate an entity X (and retrieve the agreed key) when communicating with that entity (i.e., the attacker can impersonate X to X). Obviously, such an attack will not be relevant in most well implemented systems.

The idea that an entity can exert some measure of key control in key agreement protocols by selecting a more favorable key from a selection it has generated using several different parameter sets (for example, when B chooses a nonce that gives a more favourable key in the nonce-based protocol of Section 12.5.2) was first introduced by Mitchell, Ward, and Wilson [34].

The station-to-station protocol was first proposed by Diffie, van Oorschot, and Wiener [35] in a slightly different format to the protocol discussed here. The original version did not sign A or B's identifiers but symmetrically encrypted the digital signatures under the newly established key K in order to demonstrate that both entities knew the key K. The adapted version of the protocol we use is discussed in Boyd and Mathuria [1] and has been proven secure by Bellare, Canetti, and Krawczyk [36, 37].

The Menezes-Qu-Vanstone (MQV) key agreement protocol [38] is not included in the ISO/IEC standard [9] but does appear in the IEEE 1363 [12], ANSI X9.42 [10] and ANSI X9.63 [15] standards. It uses the fact that when P is the Diffie-Hellman protocol (i.e., $P(h, g) = g^h \bmod p$), we have certain multiplicative identities:

$$P(h_1 + h_2, g) = P(h_1, g) \cdot P(h_2, g)$$
$$P(h_1 h_2, g) = P(h_1, P(h_2, g))$$

and

$$P(h, g_1 g_2) = P(h, g_1) \cdot P(h, g_2)$$

For more details, see [38].

The key transport mechanism given in Section 12.5.3 is both efficient and secure, although some concerns have been raised about the fact that the signature is only computed on publicly available information. Hence, it is possible for a malicious attacker to substitute the correct signature with his own, and thus attempt to fool B into thinking that the message was from him. This attack only works if the attacker can also change the identifier i_A that has also been encrypted, and even then the attacker still does not learn the value of the key.

Section 12.6

We have only briefly mentioned the mechanisms and the problems associated with key establishment using weak secrets (passwords). A more comprehensive study can be found in Boyd and Mathuria [1].

Section 12.7

An overview of the key establishment mechanisms used in 3GPP mobile networks can be found in Temple and Regnault [39]. As we have mentioned, the 3GPP key establishment algorithm is very similar to that found in the second generation GSM mobile networks. A good description of this earlier scheme can be found in Hillebrand [40]. Future trends in security for mobile networks are discussed in Mitchell [41].

The 3GPP key establishment scheme described in this section is standardized in 3GPP TS 33.102 [5]. The MILENAGE algorithm set and the example algorithms that 3GPP have provided for the $f1 - f5$ functions are given in a series of five standards: the general introduction [42], the algorithm specification [43], the implementors' test data [44], the conformance test data [45], and the summary and results of the design and evaluation process [46].

References

[1] Boyd, C. A., and A. Mathuria, *Protocols for Key Establishment and Authentication*, New York: Springer-Verlag, 2003.

[2] Stallings, W., *Cryptography and Network Security*, Upper Saddle River, NJ: Prentice Hall, 2003.

[3] Davies, D. W., and W. L. Price, *Security for Computer Networks*, 2nd ed., New York: John Wiley and Sons, 1989.

[4] International Organization for Standardization, *ISO/IEC 8732, Banking—Key Management (Wholesale)*, 1988.

[5] European Telecommunications Standards Institute (ETSI), *3GPP TS 33.102, 3rd Generation Partnership Project; Technical Specification Group Services and System Aspects; 3G Security; Security Architecture*, September 2003.

[6] International Organization for Standardization, *ISO/IEC 11770–2, Information Technology—Security Techniques—Key Management—Part 2: Mechanisms Using Symmetric Techniques*, 1996.

[7] Kohl, J., and C. Neuman, *RFC 1510, The Kerberos Network Authentication Service (V5)*, Internet Engineering Task Force, September 1993.

[8] Karn, P., and W. Simpson, *RFC 2522, Photuris: Session-Key Management Protocol*, Internet Engineering Task Force, March 1999.

[9] International Organization for Standardization, *ISO/IEC 11770–3, Information Technology—Security Techniques—Key Management—Part 3: Mechanisms Using Asymmetric Techniques*, 1999.

[10] Accredited Standards Committee X9—Financial Services, *ANSI X9.42, Public Key Cryptography for the Financial Services Industry: Agreement of Symmetric Keys Using Discrete Logarithm Cryptography*, 2001.

[11] Rescorla, E., *RFC 2631: Diffie-Hellman Key Agreement Method*, Internet Engineering Task Force, June 1999.

[12] Institute of Electrical and Electronics Engineers, Inc., *IEEE Standard Specifications for Public-Key Cryptography*, 2000.

[13]   Institute of Electrical and Electronics Engineers, Inc., *IEEE Standard Specifications for Public-Key Cryptography—Amendment 1: Additional Techniques*, 2004.

[14]   International Organization for Standardization, *ISO/IEC 15946, Information Technology—Security Techniques—Cryptographic Techniques Based on Elliptic Curves*, 2002.

[15]   Accredited Standards Committee X9—Financial Services, *ANSI X9.63, Public Key Cryptography for the Financial Services Industry, Key Agreement and Key Transport Using Elliptic Curve Cryptography*, 2001.

[16]   International Organization for Standardization, *ISO/IEC 11166–1, Banking—Key Management by Means of Asymmetric Algorithms—Part 1: Principles, Procedures, and Formats*, 1994.

[17]   International Organization for Standardization, *ISO/IEC 11166–2, Banking—Key Management by Means of Asymmetric Algorithms—Part 2: Approved Algorithms Using the RSA Cryptosystem*, 1994.

[18]   Dierks, T., and C. Allen, *RFC 2246, The TLS Protocol, Version 1.0*, Internet Engineering Task Force, January 1999.

[19]   Harkins, D., and D. Carrel, *RFC 2409, The Internet Key Exchange (IKE)*, Internet Engineering Task Force, November 1998.

[20]   Medvinsky, A., and M. Hur, *RFC 2712, Addition of Kerberos Cipher Suites to Transport Layer Security (TLS)*, Internet Engineering Task Force, October 1999.

[21]   Blakley, G. R., Safeguarding Cryptographic Keys, *Proceedings of the National Computer Conference*, Vol. 48, *American Federation of Information Processing Societies Proceedings*, 1979, pp. 313–317.

[22]   Shamir, A., "How to Share a Secret," *Communications of the ACM*, Vol. 22, 1979, pp. 612–613.

[23]   International Organization for Standardization, *ISO/IEC 9798–2: 1999, Information Technology—Security Techniques—Entity Authentication—Part 2: Mechanisms Using Symmetric Encipherment Algorithms*, 2nd ed., 1999.

[24]   Needham, R. M., and M. D. Schroeder, "Using Encryption for Authentication in Large Networks of Computers," *Communications of the ACM*, Vol. 21, 1978, pp. 993–999.

[25]   Bauer, R. K., T. A. Berson, and R. J. Feiertag, "A Key Distribution Protocol Using Event Markers," *ACM Transactions on Computer Systems*, Vol. 1, No. 3, August 1983, pp. 249–255.

[26]   Denning, D. E., and Sacco, G. M., "Timestamps in Key Distribution Protocols," *Communications of the ACM*, Vol. 24, 1981, pp. 533–536.

[27]   Boyd, C., "A Class of Flexible and Efficient Key Management Protocols," *9th IEEE Computer Security Foundations Workshop*, IEEE Computer Society Press, 1996, pp. 2–8.

[28]   Neuman, B. C., and T. Ts'o, "Kerberos: An Authentication Service for Computer Networks," *IEEE Communications Magazine*, Vol. 32, No. 9, September 1994, pp. 33–38.

[29]   Steiner, J. G., C. Neuman, and J. I. Schiller, "Kerberos: An Authentication Service for Open Network Systems," in *Proceedings: Usenix Association, Winter Conference 1988*, USENIX Association, Berkeley, CA, February 1988, pp. 191–202.

[30] Diffie, W., and M. E. Hellman, "New Directions in Cryptography," *IEEE Transactions on Information Theory*, Vol. 22, 1976, pp. 644–654.

[31] Matsumoto, T., Y. Takashima, and H. Imai, "On Seeking Smart Public-Key-Distribution Schemes," *Transactions of the IECE of Japan*, Vol. E69, No. 2, 1986, pp. 99–106.

[32] Burmester, M., "On the Risk of Opening Distributed Keys," in Y. Desmedt, (ed.), *Advances in Cryptology—Crypto '94*, Vol. 839, *Lecture Notes in Computer Science*, Springer-Verlag, 1994, pp. 308–317.

[33] Just, M., and S. Vaudenay, "Authenticated Multi-Party Key Agreement," in K. Kim and T. Matsumoto, (eds.), *Advances in Cryptology—Asiacrypt '96*, Vol. 1163, *Lecture Notes in Computer Science*, Springer-Verlag, 1996, pp. 36–49.

[34] Mitchell, C. J., M. Ward, and P. Wilson, "On Key Control in Key Agreement Protocols," *Electronics Letters*, Vol. 34, 1998, pp. 980–981.

[35] Diffie, W., P. C. van Oorschot, and M. J. Wiener, "Authentication and Authenticated Key Exchange," *Designs, Codes, and Cryptography*, Vol. 2, 1992, pp. 107–125.

[36] Bellare, M., R. Canetti, and H. Krawczyk, "A Modular Approach to the Design and Analysis of Authentication and Key Exchange Protocols," *30th ACM Symposium on the Theory of Computing*, ACM Press, 1998, pp. 419–428.

[37] Canetti, R, and H. Krawczyk, "Analysis of Key-Exchange Protocols and Their Use for Building Secure Channels," in B. Pfitzmann, (ed.), *Advances in Cryptology—Eurocrypt 2001*, Vol. 2045, *Lecture Notes in Computer Science*, Springer-Verlag, 2001, pp. 453–474.

[38] Law, L., "An Efficient Protocol for Authenticated Key Agreement," *Designs, Codes, and Cryptography*, Vol. 28, No. 2, 2003, pp. 119–134.

[39] Temple, R., and J. Regnault, (eds.), *Internet and Wireless Security*, New York: Institute of Electrical Engineers, 2002.

[40] Hillebrand, F., (ed.), *GSM and UMTS: The Creation of Global Mobile Communications*, New York: John Wiley and Sons, 2001.

[41] Mitchell, C. J., (ed.), *Security for Mobility*, New York: Institution of Electrical Engineers, 2004.

[42] European Telecommunications Standards Institute (ETSI), *3GPP TS 35.205, 3rd Generation Partnership Project; Technical Specification Group Services and System Aspects; 3G Security; Specification of the MILENAGE Algorithm Set: An Example Algorithm Set for the 3GPP Authentication and Key Generation Functions f1, f1*, f2, f3, f4, f5, and f5*; Document 1: General*, June 2002.

[43] European Telecommunications Standards Institute (ETSI), *3GPP TS 35.206, 3rd Generation Partnership Project; Technical Specification Group Services and System Aspects; 3G Security; Specification of the MILENAGE Algorithm Set: An Example Algorithm Set for the 3GPP Authentication and Key generation Functions f1, f1*, f2, f3, f4, f5, and f5*; Document 2: Algorithm Specification*, June 2003.

[44] European Telecommunications Standards Institute (ETSI), *3GPP TS 35.207, 3rd Generation Partnership Project; Technical Specification Group Services and System Aspects; 3G Security; Specification of the MILENAGE Algorithm Set: An Example Algorithm Set for the 3GPP Authentication and key Generation Functions f1, f1*, f2, f3, f4, f5, and f5*; Document 3: Implementors' Test Data*, June 2002.

[45]   European Telecommunications Standards Institute (ETSI), *3GPP TS 35.208,
        3rd Generation Partnership Project; Technical Specification Group Services and Sys-
        tem Aspects; 3G Security; Specification of the MILENAGE Algorithm Set: An Example
        Algorithm Set for the 3GPP Authentication and key Generation Functions f1, f1*, f2,
        f3, f4, f5, and f5*; Document 4: Design Conformance Test Data*, June 2002.

[46]   European Telecommunications Standards Institute (ETSI), *3GPP TS 35.909, 3rd
        Generation Partnership Project; Technical Specification Group Services and System As-
        pects; 3G Security; Specification of the MILENAGE Algorithm Set: An Example Algo-
        rithm Set for the 3GPP Authentication and Key Generation Functions f1, f1*, f2,
        f3, f4, f5, and f5*; Document 5: Summary and Results of Design and Evaluation*,
        May 2002.

CHAPTER

13

Contents

13.1 What is a PKI?

13.2 PKI standards

13.3 Certificate formats

13.4 Certificate management

13.5 Certificate storage and retrieval

13.6 Certificate status discovery

13.7 Certificate policies
and certification practice
statements

13.8 Notes

Public Key Infrastructures

This chapter is concerned with PKIs, as used to support the use of public key (asymmetric) cryptography (see also Chapters 4, 8, and 12). The main focus of the chapter is the generation, distribution, and ongoing management of *public key certificates*; such a certificate is simply a collection of data items including a public key, one or more identifiers for the key owner, and other data (e.g., an expiry date) all digitally signed by the TTP known as a CA. This digital signature guarantees that the the various items in the certificate are "bound" to each other.

Thus, anyone who has access to a certificate for an entity and who has a trusted copy of the public verification key for the CA that generated it, can verify the signature in the certificate and thereby obtain a trusted copy of the entity's public key. References are typically made to the *contents* of a certificate, meaning all the data items included within the scope of the CA's digital signature.

13.1 What is a PKI?

The term PKI appears to have first been used in the mid-1990s, although the concepts this term encompasses have been known for much longer. Indeed, the notion of a public key certificate, which underlies almost all practical PKIs, dates back to 1978 (i.e., almost to the origin of public key cryptography).

For the purposes of this book, a PKI can be considered as the infrastructure necessary to support the distribution of public keys to those entities who need to use them, in such a way that the recipient of a public key can be sure of its integrity and authenticity. A PKI can thus be made up of a variety of different elements depending on the technology and organizational structure used to distribute and guarantee the correctness of public keys. However, by far the most common form of PKI is one based on the generation and distribution of public key certificates.

More specifically, most practical PKIs consist of one or more management entities responsible for generating, distributing, and providing ongoing support for public key certificates.

This includes a variety of different types of entity, including:

- CAs who are responsible for generating public key certificates in accordance with a defined *certification practice statement*, and such that the certificates can be interpreted subject to a defined *certificate policy*;

- Registration authorities (RAs), who are responsible for verifying the identities of individuals requesting the generation of a certificate by a CA;

- Certificate repositories, which store and make available public key certificates,

- Certificate status servers, who provide on-line information (on request) regarding the current status of a certificate.

It is important to note that a single entity may take on more than one of the above roles—in particular, the roles of CA and RA may often be taken by the same entity, since a close trust relationship will need to exist between them. Of course, the public keys themselves will be used in conjunction with one or more applications, although we do not regard the applications themselves as being part of the PKI.

The term *digital certificate* has been introduced to cover a larger class of object than just public key certificates. A digital certificate is generated for a single entity and must contain an identifier for that entity; it will also typically contain a serial number and an expiry date. The other contents of a digital certificate will depend on its use and may be any data that needs to be securely *bound* to an entity. The two most important types of digital certificate from a practical and a standards perspective are public key certificates, containing a user public key, and *attribute certificates*, containing access control information about an individual.

Before proceeding we briefly introduce some other widely used PKI-related terminology.

- The entity whose identifier is present in a certificate is known as the *certificate subject*. This is the entity to which all the information in a certificate pertains (e.g., the entity that owns the access privileges in an attribute certificate).

- The entity that validates a digital certificate in order to obtain the *trusted binding* between the data in the certificate and the identifier of the certificate subject is known as the *relying party*.

- While a digital certificate will almost always contain an expiry date, after which it should no longer be regarded as valid, it may be necessary to *withdraw* the certificate before this date. This could arise for a variety of reasons (e.g., because of the known or suspected compromise of the private key corresponding to the public key in the certificate, or because the certificate subject no longer possesses the access rights listed in an attribute certificate). This is known as the *revocation* of the certificate. Thus, before trusting a certificate, the relying party may wish to learn its *status* (i.e., whether or not it has been revoked).

▸ One way of disseminating certificate status information is via a *certificate revocation list* (CRL) (i.e., a list of certificates that have been revoked, digitally signed by the CA that issued the revoked certificates; typically every certificate will contain a unique serial number, and the CRL then needs only contain the serial numbers of each revoked certificate). With this approach it is necessary that the CA issues a new CRL at regular intervals, so that the CRL user (who may retrieve the CRL from a third party) can always be sure that he or she has the latest CRL.

An alternative method for disseminating this information is via an on-line *certificate status service*, which might use the OCSP protocol. Certificate revocation is discussed in Section 13.6.

13.2 PKI standards

Recent years have seen a rapid growth in the number and scope of standards dealing with aspects of PKIs. This has primarily been fueled by the much increased interest in implementing PKIs, which is itself largely a result of the development of commercial and wider public use of the Internet, not least for e-commerce activities. The growth of e-commerce in particular has raised awareness of some of the security issues involved in the use of the Internet. To enable purchasers and merchants to conduct their transactions securely, there is a need for them to interwork securely. This will typically involve supporting secure communications between entities that have no prior formal relationship. PKIs are widely seen as a solution to the key management problems arising from this type of application.

With the growth in awareness of, and requirements for, PKIs, there has been a parallel increase in development effort devoted to standardizing all aspects of PKIs. The potential benefits are clear, including the possibility of large scale interworking between PKIs, and lower costs through economies of scale and increased competition.

Sources of PKI standards   PKI standardization has been carried out by a number of different bodies. In general, efforts have been made to harmonize the results of this work. Some of the most significant standardization efforts are described as follows.

▸ *ITU-T.* This body led the way in PKI standardization with the publication in 1988 of the first edition of the X.509 Recommendation, providing a standardized format for public key certificates and CRLs. In collaboration with ISO/IEC, ITU-T has continued to develop the X.509 recommendation, culminating in the fourth edition, published in 2000. Note that the first three editions of the standard contained three different versions of the basic certificate format, known as X.509 version 1, 2, and 3 public key certificates. The fourth edition of the standard also specifies version 3 public key certificates—the major innovation in this edition was the standardization of attribute certificates.

- *IETF*. As discussed in Chapter 2, the IETF is responsible for the standards governing the operation of the Internet. Over the last seven years or so, the IETF has been developing a suite of standards governing operation of an X.509-based PKI for use across the Internet. This suite of standards has the title PKIX. The Internet *PKIX roadmap* provides a useful general introduction to PKIX.

- *ISO/IEC JTC1/SC27*. Apart from the joint work with ITU-T on X.509, which has been standardized by ISO/IEC as ISO/IEC 9594-8, ISO/IEC has also been developing a series of more general PKI-related standards, including ISO/IEC 15945 on certificate management. ISO/IEC 15945 has also been adopted as an ITU-T Recommendation, X.843.

- *ISO TC68*. ISO TC68, responsible for banking standards, has recently developed a two-part standard, ISO 15782, on the topic of certificate management. Like the IETF work, it is based on X.509 certificates. Part 1, covering public key certificates, defines certificate management procedures and associated data structures. Part 2 is concerned with the *extensions* permitted in version 3 X.509 certificates.

- *ANSI X9*. ANSI X9, the U.S. national standards committee concerned with banking standards has released three standards for PKI-related topics. X9.55 defines banking-specific extensions to X.509 certificates and CRLs, and X9.57 provides a general model and set of rules for the management of certificates; these two standards have much in common with Parts 2 and 1 of ISO 15782, respectively. Finally, X9.79-1 (Part 1 of a planned multipart standard) addresses certificate policies and certification practice statements.

Types of PKI standards   Before considering individual PKI-related standards, we first consider what types of issues these standards deal with. That is, we consider which areas of operation of a PKI are covered by standards.

The most fundamental issue for a PKI is the format of the public key certificates. The development of standards in this area is discussed in more detail in Section 13.3.

Certificate management is a term used to cover a range of different types of interaction between CAs and their clients, including issues such as initial registration, certificate requests, and revocation requests. Standards for certificate management are the focus of Section 13.4.

Once certificates have been created, there is a need for certificate users to be able to retrieve them from where they are stored; this is covered in Section 13.5.

Once certified, there may be a need to withdraw a public key from use prior to the expiry date specified in the certificate—this is known as revocation. As a result there is a need for a certificate user to be able to determine the status of a certificate (i.e., whether it has been revoked). Standards covering revocation and certificate status are discussed in Section 13.6.

Finally, underlying any effective use of public key certificates must be an understanding of what a certificate means. This is dependent on the certificate policy and certification practice statement of the CA. Standards covering these issues are considered in Section 13.7.

TTP support for PKIs   One of the main reasons for the introduction of time-stamping services, as discussed in Chapter 14, has been to support long-term use of signed documents. In particular, time-stamping enables a digitally signed document to have validity after the expiry or revocation of the public key. There are a variety of other TTP services relevant to PKIs, and some of these are briefly mentioned in Chapter 14.

13.3   Certificate formats

As has already been stated, in practice, the fundamental component of any PKI is the set of public key certificates that are generated, distributed, and used. Thus we focus in some detail on possible formats for such certificates.

13.3.1   X.509 public key certificates

The key standard for certificates is ITU-T X.509 (which is aligned with ISO/IEC 9594-8). We now consider in a little more detail the main elements in an X.509 version 3 (v3) public key certificate.

ASN.1   The X.509 certificate format is specified in a language called abstract syntax notation one (ASN.1), standardized in ITU-T recommendations X.680-X.683. ASN.1 is widely used for the specification of ITU-T and ISO (and other standard) communication protocols. The purpose of ASN.1 is to have a standardized and platform-independent language with which to express data structures. For the purposes of this book a data structure can be considered as a collection of related data items, assembled for a specific purpose.

ASN.1 is accompanied by a standardized set of rules called *encoding rules*, for the transformation of the values within a data structure into a stream of bytes. This stream of bytes can then be sent on a communication channel set up by the lower layers in the stack of communication protocols (e.g., TCP/IP) or encapsulated within UDP packets (for a brief discussion of communications protocols see Chapter 3). As a result, two different applications written in two completely different programming languages running on different computers with different internal representations of data can exchange data. This frees the programmer from a great deal of work, since no code has to be written to process the format of the data prior to transport.

The ASN.1 syntax enables very complex data structures to be specified. The examples of ASN.1 data structures given in this chapter only use a small subset of the syntax. Most of the ASN.1 data structures with which we are concerned here are defined as a sequence of items, using the SEQUENCE {...} syntax. The items in the sequence each have a defined name and a defined data type (which may itself be a sequence of subsidiary elements).

As an example, consider the definition of Certificate given under the heading "Top level certificate definition" below. This data structure is the result of applying the SIGNED operation to a data structure made up of a sequence of subsidiary data items. The first element of this sequence is version with data type Version; the second element is serialNumber with data type CertificateSerialNumber; the third element is signature with data type AlgorithmIdentifier; and so on. The Version data type is simply defined to be an INTEGER (i.e., a whole number) as is the data type CertificateSerialNumber. However, the AlgorithmIdentifier data type is somewhat more complex, since this is itself a sequence of simpler data types, as defined below.

Encoding of ASN.1 data structures   When the first ITU-T recommendation on ASN.1 was released in 1988, it was accompanied by the basic encoding rules (BER) as the only option for encoding. BER is a somewhat verbose protocol. It adopts a so-called TLV (type, length, value) approach to encoding, in which every element of the encoding carries type information, length information, and the value of that element. Where the element is itself structured (i.e., it consists of other data elements) then each of these constituent elements must be stored with its type, length, and value. In summary BER is not a compact encoding but is fairly fast and easy to produce.

The BER come in three variants: the original BER, which allows options for the encoder; distinguished encoding rules (DER), which resolves all options in a particular direction; and canonical encoding rules (CER), which resolves all options in the other direction. DER and CER are unambiguous, since there are no encoding options.

A more compact encoding is achieved with the packed encoding rules (PER), which were introduced with the second edition of the ASN.1 recommendations in 1994. Use of the PER results in compact encodings that, however, require much more computation to produce than BER encodings.

Top-level certificate definition   The top-level X.509 version 3 certificate syntax is as below.

```
Certificate                     ::= SIGNED { SEQUENCE {
    version                     [0] Version DEFAULT v1,
    serialNumber                    CertificateSerialNumber,
    signature                       AlgorithmIdentifier,
    issuer                          Name,
    validity                        Validity,
    subject                         Name,
    subjectPublicKeyInfo            SubjectPublicKeyInfo,
    issuerUniqueIdentifier      [1] IMPLICIT UniqueIdentifier OPTIONAL,
                                    – If present, version must be v2 or v3
    subjectUniqueIdentifier     [2] IMPLICIT UniqueIdentifier OPTIONAL,
                                    – If present, version must be v2 or v3
    extensions                  [3] Extensions OPTIONAL
                                    – If present, version must be v3 }}
```

Translated into English, a certificate consists of a digitally signed sequence of 10 different data items, the first and the last three of which are optional.

Moreover, the last three fields can only be present in more recent versions of the X.509 certificate.

The SIGNED operation, which indicates that the certificate consists of a digitally signed version of the data items within the certificate, can be implemented in a variety of different ways. For example, it might use a reversible or a nonreversible signature scheme (see Chapter 8).

X.509 digital signatures   Before describing the 10 data fields within an X.509 certificate, we first examine the way in which the signature operation is standardized. It seems likely that the digital signature scheme used to construct X.509 certificates will typically be of the nonreversible type (see Chapter 8). In such a case a signed data string will consist of the data string together with the signature generated on that data string. Because of the importance of this case, the X.509 recommendation provides the ASN.1 specification for this possible instantiation of the SIGNED operation, as follows (although, as noted above, this is not the only way the SIGNED operation might be defined).

```
SIGNED{ ToBeSigned}        ::= SEQUENCE {
    toBeSigned             ToBeSigned,
    COMPONENTS OF          SIGNATURE { ToBeSigned }}
```

That is, in this case, the SIGNED operation simply involved taking the data to be signed and concatenating it with a signature computed on the data. This signature may have more than one component (e.g., in the case of DSA signature—see Chapter 8), which explains why the SIGNATURE operation yields a series of COMPONENTS.

Similarly, because of the historical importance of the "hash and sign" method for computing digital signatures, one possible instantiation of the SIGNATURE operation is defined in X.509:

```
SIGNATURE{ ToBeSigned}     ::= SEQUENCE {
    algorithmIdentifier    AlgorithmIdentifier,
    encrypted              ENCRYPTED-HASH { ToBeSigned }}
```

The algorithmIdentifier field contains the identifier for the cryptographic algorithm used by the CA to sign this certificate. An algorithm identifier is defined by the following ASN.1 structure.

```
AlgorithmIdentifier        ::= SEQUENCE {
    algorithm              ALGORITHM.&ID ({SupportedAlgorithms}),
    parameters             ALGORITHM.&Type ({SupportedAlgorithms}
                               {algorithm}) OPTIONAL}
```

The algorithm identifier is used to identify a cryptographic algorithm and its parameters. The ALGORITHM.&ID component identifies the algorithm (such as DSA with SHA-1—see Chapters 6 and 8) and must be chosen from the set of SupportedAlgorithms. This field would normally contain the same algorithm identifier as the signature field in the body of the certificate (see below). The X.509 recommendation does not define the set of supported algorithms—this is left to the definers of certificate profiles, such as the PKIX profile, discussed below. The contents of the optional parameters field will vary according to the algorithm identified. We next examine the 10 data items within a certificate.

Version number   The version field describes the version of the encoded certificate, which can be version 1, version 2, or version 3. The default value is version 1 (in which case this field can be omitted).

Serial number   The serialNumber is an integer assigned by the CA to each certificate. It must be unique for each certificate issued by a given CA (i.e., the issuer name and serial number identify a unique certificate). This is especially useful when constructing CRLs, where the serial number can be used to identify the certificate being revoked. The syntax of CRLs is also defined in X.509.

```
CertificateSerialNumber ::= INTEGER
```

Signature algorithm   The signature field identifies the signature method used by the CA to sign the certificate.

Validity period   The certificate validity period is the time interval during which the CA warrants that it will maintain information about the status of the certificate. The validity field is represented as a SEQUENCE of two dates: the date on which the certificate validity period begins (notBefore) and the date on which the certificate validity period ends (notAfter).

```
Validity          ::= SEQUENCE {
    notBefore     Time,
    notAfter      Time }
```

Certificate subject   The subject field identifies the individual to whom the public key in the certificate is assigned. It has type Name, a complex data type known as an *X.500 name*, which may not be appropriate for all uses of X.509 certificates and may also not always uniquely define the subject. As a result there are two other ways of including subject identification details in version 3 certificates, namely via the subjectUniqueIdentifier, discussed below, and via the *Subject alternative name* extension, discussed along with other possible extensions below.

Public key   The SubjectPublicKeyInfo field is used to carry the public key and identify the algorithm with which the key is used. The algorithm is identified using the AlgorithmIdentifier structure. The public key itself is just defined as a BIT STRING, the structure and contents of which will depend on the algorithm.

```
SubjectPublicKeyInfo      ::= SEQUENCE {
    algorithm                 AlgorithmIdentifier,
    subjectPublicKey          BIT STRING }
```

Issuer and subject unique IDs   The issuerUniqueIdentifier and subjectUniqueIdentifier fields may only appear if the X.509 certificate version is 2 or 3. They are present in the certificate to handle the possibility of reuse of subject and issuer names over time.

Extensions   The extensions field may only appear in version 3 certificates. If present, this field is a SEQUENCE of one or more certificate extensions. The extensions allow the encoding of policy information, and any other information deemed appropriate by the CA, within a certificate. The extensions field consists of a SEQUENCE of individual extension fields; each individual extension is then structured as a SEQUENCE of three items, as follows.

```
Extensions       ::= SEQUENCE OF Extension

Extension        ::= SEQUENCE {
    extnID               EXTENSION.&ID {ExtensionSet},
    critical             BOOLEAN DEFAULT FALSE,
    extnValue            OCTET STRING }
```

There are a large number of standardized extensions. The standard also allows implementers to define their own extensions. If the optional critical flag is set to TRUE then the relying party verifying a certificate must process that extension (i.e., if an extension marked as critical is not recognized by an implementation, then certificate verification must fail).

Some of the more important standardized extensions are as follows:

▸ *Key usage:* The key usage extension defines the intended use (e.g., encipherment, signature, and certificate signing) of the key contained in the certificate. This extension would typically be employed when a key that could otherwise be used for more than one operation (e.g., an RSA public key that could potentially be used for encryption and for signature verification) is to have its use restricted to some subset of the possible uses (e.g., encryption only).

▸ *Certificate policies:* A certificate policy is a named set of rules that indicates the applicability of a certificate to a particular community or class of applications with common security requirements. For example, a particular certificate policy might indicate applicability of a type of certificate to the authentication of electronic data interchange (EDI) transactions for the trading of goods within a given price range.

▸ *Subject alternative name:* The subject alternative name extension allows additional identifiers for the subject to be included in the certificate. Defined options include an Internet electronic mail address, a DNS name (see RFC 1035), an IP address (see RFC 791), and a uniform resource identifier (URI) (see RFC 1630). Other options exist, including completely local definitions. The parallel *issuer alternative name* extension allows additional identifiers for the issuer to be included in the certificate.

13.3.2   X.509 attribute certificates

As has also been mentioned above, public key certificates are not the only form of certificates, and the fourth edition of X.509 also defines a format for attribute certificates, designed to enable access control information to be securely bound to users.

The definition of an attribute certificate is very similar to that of a public key certificate; the syntax is as follows.

```
AttributeCertificate        ::= SIGNED {AttributeCertificateInfo}

AttributeCertificateInfo    ::= SEQUENCE
  {
  version                   AttCertVersion, –version is v2
  holder                    Holder,
  issuer                    AttCertIssuer,
  signature                 AlgorithmIdentifier,
  serialNumber              CertificateSerialNumber,
  attCertValidityPeriod     AttCertValidityPeriod,
  attributes                SEQUENCE OF Attribute,
  issuerUniqueID            UniqueIdentifier OPTIONAL,
  extensions                Extensions OPTIONAL }
```

The version field shall always be set to version 2 (at least in the current version of X.509). The holder identifies the entity to whom the attributes belong, and the issuer field identifies the attribute authority (AA) that issued the certificate. The signature field identifies the algorithm used to sign the certificate, and the attCertValidityPeriod indicates the period of validity of the certificate. Most importantly, the attributes contain the attributes (e.g., access control rights) assigned to the holder by the certificate. The issuerUniqueID provides additional information to identify the certificate issuer, and the extensions act in a similar way to the extensions in a public key certificate (i.e., they allow the inclusion of any other data in the certificate).

Finally note that, using the extensions field, attributes can also be included in a public key certificate. However the creation of separate attribute certificates allows the assignment of access control privileges by entities not entitled to generate public key certificates, as well as allowing short-lived attributes to be assigned without the need to generate new public key certificates.

13.3.3   X.509 certificate profiles

We next examine X.509 certificate profiles. As should be clear from the description immediately above, the X.509 certificate format is very flexible and allows a large number of options to be chosen by the implementer using the standard. As a result, in practice it is necessary to define a profile for X.509, specifying which options should be used in a given situation.

The PKIX certificate profile   The best known such profile is that defined by the IETF in RFC 3280: the PKIX X.509 profile. The goal of RFC 3280 is to facilitate the use of X.509 certificates within Internet applications. Such applications may include electronic mail, user authentication, Web-based schemes, and the IP security protocol, IPsec. In order to remove some of the obstacles to using X.509 certificates, RFC 3280 defines a profile to promote the development of certificate management systems, the development of application tools, and interoperability determined by policy.

The profile restricts the way in which an X.509 certificate can be constructed; in particular, it forces the use of a nonreversible signature scheme. The top-level X.509 version 3 certificate syntax, as constrained by the PKIX profile, is as below. For signature calculation, the data to be signed is encoded using the *type, length, value* ASN.1 DER.

```
Certificate ::= SEQUENCE {
        tbsCertificate              TBSCertificate,
        signatureAlgorithm          AlgorithmIdentifier,
        signatureValue              BIT STRING }
```

The signatureValue field contains a digital signature computed upon the ASN.1 DER-encoded field tbsCertificate, which stands for "to be signed certificate" (i.e., this is the data string that will be signed to construct the certificate). Specifically, the ASN.1 DER encoded tbsCertificate is used as the input to the signature function. This signature value is then ASN.1-encoded as a BIT STRING and included in the certificate's signature field.

Comparing the above with the definition in X.509 (given in Section 13.3.1), it should be clear that the profile forces the use of a nonreversible digital signature. The tbsCertificate field corresponds precisely to the list of data items included within the SIGNED operation for an X.509 certificate, as defined in Section 13.3.1, and has the following ASN.1 definition.

```
TBSCertificate ::= SEQUENCE {
    version                 [0]   EXPLICIT Version DEFAULT v1,
    serialNumber                  CertificateSerialNumber,
    signature                     AlgorithmIdentifier,
    issuer                        Name,
    validity                      Validity,
    subject                       Name,
    subjectPublicKeyInfo          SubjectPublicKeyInfo,
    issuerUniqueID          [1]   IMPLICIT UniqueIdentifier OPTIONAL,
                                  – If present, version must be v2 or v3
    subjectUniqueID         [2]   IMPLICIT UniqueIdentifier OPTIONAL,
                                  – If present, version must be v2 or v3
    extensions              [3]   EXPLICIT Extensions OPTIONAL
                                  – If present, version must be v3
}
```

Algorithms supported by the PKIX profile, together with defined algorithm identifiers, are listed in a separate profile document, namely RFC 3279. Examples of combinations of signature techniques and hash functions (see Chapters 6 and 8) for which IDs are defined include the following:

> ▸ RSA with MD2, RSA with MD5, and RSA with SHA-1;

> ▸ DSA with SHA-1;

> ▸ Elliptic curve DSA (ECDSA) with SHA-1.

Other profiles   A separate IETF document, RFC 3039, provides a profile for *qualified certificates*. The term was introduced by the European Commission to describe a type of certificate with specific relevance in European legal jurisdictions. Such a certificate can only be issued to individual human beings. The objective is to define a syntax independent of the legal requirements of individual jurisdictions.

Just as RFC 3280 provides a profile for X.509 certificates, PKIX profiles also exist for X.509 CRLs and X.509 attribute certificates. These profiles are defined in RFCs 3280 and 3281 respectively.

Finally, it should be noted that a separate X.509 version 3 certificate profile, X.509-WAPcert, has been defined by use with the wireless transport layer security (WTLS) protocol. WTLS is a version of the well-known transport layer security protocol, tailored for use in wireless networks.

13.3.4 Other certificate formats

Apart from the international standard certificate formats, there are a number of other certificate formats defined for use in specific application domains. It is outside the scope of this chapter to list them all, but we mention one that is of some practical importance.

This is the Europay-MasterCard-Visa *(EMV) certificate*, defined in the standards governing communications between a payment smart card (e.g., a credit or debit card) and a merchant terminal. The main reason that EMV certificates were developed (as opposed to adopting X.509 certificates) was the need to minimize the length of certificates. In the card/terminal environment, both storage space and communications bandwidth are in short supply.

EMV certificates are encoded using a tag-length-value technique, much as for BER; however, the number of fields is much less than for X.509. Moreover, the signature algorithm employed (which conforms to ISO/IEC 9796-2) minimizes data storage/bandwidth requirements by enabling as much data as possible to be recovered from the signature.

13.4 Certificate management

We next consider standards for certificate management (i.e., for protocols governing communications between a client of a CA and the CA itself). Note that in environments where the role of a RA, see Section 13.1, is distinguished from that of the CA, part of these protocols may actually be conducted between the RA and the client rather than the CA and the client.

13.4.1   The certificate management protocol (CMP)

The PKIX CMP is specified in RFC 2510. CMP is also specified in ISO/IEC 15945 (which has also been published as ITU-T X.843). At a high level, the set of operations for which management messages are defined within RFC 2510 can be grouped as follows.

CA establishment   When establishing a new CA, certain steps are required (e.g., the production of initial CRLs and the export of the CA public key).

End entity initialization   This includes importing a CA public key to the end entity and requesting information about the options supported by a PKI management entity.

Certification   Certification covers various different operations that result in the creation of new certificates.

> *Initial registration/certification:* This is the process whereby an end entity first makes itself known to a CA or RA, prior to the CA issuing a certificate or certificates for that end entity. As part of this process the RA must authenticate the end entity (the certificate subject) and make the result of this authentication known to the CA, if the RA and CA are implemented separately. The end result of this process (when it is successful) is that a CA issues a certificate for an end entity's public key and returns that certificate to the end entity or places that certificate in a public repository.
>   This process may, and typically will, involve multiple "steps," possibly including initialization of the end entity's equipment. For example, the end entity's equipment would typically need to be securely initialized with the public key of a CA to be used in validating certificates signed by the CA. Furthermore, an end entity typically needs to obtain its own key pair(s), which it can generate for itself or have provided by the CA or other TTP.

> *Key pair update:* Every end entity's key pair needs to be updated regularly (i.e., replaced with a new key pair—see Chapter 11), and when this happens a new certificate needs to be issued.

> *Certificate update:* As certificates expire they may be *refreshed* if nothing relevant in the environment has changed.

> *CA key pair update:* As with end entities, CA key pairs need to be updated regularly.

> *Cross-certification request:* This refers to the situation where one CA requests the issue of a cross-certificate from another CA. The following terms are defined. A *cross-certificate* is a certificate in which the

certificate subject is a CA and where the SubjectPublicKeyInfo field contains a signature verification key. To cover the case where it is necessary to distinguish more finely between types of cross-certificates, the following terms are also defined: A cross-certificate is called an *interdomain cross-certificate* if the subject CA and the issuer CA belong to different administrative domains; it is called an *intradomain cross-certificate* otherwise.

The above definition of cross-certificate aligns with the defined term *CA-certificate* in X.509. Note that this term is not to be confused with the X.500 cACertificate attribute type, which is unrelated. In many environments the term cross-certificate, unless further qualified, is synonymous with interdomain cross-certificate as defined above. The issue of cross-certificates may be, but is not necessarily, mutual; that is, two CAs may simultaneously issue cross-certificates for each other.

▶ *Cross-certificate update:* This operation is similar to a normal certificate update but involves a cross-certificate.

Certificate/CRL discovery operations   Some PKI management operations result in the publication of certificates or CRLs.

▶ *Certificate publication:* Having gone to the trouble of producing a certificate, some means for publishing it is needed. This might involve the use of LDAPv2 (see Section 13.5). Alternatively, RFC 2510 specifies a series of ASN.1 data structures to allow certificate information to be disseminated in a standardized way, namely the following.

  – "CA key update announcement": To notify users of this CA of the replacement of a CA public key;

  – "Certificate announcement": To announce the creation of a new certificate (of any kind);

  – "Revocation announcement": To provide information about the revocation of a certificate;

  – "CRL announcement": Notifying users of the release of a new CRL.

▶ *CRL publication:* This can also be disseminated via the use of LDAP2, or can be arranged by the use of a "CRL announcement," as above.

Recovery operations   Some PKI management operations are used when an end entity has "lost" its personal security environment (PSE) (i.e., its local store for security-related material).

One such recovery operation is *key pair recovery*. As an option, user client key material (e.g., a user's private key used for decryption purposes) may be backed up by a CA, an RA, or a key backup system associated with a CA or RA. If an entity needs to recover these backed up key materials (e.g., as a result of a forgotten password or a lost file), a protocol exchange may be needed to support such recovery.

Revocation operations   Some PKI operations result in the creation of new CRL entries or new CRLs. One example of such an operation is the *revocation request*, in which an authorized person advises a CA of an abnormal situation requiring certificate revocation. Certificate revocation is discussed in more detail in Section 13.6.

Implementing the CMP   As pointed out in RFC 2510, it is important to note that on-line protocols are not the only way of implementing the above operations. For all operations there are off-line methods of achieving the same result, and the RFC 2510 specification does not mandate use of on-line protocols. For example, when hardware tokens are used, many of the operations may be achieved as part of the physical token delivery. RFC 2510 defines a set of standard messages supporting the above operations. The protocols for conveying these exchanges in different environments (file-based, on-line, e-mail, and Web-based) are also specified.

13.4.2   Certificate request messages

At the core of RFC 2510 is the definition of a certificate request message (CRM), in which the public key subject requests the CA to issue a new certificate. The format of this message is defined in a separate document, RFC 2511—the same syntax has been adopted in ISO/IEC 15945 (which is also published as ITU-T X.843).

A certificate request message is composed of the certificate request, an optional proof of possession (POP) field, and an optional registration information field.

CertReqMessages ::= SEQUENCE SIZE (1..MAX) OF CertReqMsg

CertReqMsg ::= SEQUENCE {
    certReq   CertRequest,
    pop   ProofOfPossession   OPTIONAL,
    – content depends upon key type
    regInfo   SEQUENCE SIZE(1..MAX) of AttributeTypeAndValue
             OPTIONAL }

The POP field is used to demonstrate that the entity to be associated with the public key certificate is actually in possession of the corresponding private key. This field may be a function of the contents of the certReq field and varies in structure and content by public key algorithm type and operational mode (see also Section 13.4.3).

Use of POP is necessary to prevent certain attacks and to allow a CA/RA to properly check the validity of the binding between an end entity and a key pair. A given CA/RA is free to choose how to enforce POP (e.g., via out-of-band procedural means versus the field in the CRM) in its certification exchanges. However, it is mandated by RFC 2511 that CAs/RAs *must* enforce

POP by some means. The stated reason for mandating POP is that there are many non-PKIX operational protocols in use (various electronic mail protocols, for example) that do not explicitly check the binding between the end entity and the private key; as a result, if POP is not provided at the time of certificate generation, then use of these protocols could result in serious security vulnerabilities.

The regInfo field should only contain supplementary information related to the certification request. This information may include subscriber contact information, billing information, or other useful ancillary information.

Information directly related to certificate content should be included in the certReq field. However, inclusion of additional certReq content by RAs may invalidate the POP field. Thus data intended for inclusion in the certificate content may also be provided in the regInfo field.

13.4.3 Mechanisms for proof of possession

POP can be accomplished in different ways depending on the type of key for which a certificate is requested. For example, for signature keys, the end entity can sign a value to prove possession of the private key. Three standards documents, namely RFC 2511, RFC 2875, and ISO/IEC 15945 (or ITU-T X.843), contain mechanisms for proof of possession.

RFC 2511 proposes three different mechanisms, all of which depend on the intended use of the key pair. The first mechanism, intended for use with signature key pairs, involves the end entity proving possession of the private signing key by using it to sign a data string. The second mechanism, intended for use with encryption/decryption key pairs, requires the end entity to decrypt a specified string. This may either be a specially encrypted challenge, a decrypted version of which is presented as POP, or may simply be the certificate itself (i.e., the end entity can only obtain the certificate if he or she is in possession of the private decryption key). The third mechanism applies to key pairs used for key establishment and involves the end entity using the private key to establish a shared secret key with the CA or RA, and then proving knowledge of the secret key (e.g., by decrypting a challenge or generating a MAC).

RFC 2875 provides two methods for generating an integrity check value from a Diffie-Hellman key pair, where this value is used to provide POP. The two different approaches differ depending on whether or not they use information concerning the receiver (i.e., the CA or RA). The first solution produces a POP value that can only be verified by the intended recipient, whereas in the second solution a POP value is generated which everyone can verify.

ISO/IEC 15945 also specifies a POP mechanism. As this standard only applies to signature keys, POP is viewed purely from this perspective. The mechanisms and the syntax used for POP of signature keys are similar to those in RFC 2511.

13.4.4 Other certificate management standards

The CMP is not the only method for interaction between a certificate subject and a CA that has been promulgated by the IETF. Another system of practical importance is known as certificate management over cryptographic message syntax (CMS) (CMC).

The CMC protocol originates from industry standards devised by RSA Inc., namely PKCS #7 and PKCS #10, which we first briefly describe. PKCS #10 is itself a simple certificate management protocol—it defines formats for messages to be exchanged between an end entity and a CA or RA. Specifically it defines a format for certification requests, where such requests will contain a public key and other values to be included in the certificate. PKCS #7 specifies an ASN.1-based method for formatting cryptographic messages. A simplified form of PKCS #7 has become widely used for delivering issued certificates back to an entity that requests a certificate using PKCS #10.

The CMC certificate management protocol, specified in RFC 2797, builds upon the PKCS schemes. It is specified using CMS, which is described in RFC 2630. CMS is an ASN.1-based method for specifying messages needed to support the use of cryptography. It supports digital signatures, message authentication codes, and encryption. The syntax allows multiple encapsulation, so one CMS-encapsulated "envelope" can be nested inside another. Similarly, one party can digitally sign previously encapsulated data. CMS is similar to PKCS #7, but has a much broader role.

CMC supports two different certificate request formats, namely the PKCS #10 format and the CMP certificate request format. CMC supports proof of possession and includes functions such as revocation requests, which are not supported by PKCS #10. In fact CMC provides a similar set of functions to CMP but is designed to be backwards-compatible with industry standard approaches rather than defining everything from the ground up.

13.5 Certificate storage and retrieval

It is clear that there will be a general requirement for users of certificates (wishing to verify the binding between a public key and a different user) to have a standard means of accessing a repository for certificates. We now briefly consider various different standardized approaches to providing this access.

13.5.1 X.500 directories

As has already been mentioned, the X.509 recommendation is actually just one part of the X.500 series of ITU-T recommendations covering the directory service. These X.500 recommendations specify how directory service users can access this service to obtain information about other entities, including their public key certificate. The recommendations also specify how CRLs (with format as defined in X.509) can be retrieved.

13.5.2 Using LDAP version 2

The PKIX certificate access protocol is defined in RFC 2559 and RFC 2587. The protocol described in RFC 2559 enables access to LDAP-compliant PKI repositories for the purposes of retrieving PKI information, including certificates and CRLs. RFC 2559 also addresses requirements to add, delete, and modify PKI information in a repository. Both mechanisms are based on the lightweight directory access protocol (LDAP) v2, defined in RFC 1777, and defines a profile of that protocol for use within PKIX. It also updates the encodings for certificates and revocation lists given in RFC 1778.

13.5.3   Using FTP and HTTP

As part of the PKIX protocol suite, RFC 2585 specifies how the FTP and the hypertext transfer protocol (HTTP) can be used to obtain certificates and CRLs from PKI repositories. In brief, RFC 2585 specifies that the names of files that contain certificates should have a suffix of ".cer," and each ".cer" file shall contain exactly one certificate, encoded in DER format. Likewise, the names of files that contain CRLs must have a suffix of ".crl," and each such file shall contain exactly one CRL, again encoded in DER format.

FTP has been widely used for many years to enable files to be transferred across the Internet. As such, it is a natural mechanism to use for recovering certificates from repositories. In recent years the use of FTP has been largely superseded by HTTP, the protocol underlying the Web. As just about all Internet users are aware, HTTP can be used to recover files from remote sites, and again this is a natural vehicle for certificate distribution.

13.5.4   Delegating certification path discovery

The PKIX protocol suite also provides a pair of protocols that enable an end user to delegate some of the tasks associated with obtaining certification paths to a TTP. The delegated path discovery (DPD) and delegated path validation (DPV) protocols are defined in RFC 3379.

The DPD protocol is designed for situations where the end user wishes to validate the certification path itself but requires help in obtaining such a path. The protocol defines two messages: a request/response pair. These messages can be used to obtain from a DPD server all the information needed (such as the end-entity certificate, the CA certificates, full CRLs, and OCSP responses) to locally validate a certificate. The DPD server uses a set of rules, called a path discovery policy, to determine which information to return.

The DPV protocol is designed for the case where the end user wishes the TTP (the DPV server) to not only discover a path but also to validate it. The DPV request/response pair can be used to fully delegate path validation processing to an DPV server. The DPV server shall act according to a set of rules, called a validation policy.

RFC 3379 also specifies a third request/response pair that allows clients to obtain information regarding the policies supported by a DPV or DPD server.

13.6   Certificate status discovery

There are two standardized ways for a user of a certificate to determine its status (i.e., to determine whether or not it has been revoked). The first is the use of CRLs. The second is where a TTP (the CA or an agent of the CA) provides on-line information regarding the status of a certificate, namely whether it has been revoked. We now describe both approaches.

13.6.1   Certificate revocation lists (CRLs)

The X.509 recommendation includes a standard format for CRLs, namely lists of revoked certificates, signed by the CA. Each CRL entry contains the serial number (see Section 13.3) of the X.509 certificate being revoked. It is a general requirement of CRLs that they are updated at regular defined intervals, enabling the CRL user to verify that they are in possession of the "latest" version, although there is inevitably a delay between revocation of a certificate and its inclusion in a CRL.

13.6.2   The on-line certificate status protocol (OCSP)

An alternative approach to certificate revocation is defined in Internet RFC 2560. This document specifies the OCSP, which enables the user to determine the current status of a digital certificate without requiring CRLs. Instead of, or in addition to, checking against a periodically updated CRL, it may be necessary to obtain up-to-date information regarding the revocation status of a certificate. Examples of situations where such a cautious approach may be necessary include high-value funds transfers or large share deals. OCSP enables applications to determine the (revocation) state of an identified certificate at a precise point in time.

OCSP operates in the following way. An *OCSP client* issues a status request to an *OCSP responder* and suspends acceptance of the certificate in question until the responder provides a response. The OCSP protocol thus specifies the data that needs to be exchanged between an application checking the status of a certificate and the server providing that status. The same protocol is also defined in ISO/IEC 15945 (and in the identical document, ITU-T X.843).

13.6.3   Using proxies for status management

RFC 3029 defines the operation of a TTP known as a data validation and certification server (DVCS). A DVCS is designed to provide data validation services, such as asserting the correctness of digitally signed documents, the validity of public key certificates, and the possession or existence of data. The scope is thus more general than PKI support, as it also covers aspects of non-repudiation (see Chapter 9).

As a result of a validation, a DVCS will generate a data validation certificate (DVC). The DVC can be used to construct evidence to support the provision of a non-repudiation service. This evidence will relate to the validity and correctness of an entity's claim to possess data, the validity and revocation status of an entity's public key certificate, and/or the validity and correctness of a digitally signed document.

It is not intended that the services provided by a DVCS should replace the use of CRLs and OCSP for public key certificate revocation checking in large open environments. This is at least partially because of concerns about the scalability of the protocol. The intention is rather that DVCS should be used to support non-repudiation, or to supplement more traditional services for paperless document environments. The presence of a data validation certificate supports non-repudiation by providing evidence that a digitally signed document or public key certificate was valid at the time indicated in the DVC.

13.7 Certificate policies and certification practice statements

Internet RFC 3647 presents a framework to assist the writers of certificate policies (CPs) or certification practice statements (CPSs) for CAs and PKIs. In particular, the framework provides a comprehensive list of topics that potentially need to be covered in a CP definition or a CPS. The general requirements for TTP management are discussed in Chapter 14.

The degree to which a certificate user can trust the binding embodied in a certificate depends on several factors. These factors include: the practices followed by the CA in authenticating the subject; the CA's operating policy, procedures, and security controls; the subject's obligations (for example, in protecting the private key); and the stated undertakings and legal obligations of the CA (for example, warranties and limitations on liability). These issues are collectively covered by a CP and a CPS. The CPS addresses issues relating to the issue of certificates, and the CP indicates how a certificate should be interpreted.

A version 3 X.509 certificate may contain a field declaring that one or more specific certificate policies applies to that certificate. According to X.509, a certificate policy is "a named set of rules that indicates the applicability of a certificate to a particular community and/or class of applications with common security requirements." A CP may be used by a certificate user to help in deciding whether a certificate, and the binding therein, is sufficiently trustworthy for a particular application. The CP concept is an outgrowth of the policy statement concept developed for Internet privacy-enhanced mail (PEM)—see RFC 1422.

A more detailed description of the practices followed by a CA in issuing and otherwise managing certificates may be contained in a CPS published by or referenced by the CA. According to the ABA digital signature guidelines, "A CPS is a statement of the practices that a certification authority employs in issuing certificates."

The purpose of RFC 3647 is to establish a clear relationship between CPs and CPSs and to present a framework to assist the writers of CPs or CPSs with their tasks. It discusses the contents of a CP (as defined in X.509) or a CPS (as defined in the ABA guidelines). In particular, it describes the types of information that should be considered for inclusion in a CP or a CPS. While the framework, as presented, generally assumes the use of the X.509 version 3 certificate format, it is not intended that the material be restricted to use of that certificate format. Rather, it is intended that this framework be adaptable to other certificate formats that may come into use in the future.

The scope does not extend to defining security policies generally (such as organization security policy, system security policy, or data labeling policy) beyond the policy elements that are considered of particular relevance to CPs or CPSs.

CPs and CPSs in a banking environment   The U.S. banking standard ANSI X9.79-1 is more prescriptive in its approach than RFC 3647. It specifies elements that *must* be included in CPs and CPSs intended for use in a banking environment.

13.8   Notes

Because of the potential practical importance of PKIs, there are a number of books on this topic, including those of Adams and Lloyd [1], Austin and Huaman [2], and Feghhi, Feghhi, and Williams [3]. Ford and Baum's book on secure e-commerce also provides extensive coverage of PKI issues [4]; indeed, this latter book provides a particularly accessible introduction to PKI.

Section 13.1

The Handbook of Applied Cryptography [5, p. 587] attributes the concept of public key certificate to the 1978 thesis of Kohnfelder [6]. The idea is implicit in the Rivest-Shamir-Adleman paper of February 1978 [7], where the notion of a *public file* signing a message containing an end-user public key is described, and where every user is equipped with the public key for this public file. This public file is playing the role of the CA.

The term PKI is of much more recent origin—it does not even appear in the 1997 edition of *The Handbook of Applied Cryptography* [5]. The earliest published reference to the term appears to be April 1994, when Berkovits et al. published a study on the subject [8]. Later the same year, Chokhani discussed a U.S. national PKI [9]. In September 1995 NIST ran an invitational workshop on the subject [10]. The IETF PKIX Working Group was also established in late 1995, with the goal of developing Internet standards needed to support an X.509-based PKI. By the late 1990s, the term was ubiquitous.

Section 13.2

The first work on developing PKI standards predates the term PKI by some years. What has become known as the X.509 certificate format was first standardised in 1988 [11], as part of the first edition of the ITU-T X.500 directory services recommendations (note that they were then referred to as CCITT recommendations). For a general guide to X.500 directories, see [12].

Three subsequent editions of this ITU-T recommendation have been published [13–15], with the most recent edition (the fourth edition) published in 2000. In each case, an aligned ISO/IEC standard, ISO/IEC 9594-8, was published later, the most recent (third and fourth editions) having been published in 1998 [16] and 2001 [17], respectively.

The original work on X.509 was performed as part of the development of the X.500 directory series recommendations. The main initial "customer" for the standardized public key certificates was the parallel X.400 series of recommendations specifying the operation of an e-mail system. The 1988 version of the X.400 standards incorporated a large range of security features, the key management for which was based round the use of X.509 certificates. Interestingly, while the X.400 recommendations have hardly set the world alight, the X.509 public key certificate format dominates the field.

After the publication of the first edition of the X.509 recommendation, the next main customer for the X.509 certificate format was again a secure e-mail system—this time the Internet Privacy Enhanced Mail (PEM) system [18].

This system again used X.509 certificates as the basis of its key management; however, a number of additional certificate features were required by PEM which were incorporated into the X.509 version 2 certificate format [13]. Subsequent growing interest in deploying X.509 PKIs revealed the need for further additions to the certificate format, and these were incorporated into the version 3 certificate format [14, 16].

The PKIX Roadmap is currently only an Internet draft; at the time of this writing, the latest version had been published in January 2003 [19].

ISO/IEC 15945 [20] was published in 2002; the identically worded ITU-T recommendation, X.843, was published a little earlier [21]. ISO/IEC 15945 is concerned with the TTP services (primarily CA services) necessary to support the use of digital signatures. It is, to a large extent, based on the mechanisms specified in RFCs 2510 [22] and 2511 [23].

The two-part standard ISO 15782 significantly extends the generic PKI standards within a banking context. Part 1 [24] provides a general model and rules for certificate management. It has a significant degree of commonality with the earlier U.S. banking standard ANSI X9.57 [25]. Part 2 [26] defines banking specific extensions to X.509 certificates, and this too builds upon an earlier U.S. standard, namely, ANSI X9.55 [27].

ANSI X9.79-1 [28] provides banking-specific guidance on Certificate Policies and Certification Practice Statements.

A useful general discussion of PKI standardization and the need for additional PKI standards has been provided by Palmer [29].

Section 13.3

ASN.1 is specified in a series of ITU-T recommendations, X.680–X.683 [30–33]. ASN.1 encoding rules are given in X.690 and X.691 [34, 35]. A comprehensive guide to ASN.1 can be found in [36], and a helpful brief introduction is given in Appendix C of [4].

The formats for DNS names, IP addresses, and URIs are specified in RFCs 1035 [37], 791 [38], and 1630 [39], respectively.

The first version of the PKIX X.509 profile, RFC 2459 [40], was published in 1999; in April 2002 this was superseded by RFC 3280 [41]. Two other PKIX certificate profile documents, RFCs 3279 and 3281 [42, 43], were published at the same time, RFC 3279 superseding RFC 2528 [44].

A second, more specialized, PKIX certificate profile, RFC 3039 [45], covering Qualified Certificates, was published in 2001. RFC 3039 is based on the now-superseded PKIX certificate profile, RFC 2459. A useful introduction to qualified certificates is provided in Chapter 6 of [4].

For further details of the X.509-WAPcert and other wireless PKI issues, see [46]. The EMV certificate format is defined in Book 2 of the EMV 2000 specifications [47].

Section 13.4

The Certificate Management Protocol is specified in RFC 2510 [22] and uses the Certificate Request Message specified in RFC 2511 [23]. Both CRM and CMP are also specified in ISO/IEC 15945 [20] and the identical ITU-T recommendation X.843 [21].

A proof of possession technique appropriate for Diffie-Hellman key pairs is defined in RFC 2875 [48]. A survey of proof of possession techniques is provided in [49].

PKCS #7 and PKCS #10, while originally produced by RSA Inc., have since been published as Internet RFCs; the latest versions are available as RFC 2315 [50] (PKCS #7 v1.5) and RFC 2986 [51] (PKCS #10 v1.7)—v1.5 of PKCS #10 was previously published as RFC 2314 [52]. The CMC protocol, which builds upon PKCS #10, is specified in RFC 2797 [53]. CMC uses the Cryptographic Message Syntax (essentially a superset of PKCS #7), which is specified in RFC 2630 [54].

Section 13.5

A more detailed comparison of LDAP version 2 and the X.500 directories has been given by Hassler [55].

The PKIX certificate access protocol is defined in RFCs 2559 and 2587 [56, 57]. This is based on the IETF LDAP v2 protocol, which is defined in RFC 1777 [58]. RFC 2559 supersedes RFC 1778 [59].

The use of FTP and HTTP to distribute certificates is specified in RFC 2585 [60]. The DPD and DPV protocols for delegating certificate path discovery and validation are given in RFC 3379 [61]. Similar functionality to DPV and DPD is also supported by the *Simple Certificate Validation Protocol* (SCVP), specified in an Internet draft [62]. Despite its appearance in an Internet draft, SCVP has never been published in an RFC.

Section 13.6

OCSP is specified in RFC 2560 [63]. It is also specified in ISO/IEC 15945 [20]. The functioning of DVCS is specified in RFC 3029 [64].

SCVP [62], discussed earlier, provides functionality broadly similar to that provided by OCSP, but also incorporates functionality provided by DVD and DVP.

Section 13.7

The PKIX Certificate Policy and Certificate Management Framework was first published as RFC 2527 in 1999 [65]; this has now been superseded by RFC 3647 [66] published in November 2003.

The ABA digital signature guidelines [67], published in 1996, have been very influential in influencing the development of CPs and CPSs.

Chapter 10 of Ford and Baum [4] provides an excellent introduction to this subject.

References

[1]   Adams, C., and S. Lloyd, *Understanding PKI: Concepts, Standards, and Deployment Considerations*, 2nd ed., Reading, MA: Addison-Wesley, 2002.

[2]   Austin, T., and D. Huaman, *PKI: A Wiley Brief*, New York: John Wiley and Sons, 2001.

[3]   Feghhi, J., J. Feghhi, and P. Williams, *Digital Certificates: Applied Internet Security*, Reading, MA: Addison-Wesley, 1999.

[4]   Ford, W., and M. S. Baum, *Secure Electronic Commerce*, 2nd ed., Upper Saddle River, NJ: Prentice Hall, 2001.

[5]   Menezes, A. J., P. C. van Oorschot, and S. A. Vanstone, *Handbook of Applied Cryptography*, Boca Raton, FL: CRC Press, 1997.

[6]   Kohnfelder, L. M., "Towards a Practical Public-Key Cryptosystem," B.Sc. thesis, Department of Electrical Engineering, MIT, 1978.

[7]   Rivest, R. L., A. Shamir, and L. Adleman, "A Method for Obtaining Digital Signatures and Public-Key Cryptosystems," *Communications of the ACM*, Vol. 21, 1978, pp. 120–126.

[8]   Berkovits, S., et al., *Public Key Infrastructure Study: Final Report*, April 1994, National Institute of Standards and Techhnology.

[9]   Chokhani, S., "Toward a National Public Key Infrastructure," *IEEE Communications Magazine*, Vol. 32, No. 9, September 1994, pp. 70–74.

[10] National Institute of Standards and Technology (NIST), *Proceedings: Public Key Infrastructure Invitational Workshop*, MITRE, McLean, IR 5788, September 1995.

[11] Comité Consultatif International de Télégraphique et Téléphonique, *CCITT Recommendation X.509 (1988), The Directory—Authentication Framework*, 1988.

[12] Chadwick, D. W., *Understanding X.500: The Directory*, New York: Chapman and Hall, 1994.

[13] International Telecommunication Union, *ITU-T Recommendation X.509 (1993), The Directory—Authentication Framework*, 2nd ed., 1993.

[14] International Telecommunication Union, *ITU-T Recommendation X.509 (08/97), The Directory—Authentication Framework*, 3rd ed., 1997.

[15] International Telecommunication Union, *ITU-T Recommendation X.509 (03/2000), The Directory—Public-Key and Attribute Certificate Frameworks*, 4th ed., 2000.

[16] International Organization for Standardization, *ISO/IEC 9594–8: 1998, Information Technology—Open Systems Interconnection—The Directory: Part 8: Authentication Framework*, 3rd ed., 1998.

[17] International Organization for Standardization, *ISO/IEC 9594–8: 2001, Information Technology—Open Systems Interconnection—The Directory: Part 8: Public-Key and Attribute Certificate Frameworks*, 4th ed., 2001.

[18] Kent, S., *RFC 1422, Privacy Enhancement for Internet Electronic Mail: Part II: Certificate-Based Key Management*, Internet Engineering Task Force, February 1993.

[19] Arsenault, A., and S. Turner, *Internet Draft draft-ietf-pkix-roadmap-09, Internet X.509 Public Key Infrastructure: Roadmap*, Internet Engineering Task Force, July 2002.

[20] International Organization for Standardization, *ISO/IEC 15945: 2002, Information Technology—Security Techniques—Specification of TTP Services to Support the Application of Digital Signatures*, 2002.

[21] International Telecommunication Union, *ITU-T Recommendation X.843 (10/2000), Security—Information Technology—Security Techniques—Specification of TTP Services to Support the Application of Digital Signatures*, 2000.

[22] Adams, C., and S. Farrell, *RFC 2510, Internet X.509 Public Key Infrastructure: Certificate Management Protocols*, Internet Engineering Task Force, March 1999.

[23] Myers, M., et al., *RFC 2511, Internet X.509 Certificate Request Message Format*, Internet Engineering Task Force, March 1999.

[24] International Organization for Standardization, *ISO 15782–1: 2003, Certificate Management for Financial Services—Part 1: Public Key Certificates*, 2003.

[25] Accredited Standards Committee X9—Financial Services, *ANSI X9.57–1997, Public Key Cryptography for the Financial Services Industry: Certificate Management*, 1997.

[26] International Organization for Standardization, *ISO 15782–2: 2001, Banking—Certificate Management—Certificate Extensions*, 2001.

[27] Accredited Standards Committee X9—Financial Services, *ANSI X9.55–1997, Public Key Cryptography for the Financial Services Industry: Extensions to Public Key Certificates and Certificate Revocation Lists*, 1997.

[28] Accredited Standards Committee X9—Financial Services, *ANSI X9.79-1:2001, Part 1: Public Key Infrastructure—Practices and Policy*, 2001.

[29] Palmer, T., "PKI Needs Good Standards?" *Information Security Technical Report*, Vol. 8, No. 3, 2003, pp. 6–13.

[30] International Telecommunication Union, *ITU-T Recommendation X.680 (07/02), Information Technology—Abstract Syntax Notation One ASN.1: Specification of Basic Notation*, 2002.

[31] International Telecommunication Union, *ITU-T Recommendation X.681 (07/02), Information Technology—Abstract Syntax Notation One ASN.1: Information Object Specification*, 2002.

[32] International Telecommunication Union, *ITU-T Recommendation X.682 (07/02), Information Technology—Abstract Syntax Notation One ASN.1: Constraint Specification*, 2002.

[33] International Telecommunication Union, *ITU-T Recommendation X.683 (07/02), Information Technology—Abstract Syntax Notation One ASN.1: Parameterization of ASN.1 specifications*, 2002.

[34] International Telecommunication Union, *ITU-T Recommendation X.690 (07/02), Information Technology—ASN.1 encoding rules: Specification of Basic Encoding Rules (BER), Canonical Encoding Rules (CER) and Distinguished Encoding Rules (DER)*, 2002.

[35] International Telecommunication Union. *ITU-T Recommendation X.691 (07/02), Information Technology—ASN.1 Encoding Rules: Specification of Packed Encoding Rules (PER)*, 2002.

[36] Larmouth, J., *ASN.1 Complete*, San Francisco, CA: Morgan Kaufmann, 1999.

[37] Mockapetris, P., *RFC 1035, Domain Names—Implementation and Specification*, Internet Engineering Task Force, November 1987.

[38] Information Sciences Institute, University of Southern California, *RFC 791, DARPA Internet Program Protocol Specification*, Internet Engineering Task Force, September 1981.

[39] Berners-Lee, T., *RFC 1630, Universal Resource Identifiers in WWW*, Internet Engineering Task Force, June 1994.

[40] Housley, R., et al., *RFC 2459, Internet X.509 Public Key Infrastructure: Certificate and CRL Profile*, Internet Engineering Task Force, January 1999.

[41] Housley, R., et al., *RFC 3280, Internet X.509 Public Key Infrastructure: Certificate and Certificate Revocation List (CRL) Profile*, Internet Engineering Task Force, April 2002.

[42] Polk, W., R. Housley, and L. Bassham, *RFC 3279, Algorithms and Identifiers for the Internet X.509 Public Key Infrastructure Certificate and Certificate Revocation List (CRL) Profile*, Internet Engineering Task Force, April 2002.

[43] Farrell, S., and R. Housley, *RFC 3281, An Internet Attribute Certificate Profile for Authorization*, Internet Engineering Task Force, April 2002.

[44] Housley, R., and W. Polk, *RFC 2528, Internet X.509 Public Key Infrastructure: Representation of Key Exchange Algorithm (KEA) Keys in Internet X.509 Public Key Infrastructure Certificates*, Internet Engineering Task Force, March 1999.

[45] Santesson, S., et al., *RFC 3039, Internet X.509 Public Key Infrastructure: Qualified Certificates Profile*, Internet Engineering Task Force, January 2001.

[46] Dankers, J., et al., "PKI in Mobile Systems," in C. J. Mitchell, (ed.), *Security for Mobility*, New York: IEE, 2004, Chapter 2, pp. 11–33.

[47] EMVCo. *EMV2000: Integrated Circuit Card Specification for Payment Systems: Book 2—Security and Key Management*, December 2000.

[48] Prafullchandra, H., and J. Schaad, *RFC 2875, Diffie-Hellman Proof-of-Possession Algorithms*, Internet Engineering Task Force, July 2000.

[49] Mitchell, C. J., and R. Schaffelhofer, "The Personal PKI," in C. J. Mitchell, (ed.), *Security for Mobility*, New York: IEE, 2004, Chapter 3, pp. 35–61.

[50] Kaliski, B., *RFC 2315, PKCS #7: Certification Message Syntax v1.5*, Internet Engineering Task Force, October 1997.

[51] Nystrom, M., and B. Kaliski, *RFC 2986, PKCS #10: Certification Request Syntax Specification Version 1.7*, Internet Engineering Task Force, November 2000.

[52] Kaliski, B., *RFC 2314, PKCS #10: Certification Request Syntax v1.5*, Internet Engineering Task Force, October 1997.

[53] Myers, M., et al., *RFC 2797, Certificate Management Messages over CMS*, Internet Engineering Task Force, April 2000.

[54] Housley, R., *RFC 2630, Cryptographic Message Syntax*, Internet Engineering Task Force, June 1999.

[55] Hassler, V., "X.500 and LDAP Security: A Comparative Overview," *IEEE Network*, Vol. 13, No. 6, November/December 1999, pp. 54–64.

[56] Boeyen, S., T. Howes, and P. Richard, *RFC 2559, Internet X.509 Public Key Infrastructure: Operational Protocols—LDAPv2*, Internet Engineering Task Force, April 1999.

[57] Boeyen, S., T. Howes, and P. Richard, *RFC 2587, Internet X.509 Public Key Infrastructure: LDAPv2 Schema*, Internet Engineering Task Force, June 1999.

[58] Yeong, W., T. Howes, and S. Kille, *RFC 1777, Lightweight Directory Access Protocol*, Internet Engineering Task Force, March 1995.

[59] Howes, T., S. Kille, and W. Yeong, *RFC 1778, The String Representation of Standard Attribute Syntaxes*, Internet Engineering Task Force, March 1995.

[60] Housley, R., and P. Hoffman, *RFC 2585, Internet X.509 Public Key Infrastructure: Operational Protocols: FTP and HTTP*, Internet Engineering Task Force, May 1999.

[61] Pinkas, D., and R. Housley, *RFC 3379, Delegated Path Validation and Delegated Path Discovery Protocol Requirements*, Internet Engineering Task Force, September 2002.

[62] Malpani, A., R. Housley, and T. Freeman, *Internet Draft draft-ietf-pkix-scvp-13, Simple Certificate Validation Protocol*, Internet Engineering Task Force, October 2003.

[63] Myers, M., et al., *RFC 2560, X.509 Internet Public Key Infrastructure: Online Certificate Status Protocol—OCSP*, Internet Engineering Task Force, June 1999.

[64] Adams, C., et al., *RFC 3029, Internet X.509 Public Key Infrastructure: Data Validation and Certification Server Protocols*, Internet Engineering Task Force, February 2001.

[65] Chokhani, S., and W. Ford, *RFC 2527, Internet X.509 Public Key Infrastructure: Certificate Policy and Certification Practices Framework*, Internet Engineering Task Force, March 1999.

[66] Chokhani, S., et al., *RFC 3647, Internet X.509 Public Key Infrastructure: Certificate Policy and Certification Practices Framework*, Internet Engineering Task Force, November 2003.

[67] American Bar Association, Information Security Committee, Section of Science and Technology, *Digital Signature Guidelines*, 1996.

CHAPTER

14

Contents

14.1 Definitions and basic properties

14.2 Standards for managing TTPs

14.3 TTP requirements

14.4 TTP architectures

14.5 Time-stamping authorities

14.6 Digital archiving authorities

14.7 Notes

Trusted Third Parties

This chapter will discuss the use of trusted third parties (TTPs) to provide security services within a system. The standards that describe how TTPs can be used are quite different to many of the other standards that we discuss, because they contain very little technical detail and instead focus on the managerial aspects of security.

We will also discuss the use of time-stamping authorities and digital archiving services. These are classes of TTP, but they are not the only ones! Other types of TTPs, including certification authorities (CAs), key generation authorities, key distribution authorities, and electronic notaries, are discussed in other chapters.

14.1 Definitions and basic properties

A TTP is an entity in a system that is not under the control of that system's security authority and yet is trusted by that security authority to carry out some security related function.

Normally, this situation will occur when a system's administrator connects to a third party server in order that that server can provide some kind of security service for the system administrator's network. It is easy to see that, in this case, the system's administrator has no control over the third party server and so must trust that server to correctly and securely provide its service.

Some standards (in particular ISO/IEC TR 14516) go even further than this and state that an entity in a system is a TTP only if (1) it is not under the control of the security authority, (2) it provides a security function, and (3) the use of the TTP service has been freely agreed between the security authority and the TTP. In other words, the security authority should have a free choice of which TTP service he or she wishes to use, and the TTP should have a free choice of which clients it wishes to take on. This definition implies that any mandatory security function provided by a third party, such as a key escrow system enforced by a government, does not constitute a TTP.

This is slightly different to the definition implicit in much of the academic literature. In most of the academic literature a TTP is any self-contained entity that provides security services, regardless of whether that entity is under the control of the security authority or not. Many of the management issues that we discuss here are not relevant to TTPs that are under the direct control of the security authority.

Many different TTPs are discussed in this book, including the following:

- Electronic notaries (see Chapter 9);

- KDCs and KTCs (see Chapter 12);

- CAs (see Chapter 13).

In this chapter, we will introduce two other classes of TTP, namely *time-stamping authorities* (see Section 14.5) and *digital archiving authorities* (see Section 14.6).

The fact that a security authority must *trust* the TTP to perform its function is indicative of a security authority's inability to be sure that a TTP is performing its function correctly. If a security authority could be sure that the TTP was performing its function correctly, then it would not need to trust it! This trust can only be established via a nontechnical, business arrangement and it is a central tenet of the guidelines to using TTPs that the relationship between the TTP and the client is based on a business contract.

This contract often ends the "chain of trust" that surrounds most cryptographic applications. Almost all cryptographic applications transfer the trust one has to have in one part of the system to another part of the system. Consider, as an example, the use of digital signatures:

1. An entity in a system may trust that a message was delivered in an integral manner because it has an associated digital signature. Hence, the use of digital signature schemes transfers the need to trust that the message was delivered integrally to the need to trust that the signature was correctly generated.

2. That entity trusts that the signature has not been forged because it has access to the public key for the entity that generated the signature. In other words, the use of public keys transfers the need to trust that the digital signature was produced correctly to the need to trust that the public key is authentic.

3. That entity trusts the public key because it has access to a digital certificate that certifies that public key. Hence, the use of certificates transfers the need to trust that the public key is authentic to the need to trust that the certificate is correct.

4. That entity trusts the certificate because it trusts the certification body that issued the certificate. In other words, the use of CAs transfers the need to trust that the certificate is correct to the need to trust that the CA only issues correct certificates.

5. That entity trusts the certification body because of a contractual arrangement (either between that entity and the CA or between the CA and the owner of the public key).

A contract ends the chain of trust by defining the penalties that an entity will have to face if the service is not correctly delivered.

14.2 Standards for managing TTPs

The only standard purely dedicated to the management of TTPs is ISO/IEC TR 14516. This is not to say that this is the only standard in which this issue arises: The management of external contractors in an information security system is also discussed in the ISO standard on information security management, ISO/IEC 17799 (see Chapter 16).

Other standards deal with the management of particular TTP services, from which generic criteria can be established. For example, IETF RFC 3628 deals with the management of a time-stamping authority but specifically states that "it should be observed that these policy requirements can be used to address other needs." Another example would be ANSI X9.79, which deals with many of the managerial issues associated with using a certification authority (see Chapter 13).

One interesting difference between the ISO/IEC TR 14516 standard and the other standards dealing with specific classes of TTPs is that the ISO/IEC TR 14516 standard specifically states that it should not be used as a formal basis to assess or compare TTPs but merely to provide guidelines. Both IETF RFC 3628 and ANSI X9.79 can be used as a basis for the assessment and comparison of TTPs.

14.3 TTP requirements

It is generally agreed, between the various standards and standardization bodies, that there are several important business issues that should be resolved and understood by both the TTP and the client before the client starts to use the service offered by the TTP.

These can be loosely classified into three categories: policy and practice statements, TTP management, and legal considerations. We will discuss each of these categories in turn.

14.3.1 Policy and practice statements

It is very important for a user of a TTP service to be sure of *precisely* what kind of service is being offered. This includes not only the functionality that the TTP service is offering but also how the TTP will handle the user's confidential information (should it have access to any such information). These will be covered by a series of formal statements published by the TTP and available to the user.

Policy statement   A policy statement is a high-level statement of the services offered by the TTP. It should explain, in nontechnical language, precisely what services the TTP is offering and what level of security is used to protect those services. This will involve explaining all of the technical, physical, and organizational policies that are in place. This may well be very similar to the TTP's internal security policy (see Chapter 3)—indeed, they may very well be identical!

Practice statement   A practice statement is a technical specification of how the promises made in the policy statement are achieved. This will undoubtedly involve the use of technical language and will need to be evaluated by an independent expert. This document will undoubtedly contain information on the technical services and mechanisms used by the system (see Chapter 3). It will also need to contain a lot of information on the organizational and managerial aspects of the business.

Responsibilities   It is imperative that both the TTP and the client understand what is required of them when using the TTP service. The responsibilities of the client are often overlooked when thinking about a TTP service: In most situations a client will, at least, be responsible for making sure that it only makes legitimate queries to the TTP service. In some situations the client may have more stringent responsibilities. For example, when using a key translation or derivation center (see Chapter 12) it is usually the client's responsibility to make sure that the long-term secret key that they share with the TTP is kept secret. If this key is compromised then the security of the whole system can be called into question.

14.3.2   TTP management

For a client to trust a TTP service, that service should provide evidence that it is a well-managed service. For our purposes we split TTP management into three different categories, described in the following sections.

Business management   A TTP service should adopt good business management and organizational practices. This may include the following measures:

- Ensuring physical security;
- Ensuring environmental security (i.e., making sure that the environment in which the service is running does not affect that service);
- Ensuring staff security (e.g., vetting staff members and controlling the levels of information to which the staff have access);
- Having well documented procedures;
- Having recovery procedures, in case the service is compromised or interrupted;
- Having periodic security reviews.

While many of these issues are discussed in ISO/IEC TR 14516 (particularly in Annex A) and in IETF RFC 3628, they are discussed in a lot more depth in the ISO/IEC standard for security management—ISO/IEC 17799 (see Chapter 16).

Use of standards   A well-managed TTP service should be able to demonstrate that it is using the best available technology for supplying a security service. A simple way to do this is to implement standardized mechanisms.

Evidence collection and security audits   A well-managed TTP service should be able to demonstrate to a client that it is operating securely. Since a client can never be 100% sure that a TTP is offering a secure service, the best that a client can do is to periodically audit the TTP. This involves two things: (1) the TTP collecting and archiving evidence relevant to its security services and (2) for there to exist a method for a client to audit a TTP without compromising that TTP's security. A client's right to audit a TTP service usually needs to be specifically stated in the contract it holds with the TTP.

14.3.3   Legal considerations

Last we consider the legal aspects that should be considered when using a TTP service.

Compliance with local laws   A TTP should comply with all local, national, and international laws. This may mean, for example, that the TTP may be forced to reveal certain confidential information when requested by a law enforcement agency. A TTP should make its legal obligations clear before entering into a contract with a client.

The situation can be further confused when we consider that the client and the TTP may be in different countries. In this case, not only must the TTP explain the legal obligations under which it is forced to work to the client, but the client must also make sure that the use of the TTP does not break any of the laws to which it is subject.

Liability   Last, a TTP must accept some liability for its own service, and this liability must be clearly stated. It is very difficult to see how a client can trust a TTP service that accepts no responsibility for its own service, as that TTP could legally misuse their power over the client's system in any way it felt like.

14.4   TTP architectures

In this section we will discuss how a TTP can be effectively placed into a network. The different ways that a network can be configured to include a TTP are known as network architectures. We will examine how a TTP can be placed into a network so that it can be used by multiple users, and how the TTP can communicate with external entities.

14.4.1   Two-party TTP architectures

It is simple to see how a single entity must interact with a TTP: The entity and the TTP must communicate directly via some communications network. However, there are more choices when two (or more) entities are involved. There are three general configurations in which a TTP provides a service to two entities; these are known as *in-line*, *on-line*, and *off-line* TTP services.

In-line TTP services   An in-line TTP service is one in which entities only communicate with the TTP—see Figure 14.1. This means that any communication between two entities has to be passed though the TTP. An in-line TTP service is ideally placed to monitor communications and to ensure that any data that passes between the two entities is confidential, integral, or non-repudiable.

An example of an in-line TTP service would be a KTC that is used *without key forwarding*—see Chapter 12. In this situation, the first entity (entity *A*) generates a key and forwards it to the TTP in a confidential manner. The TTP recovers the key and forwards it to the second entity (entity *B*) in a similarly confidential manner. Entity *A* and entity *B* never communicate directly in this exchange but only ever communicate through the KTC; hence, the KTC is offering a in-line TTP service.

A second example would be to use a TTP for access control. A TTP could be used to intercept all access requests as they pass between the user and the target the user wishes to access. This TTP would be used to decide if the user has the right to access the target. Again, since the user and the target would never be able to communicate except via the TTP, the TTP would be offering an in-line service.

On-line TTP services   An on-line TTP service is one in which entities communicate directly but one (or both) of a pair of communicating entities uses the TTP to provide a security service—see Figure 14.2. An on-line TTP service can also provide confidentiality, integrity, and non-repudiation services but is perhaps better suited to providing supporting functions such as key management and time-stamping.

An example of an on-line TTP is a KDC that is used *with key forwarding*—see Chapter 12. In this situation, the first entity (entity *A*) would request that a session key be generated for use between *A* and a second entity (entity *B*). The TTP would then generate a suitable key and send two copies of it back to entity *A*: one encrypted using a key that *A* shares with the TTP and one encrypted using a key that *B* shares with the TTP. Entity *A* would then

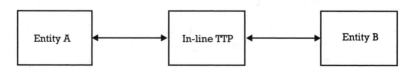

Figure 14.1   An in-line TTP service.

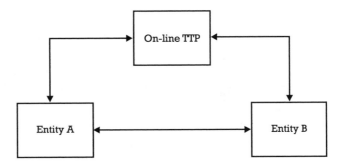

Figure 14.2 An on-line TTP service.

forward the second of these keys to entity B. Clearly, A and B communicate directly and so the KDC must be offering an on-line TTP service.

Care must be taken to make sure that an on-line TTP service is not confused with an on-line TTP. An on-line TTP is one that is actively available to perform its function. An on-line TTP service is one in which a TTP actively provides a service that is used by two communicating entities. Hence, a TTP providing an on-line TTP service must be on-line, but so must a TTP providing an in-line service.

Off-line TTP services   An off-line TTP service is one in which the TTP does not actively engage in any protocol, but merely provides pregenerated data to other entities on request—see Figure 14.3. Hence, the difference between an on-line TTP service and an off-line TTP service is that an on-line TTP service responds to a request with newly generated data. An off-line TTP service replies to a request by merely providing some data that had been produced prior to the request being made.

Off-line TTP services can be used to handle authentication, certification, non-repudiation, and some key management functions. Indeed the classic example of an off-line TTP service is the service offered by a CA (see Chapter 13). In this case, a CA will respond to a request by providing a certificate. Since these certificates have typically been precomputed by the CA, the CA is providing an off-line TTP service.

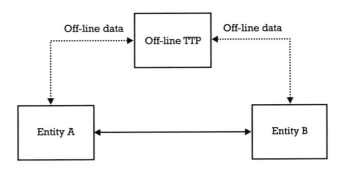

Figure 14.3 An off-line TTP service.

14.4.2   Interworking TTPs

In the provision of its service, a TTP may have to deal with other external entities besides its clients, including TTPs or law enforcement agencies. The method by which a TTP secures its communication with these external entities is at least as important as how the TTP secures its communication with its clients.

Communication between distinct TTPs may help both TTPs expand the range of services that they can offer. However, just as the basis for the communication between a user and a TTP must be based on a contractual business arrangement, so must any communication between distinct TTPs. The situation is complicated by the relationship each TTP has with its clients: suppose a user uses a TTP service offered by a third party (entity A, say) and that entity A relies on another TTP service provider (entity B, say) to help provide its service. The user trusts entity A because of a contractual business agreement between the user and A. The user has no such contract with B and yet A, and so the user, may rely on entity B to provide its security service. What assurance does the user therefore have that B is trustworthy?

This situation can only be resolved by the use of clear contracts, security policies, and practice statements. It is imperative that the user fully understands who is responsible for each part of a service that a TTP is offering, who is liable if that part fails, and who is responsible for checking that each part of a service is operating correctly. Interworked TTPs are often used in key distribution—see Section 12.4.4.

The relationship between a TTP and a law enforcement agency is quite different to the relationship between two TTPs. Some law enforcement agencies are worried that the widespread use of strong cryptographic protocols will reduce their ability to fight against crime. Many nations require TTPs and system administrators to reveal confidential information if requested by a properly authorized representative of the government. It is important that good practices are in place to allow this to happen without any other loss of confidentiality.

14.5   Time-stamping authorities

In this section we discuss one particular type of TTP—time-stamping authorities. A time-stamping authority is a TTP that offers evidence that data existed at a certain point in time (i.e., evidence that that data was generated *before* that point in time). Typically it does this by producing a *time-stamp token* (or *time-stamp*) that cryptographically binds a representative of that data to the time at which the token was issued. Normally, this token will not reveal any information about the data itself but will allow an entity that is already in possession of the data to check that it was generated before the time stated in the token.

Time-stamping authorities can be used to provide time-stamps for use in entity authentication and key establishment algorithms (see Chapters 10 and 12). Since the time-stamping authority can be used to provide evidence that some data existed at a certain point in time, it can also help provide a non-repudiation service (see Chapter 9).

If a time-stamp is to be useful, however, all parties involved must agree on a common notion of time (i.e., how to measure the current time and data). One useful common notion of time is coordinated universal time (UTC). This time scale is based on the rotation of the Earth and is defined in the ITU-R TF.460-6 standard. All IETF standards require that a time-stamping authority is synchronized with UTC.

It is a common mistake to think that a time-stamping authority's only role is in generating a time-stamp token. While this is true for the most common schemes, it is not true in general. There is no reason that a time-stamping authority cannot be involved in verifying a time-stamp token as well. This will require the verifying party to be able to contact the (authenticated) time-stamping authority itself.

Since time-stamp tokens are typically produced using cryptographic means, they often involve the use of secret keys, and these keys will need to be periodically replaced (see Chapter 11). This leads to a common problem with time-stamping authorities known as *restamping*. If a key used in producing a time-stamp is to be deactivated then all the time-stamps made using that key must be reissued with a new key *before the old key is taken out of service*. If the old key is deactivated first then the time-stamping authority will not be able to check the validity of any of the old time-stamps before reissuing them with the new key. Hence, the time-stamping authority will only be able to guarantee that the data was in existence at the time of restamping, rather than at the time that the original time-stamp token claimed. This is particularly relevant when a key is being deactivated due to suspected compromise.

There are two major standards that deal with the creation of time-stamp tokens: ISO/IEC 18014 and IETF RFC 3161. ISO/IEC 18014 is a three-part standard. Part 1 provides a general overview of time-stamping and time-stamping authorities, while parts 2 and 3 deal with mechanisms to generate time-stamp tokens. The IETF RFC also contains a mechanism for a time-stamping authority to generate a time-stamp token; however, this mechanism also appears in ISO/IEC 18014-2.

14.5.1 Time-stamping tokens

The ISO/IEC 18014-2 standard defines three mechanisms for producing time stamp tokens. These involve the use of either a digital signature (see Chapter 8), a message authentication code (see Chapter 7), or a digital archiving service (see Section 14.6).

In all cases, the time-stamping authority binds together a representative of the data that needs to be stamped with the current time (in some universally acceptable format, such as UTC). Typically, the data representative is not the data itself but a hash of the data (see Chapter 6). This means that the time-stamp token does not reveal any information about the data itself, but it does mean that it is vitally important that the hash function used is collision-resistant, or else it is possible that a registering entity might be able to repudiate the existence of a piece of data at a particular time.

The binding of the data representative with the current time can be done in three ways:

> ▸ Digitally signing a document containing the data representative and the time. This means that anyone with an authentic copy of the time-stamping authority's public key can verify the signature and, so, the time-stamping token. The time-stamping authority only needs to store the private signing key in this scenario; however, time-stamping tokens can still be verified even if the private signing key is lost.

> ▸ Producing a MAC of a document containing the data representative and the time. In order to verify this, an entity would have to present the data (including the time of stamping) and the token to the time-stamping authority. The time-stamping authority could then recompute the MAC using the data and compare it to the token, passing the result back to the user. In this scenario, the time-stamping authority has to store the secret key used to compute the MACs.

> ▸ Storing the data representative and the time-stamping token in a secure digital archive. To verify this, a user needs to present the token and the data to the time-stamping authority. The time-stamping authority then checks the veracity of the token against the stored version. In this case, the time-stamping authority does not need to store any kind of key but does need to securely store all the tokens.

The method of producing time-stamping tokens using a digital signature scheme is also standardized in IETF RFC 3161.

14.5.2   Linked tokens

A linked time-stamping token is a token that contains information about previously generated tokens. This allows the user to establish an order in which time-stamp tokens were produced without having to rely on the trustworthiness of the time-stamping authority. Thus, we can reduce the amount of trust we need to have in the time-stamping authority: it may be able to deny that a piece of data existed at the time at which a time-stamping token claims by refusing to verify the token, but it cannot easily change the order in which the tokens were produced.

Linked time-stamping tokens are generally produced when a time-stamping authority includes in a newly generated token, a hash code of the last time-stamping token it generated. This gives evidence that the previous time-stamping token must have been in existence before the new one was generated. For critical applications, hash codes computed using more than one hash function can be included. This means that even if one hash function is broken, then there is still a valid hash code attesting to the order in which tokens were produced. Hash functions are discussed in detail in Chapter 6.

However, merely including a hash code in the every newly generated token might not be enough to ensure that the order in which time-stamping tokens are produced is non-repudiable. A hash code is sufficient when the time-stamping authority produces a time-stamping token using a digital signature scheme, but it is not sufficient when the time-stamping authority produces time-stamping tokens based on the use of a MAC scheme or a digital archiving service. In these circumstances, a time-stamping authority can simply reorder and recertify all the time-stamping tokens it has produced and refuse to verify any of the original tokens. In order to produce linked tokens in these circumstances, a time-stamping authority may choose to widely publicize its tokens as they are being produced. The authority will not later be able to repudiate the order in which tokens were produced as too many independent observers will have seen the original tokens. These tokens are said to have been "widely witnessed."

14.6 Digital archiving authorities

The last class of TTPs that we will consider in this chapter is the digital archiving authorities. Such a TTP performs two functions: It stores digital documents at an appropriate level of security, and it issues copies of those documents to authorized entities. These copies will often be digitally signed by the archiving authority and include a date of registration.

The security problems associated with digital archiving are slightly different than those associated with other TTP services. While a digital archiving service must cope with all the usual problems associated with collecting and releasing digital data in an integral, and possibly confidential, manner, it must also cope with various extra problems caused by the need to store the documents for a long time.

A digital archiving service is normally used to archive documents for long periods of time. This can leads to unforeseen problems. For example, magnetic storage devices (such as magnetic tapes) decay over time, and the data on these tapes will need to be transferred onto a new storage device. Similarly, the machines used to access the storage device may become obsolete and need to be replaced or updated. It is possible that this might mean the entire archive may need to be transferred from one type of storage device (such as magnetic tapes) to another (such as CD-ROMs).

Another problem involves the use of cryptography. Since a digital archive may need to survive for years or even decades, it is important that any cryptographic techniques that are used to secure the data will be valid for that length of time. This can be quite a challenge: Who knows what developments in cryptanalysis there will be after 20 years? Realistically there are two choices: Either the cryptography used to protect data must be regularly updated (which may be a massive computational process) or the data must be protected by more than just cryptographic means (for example, be physically secured).

14.7 Notes

Sections 14.1–14.4

Several standards discuss the management of trusted third parties in some form or another. These include:

> ‣ The general ISO/IEC guideline on the use of trusted third parties, ISO/IEC TR 14516 [1], which is identical to the International Telecommunication Union recommendation, ITU-T X.842 [2];

> ‣ The IETF RFC on the management of time-stamping authorities, IETF RFC 3628 [3], which is identical to the European Telecommunications Standards Institute standard, ETSI TS 102023 [4];

> ‣ The ANSI standard on PKI policies [5];

> ‣ The ISO/IEC information security management guidelines, ISO/IEC 17799 [6].

The ISO/IEC standard on information security management will be discussed in detail in Chapter 16.

Some people are uncomfortable with a TTP service provider's obligation to reveal confidential data to law enforcement agencies. This is a classic example of the debate between civil liberty groups and law enforcement agencies about the use of strong cryptographic primitives by criminals. This debate is well documented [7, 8] but well outside the scope of this book.

Section 14.5

There are two relevant standards that specify time-stamping mechanisms: ISO/IEC 18014 and IETF RFC 3161. The ISO/IEC 18014 standard has three parts: ISO/IEC 18014-1 [9], which describes the general principles of time-stamping; ISO/IEC 18014-2 [10], which describes three mechanisms for producing independent (i.e., unlinked) time-stamping tokens; and ISO/IEC 18014-3 [11], which describes a mechanism for linking tokens. IETF RFC 3161 [12] standardizes a time-stamping mechanism that is similar to one of the mechanisms specified in ISO/IEC 18014-2.

These standards only describe the technical means by which time-stamps may be produced, but any use of a time-stamping authority must also be correctly managed. In particular, ISO/IEC 18014 recommends that a time-stamping authority should be managed according to the guidelines set down in ISO/IEC TR 14516 [1], while IETF RFC 3161 recommends that a time-stamping authority should be managed according to the guidelines in IETF RFC 3628 [3]. The specification of coordinated universal time is contained in ITU-R TF.460-6 [13].

One potential drawback with linking time-stamping tokens is that one must have copies all of the earlier time-stamps in order to verify the ordering. For example, if an entity wishes to verify that a document A was stamped before document B then that entity will have to have the time-stamp for document A, the time-stamp for document B, and all time-stamps that have been issued in between. The entity must then check that the time-stamps were issued one after the other and that each contains the hash code of the previous time-stamp. This could be quite a time-intensive job and would undoubtedly involve storing a lot of unrelated time-stamping tokens.

Of course, the time-stamping authority is not forced to include the hash code of the previous document in every time-stamping token. It is usually enough for a time-stamp to include the hash code of the last time-stamp token that the time-stamping authority issued to that entity. That entity could then determine the ordering of time-stamps that they have been issued without needing to store lots of other tokens.

More information about time-stamps and time-stamping can be found in [14–17].

References

[1] International Organization for Standardization, *ISO/IEC TR 14516, Information Technology—Security Techniques—Guidelines for the Use and Management of Trusted Third Party Services*, 2002.

[2] International Telecommunication Union, *ITU-T Recommendation X.842 (10/00), Information Technology—Security Techniques—Guidelines for the Use and Management of Trusted Third Party Services*, October 2000.

[3] Pinkas, D., N. Pope, and J. Ross, *RFC 3628, Policy Requirements for Time-Stamping Authorities (TSAs)*, Internet Engineering Task Force, November 2003.

[4] European Telecommunications Standards Institute (ETSI), *ETSI TS 102023, Electronic Signatures and Infrastructures (ESI); Policy Requirements for Time-Stamping Authorities*, January 2003.

[5] Accredited Standards Committee X9—Financial Services, *ANSI X9.79-1:2001, Part 1: Public Key Infrastructure—Practices and Policy*, 2001.

[6] International Organization for Standardization, *ISO/IEC 17799, Information Technology—Code of Practice for Information Security Management*, 2000.

[7] Diffie, W., and S. Landau, *Privacy on the Line*, Cambridge, MA; MIT Press, 1999.

[8] Hoffman, L. J., (ed.), *Building in Big Brother*, New York: Springer-Verlag, 1995.

[9] International Organization for Standardization, *ISO/IEC 18014-1, Information Technology—Security Techniques—Time-Stamping Services—Part 1: Framework*, 2002.

[10] International Organization for Standardization, *ISO/IEC 18014-2, Information Technology—Security Techniques—Time-Stamping Services—Part 2: Mechanisms Producing Independent Tokens*, 2002.

[11] International Organization for Standardization, *ISO/IEC 18014-3, Information Technology—Security Techniques—Time-Stamping Services—Part 3: Mechanisms Producing Linked Tokens*, 2004.

[12] Adams, C., et al., *RFC 3161, Internet X.509 Public Key Infrastructure Time-Stamp Protocol (TSP)*, Internet Engineering Task Force, August 2001.

[13] International Telecommunication Union, *ITU-R Recommendation TF.460-6 (02/02), Standard Frequency and Time-Signal Emissions*, February 2002.

[14] Buldas, A., et al., "Time-Stamping with Binary Linking Schemes," in H. Krawczyk, (ed.), *Advances in Cryptology–Crypto '98*, Vol. 1462, *Lecture Notes in Computer Science*, Springer-Verlag, 1998, pp. 486–501.

[15]   Buldas, A., H. Lipmaa, and B. Schoenmakers, "Optimally Efficient Accountable Time-Stamping," in H. Imai and Y. Zheng, (eds.), *Public Key Cryptography 2000*, Vol. 1751, *Lecture Notes in Computer Science*, Springer-Verlag, 2000, pp. 293–305.

[16]   Haber, S., and W. Stornetta, "How to Time-Stamp a Digital Document," *Journal of Cryptography*, Vol. 3, No. 2, 1991, pp. 99–111.

[17]   Haber, S., and W. Stornetta, "Secure Names for Bit-Strings," *Proceedings of the 4th ACM Conference on Computer and Communications Security*, 1997, pp. 28–35.

Cryptographic APIs

Contents

15.1 Introduction

15.2 Standards for crypto APIs

15.3 GSS-API

15.4 PKCS #11

15.5 Security issues

15.6 Notes

Cryptographic APIs, or simply *crypto APIs,* are a topic of considerable practical importance. When implementing an application using cryptography, it is often convenient to use a set of cryptographic functions implemented externally to the application, which can be accessed via this API. This avoids the need to implement cryptographic functions in every application and, depending on which functions are implemented, it can also offer significant security advantages.

15.1 Introduction

The term applications program interface (API) is very widely used. Although precise definitions of the term vary, in general an API is an interface offered by a computing platform to application programs running on that platform. A platform can be thought of as a combination of computer hardware (e.g., a PC), and an operating system running on the hardware. The platform may also incorporate so called *middleware* (i.e., software running on the platform and offering services to applications running over the middleware). Typically such middleware will exist to hide implementation-specific details of the underlying system and will enable applications to be written in a way independent of how the middleware functions are implemented.

An API will typically consist of a set of functions, each with a defined set of parameters, which may be invoked by an application to gain access to the services provided by the underlying platform. The exact nature of the functions will depend on the underlying platform. Also, a single platform may offer multiple APIs.

Following this introductory section, the status of crypto API standardization is reviewed in Section 15.2. This is followed by a more detailed discussion of GSS-API and PKCS #11 (in Sections 15.3 and 15.4, respectively). Finally, a discussion of security issues for crypto APIs is provided in Section 15.5.

Crypto APIs   The general notion of an API leads naturally to the more specialized concept of a crypto API. A crypto API consists of a defined set of cryptographic functions, such as *encrypt, decrypt, generate MAC, generate signature,* and *verify signature.* Associated with each such function is a set of input parameters [e.g., specifying the message to be encrypted and how it is to be encrypted (such as which algorithm is to be used and which key is to be employed)] and a set of output parameters to enable the application to be given back the results of the cryptographic operations (e.g., encrypted or decrypted data, or a MAC).

A key issue in designing and/or selecting a crypto API is what lies beneath it (i.e., what is implementing the set of functions offered by the API). There are two main possibilities: The functionality can be implemented in software or in hardware. In the former case the software could be part of the underlying platform (e.g., part of the operating system) or it could be a software package specifically present to provide cryptographic services.

In the latter case, the hardware would typically be in the form of a hardware security module of some kind. Such devices typically offer a level of physical security for stored keys and exist in many form factors. One common type of module is implemented as a board that can be installed within a PC (e.g., using a PCI slot). Hardware security modules are also briefly discussed in a more general context in Chapter 16.

Key management   In order to support the functions provided by a cryptographic API, the underlying software or hardware will typically need to have access to key material (such as secret keys, private keys, and public keys). These keys will need to be managed by some means (i.e., new keys will need to be generated, derived, imported or exported and old keys will need to be withdrawn from use or deleted), just as is discussed in Chapter 11.

While some key management functions may be offered as part of the crypto API, in a typical case these functions will only be available via a separate interface. This separate interface will also typically be more strongly protected than the crypto API. Indeed, in some cases this interface may be permanently disabled once the module has been initialized (preventing keys from ever being modified or disclosed by the module).

The reason for the use of a separate, more tightly protected interface for key management should be clear. In a PC environment, access to the crypto API is likely to be open to any software running on the PC. This may include malicious code, outside of the control of the owner or operator of the PC. While providing temporary access to the functions offered by the crypto API will no doubt be a significant security risk, this risk is typically much less than the risk posed by compromise or loss of integrity of long-term keys. Similar arguments apply to security modules operating within a network (e.g., a secure payment network). Employees will have temporary access to the modules and hence may have access to the functions offered by the crypto API; however, this should not mean that they have access to the keys used in computing the functions accessible via the crypto API.

Where the crypto API is supported by a hardware security module, it will often be the case that the module does not store all the necessary keys long term. A common practice is for the module to be equipped with a small number of secret "master keys," and for all other keys to be stored externally, encrypted and integrity-protected using the master keys. These externally stored keys would then be submitted with the relevant crypto API command (e.g., one of the parameters for an encryption command would be the (encrypted) key to be used for encrypting the data). The module can then decrypt and verify the integrity of the key before using it to encrypt the data.

Finally, it should be clear that where the crypto API is supported purely by software, protecting the secrecy and integrity of keys relies purely on the protection measures the operating system can offer. In many environments, this will be somewhat limited.

Access control   Most crypto APIs possess access control mechanisms designed to restrict access to the functionality offered by the crypto API. While such mechanisms can certainly not harm the level of security offered by the crypto API, in many environments (e.g., within a PC) the use of such mechanisms can only offer a limited level of protection. This is because the password, or other secret necessary to access the crypto API, must be possessed by the legitimate application software and hence will potentially be available to any entity with access to this software.

Access control mechanisms used for the key management interface will typically be separate from, and more robust than, those used to protect access to the crypto API. This is reasonable since the key management interface will typically be used much less frequently than the crypto API itself, and a requirement for manual intervention to access the key management interface may be acceptable. In the case of security modules, one approach is to equip the module with a separate hardware interface to which a smart card reader or other terminal can be attached and that can be used to control access to the key management interface.

15.2 Standards for crypto APIs

There are no true international standards for crypto APIs, although "standards track" IETF RFCs do exist. However, there are a number of API specifications that have achieved wide recognition. It remains to be seen which, if any, of them will be subject to international standardization.

API specifications   One of the most important is the generic security service application program interface (GSS-API). Version 2 (update 1) of this API has been published as RFC 2743, and there are a significant number of other supporting RFCs (see Section 15.3).

An alternative, widely recognized, crypto API is contained in PKCS #11, published by RSA Laboratories, the current version of which is v2.11. As discussed in Chapter 2, the PKCS series of documents are not formal standards documents, but the specifications have nevertheless become widely used.

Over the last 20 years, many different companies have designed and implemented security modules, and many of them feature proprietary crypto APIs. While most of these APIs remain confidential, the API for one important family of modules, apparently widely used in the banking industry, has been published, namely the API belonging to the IBM 4758. We discuss certain aspects of this module briefly in Section 15.5.

Related standards   Although there are no international standards for crypto APIs, there do exist standards covering a closely related topic, namely security modules (see also Chapter 16). We mention two of particular importance to crypto APIs.

NIST FIPS Pub. 140-2 specifies security requirements for cryptographic modules; these requirements are divided into four increasing levels, from 1 (lowest) to 4 (highest). Some of these requirements have a bearing on the design of the crypto API for the module. These include requirements relating to access control (for level 2 and above), and requirements for separation of the key management interface from the crypto API (for level 3 and above).

The two-part banking standard ISO 13491 is concerned with *secure cryptographic devices* (i.e., it has a somewhat similar scope to FIPS 140-2). Again, some of the requirements in this standard have a bearing on crypto API design.

15.3   GSS-API

The GSS-API, Version 2 update 1, as defined in RFC 2743, supports a range of different underlying cryptographic mechanisms in a transparent fashion. The GSS-API specification defines services and primitives at a level independent of both the underlying cryptographic mechanism and the programming language environment. For example, GSS-API services have been implemented using secret-key technologies (e.g., Kerberos—see RFC 1964) and with public-key approaches [e.g., the simple public-key GSS-API mechanism (SPKM)—see RFC 2025]. Source code for applications that make calls to this API is therefore portable between environments using different suites of cryptographic algorithms.

Because of the algorithm-independent nature of GSS-API, the base specification in RFC 2743 thus needs to be complemented by other, related specifications (discussed later). These include the following:

  ▸ Documents defining specific parameter bindings for particular language environments;

  ▸ Documents defining cryptographic mechanism-specific token formats, protocols, and procedures to be implemented in order to realize the GSS-API services provided via the API.

Because of its mechanism-independence, the GSS-API is probably most appropriate for implementation in software, rather than by a hardware security module. APIs to hardware security modules will typically be somewhat lower level, and the function calls making up the API will implicitly or explicitly define the cryptographic algorithm(s) to be used. Such APIs therefore allow much greater control over the use of the cryptographic mechanisms. Of course, one possibility would be to implement the GSS-API as a software layer running over a second cryptographic API supported by a hardware security module.

15.3.1 Properties of the API

The GSS-API is designed to be used in the following general way. A typical "user" of GSS-API services is itself a communications protocol, using the GSS-API functions in order to protect its communications. This protection might include entity authentication, data integrity, and/or data confidentiality.

The GSS-API calling process accepts *tokens* provided to it by its local GSS-API implementation and transfers the tokens to a communicating peer entity on a remote system. The peer entity passes the received tokens to its local GSS-API implementation for processing. As mentioned above, the security services available through GSS-API can be implemented using a range of underlying cryptographic mechanisms.

The GSS-API separates the operations of initializing a *security context* between communicating peer entities, including entity authentication, from the operations of providing message-specific data origin authentication and data integrity protection for messages subsequently transferred in conjunction with that context.

More specifically, there are four stages to the use of GSS-API by an application.

1. The application acquires a set of *credentials* with which it can prove its identity to other processes. The application's credentials vouch for its global identity, which may or may not be related to any local user name under which it may be running.

2. A pair of communicating applications establish a joint security context using their credentials. The security context is a pair of GSS-API data structures that contain shared state information; this information is needed to provide per-message security services. Examples of state that might be shared between applications as part of a security context are cryptographic keys and message sequence numbers. As part of the establishment of a security context, the context initiator is authenticated to the responder and may require that the responder is authenticated in turn. The initiator may optionally give the responder the right to initiate further security contexts, acting on behalf of the initiator. This transfer of rights is termed *delegation* and is achieved by creating a set of credentials similar to those used by the initiating application, but designed specifically for use by the responder.

   To establish and maintain the shared information that makes up the security context, certain GSS-API calls will return a token data structure. Such a data structure may contain cryptographically protected data. The caller of the GSS-API routine is responsible for transferring the token to the peer application, encapsulated if necessary in an application-level protocol. On receipt of such a token, the peer application should pass it to a corresponding GSS-API routine that will decode the token and extract the information, updating the security context state information accordingly.

3. Message-specific services are invoked to provide one of two possible combinations of security services for application data, listed as follows:

    ‣ Data integrity and data origin authentication;

    ‣ Data confidentiality, data integrity, and data origin authentication.

    Application data is handled by GSS-API as arbitrary strings of bytes. An application transmitting a message that it wishes to protect will call the appropriate GSS-API routine to apply protection, specifying the appropriate security context, and send the resulting token to the receiving application. The receiver will pass the received token to the corresponding decoding routine to remove the protection and validate the data.

4. At the completion of a communications session, each application calls a GSS-API routine to delete the security context. An application may also use multiple contexts (either successively or simultaneously) within a single communications association.

15.3.2 Language bindings

As discussed above, the base GSS-API specification in RFC 2743 is programming language–independent. As a result it is necessary to specify language-specific *bindings* for GSS-API, which specify the language-specific data structures to be used for the parameters associated with each GSS-API function. Two sets of language-specific GSS-API bindings are defined, one for C (in RFC 2744) and one for Java (in RFC 2853).

15.3.3 Authentication protocols

Since GSS-API operates in a cryptographic mechanism–independent fashion, it is necessary to define how particular authentication protocols should be implemented beneath the GSS-API. Two particular schemes have been specified.

RFC 1964 specifies how the Kerberos v5 authentication protocol (see Chapter 10) can be used to support the GSS-API function set. RFC 1964 defines protocols, procedures, and conventions to be employed by communicating peers implementing GSS-API when using Kerberos version 5 technology. In particular, the structure of the tokens transferred between GSS-API peers (for security context management and message protection purposes) are defined. However, the data elements exchanged between a GSS-API end-point implementation and the Kerberos KDC are not specific to GSS-API and are therefore as defined within the Kerberos specification itself.

As an alternative to Kerberos Version 5, RFC 2025 defines a GSS-API authentication mechanism based on a public key, rather than a secret key, infrastructure. This is known as SPKM. SPKM allows both unilateral and mutual authentication to be accomplished without the use of secure timestamps. This enables environments that do not have access to secure time to nevertheless have access to secure authentication. SPKM uses the signature-based authentication protocols specified in ISO/IEC 9798-3 (see Chapter 10).

15.4   PKCS #11

The PKCS #11 API is defined at a somewhat lower level than GSS-API, in that it allows more direct control over the use and computation of cryptographic functions. It is not algorithm-independent—the set of functions it provides allows the calling application to specify exactly how cryptographic operations should be performed. Neither is it programming language–independent—it uses ANSI C syntax. The API supports a large selection of different cryptographic algorithms, and future versions of the API will presumably support ever larger numbers of algorithms.

The API specified in PKCS #11 is called "Cryptoki" (pronounced "crypto-key" and short for *cryptographic token interface*). It uses an object-based approach, and is designed to permit resource sharing (i.e., to permit multiple applications to access multiple devices). It is intended to provide an interface "to devices that hold cryptographic information and perform cryptographic functions"; the device supporting the Cryptoki API is referred to as a *token*. Thus, unlike GSS-API, it is intended as an interface to a hardware security module. In fact, it "was intended from the beginning to be an interface between applications and all kinds of portable cryptographic devices, such as those based on smart cards, PCMCIA cards, and smart diskettes."

15.4.1   Data storage

All data (e.g., keys and certificates) stored by a token are stored in the form of objects. Objects are classified according to their lifetime and visibility. "Token objects" are visible to all applications connected to the token that have sufficient permission and remain on the token even after the "sessions" (connections between an application and the token) are closed and the token is removed from its slot. "Session objects" are more temporary: Whenever a session is closed, all session objects created by that session are automatically destroyed. In addition, session objects are only visible to the application which created them.

A separate classification defines access requirements. Applications are not required to log into the token to view "public objects"; however, to view "private objects," a user must be authenticated to the token by a PIN or some other token-dependent method (for example, via a biometric device—see Chapter 16).

15.4.2 Access control

Cryptoki supports two types of token user. One type is a *security officer* (SO), and the other is a *normal user*. Only a normal user is allowed access to *private objects* on the token, and that access is granted only after the normal user has been authenticated (e.g., entered the user's PIN). Some tokens may also require that a user be authenticated before any cryptographic function can be performed on the token, whether or not it involves private objects.

The role of the SO is to initialize a token and to set up the normal user PINs (or otherwise define, by some method outside the scope of Cryptoki, how normal users are authenticated), and possibly to manipulate some public objects. A normal user cannot log in until the SO has set the user's PIN. Note that, while this may require the SO to know the initial value of a user's PIN, in practice the user would typically be required to change the PIN after issue to ensure that he or she is the only person with knowledge of their PIN.

15.4.3 Sessions and concurrency

The Cryptoki API requires an application to open one or more *sessions* with a token in order to gain access to the token's objects and functions. A session provides a logical connection between the application and the token. In any session, an application can create, read, write, and destroy *session objects* and read *token objects*. However, only in a special type of session, called a *read/write session*, can an application create, modify, and destroy token objects.

After it opens a session, an application has access to the token's public objects. All threads of a given application have access to exactly the same sessions and the same session objects. (A thread is a single sequential flow of control within a program. Multithreading is when multiple threads execute the same program.)

To gain access to the token's private objects, the normal user must log in and be authenticated. When a session is closed, any session objects that were created in that session are destroyed. This holds even for session objects that are "being used" by other sessions. That is, if a single application has multiple sessions open with a token, and it uses one of them to create a session object, then that session object is visible through any of that application's sessions. However, as soon as the session that was used to create the object is closed, that object is destroyed.

Cryptoki supports multiple sessions on multiple tokens. An application may have one or more sessions with one or more tokens. In general, a token may have multiple sessions with one or more applications.

15.5 Security issues

While crypto APIs have been in use for a number of years, and many such APIs have been designed, there is a relatively small amount of academic literature on the subject. Indeed, the science of good crypto API design would appear to be underdeveloped. Historically, the main focus of standards for security modules has been on ensuring their physical security and addressing implementation issues rather than on the logical design of the crypto API.

Possibly as a result, in recent years a number of flaws have been identified in widely fielded APIs. Some examples of general categories of security issues are described as follows:

- Flaws in the key management interface have, in a specific example, allowed the integrity of keys to be compromised. Specifically, in a case where entry of a secret key in a number of "key components" is permitted [to allow split control (i.e., no single person having control over the key)] repeated entry of one of the components allowed an incorrect key to be entered.

- The presence of too much flexibility in the API can enable attacks. One example of an attack of this type allowed exhaustive attacks on PINs to be performed much more efficiently than would otherwise have been the case.

- It is important that the key management system in use enables the use of keys to be properly controlled (i.e., it must enforce *key separation*). Examples exist of cases where some aspects of MAC computations are not properly bound to a secret key, which may make certain attacks easier to perform.

- Possible problems with partial cryptographic computations have been identified. Such computations occur where a long message is to be protected (e.g., encrypted or MACed), and it is not possible to pass the entire message to the crypto API in one function call. In such a case it is necessary to divide the message into parts and make a series of function calls, with partial computation results being transferred from one call to the next. In such an environment, the "partial calls" must be designed very carefully lest it becomes possible to use such calls to perform unauthorised cryptographic operations.

One final issue we mention concerns the "statefulness" of the system supporting the crypto API. Clearly, all crypto APIs will have an inherent state, namely the set of keys managed to support the API functions. However, some APIs store additional "short-term" state information. For example, the Cryptoki API specified in PKCS #11 involves a Cryptoki token (i.e., the device implementing the API functions) storing session information. Such session information could, for example, include partial results from a multi-call cryptographic computation. While use of such state information can simplify the handling of such function calls, in some circumstances it is also a significant disadvantage. For example, if a system uses multiple tokens, (e.g., to support higher throughput than would be supportable using a single device) then the multiple API calls necessary to compute a MAC or signature on a long message must all be made to the same token. This limits the potential for load balancing across multiple tokens.

It is interesting to observe that the proprietary IBM 4758 API is not stateful in the above sense. Thus a system using multiple IBM 4758 modules can use any of these modules for cryptographic computations, as long as they all share the same basic set of keys. However, not least because there are a large number of them, we do not discuss proprietary interfaces such as that of the IBM 4758 in this book.

15.6   Notes

Section 15.1

There are many books, see, for example [1], on using cryptography within Java, including Java GSS-API. There are also a significant number of books, for example [2, 3], covering the use and functionality of smart cards, which are essentially a special type of hardware security module. Thus, some of the discussions on the interfaces offered by smart cards are also of relevance to crypto APIs.

Section 15.2

Version 2 update 1 of GSS-API is specified in RFC 2743 [4]. Previous versions of the GSS-API specification can be found in RFC 1508 [5] (version 1), and RFC 2078 [6] (version 2).

The current release of PKCS #11 is version 2.11 [7]. This and previous versions of the PKCS #11 specifications are available at http://www.rsasecurity.com/rsalabs/pkcs/index.html.

The current version of the interface to the IBM 4758 hardware security module is specified in [8].

NIST FIPS Pub. 140-2 was released in 2001 [9]; the "2" in the title indicates that this is the second revision of FIPS 140. The two parts of the ISO banking standard for secure cryptographic devices, ISO 13491, were published in 1998 [10, 11].

Section 15.3

The current version of the GSS-API C bindings are specified in RFC 2744 [12], which supersedes RFC 1509 [13]. The parallel Java bindings are given in RFC 2853 [14].

The Kerberos v5 GSS-API mechanism is described in RFC 1964 [15]. Note that Kerberos v5 itself is specified in RFC 1510 [16] (for more details, see Chapter 10). The SPKM mechanism is specified in RFC 2025 [17].

There are four other RFCs that relate to use of GSS-API. Two of these describe how GSS-API can be used to support specific functions. RFC 1961 [18] describes how GSS-API can be used to provide authentication for v5 of the SOCKS Protocol (itself specified in RFC 1928 [19]). SOCKS is designed to enable application layer protocols to traverse network firewalls. RFC 2203 [20] allows Remote Procedure Call (RPC) protocols to use GSS-API security services. The other two RFCs provide enhancements to the base GSS-API functionality. RFC 2478 [21] specifies a security negotiation mechanism for GSS-API. It enables GSS-API peers to determine whether their credentials share common cryptographic mechanism(s), and, if so, to invoke security context establishment for a selected common mechanism. This is most useful for applications using GSS-API implementations supporting multiple cryptographic mechanisms. RFC 2479 [22] extends GSS-API for applications requiring protection of a generic data unit (such as a file or message) in a "connectionless" way. It is thus suitable for applications such as secure electronic mail where data needs to be protected without any on-line connection with the intended recipient(s) of that data.

Section 15.4

The current version (v2.11 revision 1) of PKCS #11 is specified in [7]. A detailed critique of PKCS #11 has been provided by Clulow [23].

Section 15.5

Clulow's 2003 master's thesis [24] contains descriptions of a number of possible crypto API vulnerabilities in commercial hardware security modules. Attacks on the key management interface for recent versions of the IBM 4758 have been identified by Bond and Anderson [25, 26].

An example of unnecessary flexibility in a crypto API which enables an attack is described by Bond [27]. In this attack, PINs can be discovered much more efficiently than would normally be the case by the fact that a "decimalization table" (used in PIN verification computations) is a parameter to one of the API functions, although in practice the table is fixed (and hence does not need to be a parameter). This allows special "false tables" to be offered to the API, permitting fast searches of the PIN space. The existence of such an attack has independently been observed by Clulow [24].

Problems with key control for MAC keys have been identified in [28, 29]. If the degree of truncation of the MAC is not bound securely to the key (which is not the case for Cryptoki or the IBM 4758 API), then this enables accelerated attacks on MAC functions.

Finally, certain possible attacks on partial computations for MACs have been identified [30], although it is not clear whether this is a problem to which existing crypto APIs are prone (since most such APIs are at least partially confidential).

References

[1] Gong, L., G. Ellison, and M. Dageforde, *Inside Java 2 Platform Security: Architecture, API Design, and Implementation*, 2nd ed., Reading, MA: Addison-Wesley, 2003.

[2] Chen, Z., *Java Card Technology for Smart Cards: Architecture and Programmer's Guide*, Reading, MA: Addison-Wesley, 2000.

[3] Rankl, W., and W. Effing, *Smart Card Handbook*, 3rd ed., New York: John Wiley and Sons, 2003.

[4] Linn, J., *RFC 2743, Generic Security Service Application Program Interface Version 2, Update 1*, Internet Engineering Task Force, January 2000.

[5] Linn, J., *RFC 1508, Generic Security Service Application Program Interface*, Internet Engineering Task Force, September 1993.

[6] Linn, J., *RFC 2078, Generic Security Service Application Program Interface, Version 2*, Internet Engineering Task Force, January 1997.

[7]   RSA Laboratories, *PKCS #11 v2.11: Cryptographic Token Interface Standard, Revision 1*, November 2001.

[8]   IBM, *PCI Cryptographic Processor: CCA Basic Services Reference and Guide, Release 2.41*, September 2003.

[9]   National Institute of Standards and Technology (NIST), *Federal Information Processing Standards Publication 140-2 (FIPS PUB 140-2): Security Requirements for Cryptographic Modules*, June 2001.

[10]   International Organization for Standardization, *ISO 13491-1: 1998, Banking—Secure Cryptographic Devices (Retail)—Part 1: Concepts, Requirements and Evaluation Methods*, 1998.

[11]   International Organization for Standardization, *ISO 13491-2: 2000, Banking—Secure Cryptographic Devices (Retail)—Part 2: Security Compliance Checklists for Devices Used in Magnetic Stripe Card Systems*, 2000.

[12]   Wray, J., *RFC 2744, Generic Security Service API Version 2: C-Bindings*, Internet Engineering Task Force, January 2000.

[13]   Wray, J., *RFC 1509, Generic Security Service API : C-Bindings*, Internet Engineering Task Force, September 1993.

[14]   Kabat, J., and M. Upadhyay, *RFC 2853, Generic Security Service API Version 2 : Java Bindings*, Internet Engineering Task Force, June 2000.

[15]   Linn, J., *RFC 1964, The Kerberos Version 5 GSS-API Mechanism*, Internet Engineering Task Force, June 1996.

[16]   Kohl, J., and C. Neuman, *RFC 1510, The Kerberos Network Authentication Service (V5)*, Internet Engineering Task Force, September 1993.

[17]   Adams, C., *RFC 2025, The Simple Public-Key GSS-API Mechanism (SPKM)*, Internet Engineering Task Force, October 1996.

[18]   McMahon, P., *RFC 1961, GSS-API Authentication Method for SOCKS Version 5*, Internet Engineering Task Force, June 1996.

[19]   Leech, M., et al., *RFC 1928, SOCKS Protocol Version 5*, Internet Engineering Task Force, March 1996.

[20]   Eisler, M., A. Chiu, and L. Ling, *RFC 2203, RPCSEC_GSS Protocol Specification*, Internet Engineering Task Force, September 1997.

[21]   Baize, E., and D. Pinkas, *RFC 2478, The Simple and Protected GSS-API Negotiation Mechanism*, Internet Engineering Task Force, December 1998.

[22]   Adams, C., *RFC 2479, Independent Data Unit Protection Generic Security Service Application Program Interface (IDUP-GSS-API)*, Internet Engineering Task Force, December 1998.

[23]   Clulow, J., "On the Security of PKCS #11," in C. D. Walter, C. K. Koc, and C. Paar, (eds.), *Cryptographic Hardware and Embedded Systems—CHES 2003, 5th International Workshop*, Vol. 2779, *Lecture Notes in Computer Science*, Springer-Verlag, 2003, pp. 411–425.

[24]   Clulow, J., "The Design and Analysis of Cryptographic APIs for Security Devices," M.Sc. dissertation, University of Natal, Durban, South Africa, 2003.

[25]   Bond, M., "Attacks on Cryptoprocessor Transaction Sets," in C. K. Koc, D. Naccache, and C. Paar, (eds.), *Cryptographic Hardware and Embedded*

Systems—CHES 2001, Vol. 2162, *Lecture Notes in Computer Science*, Springer-Verlag, 2001, pp. 220–234.

[26] Bond, M., and R. Anderson, "API-Level Attacks on Embedded Systems," *IEEE Computer Magazine*, Vol. 34, No. 10, October 2001, pp. 67–75.

[27] Bond, M., and P. Zielinski, "Decimalisation Attacks for PIN Cracking," Preprint, Computer Laboratory, University of Cambridge, 2002.

[28] Mitchell, C. J., "Key Recovery Attack on ANSI Retail MAC," *Electronics Letters*, Vol. 39, 2003, pp. 361–362.

[29] Mitchell, C. J., "Truncation Attacks on MACs," *Electronics Letters*, Vol. 39, 2003, pp. 1439–1440.

[30] Brincat, K., and C. J. Mitchell, "Key Recovery Atacks on MACs Based on Properties of Cryptographic APIs," in B. Honary, (ed.), *Cryptography and Coding, 8th IMA International Conference*, Vol. 2260, *Lecture Notes in Computer Science*, Springer-Verlag, 2001, pp. 63–72.

Other Standards

Contents

16.1 Random bit generation

16.2 Prime number generation

16.3 Authenticated encryption

16.4 Security modules

16.5 Standards for the use of biometric techniques

16.6 Information security management

16.7 Notes

We have attempted, so far, to cover all of the major standards in all of the major areas of cryptography. It would be impossible to cover all of the different standards as there are simply too many. In this chapter we give a brief overview of some of the important standards and areas of cryptography that we have so far overlooked.

16.1 Random bit generation

Again and again within this book we have referred to the need for secure random bit generation. We have used random bits to generate secret symmetric keys, to produce asymmetric key pairs, to generate random nonces in authentication and key distribution protocols, as integral parts of digital signature schemes, and to generate starting vectors for the modes of operation of a block cipher. The ability to generate random bits is a key facet of a security system; however, it is one that is continually overlooked.

Many commonly used random bit/number generation algorithms (for example, those contained in many standard libraries for programming languages) are not sufficient for cryptographic applications. The need for a systematic approach to secure random bit generation has caused two important standardization bodies to consider the issue, and there are currently draft standards being produced by the ISO/IEC JTC1 committee (ISO/IEC 18031) and ANSI (ANSI X9.82—a three-part standard).

Prior to these efforts, advice on the secure generation of random bits was mostly given on an ad hoc basis, such as in the appendixes of ANSI X9.31 and ANSI X9.42, and in the NIST FIPS 186 digital signature standard. An early exception to this ad hoc approach is the recommendations for randomness given in IETF RFC 1750. This standard gives an excellent high-level introduction to the problems associated with generating random data.

A random bit generator (RBG) is a device or algorithm that produces a long string of bits that appear random to an external entity. Here, the word "random" means that no attacker can predict any output bit with probability significantly better than 1/2, nor find any dependence between bits.

RBGs are necessarily deterministic algorithms: They need to take some input and always give the same output when given the same inputs. They cannot be probabilistic algorithms because probabilistic algorithms need to have access to an unlimited source of randomly generated bits and that is what the RBG is itself trying to produce! However, the condition that an RBG must always give the same output when given the same input must be taken in the correct context. It means that if two RBGs are given all the same inputs (including any secret keys or other secret information) from the time that they are first used then they will produce the same output. The type of input is known as the RBG's *entropy source* or *source*.

We can classify RBGs according to the type of entropy source they use. There are two different types of sources that an RBG could use:

> ‣ *A physical input source:* A physical input source is a source that produces random output by measuring some physical event such as the decay of a unstable atom or the thermal noise in a semiconductor. A RBG that is based on one or more physical input sources is sometimes called a nondeterministic RBG (NRBG).

> ‣ *A seed:* A seed is a short input string that has typically been generated randomly from the set of all possible inputs. The RBG uses this seed to start up a cryptographic process that produces a long stream of random-looking bits. An RBG that is based on the use of a seed rather than a physical input is sometimes called a deterministic RBG (DRBG). We shall discuss each of the different types of RBGs in turn in the next two sections.

Just as it is difficult to design an RBG, it also difficult to demonstrate that an RBG is suitably secure (i.e., producing a suitably random output). A simple solution is to test the output using a series of statistical tests. While this will not give an implementor complete confidence in the randomness of a generator—there are many examples of weak RBGs that will pass all standard statistical tests—it is a good first step to assessing its quality. NIST has released a special publication detailing a series of statistical tests for testing RBGs (NIST Special Publication 800-22).

16.1.1 Nondeterministic RBGs

A good RBG is often compared to a person flipping a coin. Each coin flip comes up heads or tails with probability exactly 1/2 (assuming that the coin is unbiased and that is never lands on its edge) and each coin flip is independent of any of the others. If we generate a random sequence by flipping an unbiased coin and recording a "0" whenever it comes up heads and "1" whenever it comes up tails, then we will generate a completely random sequence of bits. This technique is still used for generating some important keys.

Flipping a coin is an example of a nondeterministic RBG. NRBGs are random bit generators where the unpredictability of the scheme is based on the unpredictability of some physical event.

The type of NRBG depends upon the nature of the physical source that it uses. Traditionally there are two types of physical sources that an NRBG can use to provide input:

- *Truly physical sources:* These are sources that are solely dependent on the characteristics of some kind of purely physical reaction; for example, the decay of a radioactive atom or the thermal noise in a semiconductor. Devices of this kind are comparatively easy to construct and analyze, however specialist hardware (such as a Geiger counter) is generally needed to measure the effects of these sources, and this can add an unnecessary expense to a system or simply be unavailable. An RBG that uses a truly physical source is often known as a *true random bit generator*.

- *Sources with some kind of human dependency:* These are unpredictable physical sources that in some way depend upon the interaction of a user with the system. Examples of these sources include the time between the user pressing a key on a keyboard or clicking a mouse, or certain types of network statistics such as the time between packets arriving at a destination. Measuring these sources can generally be done with the existing hardware within a normal computer system, but care must be taken to make sure that the sources cannot be seen by the attacker.

Regardless of the type of source used, an NRBG normally works in two stages. First, the entropy source needs to be measured, and then this input needs to be processed to give a suitable output. This latter stage is sometimes known as *postprocessing*.

Measuring the entropy source involves collecting raw data from the source (such as the time taken for an atom to decay or the time between user key presses) and turning that into a single binary digit. This is generally done by comparing the measurement to a *threshold value*. If the measurement is greater than the threshold value then a "1" digit is output, otherwise a "0" digit is output. The threshold value depends upon the particular source being used. Sometimes more than one digit can be obtained from a single measurement by comparing the measurement to a series of threshold values.

While it is necessary that the output of the entropy source be unpredictable, it is not always instantly ready for use as an RBG. It is possible the entropy sources output may be biased (so that one binary digit occurs more often than the other) or dependent (so the probability that a binary digit occurs may depend upon previous outputs). Postprocessing is designed to remove these undesirable properties.

Postprocessing can range from simple techniques such as combining several bits of output using an exclusive-or, to complicated cryptographic techniques such as are used by DRBGs.

Due to the simple nature of most NRBGs, the quality (randomness) of the output can usually be tested using standard statistical tests for randomness.

16.1.2   Deterministic RBGs

A deterministic RBG (DRBG) is vastly different to an NRBG. An NRBG provides true randomness by measuring an unpredictable physical source. A DRBG does not provide true randomness; it merely outputs a long string of random-looking data based on a secret seed value (and, possibly, some other secret information). For this reason, DRBGs are sometimes called *pseudorandom bit generators*.

A DRBG is essentially a machine with some kind of (hidden) internal state. The state is initially defined by the seed. On demand the DRBG will do two things: First, it will output a block of random-looking data, and second, it will update the internal state. Obviously, it must be computationally infeasible for an attacker to compute all of the secret information in the DRBG (the combination of the current state and any other secret information that the DRBG needs to work) from observing the output.

As the internal state must be finite, eventually internal states will start to repeat. (It is impossible for a new internal state to be generated every time!) Once the internal state starts to repeat, so will the output. Hence it is important to update the seed value before this happens. In practice, many DRBGs update the seed value fairly frequently so as to make sure that the output continues to look random. The other secret information in the scheme, for example any cryptographic keys the DRBG makes use of, will also need to be updated but typically less frequently than the seed value. For more information on the management of cryptographic keys, see Chapter 11. DRBGs are generally cheaper and faster than their nondeterministic counterparts, as they can be run using normal computing technology without any need for specialist hardware or user interaction. However, unlike an NRBG, a DRBG contains an inherent weakness in that its security is based on cryptographic techniques and so there is always a possibility that it can be cryptanalyzed.

On the simplest level, a DRBG can be broken by an exhaustive search, in which an attacker merely searches through all the possible seeds (and any other secret input) until it finds the correct one. The attacker will then be able to compute all of the output of the DRBG until the seed (or other secret information) is changed. It is therefore critical that the seed is sufficiently large as to be effectively unguessable.

There are many similarities between RBGs and keystream generators for a synchronous stream cipher (see Chapter 4), and a DRBG can always be used as a synchronous key stream generator. Here, the key for the stream cipher would be all the secret data that the DRBG uses (i.e., the seed and any other secret information). Many keystream generators can also be used as DRBGs, including the counter and output feedback modes of operation for a block cipher detailed in Chapter 5.

Of course, implementing a DRBG is not enough to guarantee a good source of cryptographically random bits. A DRBG requires that the seed it receives is suitably random and this seed must somehow be generated. It is not unusual for the seed for a DRBG to be generated by an NRBG. This may seem a bit contradictory; after all, if we have an NRBG available then why do we need to implement a DRBG at all? The answer lies in the expense and speed of an NRBG. An NRBG alone may not be able to produce the vast quantities of data that may be required by the application, nor may it be practical to implement an NRBG on every machine in a system. However it may well be practical to have a single central NRBG that periodically provides seeds for DRBGs running on many different machines.

16.1.3   Generating random numbers

Many cryptographic algorithms, especially those associated with asymmetric techniques, require more than a simple random bit generator: They require a generator that can produce random numbers from a given range in such a way that every number in that range is equally likely to occur. This requires slightly more work than merely producing a string of random bits.

Suppose that a cryptographic application requires a random number x is generated between 0 and $r - 1$ and that each number in this range is equally likely to be generated. This is a very simple task if r is a power of 2 (i.e., $r = 2^k$ for some integer k) as it is easy to interpret a block of k bits as the binary representation of a number in the required range. It is slightly more difficult when r is not a power of 2. For simplicity, we will assume that r is not a power of two and can be represented using k bits (i.e., $2^{k-1} < r < 2^k$).

The simplest solution would seem to be to use an RBG to produce a k-bit integer and reduce the integer modulo r. This is not sufficient as small values are twice as likely to occur than large values. (For example, this generator would output the number 0 if either the RBG output a bit string corresponding to the number 0 or the number r, whereas it would only output the number $r - 1$ if the RBG output a bit string corresponding to the number $r - 1$.)

The two simplest methods for generating random numbers from random bit strings are known (in the draft ISO/IEC 18031 standard) as the *discard method* and the *modular method*.

The discard method works as follows:

1. Generate a k bit string using a secure RBG. Interpret this string as an integer x between and $2^k - 1$.

2. If x is between 0 and $r - 1$, then output x. Otherwise, output "error" or return to step 1.

The discard method has one major disadvantage: The random number generator may fail to produce an output on its first attempt. However, when it finally succeeds, the output will have been selected completely at random from the required range. In any single attempt, the generator will fail with probability $(2^k - r)/2^k$.

The modular method works as follows:

1. Generate an l bit string using a secure RBG. Interpret this string as an integer x between 0 and $2^l - 1$. The exact value of l will depend upon the needs of the application but it should be fixed in advance and significantly larger than k. Most standards recommend that l is at least $k + 128$.

2. Output $x \bmod r$.

Unlike the discard method, the modular method has the advantage that it will always produce an output. However, it has two serious drawbacks. The first is that it requires a longer random input than the discard method. The second is that not every number will be output with the same frequency. Just as with the naive modular method we first discussed, smaller numbers are more likely to occur than large numbers, but (for large enough values of l) the difference in these probabilities should be so small as to have no practical significance.

16.2 Prime number generation

Almost all of the key generation algorithms for asymmetric schemes require some kind of random prime number to be generated. For example, the RSA algorithm (see Chapter 4) requires two primes p and q to be generated and multiplied together to give the modulus n, and the DSA algorithm (see Chapter 8) requires a prime *modulus p* and a prime *order q* to be generated, so that q divides $p - 1$.

Recall that an integer $x > 1$ is prime if it is only divisible by itself and 1. An integer $x > 1$ that is not prime is called composite.

Just as with random bit and random number generation (see Section 16.1), standards describing secure methods of generating prime numbers suitable for cryptographic techniques were traditionally developed as appendixes of other standards (for example, ANSI X9.31). In parallel to the work that the ANSI X9 committee and the ISO/IEC JTC1 committee have undertaken on random bit generation, both bodies have begun work on standards for prime number generation. The former published the ANSI X9.80 standard on prime number generation, primality testing and primality certificates in 2001. The latter has nearly completed the ISO/IEC 18032 standard, which covers a similar set of topics.

There are two broad classes of prime generation methods: those that make use of some kind of primality test and those that do not. A primality test is an algorithm that takes a number as input and outputs whether that number is prime or not. The simplest primality test is carried out by trial division; here an integer x is determined to be prime if no other integer y $(2 \leq y \leq \sqrt{x})$ divides into x.

Prime generation algorithms that make use of a primality test typically work in the following way. First the algorithm generates a random number in the required range (see Section 16.1.3). This number is known as the *candidate prime* and is often generated in a way that prevents certain obviously composite numbers, such as even numbers, from being generated. Next the primality of this number is checked using the primality test. If the generated number passes the test then it is output; otherwise, a new random number is generated and tested.

For many applications this "generate-and-test" method is considered to be too slow and, in those cases, a slightly different approach is used. Here a random odd candidate prime x is generated and tested for primality. If x is prime then the algorithm outputs x and terminates. If x is not prime then the algorithm adds two to x and tests this new number for primality. This "add-two-and-test" process is repeated until a prime number is generated. This algorithm is faster than the "generate-and-test" algorithm but does not output all prime numbers with equal probability (i.e., some prime numbers are more likely to be output than others).

Most of the primality tests that are currently in use are probabilistic algorithms. These algorithms occasionally output an incorrect answer (i.e., declare an integer to be prime when it is composite or declare an integer to be composite when it is prime). This drawback is usually accepted as the probability that the test will make a mistake is fairly low. Sometimes tests are repeated more than once to try to minimize the chance that it outputs an incorrect answer.

The most famous primality test is probably the Miller-Rabin test, which tests to see if the candidate prime x exhibits the same behavior as a prime number when computing arithmetic modulo x. The exact details of the test are complex and unenlightening, and are therefore omitted.

Prime generation algorithms that do not make use of a primality test are more complicated to describe. They generally involve running an algorithm multiple times; each time the algorithm takes the prime generated in the previous round as input, and outputs a longer prime. Hence, very large prime numbers can be constructed by running the algorithm enough times. The problem with these kinds of algorithms is that they are not likely to output all of the different primes of a given length with equal probability—some prime numbers are more likely to be output than others, and some prime numbers may not be output at all. This bias may help an attacker guess a prime number (if it is meant to be secret) or cryptanalyze a scheme that uses that prime.

16.3 Authenticated encryption

As we have stressed throughout the earlier chapters, it is important to realize which services a mechanism is able to offer. In particular, we have stressed that an encryption scheme (see Chapters 4 and 5) provides a confidentiality service, whereas a MAC algorithm or a digital signature scheme (see Chapters 7 and 8) provides integrity and data origin authentication services. So, what should you do if you wish to send a message that is confidential, integrity-protected and has data origin authentication? The simple answer would seem to be to use an encryption scheme and a MAC/digital signature scheme together, but the way in which this should be done has been subject to much debate over many years.

There are three ways one can attempt to use both an encryption scheme and a MAC/digital signature scheme to protect a message. The first is to both encrypt the message, and compute its MAC/signature. However, the security of the encryption is only guaranteed if no other data about the message is released. The MAC/signature may reveal enough information about the message to allow an attacker to decrypt the ciphertext.

Alternatively one could encrypt a message to give a ciphertext and then MAC/sign the ciphertext. However, it can then be argued that the MAC/signature does not provide any kind of data origin authentication because there is no evidence that the entity that computed the MAC/signature knew the message—only that it knew the ciphertext!

Lastly, one could MAC/sign the message and then encrypt it. This means the encryption algorithm has to encrypt not only the message data, but also the MAC/signature. This is computationally inefficient.

The best solution seems to be to design completely new authenticated encryption schemes (i.e., schemes that simultaneously provide confidentiality, integrity, and data origin authentication). In the symmetric arena, this means effectively finding a scheme that simultaneously symmetrically encrypts and MACs a message. This can be accomplished by developing new modes of operation for a block cipher or stream cipher (e.g., the MULTI-S01 mode of operation for a stream cipher discussed in Chapter 4). In the asymmetric arena, this means finding a scheme that simultaneously asymmetrically encrypts and signs a message. This has led to the study of a new branch of asymmetric cryptography known as "signcryption."

While signcryption is still considered too new a topic to produce standardized algorithms, work is progressing on standardizing a new mode of operation for a block cipher that provides authenticated encryption. This work is primarily being undertaken by NIST, which is attempting to standardize a single authenticated encryption mode for use with the AES encryption algorithm (see Chapter 4). Work has also recently begun on an ISO/IEC standard for authenticated encryption: ISO/IEC 19772.

The two main candidates for standardization by NIST are the CCM mode and the EAX mode, although popular alternatives exist in the form of the OCB mode and the AES key wrap mode (which is specified in IETF RFC 3394). The first draft of ISO/IEC 19772 contains the CCM, OCB, and AES key wrap modes.

16.3.1   Counter and CBC-MAC (CCM) mode

The CCM mode of operation for a block cipher was proposed by Housley, Whiting, and Ferguson in 2002. It was quickly adopted by several standards bodies: It is standardized in IETF RFC 3610, IEEE 802.11i (a standard for securing data traveling over a wireless network), and in a draft standard by NIST, NIST Special Publication 800-38C.

The CCM mode of encryption combines the use of counter mode (see Chapter 5) for confidentiality with a CBC-MAC (see Chapter 7) for integrity and data origin authentication. We will let e_K denote encryption using the underlying block cipher and a key K, and n denote the block length of the block cipher.

Generation–Encryption   The algorithm that produces the ciphertext and MAC is known as the *generation–encryption* algorithm. The CCM generation-encryption algorithm takes three inputs (besides the secret key for the underlying block cipher):

▸ The payload P. This is the data that should be sent in both a confidential and integrity-protected manner.

▸ The associated data A. This is data that needs to be sent along with the payload and should be integrity-protected, but need not be kept confidential.

▸ A nonce N. This is a short randomly generated string of bits that will be used by the encryption algorithm. A new nonce should be generated every time the algorithm is used.

The generation-encryption algorithm works as follows. First, the algorithm produces a long sequence of blocks B_0, B_1, B_2, ... These blocks contain all the data that needs to be integrity-protected. This sequence is constructed in three steps:

1. The block B_0 is constructed. This is a "control block" and contains no actual data. Instead, it consists of four things: the length of the MAC that is to be produced, the length of the payload, the length of the data string that contains the length of the payload, and the nonce. Including the nonce in B_0 means that it will be different every time a message is encrypted.

2. The blocks $B_1, \ldots, B_a$ are constructed from the associated data. These blocks are formed by splitting the associated data into blocks of length n and appending this with the length of the associated data (encoded in a special way) and as many zeroes as are required to make the length of the final block be n.

3. The blocks $B_{a+1}, \ldots B_{a+b}$ are constructed from the payload. These blocks are formed by appending the payload with as many zeroes as are required to make the length of this string a multiple of n, and splitting this string into b blocks of length n. Hence $b = \lceil |P|/n \rceil$.

The blocks $B_0, \ldots B_{a+b}$ are subject to a CBC-MAC algorithm with a starting variable consisting of n zeroes—i.e., the blocks $Y_0, \ldots Y_{a+b}$ are computed where

$$Y_0 = e_K(B_0), \quad Y_i = e_K(B_i \oplus Y_{i-1}) \quad (1 \le i \le a+b) \tag{16.1}$$

and the output MAC T is a truncated version of Y_{a+b}. CBC-MAC algorithms are discussed in detail in Chapter 7.

Next, the payload is encrypted using counter-mode encryption (see Chapter 5). The initial counter block Ctr_1 is constructed from three data values: the length of the MAC that is produced, the length of the payload and the nonce. The initial counter block is constructed in a manner that is very similar to the control block B_0, but these two blocks are constructed in such a way that they can never be confused (i.e., a control block could never be mistakenly thought to be a initial counter block for any message and vice versa).

Hence, the encryption of the payload occurs by computing b "keystream blocks"

$$S_i = e_K(Ctr_i) \quad \text{where } Ctr_i = Ctr_1 + i - 1 \bmod 2^n \quad (1 \le i \le b) \tag{16.2}$$

and computing the ciphertext

$$C = P \oplus (S_1 || \ldots || S_b)|_{|P|} \tag{16.3}$$

The algorithm outputs the pair (C, T). The generation-encryption algorithm is shown in Figure 16.1.

Verification-decryption   The algorithm that checks the integrity of the data and then, if the integrity check is valid, outputs the message is known as the *verification-decryption* algorithm. The CCM verification-decryption algorithm takes four inputs:

- The MAC T;

- The ciphertext C;

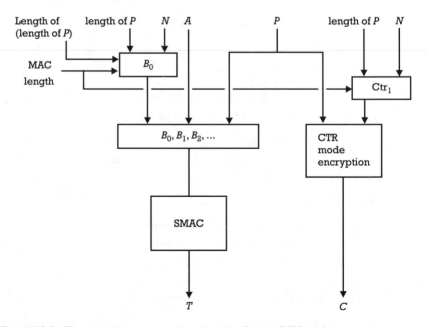

Figure 16.1 The generation-encryption algorithm for the CCM mode.

> ▸ The associated data A;

> ▸ The nonce N. This must be same nonce as was used in the generation-encryption process.

The verification-decryption algorithm works in two stages. First, the algorithm decrypts the ciphertext. It does this by first constructing the initial counter block Ctr_1 from the length of the MAC, the length of the ciphertext (which is the same as the length of the payload) and the nonce. It is then possible to recover the "keystream blocks"

$$S_i = e_K(Ctr_i) \quad \text{where } Ctr_i = Ctr_1 + i - 1 \bmod 2^n \quad (1 \le i \le b) \tag{16.4}$$

and compute the payload

$$P = C \oplus (S_1 || \ldots || S_b)|_{|C|} \tag{16.5}$$

Here $b = \lceil |C|/n \rceil$—if the message has not been altered in transit then this should be the same as in the generation-encryption algorithm. Of course, the algorithm should not output the payload at this stage: It needs to check the integrity of the message first.

Next, the algorithm computes the blocks $B_0, B_1, \ldots, B_{a+b}$ and computes the MAC for this value in exactly the same way as during the generation-encryption algorithm. The process will output a prospective MAC T'. The data is assumed to have been delivered correctly if $T = T'$. In this case the algorithm outputs the payload P; otherwise, the algorithm outputs that there has been an error.

Properties The use of a random nonce means that if the same message is enciphered twice then different ciphertexts and MACs should result.

Although this mode is thought to be secure, it has been criticized for two major reasons. First, it cannot process on-line data. The entire ciphertext must be collected before verification-decryption can begin. This is because it necessary to know the length of the payload and the tag in order to be able to construct Ctr_1. Second, the fact that the nonce and the message length must be encoded into the single block B_0 means that neither can be too long. This means that very long messages must be encrypted using very short nonces and may mean that the mode is not secure when sending these messages.

16.3.2 Counter and OMAC (EAX) mode

The most popular alternative to CCM mode appears to be EAX mode. EAX mode is similar to CCM mode in that it combines the use of a known encryption mode (CTR mode—see Chapter 5) and a known MAC algorithm (OMAC—see Chapter 7). Again, we will let e_K denote encryption using the underlying block cipher and a key K, and n denote the block length of the block cipher.

Generation-encryption   The EAX algorithm is similar in its construction to the CCM algorithm. It also takes three inputs: the payload P, the associated data A, and a nonce N. The generation-encryption algorithm works as follows:

1. Compute the MAC N_{MAC} formed by running the OMAC algorithm on the input $[0]_n||N$, where $[0]_n$ is a block of n bits that represent the number 0 (i.e., a block of n zeroes).

2. Compute the MAC A_{MAC} formed by running the OMAC algorithm on the input $[1]_n||A$, where $[1]_n$ is a block of n bits that represent the number 1 (i.e., a block of $n-1$ zeroes followed by a single one bit).

3. Compute the ciphertext C by encrypting the payload P using an initial counter of N_{MAC}. In other words, generate $m = \lceil |P|/n \rceil$ "keystream blocks" by computing

    $$S_i = e_K(Ctr_i) \quad \text{where } Ctr_i = N_{MAC} + i - 1 \bmod 2^n \quad (1 \le i \le m)$$
    (16.6)

    and then compute the ciphertext C by setting

    $$C = P \oplus (S_1||S_2||\ldots||S_m)|_{|P|}.$$
    (16.7)

4. Compute the MAC C_{MAC} formed by running the OMAC algorithm on the input $[2]_n||C$, where $[2]_n$ is a block of n bits which represent the number 2 (i.e., a block of $n-2$ zeroes followed by the bits "10").

5. Set the MAC $T = N_{MAC} \oplus A_{MAC} \oplus C_{MAC}$. If required, this value can be truncated.

6. Output the pair (C, T).

The generation-encryption algorithm is shown in Figure 16.2.

Verification-Decryption   The verification-decryption algorithm takes four inputs: the ciphertext C, the MAC T, the associated data A, and the nonce N. It works as follows:

1. Compute the MAC N_{MAC} formed by running the OMAC algorithm on the input $[0]_n||N$, where $[0]_n$ is a block of n bits that represent the number 0 (i.e., a block of n zeroes).

2. Compute the MAC A_{MAC} formed by running the OMAC algorithm on the input $[1]_n||A$, where $[1]_n$ is a block of n bits that represent the number 1 (i.e., a block of $n-1$ zeroes followed by a single one bit).

3. Compute the MAC C_{MAC} formed by running the OMAC algorithm on the input $[2]_n||C$, where $[2]_n$ is a block of n bits that represent the number 2 (i.e., a block of $n-2$ zeroes followed by the bits "10").

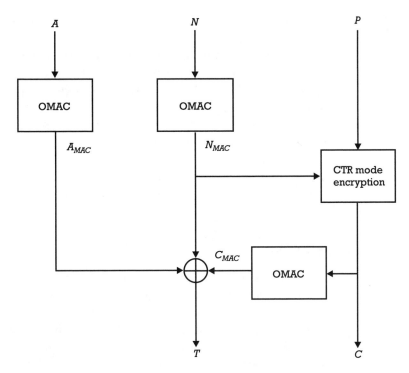

Figure 16.2 The generation-encryption algorithm for the EAX mode.

4. Compute $T' = N_{MAC} \oplus A_{MAC} \oplus C_{MAC}$ and truncate this result if required. Check that $T = T'$. If not, output that there is an error and terminate the application.

5. Compute the payload P by decrypting the ciphertext C using an initial counter of N_{MAC}. In other words, generate $m = \lceil |C|/n \rceil$ "keystream blocks" by computing

$$S_i = e_K(Ctr_i) \quad \text{where } Ctr_i = N_{MAC} + i - 1 \bmod 2^n \quad (1 \le i \le m) \tag{16.8}$$

and then compute the payload P by setting

$$P = C \oplus (S_1||S_2||\ldots||S_m)|_{|C|}. \tag{16.9}$$

6. Output the payload P.

Properties   Again, because this algorithm uses unpredictable nonces, if the same payload is enciphered twice then different ciphertexts and MACs should result.

The EAX mode has a couple of advantages over the CCM mode. Unlike the CCM mode, the EAX mode can begin to process data as it arrives (i.e., before the entire ciphertext has been received) and the size of the message does not affect the possible sizes for the nonce. Indeed, in the EAX the nonce can be of any length—it does not have to be included in a single block of data.

The EAX mode also has the advantage that it can preprocess fixed associated data. Often the associated data will be the same for large numbers of payloads. In the CCM mode, the verification-decryption algorithm must process the associated data every time it wants to verify-decrypt a payload; however, with EAX mode, the verification-decryption algorithm can store the value A_{MAC} and use this to decrypt every message it receives with associated data A.

The disadvantage of the EAX mode is that it is comparatively new and has not received the attention of many standardization bodies. In particular, unlike CCM mode, it has not been standardized by the IEEE 802 group.

16.4   Security modules

A security module is a hardware device that contains and/or processes security information. While the design and use of security modules is not strictly cryptography, it is an essential component of many cryptographic processes (e.g., the computation of session keys for use in mobile networks—see Chapter 12). Security modules are also of particular importance in the financial sector. The ANSI X9.24 key management framework (see Chapter 11) states that a key can only be used if it is protected by a security module.

There are two main standards that deal with the security of cryptographic modules: ISO 13491 and NIST FIPS 140-2.

16.4.1   Security modules in the financial sector

Secure modules are an essential part of the ANSI X9.23 key management framework, which is also standardized as ISO 11568. This framework specifically states that cryptographic keys can only exist in a useful, useable format inside a secure cryptographic module. However, it provides no guidance on what exactly constitutes a secure module. This void is filled by the two part ISO TC68 standard, ISO 13491.

Considering the length of time that the ANSI X9.24 framework has been in use, ISO 13941 is a comparatively recent development in the financial sector. It was originally envisaged as part of the ISO version of ANSI X9.24, ISO 11568, but, as the standard became more and more complicated, it was decided to cover security modules separately. The first part of ISO 13941, on the requirements and evaluation methods for security modules, was published in 1998. The second part, which covers the specific case where the security module relates to magnetic stripe cards, was published in 2000.

The general requirements for a security module are standardized in ISO 13491-1. It covers two topics: the requirements for a security module used in the retail banking environment, and the methods for evaluating such a security module. This highlights a major difference between the standards for security modules and those for "pure" cryptographic schemes such as those discussed in earlier parts of the book. Standards that describe algorithms and protocols rarely concern themselves with details of how a product could be proven to be compliant with that standard. Standards on more practical issues, such as security modules and security management techniques (see Section 16.6), are more likely to discuss evaluation methods.

The standard describes the physical, logical, and managerial security requirements for a security module under a series of different headings. It covers the physical and logical requirements by classifying the different types of attacks that a module may be subject to, and the different types of defense that it should provide. It defines three classes of defense characteristics:

> *Tamper evidence characteristics;*

> *Tamper resistance characteristics;*

> *Tamper response characteristics.*

and five classes of attacks that can be made against a security module:

> *Penetration:* Attempting to recover data directly from the module's hardware;

> *Monitoring:* Attempting to recover data by passively observing the inputs and outputs of the module (including unintentional outputs such as power consumption data, electromagnetic radiation, and timing information);

> *Manipulation:* Attempting to recover data by sending the module sequences of inputs that cause it to perform unauthorized functions;

> *Modification:* Attempting to recover data by altering the physical or logical characteristics of the device (such as replacing components in the module);

> *Substitution:* Attempting to recover data by completely replacing the module with a bogus device with the same physical and logical characteristics and observing how this device interacts with the larger system.

It may be noted that, in traditional ISO style, these security requirements do not cover the problems associated with denial of service (DoS) attacks. For each pair of attack and defense characteristics, the standard gives a series of requirements, both mandatory and recommended, that the module should satisfy. Unlike the NIST FIPS 140-2 standard discussed in Section 16.4.2, these requirements are not detailed on a sliding scale but are simple statements of the features that the module should have.

This is not to say that all security modules need to satisfy the same stringent security requirements regardless of the environment in which they will be used. The standard makes statements about how a device should react in the case of an attack but does not specify how the requirements should be implemented. Clearly, in situations where a security module protects valuable or critical data, the security module should implement the requirements with stronger mechanisms than might be used if the data is of less importance.

The standard deals with the managerial aspects of security by noting that the longer a security module is deployed, the more chance that an attacker has to compromise the functionality of that module. Hence, every security module should have a well-defined life cycle similar to that of a cryptographic key. Cryptographic life cycles are discussed, in the context of keys, in Chapter 11. The ideas contained in that chapter can easily be adapted to apply to security modules.

16.4.2 Security modules in the wider world

The main general-purpose standard on security modules is NIST FIPS Pub. 140-2, which details the general security requirements for cryptographic modules, although it specifically states that "conformance is not sufficient to ensure that a particular module is secure."

The standard defines four increasing qualitative levels of security: from security level 1 (the lowest level) to security level 4 (the highest level). Each of these levels defines a series of requirements for a security module. For simplicity, these requirements are grouped into ten categories:

- *Module specification:* All aspects of the module must be well documented.

- *Module ports and interfaces:* The module must have logically separate input/output and data/control ports (although these may all use a single physical interface). At higher levels, data ports for unsecured critical data must also be logically separated.

- *Roles, services, and authentication:* The module should support multiple roles and provide services for these roles. These roles should include a user role, a crypto-officer role, and a maintenance role. The strength of the authentication required depends upon the security level.

- *Finite state model:* The operation of a security module should be specified using a finite state model.

- *Physical security:* The module should employ physical security mechanisms to prevent unauthorized physical access to the module's memory and processes. The level of physical security depends upon the security level: from no extra requirements (security level 1) to complex tamper protection mechanisms which have to be formally tested (security level 4).

- *Operational environment:* This refers to the secure management of the software and hardware components of the module (the module's *operating environment*). These should be nonmodifiable and tested, with the level of testing determined by the security level.

- *Cryptographic key management:* All keys included in a security module should be managed using secure functions (e.g., secure key generation techniques and secure key distribution techniques). At lower security levels, keys can be entered manually but at higher security levels keys must be entered using some form of encryption or dual control.

▸ *Self tests:* The module should be able to check its own critical functions, and, at higher levels, must use statistical tests to check random number generators.

▸ *Design assurance:* There should be some assurance that the module is well designed (i.e., has the claimed functionality). This assurance ranges from documented evidence (security level 1) to a formal modeling of the module and an analysis of its security (security level 4).

▸ *Mitigation of other attacks:* The module should be able to resist all other attacks, even those for which it is not possible to systematically test a module's ability to withstand them. This includes attacks such as power analysis, timing analysis, and fault induction.

Whilst the NIST standard does not give any information about how a modules security could be tested, unlike ISO, NIST also runs a testing facility that checks whether a given security module meets the requirements for the claimed security level.

NIST FIPS Pub. 140-2 is currently being reviewed by the ISO/IEC JTC1/SC27 subcommittee and a new ISO/IEC standard on security modules (ISO/IEC 19790) is expected to be produced in the next few years.

16.5 Standards for the use of biometric techniques

There are three ways in which users can authenticate themselves to a computer system:

▸ By using something they know—such as a password or a PIN;

▸ By using something they have—such as a token, security module, or key;

▸ By displaying some particular physical or behavioral characteristic—such as their fingerprint or iris pattern.

In this section we shall be considering the last of these three options. Such measurable physical or behavioral characteristics are known as *biometrics,* and systems that make use of some kind of biometric input are known as *biometric systems.* The study of biometric systems is not, strictly speaking, cryptography, but biometrics are mostly used to provide security solutions; hence it is reasonable for us to provide an overview of the standardization work in this area.

The design, suitability, and social impact of biometric systems are major research topics, and the resulting work could easily fill an entire volume by itself. Therefore we will only attempt to sketch the basic principles of biometric systems, and comment on the work of the major standardization bodies in this area.

We will concentrate our efforts on the framework for biometric systems introduced in ANSI X9.84. This framework is designed for use within the financial services sector and specifies both the framework required to collect and process biometrics, and the ASN.1 format in which biometric data should be encoded for transmission. (The ASN.1 syntax notation is discussed in Chapter 13). It is interesting to note that, while the ANSI X9.84 biometric standard covers all of the technical aspects of a biometric system, it does not cover several of the important social aspects of biometrics. In particular, issues relating to the privacy and ownership of biometric data are specifically stated as being outside the scope of the standard.

ANSI X9.84 was published in 2003, and efforts were made by the ISO TC68 committee to convert ANSI X9.84 into an ISO standard. These efforts failed (primarily, it would seem, for political reasons). Other biometric standardization efforts are discussed in Section 16.5.5.

Biometrics can be used in one of two ways. Either a biometric can be used to verify the fact that a person is the individual that he or she claims to be (*verification* or *one-to-one authentication*) or it can be used to identify the person from a large range of possible subjects (*identification* or *one-to-many authentication*). The only difference between verification and identification is whether the user claims an identity. In a verification system, the user claims an identity and his or her biometric data is tested against the stored biometric data, the *biometric profile*, of the individual the user claims to be. In an identification system, the user does not claim to be any particular individual and so the user's biometric data is tested against all the biometric profiles in the system.

16.5.1 General requirements of a biometric

A biometric is a physical or behavioral quality that can be measured by a security system and that (practically) uniquely identifies that individual. ANSI X9.84 summarizes the qualities of a physical characteristic that make it a good biometric under four headings: *universality*, *distinctiveness*, *accuracy*, and *performance*.

Universality   Universality is the quality of a biometric that allows it to be used by the general population. This essentially comes down to two questions: Does everyone have the biometric? And is the biometric easily measurable?

For a biometric to be useful, most users of a system must possess the biometric. It is no use, for example, using freckle patterns as a biometric, as a large proportion of the population do not have freckles! Similarly, it is important that the biometric is easily measurable (a quality sometimes known as *availability*). DNA would make an excellent biometric were it not for the fact that it is comparatively difficult to measure a user's DNA profile— DNA profiling usually requires a blood or tissue sample, and many users will be reluctant to provide these samples on a regular basis.

Of course, most biometrics are not completely universal. For example, fingerprints are commonly used as a biometric but cannot be used to authenticate a user who has lost their fingers. Therefore, it is important for a system to provide a suitably secure alternative authentication method for the small number of users who cannot authenticate themselves via the biometric system.

Distinctiveness   A biometric must not only be universal but it must also uniquely identify the user (i.e., the biometric must be distinctive). The distinctiveness of a biometric usually has to be determined by statistical study: For example, there is evidence that fingerprints and iris patterns are unique to an individual. Other biometrics, such as facial recognition systems, can have problems distinguishing certain people, such as identical twins.

Accuracy   Even if a biometric is perfectly distinctive (i.e., is unique to each individual) it may not always be possible to obtain a perfect measurement of the biometric. Therefore, almost all biometric systems allow for some errors. These errors can be made in one of two ways: either there will be a *false match* or a *false nonmatch*.

A false match occurs when a user is incorrectly identified by a biometric system or manages to falsely claim the identity of another user. This may allow that user access to information or resources to which he or she has not been authorized. A false nonmatch occurs when a user is incorrectly rejected by a biometric system. This would mean that the user is not allowed access to information and resources to which he or she is authorized.

The false match and false nonmatch rates can be adjusted by forcing the biometric system to be more or less stringent about how well the biometric a user is presenting must match the stored biometric measurement. If a system is lax about checking the match between the presented and stored biometric, then the false nonmatch rate will decrease, but the false match rate will increase. If the system is strict about checking the match, then the false match rate will decrease but the false nonmatch rate will increase.

The correct levels for a system's false match and false nonmatch rate depend upon the application for which the system is being used.

Performance   For a biometric system to be effective it must also work in a timely fashion. What is the point in having a perfect biometric authentication system for a security door if the biometric measurement takes two weeks to complete?

Interestingly, the ANSI X9.84 standard does not comment on the speed of a biometric system but uses the "performance" section to comment on the degree of assurance one can have in published accuracy results (false match and false nonmatch rates).

16.5.2 Common biometrics

This section discusses the more commonly used or proposed biometrics (as described in ANSI X9.84).

Fingerprints   This is the classic biometric used by law-enforcement agencies for over a hundred years. The biometric is taken by measuring the location of different types of patterns in the friction ridges and valleys on a finger. Fingerprints appear to be be completely distinctive: Each of an individual's fingers has a different fingerprint pattern and so do identical twins. However, a fingerprint measurement can be distorted by the condition of the finger and fingerprints appear to change slightly with age.

Voice identification   Voice biometrics have been in use for over five decades. Here, the biometric system identifies users from the distinct tones of their voice. There is some evidence that this biometric is suitably distinctive and controlled by various physical aspects of the user, such as the size and shape of the voice box. A key threat against voice identification systems is the threat that a legitimate user's voice could be recorded and used by an attacker to gain some kind of unauthorized access.

Iris patterns   The iris is the colored portion of the eye that surrounds the pupil. Like fingerprints, iris patterns seem to be exceptionally distinctive and can be used for both verification and identification.

Retina patterns   The retina pattern is the structure of blood vessels inside the eye. The pattern of blood vessels in the retina is very distinctive, and this biometric typically has a very low false match rate. Conversely, it has a larger false nonmatch rate then many other biometrics. Retinal patterns are also prone to change during a person's lifetime.

Facial biometrics   Facial recognition is a commonly used technique—indeed, most of us use it every day! Facial recognition technology verifies a user's identity by measuring the location of details within a user's face (or, alternatively, the heat patterns produced by a user's face). This is probably the most "user-friendly" biometric technology but is also possibly the easiest to fool with simple changes (e.g., a change of hairstyle, expression, or makeup).

Hand geometry   This biometric is measured using cameras that establish the lengths and locations of different parts of the user's hand. Hand geometry is not a particularly distinctive biometric and is only recommended for use as a verification tool (possibly in combination with token or password authentication). A user's hand geometry can also change quite dramatically in a short period of time, due to disease, age, or accident.

Signature biometrics   Handwritten signatures have been used as a biometric for centuries. Recently, some success has been achieved in using signature biometrics as a computer biometric. This biometric measures (amongst other things) the speed, shape and pressure of a user's signature on a specially designed electronic tablet and/or with a specially designed electronic pen. This biometric is difficult to forge but requires specialist hardware that may be difficult to maintain.

16.5.3   The general biometric architecture

Most biometric systems work in the same way and are characterised by three phases: *data collection, feature extraction,* and *matching.* These phases are shown in Figure 16.3.

Data collection   Data collection is the physical process of measuring a user's biometric. This may involve the use of cameras, scanners, sound recorders, or a signature pen or tablet. These devices need to be correctly maintained and calibrated so that each device measures the biometric in the same way.

Another important point in data collection is *liveness.* Since biometric data is usually freely available in some form or another (e.g., faces can be photographed and voices can be recorded), it is important that the biometric system can distinguish between a live user's biometric and an attempt to copy another user's biometric. This is known as a "liveness test."

Feature extraction   The raw biometric data produced by the data collection process is generally very large. This data usually contains a lot of redundant information and is difficult to compare to the user's stored biometric data profile. In order to reduce the size of the data and to allow for quick comparison, the features of the biometric are extracted. These may be, for example, the location of the minutiae in the fingerprint. This reduced data set is then presented to the matching process.

Matching   The matching process is the comparison between the biometric data presented by the user and the user's stored biometric profile. If the biometric system is being used to verify a user, then the data is only compared to the stored biometric profile of the individual that the user is claiming to be. If the biometric system is being used to identify a user, then the data is compared to all the biometric profiles in the system's database.

It is unlikely that the presented data will exactly correspond to the user's biometric profile, hence it is critical that the system tolerate a small number of discrepancies between the two sets of data. Whether the presented data is sufficiently close to a particular biometric profile to verify or identify the user depends upon the system's *decision policy.*

After the matching phase, the biometric system will present the application using the system with either an authentication decision (in an verification system), or either the identity of the user or an "invalid" response (in an identification system).

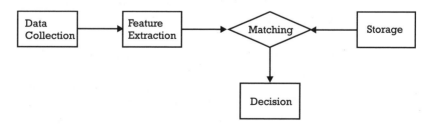

Figure 16.3   The general biometric architecture.

16.5.4 Supporting functions

While we describe the main parts of a biometric system in Section 16.5.3, these main processes must be supported by several other functions. In particular, a biometric system must include functionality for:

- Enrollment;
- Transmission and storage;
- Updating biometric profiles.

A biometric system must have an enrollment service to allow a user's biometric profile to be initially entered in the system. The enrollment system must combine the checking of a user's access rights and the creation of the user's initial biometric profile. It is important that the user is correctly identified before any access rights are given to them (as the biometric system will bind the user's access rights to a physical person rather then to some kind of computer identity). The creation of an initial biometric profile merely involves carefully sampling the user's biometric.

The transmission and storage of biometric data is also critical. If an attacker can read a user's biometric data, then that attacker will know *exactly* which features they will have to copy in order to impersonate that user to the system. If an attacker can modify a user's biometric data then he or she can break the system by inserting his or her own biometric data into a legitimate user's biometric profile.

Many biometrics change over time. In order to cope with this fact, users may be forced to periodically resubmit their biometric data in a manner that is very similar to enrollment. Indeed, this process is often called *reenrollment*. An alternative approach is to update a user's biometric profile every time the user is successfully authenticated. This process is known as *adaptation*.

16.5.5 Biometric standards

The only major standardization body that has released a standard on biometric systems is the ANSI X9 committee, which has produced ANSI X9.84. However, other standardization bodies are currently working on new standards.

The ISO/IEC JTC1 committee have set up a new subcommittee, ISO/IEC JTC1/SC37, specifically to standardize biometric techniques. This subcommittee has working groups on vocabulary, technical interfaces, data interchange formats, profiles, testing, and the societal aspects of biometrics. This subcommittee is currently working on many new standards, but of particular interest is ISO/IEC 19792, which presents a general biometric framework. This framework is similar to, but not based on, the ANSI X9.84 framework which we have presented here.

Many of the other organizations that are working to develop biometric standards are conglomerations of businesses, rather than "traditional" standardization bodies. These include the Biometric Consortium, the BioAPI consortium, and OASIS. The BioAPI consortium is a collection of over 100 businesses and organizations, including NIST and the NSA. It was formed to develop a common API (see Chapter 15) for use with various biometric technologies.

The Biometric Consortium is another collection of businesses and organizations, including NIST. Its main achievement seems to be the development of the common biometric exchange file format (CBEFF). This a standardised data format designed to allow biometric data to be sent electronically in a product-independent way.

The Organization for the Advancement of Structured Information Standards (OASIS) is a standardization body that seeks to promote the use of e-business. Amongst other things, OASIS have produced the XML language format, which is designed to aid the passing of large volumes of data securely. In the area of biometrics, the OASIS body have produced a version of XML for use with biometric data: the OASIS XML common biometric format (OASIS XCBF). This method for passing biometric data is gaining popularity among vendors and may be adopted by other standards bodies such as the ANSI X9 committee or the ISO/IEC joint technical committee.

16.6   Information security management

This book has concentrated on technical solutions to digital information security problems (i.e., how to ensure information security when manipulating information on a computer system). However, most information security incidents occur because of some kind of human failing rather than due to a technical problem or flaw. Hence, if we are attempting to secure information within a company or organization, we need to look at all the places where information is used and not just the way information is passed around a computer system.

The management of information in a secure way (information security management) is another huge topic, worthy of a book of its own, and we will not attempt to cover the whole subject here. We note, however, that standards are beginning to emerge that deal with this area. In particular, the BS 7799 information security management standard, produced by the BSI, has been widely adopted as a good basis for information security management within large companies and organizations.

BS 7799 is actually a two-part standard: The first part provides guidelines as to how information can be securely managed within an organization, and the second provides a basis for an external third party to audit an organization's information security management techniques. Companies that pass an inspection by an approved auditor will be issued with a certificate of compliance by the BSI. The first part of the BS 7799 standard has already been adapted for international use as ISO/IEC 17799. The second part is currently being reviewed by ISO/IEC JTC1/SC27.

The standard focuses on securing a process rather than a piece of technology (like a network) or a site. It ensures that all information that is used and/or manipulated by that process is dealt with in a manner that conforms to the security policy (see Chapter 3). It pays particular attention to making sure that information is, at all times, sufficiently confidential, integral, and available.

To help assess whether a process is handling data in a way that conforms to the security policy, it defines 127 "controls" grouped into 10 "disciplines." Each control represents an area in which security could be compromised if the appropriate controls are not in place. The 10 groups of controls are described as follows:

- *Security policy:* These controls are designed to ensure that an effective security policy is in place, and that all the relevant staff are aware of it.

- *Organizational security:* These controls are meant to ensure that the structure of the organisation is sufficient to protect security (e.g., that each member of an organization is aware of their security responsibilities and that there are channels for reporting security incidents to the relevant security authority).

- *Asset clarification and control:* These controls are designed to ensure that (digital or physical) assets are suitably labeled according to their security needs, and that these assets are dealt with in a suitably secure way.

- *Personnel security:* These controls deal with the risks to information security that come from the organization's staff (whether these risks come from error, theft, fraud, or the misuse of the organisation's information).

- *Physical and environmental security:* These ensure that the physical site in which information is held is suitably secure and that the site itself is not a threat to the data (for example, by being prone to flooding).

- *Communications and operations management:* These controls seek to make sure that there are procedures in place for every possible eventuality, and that these procedures are suitably secure. They also make sure that all supporting systems (such as a computer network) are secure.

- *Access control:* These controls are designed to make sure that information is only accessed, modified, or made available by authorized personnel.

- *Systems' development:* These controls are meant to make sure that security is built into an organization's systems and processes (computer-based and otherwise).

- *Business continuity management:* These controls are designed to ensure that a business can still function after a major incident (such as a fire or the destruction of a server).

- *Compliance:* These controls seek to make sure that the information security management structure complies with local, national, and international laws.

The standard recommends that these 127 controls are reviewed to see which ones are relevant to this particular organization, and then that a risk assessment is used to check that the appropriate security measures are in place for each of the relevant controls. If an organization's current security provision is not sufficient then it will need to be updated. The standard also recommends that all potential security issues are regularly checked (both by the relevant departmental managers and by an independent internal auditor).

16.7 Notes

Section 16.1

There are three standards that discuss the generation of random bits in a systematic and self contained way: IETF RFC 1750 [1], ISO/IEC 18031 [2], and ANSI X9.82 [3]. Of these, only the IETF RFC is currently available. Both ANSI X9.82 and ISO/IEC 18031 should be published in the next couple of years.

While it is generally true that an NRBG based on a physical source needs specialist hardware to measure the source, this does not mean that the physical sources must themselves be new components. IETF RFC 1750 points out that many existing computer systems naturally contain phenomena that could be used as entropy sources. The standard suggests that audio input to a machine or the random fluctuations in the rotational speed of a disk drive could both be used as effective entropy sources, if hardware was put into place to measure the phenomena.

A large body of academic work has been published on the subject of deterministic random bit generators. For example, Yao [4] has shown that a random bit generator is secure (produces bits which are effectively unbiased and independent), and, if not, an efficient attacker can determine the next bit of the RBGs output with probability significantly greater than one/half. A good, if somewhat technical, overview of this theory is given by Goldreich [5].

Examples of DRBGs include the use of a suitably secure block cipher in counter or output feedback mode (a proof that the CTR mode of operation provides suitably random output if the underlying block cipher is perfect is given by Bellare et al. [6]), the Micali-Schnorr generator [7, 8] and the Blum-Blum-Shub generator [9, 10]. Details of all of these deterministic random bit generators can be found in Menezes et al. [11].

The NIST statistical tests for random bit generators are currently available as a special publication: NIST Special Publication 800-22 [12]. Code for these tests is also available on the NIST Web site: http://csrc.nist.gov/rng/.

Section 16.2

The first attempt to produce some kind of standardized advice for choosing primes was probably the 1986 patent submitted by Hellman and Back (U.S.

patent #4,633,036). This defined a cryptographically strong prime as a prime number p where

- $p - 1$ has a large prime factor r.

- $p + 1$ has a large prime factor s.

- $r - 1$ has a large prime factor r'.

- $s - 1$ has a large prime factor s'.

It was thought, at the time, that the product of two primes of this form would make an ideal RSA modulus. This advice has now been largely superseded, as the difficulty in factoring an RSA modulus now appears to depend on other properties.

Both the ANSI X9 committee and ISO/IEC JTC1 have recently been working on standards on prime number generation. These are ANSI X9.80 [13], released in 2001, and ISO/IEC 18032 [14], which is due to be published in the next couple of years.

A discussion of the problems associated with the "add-two-and-test" method of using a probabilistic primality test to generate a prime number is given by Brandt [15].

There are several popular primality tests that are currently in use. These include the Miller-Rabin test [16], the Frobenius-Grantham test [17], and the Lehmann test [18]. These algorithms are all probabilistic and have (relatively small) error probabilities.

Recently, a new primality test has been proposed by Agrawal, Saxena, and Kayal [19]. This paper is very interesting from a mathematical point of view, as it proposes a fast (using a mathematical definition of the word "fast"), deterministic method for testing the primality of a number. Unfortunately, even though the algorithm is mathematically classed as a "fast" algorithm, in practice, the algorithm is very slow when compared to the probabilistic tests mentioned above. Hence, it is not thought to be of significant use for generating primes for cryptographic applications.

Prime number generation algorithms that do not make use of primality tests include Maurer's algorithm [20] and the Shawe-Taylor algorithm [21].

Section 16.3

While the problems of authenticated encryption, and, in particular, the order in which one should apply an encryption and MAC algorithm, have been discussed for many years, we have recently begun to see some formal analysis of the problem. Bellare and Namprempre [22] have analyzed the problem to see what can be proven about the different types of schemes and have come to the conclusion that the encrypt-then-MAC approach is best.

The idea of a signcryption scheme—an asymmetric scheme that acts as both an asymmetric encryption and digital signature scheme—was first introduced by Zheng [23]. Again, there has been some recent research that has analyzed the problem of signcryption from a "provable security" point of view. Papers by An [24] and An, Dodis, and Rabin [25] have proposed security models that discuss the security properties that a signcryption scheme should have and have also examined the question of whether it is possible to get this security just by signing and encrypting a message (in some order).

NIST is attempting to standardize a single mode of operation for a block cipher that provides authenticated encryption. Currently, a draft standard exists that contains the CCM mode [26]. This choice has been the subject of fierce debate. Many of the arguments for and against CCM mode are summarized on the relevant section of the NIST Web site: http://csrc.nist.gov/CryptoToolkit/modes.

The work on the ISO/IEC standard on authenticated encryption is at a very early stage. It is unclear which algorithms will be included in this standard.

The CCM mode of a block cipher has been proposed by Housley, Whiting and Ferguson [27] and is included in IETF RFC 3610 [28], IEEE 802.11i [29] and the draft NIST standard [30]. A proof of security for this mode was produced by Jonsson [31]. Despite this, it has been heavily criticized, particularly by Rogaway and Wagner [32].

The EAX mode was proposed by Bellare, Rogaway, and Wagner [33] to provide an alternative to the CCM mode. Another proposed alternative to the CCM mode is the OCB mode [34]. However, this mode has the disadvantage of having been patented and has not been made freely available—instead it can be licensed under reasonable and nondiscriminatory terms. The final alternative, AES key wrap mode, is given in IETF RFC 3394 [35], but does not seem to be a serious contender for inclusion in the NIST standard.

The first draft of the ISO/IEC standard on authenticated encryption, ISO/IEC 19772 [36], contains specifications for the CCM, OCB, and AES key wrap modes of operation of a block cipher.

Section 16.4

The general security requirements for a security module that is to be used in the retail banking sector are described in ISO 13491-1 [37]. The second part of the standard, ISO 13491-2 [38], describes specific requirements for systems using magnetic card stripe systems (both requirements for the cards themselves and the terminals which interact with them). It may be thought, since we have motivated the discussion of security modules via the ANSI key management framework [39–42], that key management is the only function for which security modules are used in the financial sector. This is not true. ISO 13491-1 states that security modules can be "used to protect messages, cryptographic keys and other sensitive information used in a retail banking environment," while ISO 13491-2 describes specific requirements not only for devices involved with PIN or key creation or manipulation, but also devices with MAC and digital signature functionality.

The main general standard on security (cryptographic) modules is NIST FIPS Pub. 140-2 [43]. The corresponding ISO/IEC standard that is currently being developed is ISO/IEC 19790 [44].

NIST also runs a certification service for FIPS 140-2 (and for the preceding standard, NIST FIPS Pub. 140-1 [45]). Vendors can submit security modules to the certification service which will check whether the module achieves the claimed security level. At the time of this writing, the NIST Cryptographic Module Validation Program (CMVP) had certified 374 products, with 111 more products under review. More information about the CMVP can be found at http://csrc.nist.gov/cryptval/.

Section 16.5

Biometric identification and authentication is a huge topic and several books have been written on the subject. For more information on biometrics, the reader is referred to Jain, Bolle, and Pankanti [46] and Nanavati, Thieme, and Nanavati [47]. This chapter concentrates on the work contained in the (published) ANSI X9.84 standard [48]. Other (draft) standards include the ISO/IEC 19792 standard [49] (work on which is at a very early stage), the BioAPI specification [50], the Common Biometric Exchange File Format [51], and the OASIS XCBF format standard [52].

It should be emphasized that the liveness of a biometric should be checked before the biometric measurement is trusted. There are cases where criminals have fooled fingerprint sensors using dead fingers that have forcibly been removed from the bodies of authorised personnel. More recently, Matsumoto et al. [53] have shown that it is often possible to fool fingerprint sensors by making false fingerprints from melted gummy bears. These "gummy" fingers have fooled both the biometric measurement system and the liveness test.

Section 16.6

The ISO/IEC standard on information security management, ISO/IEC 17799 [54], is based on the British Standard BS 7799-1 [55]. This standard consists of a series of guidelines for good information security management. A second part to this national standard, BS 7799-2 [56], deals with certification that an organization is compliant with BS 7799-1. This standard is currently being reviewed by ISO/IEC JTC1/SC27.

References

[1]   Eastlake, D., S. Crocker, and J. Schiller, *RFC 1750, Randomness Recommendations for Security*, Internet Engineering Task Force, December 1994.

[2]   International Organization for Standardization, *ISO/IEC CD 18031, Information Technology—Security Techniques—Random Bit Generation*, 2004.

[3]   Accredited Standards Committee X9—Financial Services, *ANSI X9.82, Random Number Generation (Draft)*, 2003.

[4]   Yao., A. C., "Theory and Applications of Trapdoor Functions," *27th IEEE Symposium on Foundations of Computer Science (FOCS)*, 1982, pp. 80–91.

[5]   Goldreich, O., *Foundations of Cryptography: Basic Tools*, Cambridge, England: Cambridge University Press, 2001.

[6] Bellare, M., et al., "A Concrete Security Treatment of Symmetric Encryption," *Proceedings of the 38th IEEE Symposium on Foundations of Computer Science*, 1997, pp. 394–403.

[7] Micali, S., and C. P. Schnorr, "Efficient, Perfect Random Number Generators," in S. Goldwasser, (ed.), *Advances in Cryptology—Crypto '88*, Vol. 403, *Lecture Notes in Computer Science*, Springer-Verlag, 1988, pp. 173–198.

[8] Micali, S., and C. P. Schnorr, "Efficient, Perfect Polynomial Random Number Generators," *Journal of Cryptography*, Vol. 3, 1991, pp. 157–172.

[9] Blum, L., M. Blum, and M. Shub, "Comparison of Two Pseudo-Random Number Generators," in D. Chaum, R. L. Rivest, and A. T. Sherman, (eds.), *Advances in Cryptology—Crypto '82*, Plenum Publishing, 1982, pp. 61–78.

[10] Blum, L., M. Blum, and M. Shub, "A Simple Unpredictable Pseudo-Random Number Generator," *SIAM Journal on Computing*, Vol. 15, 1986, pp. 364–383.

[11] Menezes, A. J., P. C. van Oorschot, and S. A. Vanstone, *Handbook of Applied Cryptography*, Boca Raton, FL: CRC Press, 1997.

[12] National Institute of Standards and Technology (NIST), *NIST Special Publication 800-22: A Statistical Test Suite for Random and Pseudorandom Number Generation for Cryptographic Applications*, May 2001.

[13] Accredited Standards Committee X9—Financial Services, *ANSI X9.80, Prime Number Generation, Primality Testing, and Primality Certificates*, 2001.

[14] International Organization for Standardization, *ISO/IEC CD 18032, Information Technology—Security Techniques—Prime Number Generation*, 2003.

[15] Brandt, J., and I. Damgård, "On Generation of Probable Primes by Incremental Search," in E. F. Brickell, (ed.), *Advances in Cryptology—Crypto '92*, Vol. 740, *Lecture Notes in Computer Science*, Springer-Verlag, 1992, pp. 358–370.

[16] Rabin, M. O., "Probabilistic Algorithm for Testing Primality," *Journal of Number Theory*, Vol. 12, 1980, pp. 128–138.

[17] Grantham, J., "A Probable Prime Test with High Confidence," *Journal of Number Theory*, Vol. 72, 1998, pp. 32–47.

[18] Lehmann, D. J., "On Primality Tests," *SIAM Journal of Computing*, Vol. 11, No. 9, 1982, pp. 374–375.

[19] Agrawal, M., N. Kayal, and N. Saxena, "PRIMES Is in P," http://www.cse.iitk.ac.in/news/primality.html, 2002.

[20] Maurer, U., "Fast Generation of Prime Numbers and Secure Public-Key Cryptographic Parameters," *Journal of Cryptography*, Vol. 8, 1995, pp. 123–155.

[21] Shawe-Taylor, J., "Generating Strong Primes," *Electronics Letters*, Vol. 22, No. 16, 1986, pp. 875–877.

[22] Bellare, M., and C. Namprempre, "Authenticated Encryption: Relations Among Notions and Analysis of the Generic Composition Paradigm," in T. Okamoto, (ed.), *Advances in Cryptology—Asiacrypt 2000*, Vol. 1976, *Lecture Notes in Computer Science*, Springer-Verlag, 2000, pp. 531–545.

[23] Zheng, Y., "Digital Signcryption or How to Achieve Cost(Signature & Encryption) << Cost(Signature) + Cost(Encryption)," in B. Kaliski, (ed.), *Advances in Cryptology—Crypto '97*, Vol. 1294, *Lecture Notes in Computer Science*, Springer-Verlag, 1997, pp. 165–179.

[24]   An, J. H., "Authenticated Encryption in the Public-Key Setting: Security No-
        tions and Analyses," http://eprint.iacr.org/2001/079, 2001.

[25]   An, J. H., Y. Dodis, and T. Rabin, "On the Security of Joint Signature and
        Encryption," in L. Knudsen, (ed.), *Advances in Cryptology—Eurocrypt 2002*, Vol.
        2332, of *Lecture Notes in Computer Science*, Springer-Verlag, 2002, pp. 83–107.

[26]   National Institute of Standards and Technology (NIST), *NIST Special Publication
        800-38C, Draft Recommendation for Block Cipher Modes of Operation: The CCM Mode
        For Authentication and Confidentiality*, September 2003.

[27]   Housley, R., D. Whiting, and N. Ferguson, "Counter with CBC-MAC,"
        http://csrc.nist.gov/CryptoToolkit/modes/proposedmodes/, 2002.

[28]   Whiting, D., R. Housley, and N. Ferguson, *RFC 3610, Counter with CBC-MAC
        (CCM)*. Internet Engineering Task Force, September 2003.

[29]   Institute of Electrical and Electronics Engineers, Inc., *IEEE Draft Supple-
        ment to Standard for Telecommunications and Information Exchange Between
        Systems—LAN/MAN Specific Requirements—Part 11: Wireless Medium Access Control
        (MAC) and Physical Layer (PHY) Specifications: Specification for Enhanced Security*,
        2002.

[30]   National Institute of Standards and Technology (NIST), *NIST Special Publication
        800-38C, Draft Recommendation for Block Cipher Modes of Operation: The CCM Mode
        For Authentication and Confidentiality*, September 2003.

[31]   Jonsson, J., "On the Security of CTR + CBC-MAC," in K. Nyberg and H. M.
        Heys, (eds.), *Selected Areas in Cryptography (SAC 2002)*, Vol. 2595, *Lecture Notes in
        Computer Science*, Springer-Verlag, 2002, pp. 76–93.

[32]   Rogaway, P., and D. Wagner, "A Critique of CCM," http://www.cs.ucdavis.edu/
        ~rogaway/papers/, 2003.

[33]   Bellare, M., P. Rogaway, and D. Wagner, "The EAX Mode of Operation," in
        R. Bimal and W. Meier, (eds.), *Proceedings of the 11th Workshop on Fast Software
        Encryption (FSE 2004)*, Vol. 3017, *Lecture Notes in Computer Science*, Springer-
        Verlag, 2004, pp. 391–408.

[34]   Rogaway, P., et al., "OCB: A Block-Cipher Mode of Operation for Efficient
        Authenticated Encryption," *Proceedings of the Eighth ACM Conference on Computer
        and Communications Security (CCS-8)*, 2001, pp. 196–205.

[35]   Schaad, J., and R. Housley, *RFC 3394, Advanced Encryption Standard (AES) Key
        Wrap Algorithm*, Internet Engineering Task Force, September 2002.

[36]   International Organization for Standardization, *ISO/IEC WD 19772, Information
        Technology—Security Techniques—Data Encapsulation Mechanisms*, 2004.

[37]   International Organization for Standardization, *ISO 13491-1: 1998, Banking—
        Secure Cryptographic Devices (Retail)—Part 1: Concepts, Requirements and Evaluation
        Methods*, 1998.

[38]   International Organization for Standardization, *ISO 13491-2: 2000, Banking—
        Secure Cryptographic Devices (Retail)—Part 2: Security Compliance Checklists for Devices
        Used in Magnetic Stripe Card Systems*, 2000.

[39]   American Bankers Association, *ANSI X9.24–2002, Retail Financial Services—
        Symmetric Key Management—Part 1: Using Symmetric Techniques*, 2002.

[40]   International Organization for Standardization, *ISO/IEC 11568–1, Banking—Key
        Management (Retail)—Part 1: Introduction to Key Management*, 1994.

[41]   International Organization for Standardization, *ISO/IEC 11568–2, Banking—Key Management (Retail)—Part 2: Key Management Techniques for Symmetric Ciphers*, 1994.

[42]   International Organization for Standardization, *ISO/IEC 11568–3, Banking—Key Management (Retail)—Part 3: Key Life Cycle for Symmetric Ciphers*, 1994.

[43]   National Institute of Standards and Technology (NIST), *Federal Information Processing Standards Publication 140-2 (FIPS PUB 140-2): Security Requirements for Cryptographic Modules*, June 2001.

[44]   International Organization for Standardization, *ISO/IEC WD 19790, Information Technology—Security Techniques—Security Requirements for Cryptographic Modules*, 2004.

[45]   National Institute of Standards and Technology (NIST), *Federal Information Processing Standards Publication 140-1 (FIPS PUB 140-1): Security Requirements for Cryptographic Modules*, January 1994.

[46]   Jain, A., R. Bolle, and S. Pankanti, (eds.), *Biometrics: Personal Identification in Networked Society*, Boston, MA: Kluwer Academic Press, 1999.

[47]   Nanavati, S., M. Thieme, and R. Nanavati, *Biometrics: Identity Verification in a Networked World*, New York: John Wiley and Sons, 2002.

[48]   Accredited Standards Committee X9—Financial Services, *ANSI X9.84–2003, Biometric Information Management and Security for the Financial Services Industry*, 2003.

[49]   International Organization for Standardization, *ISO/IEC WD 19792, Information Technology—Security Techniques—A Framework for Security Evaluation and Testing of Biometric Technology*, 2003.

[50]   The BioAPI Consortium, *BioAPI Specification Version 1.1*, March 2001.

[51]   National Institute of Standards and Technology (NIST), *Common Biometric Exchange File Format (CBEFF)*, January 2001.

[52]   Organization for the Advancement of Structured Information Standards, *OASIS XML Common Biometric Format, Committee Specification 1.1*, June 2003.

[53]   Matsumoto, T., et al., "Impact of Artificial Gummy Fingers on Fingerprint Systems," in R. L. van Renesse, (ed.), *Optical Security and Counterfeit Deterrence Techniques IV—Proceedings of SPIE*, Vol. 4677, 2002, pp. 275–289.

[54]   International Organization for Standardization, *ISO/IEC 17799, Information Technology—Code of Practice for Information Security Management*, 2000.

[55]   British Standards Institute (BSI), *BS 7799-1, Information Technology, Code of Practice for Information Security Management*, 2000.

[56]   British Standards Institute (BSI), *BS 7799-2, Information security Management, Specification with Guidance for Use*, 2002.

Standards: The Future

It is not much easier to predict the future of cryptographic standards than it is to predict the future of cryptography itself. New standardized cryptographic schemes will grow out of current and future research. However, current trends in research give some sort of indication about the direction that standards bodies may follow in the near future, and we will use this chapter to try and "second-guess" some of these trends.

The general toolbox will be completed   Over the past 20 years, standards bodies have defined an extensive toolbox of cryptographic schemes that can be applied to any network or system. The schemes in this generic toolbox are all well-established and widely trusted: By and large they have a long history and have withstood attempted attacks by many expert cryptographers. In every sense, they have stood the test of time. However, the generic toolbox has a few notable gaps.

In particular, standards bodies are only just beginning to turn their attention toward the problem of authenticated encryption (see Section 16.3). NIST is currently attempting to standardize an authenticated encryption mode of operation for a block cipher, and the ISO/IEC joint technical committee is following their work closely with a view to standardizing several authenticated encryption modes; in fact, a first working draft for such a standard, WD 19772, was produced in March 2004. The draft ISO/IEC standard on stream ciphers (ISO/IEC 18033-4—see Chapter 4) also contains a mode of operation for a stream cipher that provides both integrity and confidentiality.

These emerging standards focus on authenticated encryption for symmetric encryption; the logical extension of this work is to standardize asymmetric authenticated encryption (or "signcryption") schemes. These schemes would provide all the benefits of a signed encrypted message (i.e., confidentiality, integrity, origin authentication, and non-repudiation) but in a potentially more efficient and more secure way.

After these new security mechanisms have been standardized, the next step will be to examine the ways that these mechanisms can be used to provide useful security services; this could result in further new or revised standards. For example, it is very easy to see that the combination of a time-stamp and a signcryption scheme provides a simple but effective asymmetric key transport mechanism (see Chapter 12).

A further area in which work is only now being developed relates to the support of user *privacy*. While existing security mechanisms such as encryption techniques can be used to provide privacy functions (e.g., by hiding the contents of communications sessions from eavesdroppers), confidentiality by itself cannot provide anonymity for users. However, over the last 20 years a whole range of privacy-enhancing technologies have been developed, offering, for example, services such as anonymous electronic payment and anonymous credential management. A 1-year privacy study group was launched in early 2004 by JTC1 of ISO/IEC, with the goal of deciding what new standards are required to support user privacy. One possible finding of this group may be that some of the key privacy technologies should be standardized.

Finally, we observe that none of the standardized security technologies are designed to maximize the *availability* of end-user systems. While offering complete protection against network-based DoS attacks appears extremely difficult, if not impossible, recent research has suggested that designing protocols with care can reduce the degree of exposure to such threats. For example, it has become widely accepted that authentication and key establishment protocols in which the server remains stateless are to be preferred. Generic standards for such protocols have yet to be produced, although protocols of this type have been introduced into application standards such as the emerging IKEv2 Internet key establishment protocol. It would therefore appear reasonable to expect that generic protocol standards will emerge containing protocols optimized for availability protection.

New technologies will drive new standards   The development of new cryptographic schemes and techniques will result in the development of new generic cryptographic standards. In addition, the development of new cryptographic technologies will drive the development of new cryptographic schemes that are designed specifically to work with that technology.

In Chapter 16 we discussed two emerging security technologies: security modules and biometrics. Both of these technologies are in the process of being standardized, and with their standardization comes the opportunity to custom-build cryptographic schemes for these environments. For example, we may see the development of more standardized algorithms designed to run on limited platforms (such as are typically associated with security modules) or via cryptographic APIs (see Chapter 15). Alternatively, schemes may be developed to securely store or transmit the highly redundant data associated with raw biometric measurements (see Chapter 16).

New situations will require new standards   The need for new standards does not only arise out of technological advances, but also from the needs of society. As society demands more and more versatility and functionality from technology, new standards will have to be produced to keep pace with these demands. We point out three different areas that are currently of some interest to standardization bodies.

The first example is in the area of mobile computing devices. Security standards already exist for a variety of types of mobile computing devices, such as the 3GPP standards for mobile (cell) phone networks and the IEEE 802.11 standards for wireless local area networks (wireless LANs). However, the research community is currently responding to society's demand that all of a user's mobile devices be able to communicate with each other to form a personal area network (PAN). Standards will need to be written to ensure that a PAN functions securely and that all user devices are interoperable in a secure way.

Our second example concerns Web services. A Web service is, as might be expected, a computing service that is offered via the World Wide Web. Such Web-based applications often use the Extensible Markup Language (XML) developed by the OASIS standardization body and briefly mentioned in Section 16.5.5. The XML language allows documents to be sent over the Internet in both encrypted and signed forms. The standardized XML language is beginning to gain widespread acceptance in the business community, but there is major scope for security standards to be produced in this area, as exemplified by the emerging Web service security proposals.

The last example is a little more speculative in that, to our knowledge, no standardization work has yet been done in this area. Over the past 10 years, the topic of electronic voting has gained a lot of attention from both cryptographers and from political bodies. The challenges of electronic voting are immense: any e-voting system must be simple to use but offer such features as anonymity for individual voters and the ability for a vote's acceptance by the system to be checked by the electorate or by some trusted representative. These challenges have not yet been fully solved by the academic community, but it is possible that, when fully functional schemes have been developed, standards will be introduced to ensure that e-voting schemes are properly and securely deployed.

The number of evaluation bodies will increase   All the previous discussion has been about the areas in which new standards can be developed, but it is useful to consider whether the standardization process itself will also change in the future. There are currently a large number of standardization bodies, each with their own specialization and agenda. Indeed, it is possible to argue that there are too many standardization bodies: If two companies follow the advice of separate standardization bodies then their products will not be interoperable—a key aim for standardized products. Hence, it is unlikely that many new important standardization bodies will appear in the future.

Recently, however, the work of several evaluation bodies has been widely applauded. The European Union's NESSIE project (see Chapter 2) provided an opportunity for new algorithms to be compared to existing standards in an unbiased way, and the results appear to have been widely disseminated and accepted. The Japanese Cryptrec project is also being used as a ongoing source for independent and unbiased appraisals of cryptographic algorithms, and it seems likely that the EU's ECRYPT project will include a subproject to evaluate recently developed stream ciphers. Even the NIST AES process more closely resembled the work of an evaluation body than a traditional standardization body.

We would therefore suggest that the number of evaluation bodies and projects may increase in the future, so that standardization bodies can rely upon the advice of impartial researchers without having to fund expensive research activities themselves.

Contents

A.1 3GPP standards

A.2 ANSI standards

A.3 BSI standards

A.4 ETSI standards

A.5 IEEE standards

A.6 IETF requests for comments (RFCs)

A.7 ISO standards

A.8 ITU-T Recommendations

A.9 NIST FIPS

A.10 RSA PKCS

A.11 SECG standards

Table of Standards

In this appendix we provide tables of standards documents listed in numerical order. This should enable the reader, faced with just a standard number, to find out what the title of the standard is and where it is discussed in this book.

A.1 3GPP standards

The 3GPP standards that are discussed in this book are given in Table A.1. These standards are published by ETSI.

Table A.1 3GPP Standards

3GPP No.	Title	Relevant Chapter(s)
TS 33.102	Security Architecture	12
TS 33.105	Cryptographic Algorithm Requirements	4
TS 35.201	Specification of the 3GPP Confidentiality and Integrity Algorithms; Document 1: $f8$ and $f9$ Specification	4
TS 35.202	Specification of the 3GPP Confidentiality and Integrity Algorithms; Document 2: KASUMI Specification	4
TS 35.205	Specification of the MILENAGE Algorithm Set: An example algorithm set for the 3GPP authentication and key generation functions $f1$, $f1^*$, $f2$, $f3$, $f4$, $f5$, and $f5^*$; Document 1: General	12
TS 35.206	Specification of the MILENAGE Algorithm Set: An example algorithm set for the 3GPP authentication and key generation functions $f1$, $f1^*$, $f2$, $f3$, $f4$, $f5$, and $f5^*$; Document 2: Algorithm Specification	12
TS 35.207	Specification of the MILENAGE Algorithm Set: An example algorithm set for the 3GPP authentication and key generation functions $f1$, $f1^*$, $f2$, $f3$, $f4$, $f5$, and $f5^*$; Document 3: Implementors' Test Data	12
TS 35.208	Specification of the MILENAGE Algorithm Set: An example algorithm set for the 3GPP authentication and key generation functions $f1$, $f1^*$, $f2$, $f3$, $f4$, $f5$, and $f5^*$; Document 4: Design Conformance Test Data	12
TS 35.909	Specification of the MILENAGE Algorithm Set: An example algorithm set for the 3GPP authentication and key generation functions $f1$, $f1^*$, $f2$, $f3$, $f4$, $f5$, and $f5^*$; Document 5: Summary and results of design and evaluation	12
TS 55.216	Specification of the A5/3 Encryption Algorithm for GSM and ECSD, and the GEA3 Encryption Algorithm for GPRS; Document 1: A5/3 and GEA3 Specifications	4

A.2   ANSI standards

The ANSI standards discussed in this book are listed in Table A.2.

Table A.2   ANSI X Series Standards

ANSI No.	Title	Relevant Chapter(s)
X3.92	Data Encryption Algorithm	4
X3.106	American National Standard for Information Systems—Data Encryption Algorithm—Modes of Operation	5
X9.9	Financial Institution Message Authentication (Wholesale)	7
X9.17	Financial institution Key management (wholesale)	11
X9.19	Financial Institution Retail Message Authentication	7
X9.24	Retail Financial Services—Symmetric Key Management— Part 1: Using Symmetric Techniques	11,12
X9.30.1	Public Key Cryptography for the Financial Services Industry— Part 1: The Digital Signature Algorithm (DSA)	8
X9.31	Digital Signatures Using Reversible Public Key Cryptography for the Financial Services Industry (rDSA)	8,16
X9.42	Public Key Cryptography for the Financial Services Industry: Agreement of Symmetric Keys Using Discrete Logarithm Cryptography	12, 16
X9.52	Triple Data Encryption Algorithm Modes of Operation	5
X9.55	Public Key Cryptography for the Financial Services Industry: Extensions to Public Key Certificates and Certificate Revocation Lists	13
X9.57	Public Key Cryptography for the Financial Services Industry: Certificate Management	13
X9.62	Public Key Cryptography for the Financial Services Industry: The Elliptic Curve Digital Signature Algorithm (ECDSA)	8
X9.63	Public Key Cryptography for the Financial Services Industry, Key Agreement and Key Transport Using Elliptic Curve Cryptography	12
X9.69	Framework for Key Management Extensions	12
X9.71	Keyed Hash Message Authentication Code	7
X9.79-1	Part 1: Public Key Infrastructure—Practices and Policy	13,14
X9.80	Prime Number Generation, Primality Testing, and Primality Certificates	16
X9.82	Random Number Generation	16
X9.84	Biometric Information Management and Security for the Financial Services Industry	16

A.3   BSI standards

The BSI standards discussed in this book are listed in Table A.3.

Table A.3   BSI Standards

BSI No.	Title	Relevant Chapter(s)
7799-1	Information Technology. Code of Practice for Information Security Management	16
7799-2	Information Security Management. Specification with Guidance for Use	16

A.4   ETSI standards

ETSI standards that are included in this book are given in Table A.4.

Table A.4   ETSI Standards

ETSI No.	Title	Relevant Chapter(s)
SR 002176	Electronic Signatures and Infrastructures (ESI); Algorithms and Parameters for Secure Electronic Signatures	8
TS 102023	Electronic Signatures and Infrastructures (ESI); Policy Requirements for Time-stamping Authorities	14

A.5   IEEE standards

The IEEE standards included in this book are detailed in Table A.5.

Table A.5   IEEE Standards

IEEE No.	Title	Relevant Chapter(s)
802.11i	IEEE Draft Supplement to Standard for Telecommunications and Information Exchange Between Systems LAN/MAN—Specific Requirements—Part 11: Wireless Medium Access Control (MAC) and Physical Layer (PHY) Specifications: Specification for Enhanced Security	16
1363	IEEE Standard Specifications for Public-Key Cryptography	4, 8, 12
1363a	IEEE Standard Specifications for Public-Key Cryptography—Amendment 1: Additional Techniques	4, 8, 12
1363.1	IEEE Standard Specification for Public Key Cryptographic Techniques Based on Hard Problems over Lattices	4
1363.2	IEEE Standard Specification for Password-Based Public Key Cryptographic Techniques	4, 12

A.6   IETF requests for comments (RFCs)

The IETF RFCs discussed in this book are listed in Table A.6 in ascending numerical order.

Table A.6   Internet RFCs

RFC No.	Title	Relevant Chapter(s)
791	DARPA Internet Program Protocol Specification	13
1035	Domain Names—Implementation and Specification	13
1118	The Hitchhikers Guide to the Internet	2
1305	Network Time Protocol (Version 3): Specification, Implementation, and Analysis	10
1319	The MD2 Message-Digest Algorithm	6
1320	The MD4 Message-Digest Algorithm	6
1321	The MD5 Message-Digest Algorithm	6
1422	Privacy Enhancement for Internet Electronic Mail: Part II: Certificate-Based Key Management	13
1507	DASS: Distributed Authentication Security Service	10
1508	Generic Security Service Application Program Interface	15
1509	Generic Security Service API : C-Bindings	15

Table A.6 Internet RFCs (Continued)

RFC No.	Title	Relevant Chapter(s)
1510	The Kerberos Network Authentication Service (V5)	10, 12, 15
1630	Universal Resource Identifiers in WWW	13
1704	On Internet Authentication	10
1750	Randomness Recommendations for Security	16
1760	The S/KEY One-Time Password System	10
1777	Lightweight Directory Access Protocol	13
1778	The String Representation of Standard Attribute Syntaxes	13
1928	SOCKS Protocol Version 5	15
1961	GSS-API Authentication Method for SOCKS Version 5	15
1964	The Kerberos Version 5 GSS-API Mechanism	15
2025	The Simple Public-Key GSS-API Mechanism (SPKM)	15
2026	The Internet Standards Process—Revision 3	2
2030	Simple Network Time Protocol (SNTP) Version 4 for IPv4, IPv6 and OSI	10
2078	Generic Security Service Application Program Interface, Version 2	15
2104	HMAC: Keyed-Hashing for Message Authentication	7
2202	Test Cases for HMAC-MD5 and HMAC-SHA-1	7
2203	RPCSEC_GSS Protocol Specification	15
2246	The TLS Protocol, Version 1.0	12
2314	PKCS #10: Certification Request Syntax v1.5	13
2315	PKCS #7: Certification Message Syntax v1.5	13
2409	The Internet Key Exchange (IKE)	12
2459	Internet X.509 Public Key Infrastructure: Certificate and CRL Profile	13
2478	The Simple and Protected GSS-API Negotiation Mechanism	15
2479	Independent Data Unit Protection Generic Security Service Application Program Interface (IDUP-GSS-API)	15
2510	Internet X.509 Public Key Infrastructure: Certificate Management Protocols	13
2511	Internet X.509 Certificate Request Message Format	13
2522	Photuris: Session-Key Management Protocol	12
2527	Internet X.509 Public Key Infrastructure: Certificate Policy and Certification Practices Framework	13
2528	Internet X.509 Public Key Infrastructure: Representation of Key Exchange Algorithm (KEA) Keys in Internet X.509 Public Key Infrastructure Certificates	13
2559	Internet X.509 Public Key Infrastructure: Operational Protocols—LDAPv2	13
2560	X.509 Internet Public Key Infrastructure: Online Certificate Status Protocol—OCSP	13
2585	Internet X.509 Public Key Infrastructure: Operational Protocols: FTP and HTTP	13
2587	Internet X.509 Public Key Infrastructure: LDAPv2 Schema	13
2630	Cryptographic Message Syntax	13
2631	Diffie-Hellman Key Agreement Method	12
2712	Addition of Kerberos Cipher Suites to Transport Layer Security (TLS)	12
2743	Generic Security Service Application Program Interface Version 2, Update 1	15
2744	Generic Security Service API Version 2: C-Bindings	15
2797	Certificate Management Messages over CMS	13
2853	Generic Security Service API Version 2: Java Bindings	15
2875	Diffie-Hellman Proof-of-Possession Algorithms	13
2986	PKCS #10: Certification Request Syntax Specification Version 1.7	13
2994	A Description of the MISTY1 Encryption Algorithm	4
3029	Internet X.509 Public Key Infrastructure: Data Validation and Certification Server Protocols	13
3039	Internet X.509 Public Key Infrastructure: Qualified Certificates Profile	8, 13

Table A.6   (Continued)

RFC No.	Title	Relevant Chapter(s)
3075	XML-Signature Syntax and Processing	8
3161	Internet X.509 Public Key Infrastructure Time-Stamp Protocol (TSP)	14
3174	US Secure Hash Algorithm (SHA-1)	6
3279	Algorithms and Identifiers for the Internet X.509 Public Key Infrastructure Certificate and Certificate Revocation List (CRL) Profile	13
3280	Internet X.509 Public Key Infrastructure: Certificate and Certificate Revocation List (CRL) Profile	13
3281	An Internet Attribute Certificate Profile for Authorization	13
3379	Delegated Path Validation and Delegated Path Discovery Protocol Requirements	13
3394	Advanced Encryption Standard (AES) Key Wrap Algorithm	5
3610	Counter with CBC-MAC (CCM)	5, 16
3628	Policy Requirements for Time-Stamping Authorities (TSAs)	14
3647	Internet X.509 Public Key Infrastructure: Certificate Policy and Certification Practices Framework	13

A.7   ISO standards

The ISO and ISO/IEC standards discussed in this book are listed in Table A.7. Note that, in Table A.7, the title given is that of the most recent edition of the standard.

Table A.7   ISO and ISO/IEC Standards

ISO No.	Title	Relevant Chapter(s)
7498-1	Information Technology—Open Systems Interconnection—Basic Reference Model—The Basic Model	3
7498-2	Information Processing Systems—Open Systems Interconnection—Basic Reference Model—Part 2: Security Architecture	3
7498-4	Information Processing Systems—Open Systems Interconnection—Basic Reference Model—Part 4: Management Framework	3
8372	Information Processing—Modes of Operation for a 64-bit Block Cipher Algorithm	5
8730	Banking—Requirements for Message Authentication (wholesale)	7
8731-1	Banking—Approved Algorithm for Message Authentication—Part 1: DEA	7
8731-2	Banking—Approved Algorithm for Message Authentication—Part 2: Message Authenticator Algorithm	7
8732	Banking—Key Management (wholesale)	11, 12
9594-8	Information Technology—Open Systems Interconnection—The Directory: Part 8: Public-Key and Attribute Certificate Frameworks	10, 13
9796	Information Technology—Security Techniques—Digital Signature Scheme Giving Message Recovery	8
9796-2	Information Technology—Security Techniques—Digital signature Schemes Giving Message Recovery—Part 2: Integer Factorization Based Mechanisms	8
9796-3	Information Technology—Security Techniques—Digital Signature Schemes Giving Message Recovery—Part 3: Discrete Logarithm Based Mechanisms	8
9797-1	Information Technology—Security Techniques—Message Authentication Codes (MACs)—Part 1: Mechanisms Using a Block Cipher	5, 6, 7
9797-2	Information Technology—Security Techniques—Message Authentication Codes (MACs)—Part 2: Mechanisms Using a Hash-Function	7

Table A.7 ISO and ISO/IEC Standards (Continued)

ISO No.	Title	Relevant Chapter(s)
9798-1	Information Technology—Security Techniques—Entity Authentication—Part 1: General	10
9798-2	Information Technology—Security Techniques—Entity Authentication—Part 2: Mechanisms Using Symmetric Encipherment Algorithms	10
9798-3	Information Technology—Security Techniques—Entity Authentication—Part 3: Mechanisms Using Digital Signature Techniques	10
9798-4	Information Technology—Security Techniques—Entity Authentication—Part 4: Mechanisms Using a Cryptographic Check Function	10
9798-5	Information Technology—Security Techniques—Entity Authentication—Part 5: Mechanisms Using Zero Knowledge Techniques	10
9798-6	Information Technology—Security Techniques—Entity Authentication—Part 6: Mechanisms Using Manual Data Transfer	10
9807	Banking and Related Financial Services—Requirements for Message Authentication (Retail)	7
9979	Information Technology—Security Techniques—Procedures for the Registration of Cryptographic Algorithms	4
10116	Information Technology—Security Techniques—Modes of Operation for an n-bit Block Cipher	5
10118-1	Information Technology—Security Techniques—Hash-Functions—Part 1: General	6
10118-2	Information Technology—Security Techniques—Hash-Functions—Part 2: Hash-Functions Using an n-bit Block Cipher	6
10118-3	Information Technology—Security Techniques—Hash-Functions—Part 3: Dedicated Hash-Functions	6
10118-4	Information Technology—Security Techniques—Hash-Functions—Part 4: Hash-Functions Using Modular Arithmetic	6
10181-1	Information Technology—Open Systems Interconnection—Security Frameworks for Open Systems—Part 1: Overview	3
10181-2	Information Technology—Open Systems Interconnection—Security Frameworks for Open Systems—Part 2: Authentication Framework	3
10181-3	Information Technology—Open Systems Interconnection—Security Frameworks for Open Systems—Part 3: Access Control Framework	3
10181-4	Information Technology—Open Systems Interconnection—Security Frameworks for Open Systems—Part 4: Non-repudiation Framework	3
10181-5	Information Technology—Open Systems Interconnection—Security Frameworks for Open Systems—Part 5: Confidentiality Framework	3
10181-6	Information Technology—Open Systems Interconnection—Security Frameworks for Open Systems—Part 6: Integrity Framework	3
10181-7	Information Technology—Open Systems Interconnection—Security Frameworks for Open Systems—Part 7: Security Audit and Alarms Framework	3
10745	Information Technology—Open Systems Interconnection—Upper Layers Security Model	3
11166-1	Banking—Key Management by Means of Asymmetric Algorithms—Part 1: Principles, Procedures and Formats	12
11166-2	Banking—Key Management by Means of Asymmetric Algorithms—Part 2: Approved Algorithms Using the RSA Cryptosystem	12
11568-1	Banking—Key Management (Retail)—Part 1: Introduction to Key Management	11
11568-2	Banking—Key Management (Retail)—Part 2: Key Management Techniques for Symmetric Ciphers	11
11568-3	Banking—Key Management (Retail)—Part 3: Key Life Cycle for Symmetric Ciphers	11

Table A.7   (Continued)

ISO No.	Title	Relevant Chapter(s)
11568-4	Banking—Key Management (Retail)—Part 4: Key Management Techniques for Public Key Cryptosystems	11
11568-5	Banking—Key Management (Retail)—Part 5: Key Life Cycle for Public Key Cryptosystems	11
11568-6	Banking—Key Management (Retail)—Part 6: Key Management Schemes	11
11770-1	Information Technology—Security Techniques—Key Management— Part 1: Framework	11
11770-2	Information Technology—Security Techniques—Key Management— Part 2: Mechanisms Using Symmetric Techniques	12
11770-3	Information Technology—Security Techniques—Key Management— Part 3: Mechanisms Using Asymmetric Techniques	12
13491-1	Banking—Secure Cryptographic Devices (Retail)—Part 1: Concepts, Requirements and Evaluation Methods	15, 16
13491-2	Banking—Secure Cryptographic Devices (Retail)—Part 2: Security Compliance Checklists for Devices Used in Magnetic Stripe Card Systems	15, 16
13594	Information Technology—Lower Layers Security	3
13888-1	Information Technology—Security Techniques—Non-Repudiation— Part 1: General	9
13888-2	Information Technology—Security Techniques—Non-Repudiation— Part 2: Mechanisms Using Symmetric Techniques	9
13888-3	Information Technology—Security Techniques—Non-Repudiation— Part 3: Mechanisms Using Asymmetric Techniques	9
14516	Information Technology—Security Techniques—Guidelines for the Use and Management of Trusted Third Party Services	14
14888-1	Information Technology—Security Techniques—Digital Signatures with Appendix—Part 1: General	8
14888-2	Information Technology—Security Techniques—Digital Signatures with Appendix—Part 2: Identity-Based Mechanisms	8
14888-3	Information Technology—Security Techniques—Digital Signatures with Appendix—Part 3: Certificate-Based Mechanisms	8
15408-1	Information Technology—Security Techniques—Evaluation Criteria for IT Security—Part 1: Introduction and General Model	3
15408-2	Information Technology—Security Techniques—Evaluation Criteria for IT Security—Part 2: Security Functional Requirements	3
15408-3	Information Technology—Security Techniques—Evaluation Criteria for IT Security—Part 3: Security Assurance Requirements	3
15764	Road Vehicles—Extended Data Link Security	7
15782-1	Certificate Management for Financial Services—Part 1: Public key Certificates	13
15782-2	Banking—Certificate Management—Certificate Extensions	13
15816	Information Technology—Security Techniques—Security Information Objects for Access Control	3
15945	Information Technology—Security Techniques—Specification of TTP Services to Support the Application of Digital Signatures	13
15946	Information Technology—Security Techniques—Cryptographic Techniques Based on Elliptic Curves	8, 12
15947	Information Technology—Security Techniques—IT Intrusion Detection Framework	3
17799	Information Technology—Code of Practice for Information Security Management	14, 16
18014-1	Information Technology—Security Techniques—Time-Stamping Services—Part 1: Framework	14
18014-2	Information Technology—Security Techniques—Time-Stamping Services—Part 2: Mechanisms Producing Independent Tokens	14

Table A.7   ISO and ISO/IEC Standards (Continued)

ISO No.	Title	Relevant Chapter(s)
18014-3	Information Technology—Security Techniques—Time-Stamping Services—Part 3: Mechanisms Producing Linked Tokens	14
18031	Information Technology—Security Techniques—Random Bit Generation	16
18032	Information Technology—Security Techniques—Prime Number Generation	16
18033-1	Information Technology—Security Techniques—Encryption Algorithms—Part 1: General	4
18033-2	Information Technology—Security Techniques—Encryption Algorithms—Part 2: Asymmetric Ciphers	4
18033-3	Information Technology—Security Techniques—Encryption Algorithms—Part 3: Block Ciphers	4
18033-4	Information Technology—Security Techniques—Encryption Algorithms—Part 4: Stream Ciphers	4
19772	Information Technology—Security Techniques—Authenticated Encryption Mechanisms	5, 16
19790	Information Technology—Security Techniques—Security Requirements for Cryptographic Modules	16
19792	Information Technology—Security Techniques—A Framework for Security Evaluation and Testing of Biometric Technology	16

A.8   ITU-T Recommendations

The ITU-T Recommendations discussed in this book are listed in Table A.8.

Table A.8   ITU-T Recommendations

ITU-T No.	Title	Relevant Chapter(s)
X.509	The Directory—Public-Key and Attribute Certificate Frameworks	10, 13
X.680	Information Technology—Abstract Syntax Notation One ASN.1: Specification of Basic Notation	13
X.681	Information Technology—Abstract Syntax Notation One ASN.1: Information Object specification	13
X.682	Information Technology—Abstract Syntax Notation One ASN.1: Constraint Specification	13
X.683	Information Technology—Abstract Syntax Notation One ASN.1: Parameterization of ASN.1 Specifications	13
X.690	Information Technology—ASN.1 Encoding Rules: Specification of Basic Encoding Rules (BER), Canonical Encoding Rules (CER) and Distinguished Encoding Rules (DER)	13
X.691	Information Technology—ASN.1 Encoding Rules: Specification of Packed Encoding Rules (PER)	13
X.800	Data Communication Networks: Open Systems Interconnection (OSI); Security, Structure and Applications—Security Architecture for Open Systems Interconnection for CCITT Applications	3
X.802	Data Networks and Open System Communications—Security—Information Technology—Lower Layers Security Model	3
X.803	Data Networks and Open System Communications—Security—Information Technology—Open Systems Interconnection—Upper Layers Security Model	3
X.805	Security—Security Architecture for Systems Providing End-to-end Communications	3
X.810	Data Networks and Open System Communications—Security—Information Technology—Open Systems Interconnection—Security Frameworks for Open Systems: Overview	3

Table A.8 (Continued)

ITU-T No.	Title	Relevant Chapter(s)
X.811	Data Networks and Open System Communications—Security—Information Technology—Open Systems Interconnection—Security Frameworks for Open Systems: Authentication Framework	3
X.812	Data Networks and Open System Communications—Security—Information Technology—Open Systems Interconnection—Security Frameworks for Open Systems: Access Control Framework	3
X.813	Data Networks and Open System Communications—Security—Information Technology—Open Systems Interconnection—Security Frameworks for Open Systems: Non-repudiation Framework	3
X.814	Data Networks and Open System Communications—Security—Information Technology—Open Systems Interconnection—Security Frameworks for Open Systems: Confidentiality Framework	3
X.815	Data Networks and Open System Communications—Security—Information Technology—Open Systems Interconnection—Security Frameworks for Open Systems: Integrity Framework	3
X.816	Data Networks and Open System Communications—Security—Information Technology—Open Systems Interconnection—Security Frameworks for Open Systems: Security Audit and Alarms Framework	3
X.841	Security—Information Technology—Security Techniques—Security Information Objects for Access Control	3
X.842	Information Technology—Security Techniques—Guidelines for the Use and Management of Trusted Third Party Services	14
X.843	Security—Information Technology—Security Techniques—Specification of TTP Services To Support the Application of Digital Signatures	13

A.9 NIST FIPS

The NIST FIPS that are discussed in this book are listed in Table A.9. Note that only the most recent editions are listed. The NIST special publications are listed in Table A.10.

Table A.9 NIST FIPS

NIST FIPS No.	Title	Relevant Chapter(s)
46-3	Data Encryption Standard	4
81	DES Modes of Operation	5
140-2	Security Requirements for Cryptographic Modules	16
180-2	Secure Hash Standard	6
186-2	Digital Signature Standard	8
196	Entity Authentication Using Public Key Cryptography	10
197	Specification for the Advanced Encryption Standard (AES)	4
198	The Keyed-Hash Message Authentication Code (HMAC)	7

Table A.10   NIST Special Publications

NIST SP No.	Title	Relevant Chapter(s)
800-22	A Statistical Test Suite for Random and Pseudorandom Number Generation for Cryptographic Applications	16
800-38A	Recommendation for Block Cipher Modes of Operation: Methods and Techniques	5
800-38B	Draft Recommendation for Block Cipher Modes of Operation: The RMAC Authentication Mode	7
800-38C	Draft Recommendation for Block Cipher Modes of Operation: The CCM Mode for Authentication and Confidentiality	5, 16

A.10   RSA PKCS

The RSA PKCS that are discussed in this book are detailed in Table A.11.

Table A.11   RSA PKCS Standards

PKCS No.	Title	Relevant Chapter(s)
1	RSA Cryptography Standard	4
3	Diffie-Hellman Key Agreement Standard	4, 12
5	Password-Based Cryptography Standard	4
7	Cryptographic Message Syntax Standard	13
8	Private-Key Information Syntax Standard	4
10	Certification Request Syntax Standard	13
11	Cryptographic Token Interface Standard	15
13	Elliptic Curve Cryptography Standard	4

A.11   SECG standards

The SECG has only produced two standards. These are listed in Table A.12.

Table A.12   SECG Standards

SECG No.	Title	Relevant Chapter(s)
SEC 1	Elliptic Curve Cryptography	4
SEC 2	Recommended Elliptic Curve Domain Parameters	4

About the Authors

Alexander W. Dent studied for his undergraduate degree in mathematics at St. Peter's College, University of Oxford, and graduated with a first class degree in 1998. Then he moved to Royal Holloway and Bedford New College, University of London, to study for his doctorate in design theory. He was awarded his Ph.D. in 2002, and began to work on cryptography full time. Since then, Dr. Dent has worked for the highly regarded NESSIE algorithm evaluation project, taught the M.Sc. course in "Standards and Evaluation Criteria" at Royal Holloway, and, more recently, been awarded a prestigious EPSRC Junior Research Fellowship.

Dr. Dent works with the information security subcommittee of the ISO/IEC Joint Technical Committee on information technology (ISO/IEC JTC1/SC27). He is the coeditor of the ISO/IEC standard on random bit generation (ISO/IEC 18031). His research interests are concentrated mainly in the field of provable security, particularly the provable security properties of asymmetric encryption algorithms.

Chris J. Mitchell received a B.Sc. and a Ph.D. in mathematics from Westfield College, University of London, in 1975 and 1979, respectively. Prior to his appointment in March 1990 as a professor of computer science at Royal Holloway, University of London, he was a project manager in the Networks and Communications Laboratory of Hewlett-Packard Laboratories in Bristol, which he joined in June 1985. Between 1979 and 1985, he was at Racal-Comsec Ltd. (Salisbury, United Kingdom), part of Racal Electronics Plc, latterly as chief mathematician.

Since joining Royal Holloway in 1990, Dr. Mitchell has played a role in the development of the Information Security Group and helped launch the M.Sc. in information security in 1992 and the M.Sc. in secure electronic commerce in 1999. His research interests mainly focus on the applications of cryptography. He has played an active role in a number of international collaborative projects, including the ongoing Mobile VCE Core 3 program, the recently completed Mobile VCE Core 2 program, four recent EU 5th Framework projects (SHAMAN and PAMPAS on mobile security, USB_Crypt dealing with novel security tokens, and the Finger_Card project combining smart cards and biometrics), and two EU ACTS projects on security for third generation mobile telecommunications systems (USECA and ASPeCT). Dr. Mitchell is currently the convenor of Technical Panel 2 of BSI IST/33, dealing with security mechanisms and providing input to ISO/IEC JTC1/SC27, on which he has served as a U.K. expert since 1992. He has edited eight international security standards and published more than 150 research papers. He is the academic editor of *Computer and Communications Security Abstracts* and a member of the editorial advisory board for the journals of the London Mathematical Society. Dr. Mitchell is a member of Microsoft's Trustworthy Computing Academic Advisory Board and continues to act as a consultant on a variety of topics in information security.

Index

3GPP, 14
  KASUMI and, 52
  key establishment, 263
  network architecture, 255
  standards, 359
3GPP-MAC scheme, 130

A

Access control, 22, 23
  crypto API, 311
  defined, 22
  framework, 37
  PKCS #11, 316
  protection, 23
  techniques, 27–28
Advanced Encryption Standard
    (AES), 52
  submissions, 52
  unusual properties, 65
AKEP2 protocol, 210
American National Standards Institute
    (ANSI), 13
  DSA, 150–51
  rDSA, 150–51
  standards, 360
  X9 standardization group, 141
  X9.17, 216
  X9.23, 336
  X9.24, 216, 225–29, 336
  X9.84, 340, 341, 344
ANSI X9.24, 216, 225–29, 336
  defined, 225
  general requirements, 225–27
  key destruction and archival, 228
  key distribution, 227
  key generation, 227
  key replacement, 228
  key utilization, 227
  See also Key management
Archive key service, 232
ASN.1, 271–72, 288
  data structures, encoding, 272
  defined, 271

encoding rules, 271
  syntax, 271
Asymmetric ciphers, 46–47, 56–63
  basis, 47
  complexity, 56
  digital signatures relationship, 137–38
  IEEE 1363, 60–61
  industry standards, 59–60
  ISO/IEC 18033, 61–63
  RSA scheme, 57–59
  values, 46–47
  See also Encryption
Asymmetric cryptography, 194–200
  key establishment mechanisms with,
    246–54
  mutual authentication mechanisms,
    197–200
  unilateral mechanisms, 195–97
  See also Cryptography; Symmetric
    cryptography
Asymmetric encryption
  authentication using, 199–200
  using, 178–79
  See also Encryption
Attackers, 45
Attacks, 47–48
  birthday, 103
  classes, 337
  DES, 50
  digital signature, 136–37
  DoS, 106
  key recovery, 47
  malicious third-party, 185
  man-in-the-middle, 200
  message recovery, 48
  preplay, 181
Attribute certificates, 268
Audit and alarms framework, 38
Authenticated encryption, 329–36
  CCM mode, 330–33
  EAX mode, 333–36
  modes, 87
  See also Encryption

Authentication, 22, 23
   with asymmetric cryptography, 194–200
   data origin, 22, 23
   entity, 22, 23, 173
   framework, 37
   Kerberos, 192–94
   key, 234
   mutual, 174
   one-to-many, 340
   one-to-one, 340
   protocols, 28
   with symmetric cryptography, 181–94
   unilateral, 174
Authentication protocols, 173–210
   choice factors, 205–7
   cryptographic mechanisms, 176–79
   entity, 173
   GSS-API, 314–15
   introduction to, 174–75
   key establishment and, 233–34
   keying relationship, 206
   manual, 200–205
   mutual, 185–89
   selecting, 205–7
   S/KEY, 183–85
   standards, 175–76
   timeliness checking mechanisms,
      179–81
   unilateral, 181–85

B

BioAPI, 344–45
Biometric profiles, 340
Biometrics, 339–45
   accuracy, 341
   architecture, 343
   data collection, 343
   defined, 339
   distinctness, 341
   facial patterns, 342
   feature extraction, 343
   fingerprints, 342
   general requirements, 340–41
   hand geometry, 342
   iris patterns, 342
   matching, 343
   performance, 341
   retina patterns, 342
   signature biometrics, 342
   standards, 344–45
   supporting functions, 344
   system frameworks, 340
   universality, 340–41
   usage methods, 340
   voice identification, 342

Birthday attacks, 103
Birthday paradox, 103, 108
Block cipher hash function 1, 99–101, 107–8
   defined, 99–100
   round function, 100
Block cipher hash function 2, 101–3
   defined, 101
   output transformation, 102
   parameters, 101
   round function, 102, 103
   security, 102
Block ciphers, 48–53
   cryptanalysis of, 64
   defined, 46
   DES, 49–51
   IDEA, 64
   Lucifer, 49
   MISTY1, 64
   modes of operation, 49, 71–89
   notation, 48
   problems, 48–49
   selecting, 84–85
   See also Encryption
British Standards Institute (BSI), 13, 360

C

Canonical encoding rules (CER), 272
CBC-MACs, 114, 115, 116–26
   functions, selecting, 125–26
   general model, 119
   output transformations, 119–21
   padding methods, 117–19
   revised general model, 123
   SMAC, 116–17
   standardized algorithms, 121
   standards, 15
   variants, 115
   See also Message authentication codes (MACs)
Certificate management, 270, 278–83
   CA establishment, 279
   certificate/CRL discovery operations, 280
   certification, 279–80
   CMP, 279–81
   end entity initialization, 279
   proof of possession mechanisms, 282
   recovery operations, 280–81
   request messages, 281–82
   revocation operations, 281
   standards, 282–83
Certificate management over CMS (CMC), 283
Certificate Management Protocol (CMP),
      279–81
   implementation, 281
   operations, 279–81
   specification, 279, 288

Certificate policies (CPs), 286
Certificate request messages (CRMs), 281–82
Certificate revocation lists (CRLs), 269, 285
Certificates
    EMV, 278
    formats, 271–78
    path discovery, 284–85
    qualified, 278
    status service, 269
    subjects, 268
    X.509, profiles, 276–78
    X.509 attribute, 276
    X.509 public key, 271–76
Certification authority (CA), 149
Certification practice statements (CPSs), 286
Cipher block chaining (CBC) mode, 74–77
    decryption, 75
    encryption, 74–75
    padding issues, 76–77
    parallelized, 77
    "proof of security," 88
    properties, 75–76
    See also Modes of operation
Cipher feedback (CFB) mode, 81–84, 88
    decryption, 83
    defined, 81
    encryption, 82
    feedback buffer, 83
    generalized, encryption, 84
    original, 81–82
    pipelined, 82–83
    properties, 83–84
    See also Modes of operation
Ciphertext, 45
Common biometric exchange file format (CBEFF), 345
Connection confidentiality, 24
Connection integrity, 24
Connectionless confidentiality, 24
Connectionless integrity, 24
Counter and CBC-MAC (CCM) mode, 330–33, 349
    algorithm illustration, 332
    defined, 330–31
    generation-encryption, 331–32
    properties, 333
    verification-decryption, 332–33
    See also Authenticated encryption
Counter and OMAC (EAX) mode, 333–36, 349
    advantages/disadvantages, 336
    algorithm illustration, 335
    defined, 333
    generation-encryption, 334
    preprocessing, 336

    properties, 335–36
    verification-decryption, 334–35
    See also Authenticated encryption
Counter (CTR) mode, 77–79
    decryption, 79
    defined, 77
    encryption, 77–78
    properties, 78–79
    See also Modes of operation
Cryptanalysis, 2, 64
Cryptographic APIs, 309–19
    access control, 311
    defined, 309, 310
    introduction, 309–11
    key management, 310–11
    security issues, 316–18
    standards, 311–12
Cryptographic check functions, 177
Cryptographic evaluation bodies, 16
Cryptographic hash functions, 93–109
Cryptographic message syntax (CMS), 283
Cryptographic Module Validation Program (CMVP), 350
Cryptographic standards
    disadvantages, 10
    ISO, 11, 12
    ITU-T, 12
    key objectives, 16
    need for, 9–10
    See also Standards
Cryptography
    asymmetric, 194–200
    evolution, 2
    identity-based, 152
    lattice-based, 61
    symmetric, 181–94
CRYPTREC, 16

D
Data confidentiality, 21, 24
    defined, 22
    types, 24
Data encryption standard (DES), 49–51
    attacks, 50
    defined, 49
    key length, 50
    keys, 50–51
Data integrity, 22, 24
    defined, 22
    framework, 38
    mechanisms, 28
    types, 24
Data origin authentication, 22, 23
Data validation and certification server (DVCS), 285

Decryption
    algorithm, 47
    CBC mode, 75
    CFB mode, 83
    CTR mode, 79
    ECB mode, 74
    OFB mode, 81
    RSA scheme, 58–59
Dedicated hash functions, 103–4
    defined, 103
    properties, 104
    RIPEMD, 104
Delegated path discovery (DPD), 284
Delegated path validation (DPV), 284
Delegation, 313
Denial of service (DoS) attacks, 206
Derive key service, 232
Deterministic RBGs (DRBGs), 326–27, 347
    defined, 326
    implementation, 326–27
    seed value update, 326
    as synchronous key stream generator, 326
    See also Random bit generators (RBGs)
Diffie-Hellman key agreement protocol, 66, 67,
       201, 250–51
    function, 248–49
    functioning, 250
    key control, 351
    public keys, 203
Digital archiving authorities, 305
Digital signature algorithm (DSA), 142–44,
       153–54
    advantages, 144
    defined, 142
    key generation, 143
    rDSA, 150–51
    selection, 150–51
    signing, 143–44
    verification, 144
Digital signatures, 27, 135–56
    asymmetric encryption relationship, 137–38
    attacks against, 136–37
    authentication with, 197–99
    certificate-based scheme, 140–41
    certification authorities, 149
    deterministic scheme, 138–39
    DSA, 142–44
    EU legislation, 149–50
    identity-based scheme, 140–41
    key generation algorithm, 135
    key transport with, 253–54
    law and, 147–50
    non-repudiation of delivery with, 169
    non-repudiation of origin with, 168–69
    nonreversible scheme, 139–40

    probabilistic scheme, 138–39
    properties, 135–41
    reversible scheme, 139–40
    RSA-based schemes, 144–46
    scheme notation, 139
    scheme selection, 150–51
    signing algorithm, 135
    standards, 141–42
    use of, 296–97
    U.S. legislation, 147
    verification algorithm, 136
Direct communication, 239–41
Discrete logarithms, 195–96
    problem, 7, 195
    unilateral authentication using, 196
Distinguished encoding rules (DER), 272
Distributed Authentication Security Service
       (DASS) protocol, 208
Distribute key service, 232
Dual control, 238

E
Electronic code book (ECB) mode, 73–74, 88
    acceptability, 85
    decryption, 74
    encryption, 74
    properties, 74
    See also Modes of operation
Electronic Communications Act, 150
Encipherment mechanisms, 27
Encryption, 45–67
    algorithms, 47
    asymmetric, 46–47, 178–79
    asymmetric ciphers, 46–47, 56–63
    attacks, 47–48
    authenticated, 329–36
    block ciphers, 48–53
    CBC mode, 74–75
    CFB mode, 82, 84
    CTR mode, 77–78
    ECB mode, 74
    family tree, 46
    KEM/DEM cipher, 62
    mutual authentication with, 186–87
    OFB mode, 80
    RSA, 58, 138
    schemes, 45
    stream ciphers, 53–56
    symmetric, 46, 176–77
    symmetric ciphers, 46
    unilateral authentication with, 181–83
Entity authentication, 22, 23
    applications, 173
    defined, 173
Equivalence relation, 6

Error propagation, 74, 85, 88
ESIGN Act, 147–48
Europay-MasterCard-Visa (EMV) certificates, 278
European Telecommunication Standard Institute (ETSI), 14, 361
Event detection, 30
Evidence, 159
   collection, 299
   types of, 162

F
Facial patterns, 342
Fingerprints, 342
Firewalls, 33
Frameworks, 36–38
   access control, 37
   audit and alarms, 38
   authentication, 37
   integrity, 38
   non-repudiation, 37–38
   overview, 37
   role, 36–37
FTP, 284

G
Generate key service, 232
Generic security service API (GSS-API), 311, 312–15
   algorithm-independent nature, 312
   authentication protocols, 314–15
   credential acquisition, 313
   defined, 312
   joint security context, 313
   language bindings, 314
   message-specific services, 312
   properties, 313
   SPKM, 312

H
The Handbook of Applied Cryptography, 7, 287
Hand geometry, 342
Hash-based MAC functions, 126–28
   classes, 126
   HMAC, 127–28
   MDx-MAC, 127
   MDx-MAC variant, 128
   selecting, 128
Hash functions, 93–109
   block cipher hash function 1, 99–101
   block cipher hash function 2, 101–3
   collision resistance, 94
   dedicated, 103–4

   extensible property, 96
   hashing, 95
   indistinguishable from random, 94
   initialization, 95
   iterative, 95–97
   keyed, 94
   looping, 95
   MACs based on, 126–28
   MASH, 105, 109
   MD, 104, 108
   modular arithmetic, 105
   output transformation, 95
   padding, 95, 98–99
   preimage resistance, 94
   second preimage resistance, 94, 106
   security, 93–95
   selecting, 105–6
   SHA-1, 104, 106
   splitting, 95
   standardized, 95
   standards, 97
   unkeyed, 94
Hashing, 95
HMAC, 127, 129
HTTP, 284

I
IDEA block cipher, 64
Identity-based cryptography, 152
Industrial standardization organizations, 13–16
Information security management, 345–47
   control groups, 346
   defined, 345
Initialization, 95
In-line TTP services, 300
Institute of Electrical and Electronics Engineers (IEEE), 14
   IEEE 1363, 60–61
   standards, 361
International Electrotechnical Commission (IEC). *See* ISO
International standardization organizations, 10–12
International Telecommunication Union (ITU), 12
   ITU-T PKI standards, 269–70
   ITU-T Recommendations, 366–67
   ITU-T X.843, 282
Internet Engineering Task Force (IETF), 14–15
   PKI standards, 270
   RFCs, 361–63
Internet key exchange (IKE) protocol, 237, 252
Internet model, 33–34
Internet Research Task Force (IRTF), 17
Iris patterns, 342

ISO, 10–12
   7498-2, 20, 31
   8372, 72
   8732, 241
   13491, 312
   DIS drafts, 12
   FDIS drafts, 12
   IEC 9796, 141–42
   IEC 9797-1, 120, 122, 124
   IEC 9798, 175
   IEC 10116, 72
   IEC 10118, 97
   IEC 11770-2, 238, 239, 240, 244
   IEC 11770-3, 247, 248
   IEC 15816, 20
   IEC 15945, 282
   IEC 18014-2, 303
   IEC 18033, 53, 61–63, 355
   IEC 19772, 330
   IEC JTC1, 141, 142
   IEC TR 15947, 21
   register of cryptographic algorithms, 51–52
   standard numbering, 11
   standards, 11, 12, 363–66
   TC68, 270
   See also Standardization organizations
Iterative hash functions, 95–97

K

KASUMI, 52
KEM/DEM cipher, 61–63
   construction, 67
   defined, 61
   DEM parts, 62
   encryption/decryption, 62
   KEM parts, 61–62
Kerberos, 192–94
   defined, 192
   development, 208
   functioning, 192–93
   with guessable password, 209
   illustrated, 193
   KDC use, 244
   message contents, 194
   messages, 193–94
   standardization, 260
   tickets, 194
Key agreement
   defined, 232
   mechanisms, 231, 249–53
   MQV, 262
   with nonces, 240–41, 251–52
   with time-stamps and KDC, 242–44
Key control, 234–35
   defined, 218
   TTPs and, 235

Key distribution centers (KDCs), 235, 241–44
   defined, 242
   Kerberos use of, 244
   key agreement with, 242–44
Key establishment, 231–63
   3GPP, 263
   authentication protocols and, 233–34
   based on weak secrets, 254–55
   between different security domains, 246
   categories, 231
   dual control, 238
   interoperability and, 258
   key agreement mechanisms, 231
   key authentication property, 234
   key confirmation property, 234
   key control property, 234–35
   key transport mechanisms, 231
   mechanisms using asymmetric cryptography, 246–54
   mechanisms using symmetric cryptography, 238–46
   for mobile networks, 255–57
   physical mechanisms, 237–38
   properties, 231, 234–35
   scheme selection, 258–59
   standards, 231, 235–37
   standards with asymmetric techniques, 236–37
   standards with symmetric techniques, 235–36
Key generation, 221–23
   algorithm, 47
   create key certificate, 222
   distribute key, 222
   generate key, 222
   register key, 222
   store, 223
Keying material, 217–18
Key management, 215–29
   ANSI X9.24, 225–28
   crypto API, 310–11
   modes of operation, 86
   properties, 216–19
   standards, 215–16
Key recovery attacks, 47
Keys
   activation, 223
   archiving, 224, 228
   authentication, 234
   confirmation, 234
   deactivation, 223–24
   defined, 217
   deregistering, 224
   deriving, 223
   destruction, 224–25, 228
   distribution, 222, 227

encrypting, 226
extraction, 239
forwarding, 242
generation, 222, 227
hierarchies, 218–19
installing, 223
life cycle, 215
life cycle illustration, 220
protection, 216–17
public, 203, 249
reactivation, 224
registering, 222
replacement, 228
revoking, 223
secret, 226
separation, 218, 317
storing, 223
threats, 216–17
transaction, 226
usage lifetime, 215
utilization, 227
Key splitting, 261
Key states, 219–20
active, 220
pending active, 219
postactive, 220
Keystream generators, 54, 55
Key transitions, 220–21
activation, 220
deactivation, 220
destruction, 220–21
generation, 220
reactivation, 220
Key translation centers (KTCs), 235,
244–46
defined, 244
key transport using, 244–46
Key transport
defined, 232
mechanisms, 231, 253–54
with nonces and KTC, 244–46
with time-stamps, 239–40
with time-stamps and signatures, 253–54

L
Language bindings, 314
Lattice-based cryptography, 61
Layers (Internet model), 33–34
list of, 32
security functionality and, 33
Layers (OSI), 32–33
Lightweight directory access protocol (LDAP)
v2, 283–84
Linked tokens, 304–5
Looping, 95

M
MAA, 128, 131
MAC algorithm 1, 127, 128
MAC algorithm 2, 127
MAC algorithm 3, 122
MAC algorithm 4, 122–23
MAC algorithm 5, 124
MAC algorithm 6, 124
Management information base (MIB), 34
Man-in-the-middle attack, 200
Manipulation detection codes (MDCs), 93, 177
calculating, 177
symmetric encryption with, 208
Manual authentication, 200–205
with full-length MAC function, 203–5
protocol list, 201
protocols, 200–205
with short check-value, 202–3
See also Authentication
MASH hash function, 105, 109
Menezes-Qu-Vanstone (MQV) key agreement,
262
Message authentication codes (MACs), 113–31
CBC, 114, 115, 116–26
computation, 114
defined, 113
functions, 115
hash functions, 126–28
manual authentication with, 203–5
mutual authentication with, 187–89
non-repudiation of delivery using, 166–68
non-repudiation of origin using, 164–66
properties, 113–15
standards, 115
unilateral authentication with, 183
uses, 113, 114
using, 177
Message digest (MD) hash functions, 104, 108
Message recovery attacks, 48
Message representation, 145
Miller-Rabin test, 329, 348
MISTY1 block cipher, 64
Mobile networks
handsets, 255
key establishment for, 255–57
Modes of operation (block ciphers), 49, 71–89
authenticated encryption, 87
CBC mode, 74–77
CFB mode, 81–84
CTR mode, 77–79
ECB mode, 73–74
OFB mode, 79–81
padding methods, 72–73
parameter selection, 85–86
properties, 71

Modes of operation (block ciphers) (*Continued*)
    selecting, 84–86
    standards, 72
    SVs and key management, 86
    Triple-DES, 86
Modes of operation (stream ciphers), 54, 55
Modular arithmetic, 5–7
    computational effort, 6
    defined, 5
    simple operations, 6
    use of, 6
Modulus, 5
Monitoring authorities, 162
Mutual authentication, 174
    with nonces and encryption, 186–87
    with nonces and MACs, 188–89
    protocols, 185–89
    three-pass, 209
    with time-stamps and MACs, 187–88
    with time-stamps and signatures, 197–99
    TTP-aided, 189
    See also Authentication

N

National Institute of Standards and Technology
        (NIST), 13, 52
    block cipher standardization effort, 52
    FIPS, 367–68
National standardization organizations, 12–13
Network Time Protocol (NTP), 208
New European Schemes for Signatures,
        Integrity, and Encryption (NESSIE)
        project, 16, 64, 357
Nonces, 180–81
    defined, 180
    key agreement using, 240–41, 251–52
    key transport using, 244–46
    mutual authentication with, 186–87, 188–89
    one-time property, 181
    random selection, 181
    TTP-aided authentication with, 191–92
    unilateral authentication with, 183
Nondeterministic RBGs (NRBGs), 324–26, 347
    example, 324–25
    physical sources, 325
    postprocessing, 325
    See also Random bit generators (RBGs)
Non-repudiation, 22
    of creation, 163
    evidence, 159
    framework, 37–38
    of knowledge, 163
    mechanisms, 159–70
    model, 161–62
    policy, 16

    of receipt, 163
    of sending, 163
    services, 162–63
    standards for, 160
    of submission, 162
    with symmetric cryptography, 164–68
    time-stamping and, 170
    tokens, 163
    of transport, 162
Non-repudiation of delivery, 159, 162
    defined, 162
    with MACs, 166–68
    with signatures, 169
Non-repudiation of origin, 159, 162
    defined, 162
    with MACs, 164–66
    with signatures, 168–69
Notarization, 29
NTRU public-key cryptosystem, 66

O

Off-line TTP services, 301–2
One-to-many authentication, 340
One-to-one authentication, 340
On-line certificate status protocol
        (OCSP), 285
On-line TTP services, 300–301
Organization for the Advancement of
        Structured Information Standards
        (OASIS), 345, 357
OSI model, 31–32
    defined, 19
    layers, 32
    reference, 31
    security management, 36
Output feedback (OFB) mode, 79–81
    decryption, 81
    defined, 79
    encryption, 80
    proof of security, 88
    properties, 80–81

P

Padding
    CBC-MAC, 117–19
    CBC mode, 76–77
    hash functions based on block ciphers,
        98–99
    iterative hash functions, 95
    methods, 72–73
    SMAC, 116
    unambiguous, 73
    zero, 73
Parallelized CBC mode, 77
Personal area networks (PANs), 357

Pervasive security mechanisms, 29–30
PKCS #11, 315–16
    access control, 316
    data storage, 315
    defined, 315
    sessions and concurrency, 316
    See also Public-Key Cryptography Standards
        (PKCSs)
PKIX
    certificate access protocol, 289
    Certificate Management Framework, 289
    Certificate Policy, 289
    Roadmap, 288
    X.509 profile, 277–78
PMAC, 129, 131
Preplay attack, 181
Prime number generation, 328–29
    algorithms, 328–29
    primality tests, 329
Proxies, 285
Public-Key Cryptography Standards (PKCSs),
        15–16, 59–60
    PKCS #11, 315–16
    standards, 368
Public Key Infrastructures (PKIs), 149, 267–89
    defined, 267
    entity types, 268
    standards, 269–71
    standard types, 270–71
    TTP support, 271
Public keys
    authentic, distributing, 249
    Diffie-Hellman, 203
    X.509 certificates, 274–75
    See also Keys

R
RACE Integrity Primitives Evaluation (RIPE)
        project, 16
Random bit generators (RBGs), 323–28
    defined, 323–24
    deterministic, 326–27
    entropy source, 324
    nondeterministic, 324–26
    physical input source, 324
    seed, 324
Random number generation, 327–28
    discard method, 327
    modular method, 328
Register key service, 232
Registration authorities, 219
Retina patterns, 342
RIPEMD hash functions, 104
Rivest-Shamir-Adleman (RSA) scheme, 57–59
    decryption, 58–59

defined, 57
encryption, 58, 138
key generation, 57–58
PKCS standards, 59–60, 368
See also Asymmetric ciphers
Routing control, 28–29
RSA-based signature schemes, 144–47, 155
    defined, 144
    key generation, 145
    signing, 145–46
    verification, 146

S
Security
    audit trails, 30
    authority, 37
    context, 313
    crypto APIs, 316–18
    domains, 21, 37
    frameworks, 36–38
    hash function, 93–95
    labels, 30
    life cycle, 21
    model, 21
    recovery, 30
    semantic, 48
    standards, 20–21
    threats, 21
Security management, 34–36
    assurance, 36
    mechanism, 35–36
    OSI, 36
    service, 35
    system, 35
Security mechanisms, 26–31
    access control, 27–28
    authentication protocols, 28
    data integrity, 28
    defined, 21
    digital signatures, 27
    encipherment, 27
    event detection, 30
    management, 35–36
    notarization, 29
    pervasive, 29–30
    routing control, 28–29
    security audit trails, 30
    security labels, 30
    security recovery, 30
    security services and, 31
    selection of, 30–31
    summary, 29
    traffic padding, 28
    trusted functionality, 29
    types of, 26–29

Security modules, 336–39, 349
    attack classes, 337
    cryptographic key management, 338–39
    defense characteristics classes, 337
    defined, 336
    design assurance, 339
    in financial sector, 336–38
    finite state model, 338
    mitigation of attacks, 339
    operational environment, 338
    physical security, 338
    ports and interfaces, 338
    requirements, 338–39
    roles, services, authentication, 338
    self tests, 339
    specifications, 338
    in wider world, 338–39
Security policies, 21–22
    authorization, 22
    defined, 21, 37
    generic, 22
    identity-based, 22
    rule-based, 22
Security services, 22–26
    access control, 22, 23
    authentication, 22, 23
    data confidentiality, 22, 24
    data integrity, 22, 24
    defined, 21
    management, 35
    non-repudiation, 22, 25
    security mechanisms and, 31
    summary, 25–26
Selective field confidentiality, 24
Selective field integrity, 24
Self-synchronous stream ciphers, 55
Semantic security, 48
SHA-1 hash function, 104, 106
Signature biometrics, 342
Signcryption, 330, 348
Signing keys, 178
Simple Certificate Validation Protocol (SCVP), 289
Simple MAC (SMAC), 116–17
Simple Network Time Protocol (SNTP), 208
S/KEY user authentication protocol, 183–85
    defined, 183–84
    illustrated, 184
    limitations, 209
    predictability, 185
Splitting, 95, 117
Standardization organizations, 10–16
    3GPP, 14
    ANSI, 13

BSI, 13
ETSI, 14
IEC, 12
IEEE, 14
IETF, 14–15
industrial, 13–16
international, 10–12
ISO, 10–12
ITU, 12
national, 12–13
NIST, 13
PKCSs, 15–16
SECG, 15
Standards, 359–68
    3GPP, 359–60
    ANSI X series, 360
    biometrics, 344–45
    BSI, 360
    certificate management, 282–83
    cryptographic APIs, 311–12
    digital signature, 141–42
    entity authentication protocol, 175–76
    ETSI, 361
    future, 355–58
    hash function, 97
    IEEE, 361
    IETF RFCs, 361–63
    ISO, 363–66
    ITU-T Recommendations, 366–67
    key establishment, 231, 235–37
    key management, 215–16
    MACs, 115
    modes of operation, 72
    NIST FIPS, 367–68
    for non-repudiation, 160
    PKI, 269–71
    RSA PKCS, 368
    SECG, 368
    security, 20–21
    time-stamp token creation, 303
    TTP management, 297
    See also Cryptographic standards
Standards for Efficient Cryptography Group (SECG), 15, 368
Station-to-station (STS) protocol, 249, 252–53
    defined, 252
    message exchange, 252
Status management, 285
Store key service, 232
Stream ciphers, 53–56
    A5/1, 65
    A5/2, 65
    defined, 46
    GSM encryption example, 54

keystream generators, 54
message encryption steps, 55
mode of operation, 54, 55
security, 53
security definition, 56
self-synchronous, 55
synchronous, 55
See also Encryption
Structure, this book, 3–4
Symmetric ciphers, 46
Symmetric cryptography, 181–94
key establishment mechanisms with,
238–46
mutual authentication protocols, 185–89
third party-aided mechanisms, 189–94
unilateral authentication protocols, 181–85
See also Asymmetric cryptography;
Cryptography
Symmetric encryption
with MDC, 208
using, 176–77
See also Encryption
Synchronous stream ciphers, 55
System security management, 35

T
Tamper resistant security module
(TRSM), 226
Terminology, this book, 4–5
Third Generation Partnership Project.
See 3GPP
Time-stamping authorities (TSAs), 163, 302–5
linked tokens, 304–5
time-stamping tokens, 303–4
use of, 302
Time-stamping tokens, 303–4
creation standards, 303
defined, 302
linked, 304–5
Time-stamps, 179–80
acceptance window, 179–80
key agreement using, 242–44
key transport using, 239–40, 253–54
logical, 180
mutual authentication with, 187–88,
197–99
TTP-aided authentication, 190–91
unilateral authentication with, 181–83
uses, 179
TMAC, 125
Traffic flow confidentiality, 24
Traffic padding, 28
Transaction keys, 226
Transport layer security (TLS) protocol, 237
Triple-DES modes, 86

Trusted binding, 268
Trusted functionality, 29
Trusted third parties (TTPs), 189, 295–307
architectures, 299–302
authentication with nonces, 191–92
authentication with time-stamps, 190–91
business management, 298–99
compliance with local laws, 299
defined, 295
digital archiving authorities, 305
evidence collection and security
audits, 299
in-line services, 300
with Kerberos authentication, 192–94
key control and, 235
law enforcement relationship, 302
legal considerations, 299
liability, 299
management, 298–99
management standards, 297
mutual authentication protocols, 189
off-line services, 301–2
on-line services, 300–301
PKI support, 271
policy/practice statements, 297–98
properties, 295–97
requirements, 297–99
responsibilities, 298
standards use, 299
time-stamping authorities, 302–5
two-party architectures, 300–302
types of, 296
Two-party TTP architectures, 300–302

U
Unambiguous padding, 73
Unilateral authentication, 174
with asymmetric crypto, 195
with discrete logs, 196
ID-based, 209
with nonces and MACs, 183
protocols, 181–85
with time-stamps and encryption, 181–83
See also Authentication

V
Verification keys, 178
Voice identification, 342

W
Weak secrets
defined, 254
key establishment based on, 254–55
WHIRLPOOL algorithm, 104, 108

Wireless local area networks (WLANs), 357
Wireless transport layer security (WTLS)
      protocol, 278

X
X.500 directories, 283
X.509 certificate profiles, 276–78
   defined, 276–77
   PKIX, 277
   qualified, 278
X.509 certificates, 271–76, 287
   attribute, 276
   certificate policies, 275
   certificate subject, 274

extensions, 275–76
issuer and subject unique IDs, 275
key usage, 275
public key, 271–76
serial number, 274
signature algorithm, 274
subject alternative names, 275–76
validity period, 274
version number, 274
XCBC, 124–25, 130

Z
Zero-knowledge protocols, 178
Zero padding, 73

Recent Titles in the Artech House Computer Security Series

Rolf Oppliger, Series Editor

Bluetooth Security, Christian Gehrmann, Joakim Persson and Ben Smeets

Computer Forensics and Privacy, Michael A. Caloyannides

Computer and Intrusion Forensics, George Mohay, et al.

Defense and Detection Strategies against Internet Worms, Jose Nazario

Demystifying the IPsec Puzzle, Sheila Frankel

Developing Secure Distributed Systems with CORBA, Ulrich Lang and Rudolf Schreiner

Electric Payment Systems for E-Commerce, Second Edition, Donal O'Mahony, Michael Peirce, and Hitesh Tewari

Evaluating Agile Software Development: Methods for Your Organization, Alan S. Koch

Implementing Electronic Card Payment Systems, Cristian Radu

Implementing Security for ATM Networks, Thomas Tarman and Edward Witzke

Information Hiding Techniques for Steganography and Digital Watermarking, Stefan Katzenbeisser and Fabien A. P. Petitcolas, editors

Internet and Intranet Security, Second Edition, Rolf Oppliger

Java Card for E-Payment Applications, Vesna Hassler, Martin Manninger, Mikail Gordeev, and Christoph Müller

Multicast and Group Security, Thomas Hardjono and Lakshminath R. Dondeti

Non-repudiation in Electronic Commerce, Jianying Zhou

Outsourcing Information Security, C. Warren Axelrod

Privacy Protection and Computer Forensics, Second Edition, Michael A. Caloyannides

Role-Based Access Controls, David F. Ferraiolo, D. Richard Kuhn, and Ramaswamy Chandramouli

Secure Messaging with PGP and S/MIME, Rolf Oppliger

Security Fundamentals for E-Commerce, Vesna Hassler

Security Technologies for the World Wide Web, Second Edition, Rolf Oppliger

Techniques and Applications of Digital Watermarking and Content Protection, Michael Arnold, Martin Schmucker, and Stephen D. Wolthusen

User's Guide to Cryptography and Standards, Alexander W. Dent and Chris J. Mitchell

For further information on these and other Artech House titles, including previously considered out-of-print books now available through our In-Print-Forever® (IPF®) program, contact:

Artech House
685 Canton Street
Norwood, MA 02062
Phone: 781-769-9750
Fax: 781-769-6334
e-mail: artech@artechhouse.com

Artech House
46 Gillingham Street
London SW1V 1AH UK
Phone: +44 (0)20 7596-8750
Fax: +44 (0)20 7630-0166
e-mail: artech-uk@artechhouse.com

Find us on the World Wide Web at: www.artechhouse.com